Kickstart Blockchain and Cryptography Fundamentals

Navigate the Intricacies of Modern Blockchain, Cryptography, Smart Contracts and Hyperledger for Driving Real-World Transformations

Prof. Veerendra Kumar Jain

www.orangeava.com

First Published: September 2024

Published By: Orange Education Pvt Ltd, AVA™

Address: 9, Daryaganj, Delhi, 110002, India

275 New North Road Islington Suite 1314 London,
N1 7AA, United Kingdom

ISBN (PBK): 978-81-97651-19-9
ISBN (E-BOOK): 978-81-97651-10-6

Scan the QR code to explore our entire catalogue

www.orangeava.com

Dedicated To

My wife, Heera Jain, for providing day and night support in many ways during the compilation of this volume

About the Author

Prof. V. K. Jain obtained a degree in Electrical Engineering in 1966 from MACT (Maulana Azad College of Technology), Bhopal. He completed his M.Tech in 1968 From MACT and BHEL (Bharat Heavy Electricals), Bhopal, in the Design and Production of Heavy Electrical Equipments. This industry-oriented course was run under the sponsorship of UNESCO at Vikram University, Ujjain, in 1968. He was assigned to the Electronics Application Engineering Department at BHEL.

He presented a thesis on "Analysis of the Performance of Speed and Excitation Regulation System Using Fast-Acting Integrator Type AVR for a Large Hydro-generator (15 MW)". This focused on studying power systems from the viewpoint of electronic control systems (based on Nyquist Criteria) through both analog and digital computers at one of India's premier institutions, IIT (Indian Institute of Technology), Kanpur. He personally prepared a digital computer program in FORTRAN IV as early as 1968 at IIT Kanpur and compiled it on the IBM 7044 Main Frame Computer, the fastest computer in India at that time.

He joined CPWD as an Electrical Engineer on May 20, 1968, based on an All India Competitive Examination for Central Electrical Engineering Services (now known as IES) through the Union Public Service Commission of India and served CPWD for 35 years.

Prof. V. K. Jain is a well-known practical engineer who has authored more than 125 books on engineering, management, and computer science. He is particularly famous for his following books:

1. Modern Cryptography
2. Information Technology (For librarians)
3. Software Testing and Analysis
4. Big Data and Hadoop
5. Data Science and Analytics
6. Machine Learning and Deep Learning
7. Internet of Things
8. Artificial Intelligence

Acknowledgements

There are a few people I want to thank for the continued and ongoing support they have given me during the writing of this book. First and foremost, I would like to thank my wife and grandson for continuously encouraging me to write the book – I could have never completed this book without their support.

I am grateful to the course organizers, such as the All India Council of Technical Education (AICTE), for approving my books on emerging technology. This book will be the fourth. I also extend my gratitude to the Orange AVA team for their efficient publication process and the invaluable guidance they provided throughout the editing and improvement stages.

Preface

Cryptocurrency and its underlying "Blockchain" technology have created much excitement in the technology community. The financial technology sector sees high potential value in cryptocurrency blockchain protocols or distributed-ledger technology. Cryptocurrency is a digital currency in which transactions are checked, and the ledger is shared, through a decentralized system. The transactions and ledger are kept secure using cryptography, rather than by a centralized authority like a bank. Cryptography is a way of protecting information using mathematics.

Cryptocurrencies as a payment medium are not regulated or issued by any central authority in India. There are no guidelines laid down for sorting disagreements when dealing with cryptocurrency. So, if you wish to trade in crypto, do so at your own risk. According to Zippia, more than 300 million people, which is equal to 3.9% of the global population, use blockchain for cryptocurrency. As of 2024, there are 82 million blockchain wallet users worldwide.

The best use of blockchain is in digital agreements and possibly in mass online voting systems for countries like India. Investing in cryptocurrencies may seem lucrative and profitable, but investors should also consider some disadvantages. Cryptocurrencies claim to be an anonymous form of transaction, but they are actually pseudonymous, meaning they leave a digital trail that any country's Federal Bureau of Investigation can decode.

Cryptocurrencies like Bitcoin and Ethereum are barely used for retail transactions in India. They are mostly used for cross-border transfers outside of India.

From a sustainability, social, and ethical point of view, blockchain is not only a subpar technology but also a bad vision for the future. Its use is energy-expensive, leading to a society where profit is everything. It encourages earning from illegal means and disrupts the idea of possessing property beyond someone's legal and valid religious requirement, that is, aparigraha.

Get a Free eBook

We hope you are enjoying your recently purchased book! Your feedback is incredibly valuable to us, and to all other readers looking for great books.

If you found this book helpful or enjoyable, we would truly appreciate it, if you could take a moment to leave a short review with a 5 star rating on Amazon. It helps us grow, and lets other readers discover our books.

As a thank you, we would love to send you a free digital copy of this book, and a **30%** discount code on your next cart value on our official websites:

www.orangeava.com

www.orangeava.in (For Indian Subcontinent)

☑ **Here's how:**

Leave a review for the book on Amazon.

Take a screenshot of your review, and send an email to **info@orangeava.com** (it can be just the confirmation screen).

Once, we receive your screenshot, we will send you the digital file, within 24 hours.

Thank you so much for your support – it means a lot to us!

Colored Images

Please follow the links or scan the QR codes to download the ***Images*** of the book:

You can find code bundles of our books on our official Github Repository. Go to the following link to and QR code to explore the further:

https://github.com/orgs/ava-orange-education/repositories

Please follow the link to download the Colored Images of the book:
https://rebrand.ly/09112f

In case there's an update to the code, it will be updated on the existing GitHub repository.

Errata

We take immense pride in our work at **Orange Education Pvt Ltd,** and follow best practices to ensure the accuracy of our content to provide an indulging reading experience to our subscribers. Our readers are our mirrors, and we use their inputs to reflect and improve upon human errors, if any, that may have occurred during the publishing processes involved. To let us maintain the quality and help us reach out to any readers who might be having difficulties due to any unforeseen errors, please write to us at :

errata@orangeava.com

Your support, suggestions, and feedback are highly appreciated.

DID YOU KNOW

Did you know that Orange Education Pvt Ltd offers eBook versions of every book published, with PDF and ePub files available? You can upgrade to the eBook version at **www.orangeava.com** and as a print book customer, you are entitled to a discount on the eBook copy. Get in touch with us at: **info@orangeava.com** for more details.

At **www.orangeava.com**, you can also read a collection of free technical articles, sign up for a range of free newsletters, and receive exclusive discounts and offers on AVA™ Books and eBooks.

PIRACY

If you come across any illegal copies of our works in any form on the internet, we would be grateful if you would provide us with the location address or website name. Please contact us at **info@orangeava.com** with a link to the material.

ARE YOU INTERESTED IN AUTHORING WITH US?

If there is a topic that you have expertise in, and you are interested in either writing or contributing to a book, please write to us at **business@orangeava.com**. We are on a journey to help developers and tech professionals to gain insights on the present technological advancements and innovations happening across the globe and build a community that believes Knowledge is best acquired by sharing and learning with others. Please reach out to us to learn what our audience demands and how you can be part of this educational reform. We also welcome ideas from tech experts and help them build learning and development content for their domains.

REVIEWS

Please leave a review. Once you have read and used this book, why not leave a review on the site that you purchased it from? Potential readers can then see and use your unbiased opinion to make purchase decisions. We at Orange Education would love to know what you think about our products, and our authors can learn from your feedback. Thank you!

For more information about Orange Education, please visit **www.orangeava.com**.

Table of Contents

CHAPTER 1
Overview of Blockchain Technology

Introduction

In this chapter, we will explore the fascinating world of blockchain technology. You will learn about the fundamental concept of blockchain and its working, including the different types of ledgers as well as the difference between public ledgers and conventional ledger systems. Then, we will discuss Bitcoin, smart contracts, and the building blocks that form the foundation of blockchain. We will learn about transaction types, distributed consensus, and the permissioned model of blockchain. Finally, we will address the security aspects, benefits, and drawbacks, as well as the evolution of blockchain technology.

Structure

In this chapter, we will cover the following topics:

- Blockchain and its Working
- Types of Digital Ledgers and Differences with Conventional Ledger Systems
- Building Blocks of Blockchain
- Smart Contracts
- Distributed Consensus and Networking
- Types of Transactions
- Cryptocurrencies: Bitcoins and Ethereum
- Permissioned Model of Blockchain
- Blockchain Security
- Benefits and Drawbacks of Blockchain
- Evolution of Blockchain

Introduction to Blockchain Technology

Blockchain technology is most simply defined as a *decentralized, distributed ledger* that records all attributes, possessions, and origins (provenance) of digital assets. Blockchain is currently internet based, and all data/information is saved as a chain of several blocks. By inherent design, the data so stored on a blockchain cannot be modified later on, which makes it a legitimate disruptor for industries, such as *payments, cybersecurity, and healthcare.*

Blockchain technology is recognized as Distributed Ledger Technology (DLT). When utilized practically, blockchain makes:

- The history of any digital asset unalterable
- Transparent through the use of decentralization and cryptographic hashing

We can relate analogically to the action of using Google Docs. When we create a document in Google Docs and share it with a group of people:

- The document is distributed rather than getting copied or transferred. This amounts to the creation of a decentralized distribution chain that gives everyone access to the document at the same time.
- In addition, no user (a party) is locked out of the action awaiting changes from another party. All modifications to the doc are being recorded in real-time, making changes completely transparent.

A blockchain[1] is a:

- Source of transactions without any centralized control and administrator (country-wise or area-wise) but with a very small amount of fees.
- Shared distributed ledger technology maintaining records digitally of all required *transactions, assets, cryptocurrencies, or properties* in a public or private tamper-evident manner.
- Peer-to-peer (that is, master-to-master) internet-based network, distributed to all member nodes in the network, each having equal rights.
- Ledger permanently maintaining records in a sequential chain of cryptographic hash-linked blocks.
- System in which an infinite number of members within a dictated limit in a blockchain network can view only those transactions that are relevant to them.
- Tamper-evident packaging that alerts the consumer to foul play or damage to the product. When tamper-evident packaging is triggered by attempted removal or manipulation, it leaves evidence of these actions behind. Any would-be consumers are alerted of the fact that the product has been tampered with and is not safe to use or consume.

The term "blockchain" originates from the idea that each transaction block, once verified and confirmed, is connected to the subsequent block at the start of the chain. A distributed ledger of blocks is exchanged among nodes within a computer network. Functioning as a database, blockchain digitally holds data electronically. It is recognized for its significant contribution to the security and distribution of business data within cryptocurrency systems, including Bitcoin.

The blockchain was devised with an in-built guarantee of wide fidelity and security for a record of data that has generated worldwide trust without the need for a central trusted third party like a government or banking system.

Peer-to-peer (P2P) networking is a type of networking system in which a group of computers are linked together with equal permissions and responsibilities for processing data. Compared with traditional client-server networking deployed on the internet, no devices in a P2P network are designated solely to serve or to receive data.

A key difference between a typical database and a typical blockchain is data structuring. In the case of a blockchain, data lies in a structured chain of information in groups known as blocks. These blocks hold a set of information of many types. Blocks of secret information automatically decide their storage holding capacity. After being filled and closed, they get linked to the previously filled block, creating a chain of data (belonging to one bonafide party), and thus known as blockchain.

To understand the type of data system the blockchain is, let's take a look at the kinds of data software and systems we deal with in everyday scenarios.

We have been dealing with the following database technologies in the past:

- A spreadsheet or table on the user's computer
- A spreadsheet in the data management system of a company/ department of the user
- A remote cloud-based working model

Instead of all these, currently, it is the Blockchain.

We need to understand that a blockchain is a type of shared database in which data is stored in blocks that are then linked together via cryptography, typically on the internet.

When new data comes in, it is entered into a fresh block. Once the block is filled with data, it is chained onto the previous block, which makes the data chained together in chronological order. This is further elaborated in the section "*Working of a Blockchain.*"

Blockchain derives its name from the fact that all the transaction blocks that are already confirmed and validated are linked and chained from the beginning of the chain to the most current block.

The distributed database of the block is shared among the nodes of a computer network. As a database, a blockchain stores information electronically in a digital format. Blockchains are currently best known for their crucial role in cryptocurrency systems, such as Bitcoin, for maintaining a secure and decentralized record of transactions.

Blockchain technology is devised as a chain of confidential data known as blocks (or otherwise chunks). This chain is purposely sent over the network in a decentralized manner. This data structure of blockchain is inherently designed to be an irreversible timeline of data.

New data is added to a new block whenever it is received. The data is chained together chronologically once a block is filled with data and is attached to the one before it. All database applications that reference a remote server using a standard database link establish a connection between the *local database* and the *remote database*. In the case of a blockchain application, it is simply a new type of database where data is not stored as in traditional databases (SQL or NoSQL, which are controlled by single entities). Instead, blockchain can be shared by a group of non-trusting parties without requiring a *central administrator* in the case of smart contracts or any cryptocurrency application.

In order to allow other nodes to process and utilize the user data from the repository effectively, it is transformed into an open data format and shared via a blockchain stream. The smart contract rewards the user with digital tokens after confirming and carrying out the agreed-upon terms of use for the data. Decentralization is the idea that all users collectively maintain control rather than any one individual or group having that authority. Since every one of these decentralized blockchains is immutable, any data entered cannot be undone. This implies that transactions involving Bitcoin are publicly visible and permanently recorded.

Since Bitcoin is built on blockchain, which is a public ledger, the address of your crypto wallet is visible to everyone. The ledger, that is, blockchain is stored on every computer (node) that participates in the network. As such there is no central hub that manages everything, it is a decentralized network that cannot be taken down at any specific point; it cannot be 'muted'.

Blockchain Architecture

- Like all data management systems, a blockchain system is composed of hardware, software, and a protocol.
- The blockchain hardware is made up of specialized computers that are used to enforce the network consensus rules.
- The blockchain protocol establishes the rule set that governs the network and its participants. According to the Bitcoin white paper, this is based on proof-of-work, where one CPU equals one vote to incentivize honest activity.

- The blockchain software provides the bridge between the transaction processors and protocol rule set that delivers the work to the rest of the network.

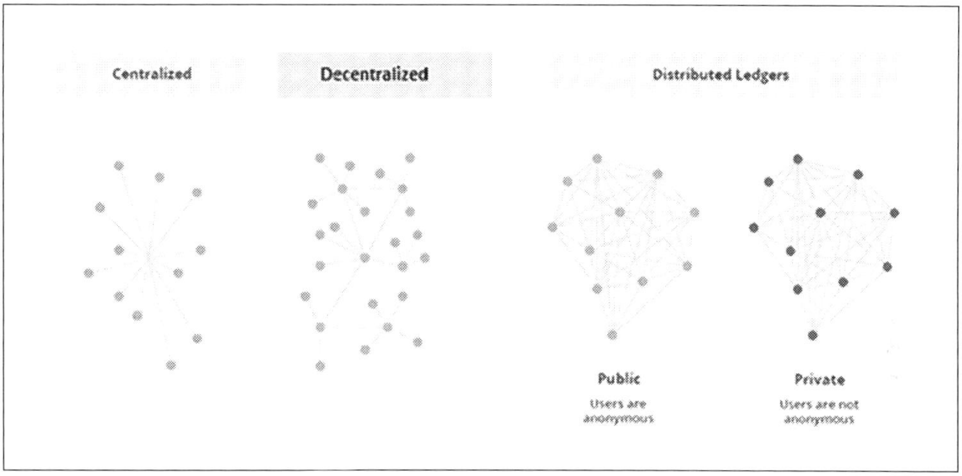

Figure 1.1: *Blockchain*

Working of a Blockchain

As per MIT Technology Review, utilizing a blockchain is all about enabling safe and unchangeable data sharing between parties, especially those who don't trust one another. Blocks, nodes, and miners are the three key ideas in blockchain technology.

- **Blocks**

Each chain is made up of several blocks, and each block has three fundamental components[2]:

- The block's data
- A nonce, which is a whole number of 32 bits. When a block is created, the nonce is generated at random, which results in the block header hash
- The nonce and a 256-bit integer make up the hash. The hash starts with an enormous amount of zeroes (that is, it needs to be minuscule).

A nonce generates the cryptographic hash at the creation of the first block in a chain. Until it is mined, the data in the block is deemed signed and permanently linked to the nonce and hash. An arbitrary number that can only be used once in a cryptographic communication is known as a **nonce**, short for "number once".

However, in order to prevent previous communications from being used in replay attacks, an authentication protocol frequently assigns a random or pseudo-random number. A 32-bit (4-byte) field called the Nonce is randomly assigned a whole number by the miners, which makes it suitable for hashing the block value.

A nonce, in cryptography, is a number used to protect private communications by preventing replay attacks. *Authentication protocols* attach a number for communications, which have to be *random or pseudo-random* numbers for security purposes. Nonce is a number added to an encrypted block in a blockchain, which when rehashed, meets the *difficulty level limitations*. The nonce is the number that digital miners are solving for, and when a solution is found, blockchain miners are awarded cryptocurrency in exchange.

To prevent an attacker from replaying a request in a different context, nonces are used to make each request unique. It makes no difference if the attacker obtains the nonce; rather, the idea is that the attacker won't be able to use the data because it contains a nonce. Each Ethereum transaction has a unique nonce. The total number of transactions sent from a particular address is known as the nonce. The nonce increases by 1 each time you send a transaction. The nonce is used to enforce certain rules about what constitutes a valid transaction.

A perfect nonce is the time of day; for example, 12.53 seconds past 5:13 pm on 18th January 2012 can only occur once. Pronounced like the "nons" in "nonsense," nonce is actually an English word that means "for the present occasion or time"; the present or particular occasion.

A nonce is a method used to sequence and organize transactions on platforms like the Ethereum blockchain. It is a unique number that helps secure communications in cryptography. Nonces can be random or pseudo-random numbers attached to communications for authentication protocols. The concept of nonce will be discussed in *Chapter 2, Cryptographic Hash Function* (CHF), of this book.

After sending a transaction that is successfully mined, your account will increase a value known as the nonce by one. This nonce serves as a record of how many transactions have been sent from a particular address over time. It is important to note that the nonce only counts transactions sent from the address and does not include transactions received by the address.

The nonce is one of the most important and least understood components of an Ethereum transaction.

- **Nodes**

To have communication in any blockchain application, decentralization is one of the key ideas in blockchain technology. The chain cannot be owned by one computer or one organization. Rather, it functions as a distributed ledger through the chain's nodes. Any type of electronic device that keeps copies of the blockchain and keeps the network running can be called a node. Blockchains allow for easy checking and viewing of every ledger transaction because they are transparent. An individual alphanumeric identification number that displays their transactions is provided to each participant. Each node has a copy of the blockchain, and for the chain to be updated, trusted, and validated, the network must algorithmically approve each newly mined block. Combining blockchain's public information with a check-and-balance system aids in the blockchain's integrity maintenance and fosters user trust. In essence, blockchains are just the technological scalability of trust.

- **Miners**

Some form of data mining must be used to obtain cryptocurrency or, for that reason, use any blockchain technology. Mining is the process by which miners add new blocks to the chain. Mining a block in a blockchain is difficult, especially on long chains, because each block has a unique nonce and hash and also refers to the hash of the block before it is in the chain. The exceedingly difficult math problem of locating a nonce that produces an accepted hash is solved by miners using specialized software. There are about four billion possible nonce-hash combinations that must be mined before the correct one is found because the nonce is only 32 bits and the hash is 256. Miners are said to have discovered the "golden nonce" at that point, and their block is appended to the chain. Blockchain technology is very hard to manipulate because, to make a simple change to any (data in) block earlier in the chain, all subsequent blocks must be mined again, not just the block with the change. Consider it "safety in math," since the process of locating golden nonces takes a great deal of time, computing power, and electrical energy. When a block is successfully mined and all of the network's nodes accept the change, the miner receives financial compensation. This is shown in *Figure* 1.2 pictorially.

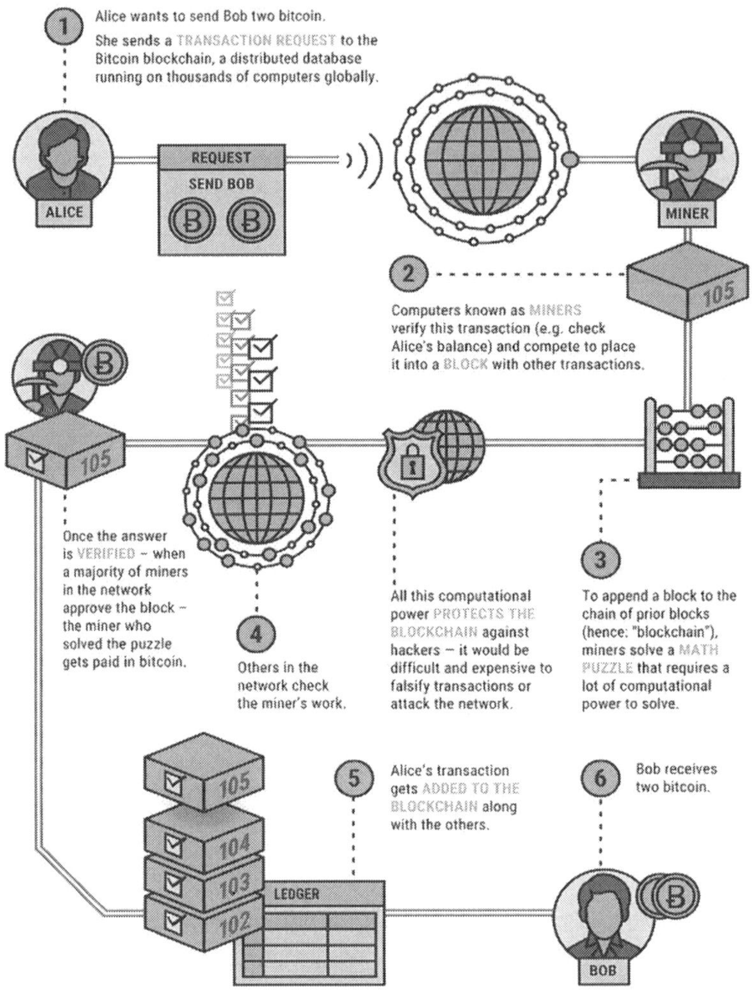

***Figure 1.2**: The Total Process of Bitcoin Transfer*

There are two types of nodes in blockchain: *full node* and *lightweight node.*

Full nodes are the nodes that need to have a copy of the entire blockchain, so every transaction and block that has ever taken place on the blockchain must be downloaded.

Lightweight nodes confirm transactions through simplified payment verification (SPV). This method enables a node to check if a transaction has been added to a block without needing to download the entire blockchain. Full nodes support lightweight nodes by facilitating their connection to the network and informing them of any relevant transactions. A lightweight node only needs to download the block headers from the blockchain, which means that download and storage requirements are significantly less intensive than that of a full node.

The legality of Bitcoin mining depends entirely on your geographic location. The concept of Bitcoin has threatened the dominance of all current fiat currencies and therefore government control over the financial markets. For this reason, Bitcoin is completely illegal in certain places.

Characteristics	Compliance
Public	Public, global distribution of data
Transparency & Auditability	Timestamp ledger, with business events (payments and data transactions) recorded in chronological orde
Immutability	Tamper-proof record keeping, so data is immutable
Fast & Low Cost	Fast, efficient, and low-cost payment system
Privacy With Traceability	Transactions have privacy but are traceable (not anonymous)

Figure 1.3: *Characteristic Features of Bockchain*

However, not all "Blockchains" are actually blockchains. Some supposed "blockchains" are just private and permissioned ledgers, which do not guarantee immutability.

Not-True Blockchain	True Blockchain
Some supposed "blockchains" are just private and permissioned ledgers, which do not guarantee immutability	A true blockchain should be kept in a distributed fashion and publicly verifiable, which helps (along with proof-of-work) ensure its immutability
Certain technologies, such as DLT, do not have cryptographically linked blocks of time-ordered transactions	A true blockchain should record a time-ordered record of business events (payment or data transactions), and secure them via cryptographically linked blocks of such transactions

Table 1.1: *Difference Between True Blockchain and Not-True Blockchain*

Public Ledger

A blockchain is a form of public ledger, which is a series (or chain) of blocks on which transaction details are recorded after suitable authentication and verification by the designated participants. Blockchain supports immutability, which means that data once is written cannot be erased or replaced. The concept of immutability means that no data tampering is possible within the network. Traditional databases don't exhibit immutability and hence are more prone to being manipulated by a rogue administrator or third-party hacks.

Distributed ledgers utilize independent computers known as nodes to record, share, and synchronize transactions within their electronic ledgers, rather than centralizing data as seen in traditional ledgers. These ledgers organize data into blocks that are linked together in an append-only fashion. This technology has the potential to revolutionize the financial sector, making it more efficient, resilient, and reliable.

In essence, Blockchain and Distributed Ledger Technology (DLT) are the foundation for creating and transferring value over the internet. They allow for the recording of interactions and transfer of this value peer-to-peer, without the need for a central coordinating entity. This value can encompass ownership of assets such as money, securities, land titles, voting rights, and artwork, as well as ownership of personal information like identity and health records. This presented persistent challenges in the field of the financial sector and the changing roles of financial sector stakeholders. DLT has the potential to transform various other sectors as well, such as manufacturing, government financial management systems, and clean energy.

Since this technology is still nascent, the World Bank Group doesn't have general recommendations about its use for international development. We are in dialogue with standard-setting bodies, governments, central banks, and other stakeholders to monitor, research, and pilot applications based on blockchain and DLT.

Distributed Ledgers

A distributed ledger (see *Figure 1.4*) is a novel kind of database that members of a decentralized network share, replicate, and synchronize. The distributed ledger keeps track of all network participant transactions, including the exchange of assets and data. The updates to the ledger's records are decided upon by consensus among all potential network participants. There is no involvement from a clearinghouse, financial institution, or other central authority or third-party mediator. The distributed ledger is an auditable and unchangeable record of all transactions, since each record has a timestamp and a distinct cryptographic signature in the network.

Blockchain's distributed ledger technology is revolutionizing the way organizations conduct their business transactions.

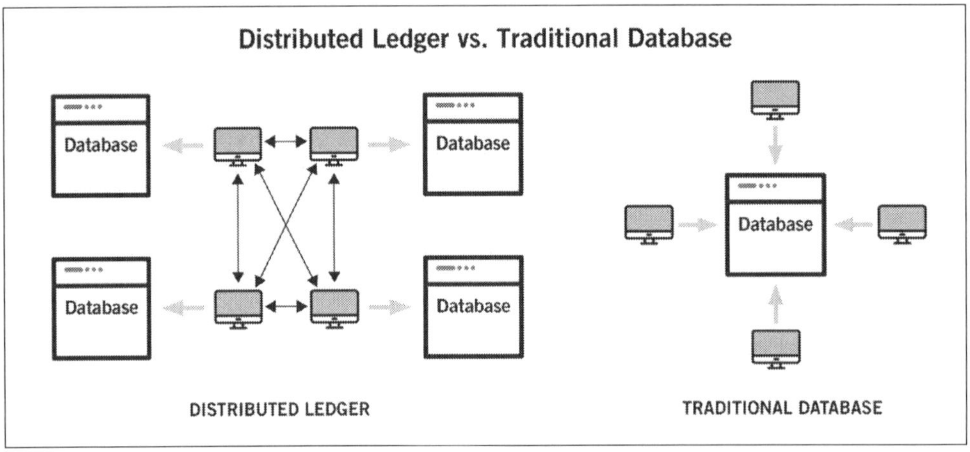

Figure 1.4: *Concept of Distributed vs. Traditional Ledger*

Business Ledger

In today's connected and integrated world, economic activity takes place in business networks that span *national*, *geographic*, and *jurisdictional* boundaries. When producers, consumers, suppliers, partners, market makers/enablers, and other stakeholders own, control, and exercise their rights, privileges, and entitlements over valuable objects known as assets, they form business networks. Intangible and virtual assets like stock certificates, patents, and deeds can be just as valuable as tangible ones like cars, houses, and strawberries. Value in a business network is created by transactions involving asset ownership and transfers. All parties involved in a transaction, including buyers, sellers, and intermediaries (banks, auditors, or notaries), have contracts and business agreements that are documented in ledgers. Multiple ledgers are usually used by a business to record asset ownership and transfers between its various business lines' participants. The systems of record for the financial operations and pursuits of a business are called ledgers.

Assets can be *tangible* and *physical*, such as cars, homes, or strawberries, or intangible and virtual, such as deeds, patents, and stock certificates. Asset ownership and transfers are the transactions that create value in a business network.

Transactions typically involve various participants like *buyers, sellers, and intermediaries* (such as banks, *auditors*, or *notaries*) whose business agreements and contracts are recorded in ledgers. A business typically uses multiple ledgers to keep track of asset ownership and asset transfers between participants in its various lines of business. Ledgers are the systems of record for a business's economic activities and interests.

A typical ledger may look like this:

LEDGER					
ACCOUNT TYPE	CASH				
TRANSACTION DATE	TRANSACTION DETAIL	REFERANCE	DEBIT	CREDIT	BALANCE
13/02/2022	Expenses for February	Ref#1	$200		$200
13/02/2023	Tax deducted	Ref#2		$220	(-$20)

Figure 1.5: *A Typical Ledger*

Problems with Conventional Business Ledgers

The methods employed in current modern business ledgers are flawed in numerous aspects. They can be abused and manipulated, and they are expensive and ineffective. Disputes are caused by a lack of transparency as well as vulnerability to fraud and corruption. Resolving disputes and potentially reversing transactions or offering transaction insurance is an expensive process. Business opportunities that are lost are a result of these risks and uncertainties. Moreover, misguided business decisions based on erroneous and temporary data are caused by out-of-sync copies of business ledgers on each network participant's systems. Reconciling disparate copies of the ledgers causes, at most, a delay in the ability to make a fully informed decision.

Hyperledger

The Hyperledger is an open-source effort to advance cross-industry blockchain technolog ies for business use. It's a global collaboration, hosted by The Linux Foundation®, including leaders in finance, banking, the Internet of Things, supply chain, manufacturing, and technology. These 183+ diverse members and nine ongoing projects, including Hyperledger Fabric, work in concert to create an open, standardized, and enterprise-grade distributed ledger framework and code base.

To make it effective, the Hyperledger Fabric framework supports distributed ledger solutions on permissioned networks, where the members are known to each other, across a wide range of industries. Its modular architecture maximizes the confidentiality, resilience, and flexibility of blockchain solutions.

We shall read about Hyperledger and Hyperledger Fabric framework in detail in *Chapter* 8 of this book.

Blockchain Decentralization

Consider a scenario where a business possesses a server farm consisting of 10,000 computers dedicated to managing a database housing the account details of all its customers. The company also possesses a single warehouse containing all these computers, giving it complete authority over each machine and the data it holds. While this setup offers convenience, it also presents a significant vulnerability. There are various potential risks to consider:

1. How would the company cope if the power supply to the warehouse suddenly failed?
2. How would it handle a situation where its Internet connection was disrupted?
3. What would be the response if the warehouse were to suffer fire damage?
4. How would it recover if a malicious individual were to delete everything using a single keystroke? The result is that in such cases, the data is lost or corrupted.

To tackle this problem, the blockchain facilitates the dispersion of the data stored in that database across multiple network nodes situated at different locations. This preserves the integrity of the data stored there and adds redundancy. For example, if a bad actor were to try to change a record at one database node, it would not affect the other nodes and deter them from doing so. All other nodes would be able to cross-reference one another and quickly identify the node that has the false information if one user tampered with Bitcoin's transaction log. This kind of system aids in establishing a precise and obvious sequence of events. In this manner, no single node in the network can change any of the data stored there. The information and history (such as cryptocurrency transactions) are irreversible due to this clause. A blockchain can store a range of other data, including contracts, state identities, and a company's product inventory. For example, it can store a list of transactions (like those involving cryptocurrencies). Every time a block is added, new records or entries are automatically validated. To approve of this, the decentralized network's processing power must be in the majority. A consensus mechanism, such as Proof of Work (PoW) or proof of stake (PoS), secures blockchains to stop malicious actors from validating fraudulent transactions or double-spending. When there isn't a single node in control, these mechanisms still enable agreement.

Transparency

Due to the decentralized nature of the Bitcoin blockchain, every node has a copy of the chain that is updated when new blocks are added and confirmed. This means that all transactions can be transparently viewed by anyone using either a personal node or blockchain explorers that enable anyone to see transactions occurring live. This implies that you could follow Bitcoin wherever it travels if you so desired. For instance, there have been hacks into exchanges in the past, where users who had Bitcoin on the exchange lost everything. The extracted Bitcoins can be easily tracked down, even though the hacker may remain completely anonymous. In any case, it would be public knowledge if the Bitcoins taken in some of these hacks were transferred or spent. Naturally, records kept on the Bitcoin blockchain (and most other blockchains) are encrypted. This means that a record can only be decrypted (using a public-private key pair) by its owner to reveal their identity. Users of blockchains can therefore maintain transparency while staying anonymous.

Bitcoins

Bitcoin (₿), like many other blockchain currencies, is a decentralized digital currency without a single administrator (central or reserve bank). It can be sent from user to user on the peer-to-peer bitcoin network without the need for intermediaries. Transactions are verified by network nodes through cryptography and recorded in a public distributed ledger called a blockchain.

Cryptocurrency was invented in 2008 by an unknown person or group of people using the name **Satoshi Nakamoto**. Bitcoin came into use in 2009 when its implementation was released as open-source software. As of 13th June, 1:22 pm, one bitcoin is equivalent to approximately INR **56,65,129.18** compared to INR **29,86,942.83** on 16 February 2022.

The financial crisis in the USA in 2008 caused a lot of people to lose faith in banks as trusted third parties in the country. This happened in India in many banks as well. Many users and prospective investors have doubts and questioned whether banks are the best guardians of the global financial system. Bad investment decisions by major banks had proved catastrophic, with rippling consequences. Bitcoin, also proposed in 2008, provided an alternative.

Bitcoin is a "peer-to-peer (one node to many others each with equal authority and privileges) electronic cash system" based on blockchain technology that "allow[s] for online payments to be sent directly from one party to another without going through a financial institution."

Trustworthiness of Bitcoins

Digital transactions without a "trusted intermediary" were made possible by Bitcoin. The technology made it possible for this to occur on a large scale, throughout the world, with cryptography performing the functions that financial regulators, central banks, and commercial banks once performed: confirming the validity of transactions and preserving the integrity of the underlying asset. Since the ledger is not under the control of a reliable third party, Bitcoin is a decentralized public ledger. Anyone with bitcoin can send and receive bitcoin, use the network, and if they would like, keep a copy of this ledger. The ledger is transparent and "trustless" in that regard. It's feasible for newly arrived parties to do this. One asset is tracked and maintained by the Bitcoin ledger, that is, Bitcoin.

(**Note:** *Lowercase "bitcoin" refers to the money or an account unit on the Bitcoin ledger, while capital "bitcoin" refers to the Bitcoin ledger or protocol*). We shall read about the process of getting a bitcoin in the section '*Creation of Bitcoins*' of *Chapter* 3 of this book.

The following rules made it more popular and trustworthy:

- The ledger is maintained with several rules encoded into it that must be followed; one of which states that there will only ever be 21M bitcoin produced. Because of this limitation (cap) on the number of bitcoins in circulation, cryptocurrency is designed to be resistant to inflation stemming from a lack of scarcity. There is no scope for creating anymore bitcoin on a whim and reduce the overall value of the currency. It is currently worth INR 6.3 thousand million or 6.3 Peta (that is, 10^9) INR.

- Very important aspect of bitcoin system is that all participants must agree to the ledger's rules in order to use it.
- Any participant is assigned one single proprietary node of this network. Bitcoin is politically decentralized – no single entity runs bitcoin – but all participants (nodes) agree on the state of the ledger and its rules. This is known as consensus.
- A bitcoin or a transaction can't be changed, erased, copied, or forged.
- This topic is further elaborated in *Chapter* 3 of this book.

Bitcoin was the first digital currency based on a blockchain, and it was mined by millions of people in various parts of the globe. The anonymous creator of Bitcoin, Satoshi Nakamoto, created its decentralized system so that anyone could use it, but no one could own it. Coincidentally, Bitcoin transactions were supposed to be anonymous, even though they were accessible to all. The goal behind the creation of Bitcoin in 2009 was to create global electronic money that could be transferred in a matter of minutes. However, Bitcoin also functions as a store of value and a payment network, thanks to certain features. Big Banks and even Wall Street were initially piqued by the exponential rise in the price of Bitcoin.

Bitcoin has the least ownership concentration among the cryptocurrencies. The top 100 Bitcoin holders control only 17.3% of the total supply, whereas, with Ether, the top 100 investors control 40% of all the issued currency. With other blockchain-based coins such as *Gnosis*, *Storj*, and *Qtum*, large owners control 90%, and they are all part of the teams managing these projects. Industry watchers estimate that perhaps about 1,000 users hold 40% of Bitcoin.

We can imagine the worth of their existence in the market. Since the viability of cryptocurrencies rests on their network size, Bitcoin is worth four times that of American Airlines and twice as much as Uber. Needless to say, Bitcoin creator is now the 15th richest person in the world, say in 2021.

Nakamoto owns between 750,000 and 1,100,000 bitcoin. As of November 2021, this puts his net worth at up to 73 billion US dollars, which would make him the 15th-richest person in the world[3].

People who hold large amounts of Bitcoin are known as **whales** in the industry. The whales stuck by Bitcoin through the pioneering days when it was derided and have known one another for years. The largest Bitcoin exchange is Mt. Gox, which got declared bankrupt. A few years ago, **Mt. Gox, the Bitcoin exchange**, built on the blockchain, burned and crashed. When it filed for bankruptcy, a large number of Bitcoins went missing from the accounts because of a problem with its code.

When discussing technical matters, Nakamoto has never disclosed personal information, but has occasionally shared views on banking and fractional-reserve banking. According to his P2P Foundation profile in 2012, Nakamoto claimed to be a 37-year-old male residing in Japan. However, some experts doubted his Japanese nationality due to his fluent English writing style.

Speculation arose that Nakamoto could be a team of individuals rather than a single person. Dan Kaminsky, a security researcher who reviewed the bitcoin code, suggested that Nakamoto might be either a "team of people" or a "genius".

It is widely known that Nakamoto worked with other developers on the bitcoin software until mid-2010, managing all modifications to the source code himself. He later handed over control of the source code repository and network alert key to Gavin Andresen, transferred various related domains to key members of the bitcoin community, and ceased his visible participation in the project.

Nevertheless, the blockchain technology underlying Bitcoin makes it possible to create a singular, rare digital asset in which every user is aware of its past. The same supply and demand dynamics that govern any market apply to bitcoin, meaning its value isn't intrinsic. The price of bitcoin increases in direct proportion to the growth in demand for it. The value of an asset is determined by its intrinsic value. Rather than utilizing the asset's current market price, this measure is determined through an objective calculation or intricate financial model. Among many other things, institutional investors diversifying their portfolios, retail investors buying into a trendy asset, and supporters of bitcoin's decentralized philosophy could all be driving forces behind demand. Extreme volatility in the value of bitcoin, akin to bubble-like behavior in the past, has been caused by shifting demand. In the end, investor sentiment and whether or not users continue to find value in Bitcoin will determine whether or not it is regarded as a "bubble". Though not guaranteed, a crash is always a possibility. By the end of October 2021, Bitcoin will have a total market value of approximately $1 trillion.

COVID-19's Impact on Bitcoin

One of the biggest drops in the history of cryptocurrency asset prices occurred as a result of the global market crash that was brought on by COVID-19 in March 2020. The price of Bitcoin dropped by almost 50% in a single day during this time. However, in the months that followed, prices rose along with safe-haven investments like gold and other bullions, as investors sought out value stores in the face of volatile markets. Bitcoin's price increased 16 times to over $64,000 by April 2021 from its low point just over a year earlier. Additionally, it is accurate to say that some analysts believe COVID-19 may boost demand for Bitcoin by enhancing the idea that cryptocurrency is a safe-haven asset. Other similar but most popular cryptocurrencies in the world are as follows:

Two of the biggest competitors of Bitcoin are *Ethereum and Darkcoin* (Now Dash).

No doubt that **Ethereum**, the second-most famous cryptocurrency after Bitcoin, runs on a unique protocol using blockchain. Ethereum not only does currency but also allows programs and platforms to run on top. Firms such as ConsenSys have partnered with Microsoft to work on Ethereum applications. As the organizations that utilize it increases, blockchain technology will be ubiquitous.

As a rival to bitcoin, this new payment method needs to be quicker, safer, and more user-friendly than the competition to draw in users. On each of these three criteria, Bitcoin and the other available digital currencies fall short. Dash offers features and functions that address these issues and shortcomings not addressed by most others. Additionally, Dash provides its users with a quick send option that is just as simple as using a credit card. Furthermore, any future projects must be submitted for voting to those who own 1,000 coins or more. A system like this has the advantage of being a decentralized network, which enables quick decision-making and prevents conflicts like those found in Bitcoin, which lacks the ability to force users to adopt new versions. Dash's upcoming version will have features like moderated transactions to ward against fraud and theft. With the help of such a feature, money could only be released after goods are received and vault accounts could prevent an upcoming withdrawal of funds within a day. The idea is to have a medium of exchange that makes regular business transactions easier. Dash's unique governance structure is by far its most innovative feature and is unreplicable.

Smart Contracts

A mutual contract is an agreement between two entities or individuals, which serves as legal protection for both parties involved in a potential business deal across the boundary.

The main legal tool used by businesses to reduce their risks when operating in global or international markets is international contracts, which is a useful feature. One or more contracts from various parties, such as freight forwarders and sales tax agents, will probably be necessary when a business intends to expand its goods or services into the international market. The General Agreement on Tariffs and Trade (GATT) was a historical type of international trade agreement. It was signed in 1947 by 23 countries – including Canada – and went into force on 1st January 1948. Eight rounds of negotiations resulted in its refinement and the World Trade Organization's (WTO) founding. A legal agreement known as the General Agreement on Tariffs and Trade (GATT) reduced or eliminated tariffs, quotas, and subsidies while maintaining a number of important regulations, thereby minimizing obstacles to international trade.

WTO replaced GATT as it is better than GATT in three respects:

- The WTO covers services and intellectual property.
- The WTO dispute settlement system is faster and more automatic than the old GATT system.

- Its rulings cannot be blocked.

One of the main reasons behind the collapse of the GATT was that the organization was in favor of the industrial countries, and lost confidence among the developing countries.

Most escrow (earnest money) agreements are put into place when one party wants to make sure the other party meets certain conditions or obligations before it moves forward with a deal. In an escrow agreement, a party usually a depositor deposits the funds or assets with the escrow agent (third gyranter party) until the time the agreement is fulfilled. Once the contractual conditions are fulfilled, the escrow agent then will deliver the funds or the assets to the beneficiary under the agreement. Escrow is a type of legal holding account for items, which can't be released until predetermined conditions are satisfied. Typically, items are held in escrow until the process involving a financial transaction has been completed. Valuables held in escrow can include real estate, money, stocks, and securities. For instance, a seller may set up an escrow agreement to ensure a potential homebuyer can secure financing before the sale goes through.

Blockchain-based smart contracts are proposed contracts that can be partially or fully executed or enforced without human interaction. One of the many other main objectives of a smart contract is automated escrow. The escrow provides both the developers and users of technology with valuable peace of mind. When you create an escrow contract, software source code or other IP from the developer is placed in a secure escrow account held by an escrow agent – a trusted independent third party.

Smart contracts are characterized by their ability to execute contracts automatically by the blockchain network, negating the need for a trusted third party, such as a trustee, to mediate disputes between contracting parties. As a result, there might be less conflict and friction when transferring value between entities, which could pave the way for more advanced transaction automation. An organization of 190 nations, the International Monetary Fund (IMF) seeks to secure financial stability, facilitate international trade, encourage high employment and sustainable economic growth, and lessen poverty on a global scale. The money that nations pay the IMF as their capital subscription (quotas) when they join the organization provides the majority of its funding. Every IMF member is given a quota that is primarily determined by how they rank in the global economy. When nations encounter financial difficulties, they can then borrow from this pool.

An International Monetary Fund's staff discussion from 2018 reported that smart contracts based on blockchain technology might reduce moral hazards and optimize the use of contracts in general. However, "no viable smart contract systems have yet emerged". Due to the lack of widespread use, their legal status was unclear. This topic is further elaborated in *Chapter* 8 of this book.

It is becoming more and more important to figure out how to create trustworthy digital business agreements as processes become more digitalized. Traditional contracts, which are frequently intricate, time-consuming, and costly, can be effectively replaced with smart contracts. Smart contracts are becoming more widely used and simpler to create globally in a very short amount of time. The development of blockchain consortiums like Hyperledger has made smart contracts available today to optimize a wide range of financial and business processes. It is now essential to figure out how to create trustworthy digital business agreements in light of the growing digitalization of society. In this regard, smart contracts are an excellent substitute for traditional contracts, which are frequently intricate, cumbersome, and costly. A smart contract, as defined by its explicit terms and conditions, is a self-executing, self-enforcing protocol that uses blockchain technology to store and execute contractual clauses. In order to enter into a blockchain-based smart contract, the involved parties must first discuss and agree upon the terms of the contract before memorializing them, partially or fully, in the smart contract code that is kept on the blockchain. The most advantageous aspect of smart contracts is their ability to conduct trustworthy transactions without the involvement of other parties. Because it is a decentralized approach, middlemen are not needed at the time of deal confirmation. Smart contracts run on their own schedule[4].

Essential Elements of Smart Contracts

Smart contracts are made up of several essential elements, including *signatories, subjects, and specific terms*:

- The signatories of the smart contract may be any of two or more parties who provide their final "go forward". By signing digitally, they confirm that they both agree to the suggested terms.
- The subject matter of the agreement, which is restricted to the smart contract's surroundings, is the second essential element.
- The smart contract's precise terms come as the third essential element. Their implementation in a programming language must be compatible with the blockchain of the smart contract and include a detailed mathematical description.

The contract will be carried out automatically based on these three terms at the very least.

Smart Contracts and Blockchain

The technology of Smart contracts uses blockchain technology to verify, validate, capture, and enforce agreed-upon terms between multiple parties. The key to these contracts is the **decentralized network** known as blockchain.

Key Features of Smart Contracts:

- Smart contracts on the blockchain allow for transactions and agreements to be carried out among anonymous parties.
- Agreements are mutual without the need for a central entity, external enforcement, or legal system.
- The transactions are transparent.
- The transactions are irreversible and traceable.
- The transactions are easily traceable but with valid internal and external keys.
- Blockchain is the perfect environment for smart contracts, as all the data stored is immutable and secure.
- The data of a smart contract is encrypted and exists on a ledger, meaning that the information recorded in the blocks can never be lost, modified, or deleted.

This topic is dealt in detail in *Chapter* 8 of this book.

Smart Contract Platforms

Nowadays, there are a number of smart contract platforms. They could be subdivided on the basis of technology, end-user (banking, government, supply chain, real estate, insurance, and so on), and region (Europe, North America, Asia, or the rest of the world oriented).

The differences among various platforms are:

- In their use of the type of programming languages
- Method of establishing blockchain consensus
- Cost of maintaining an application's smart contracts
- Differences in blockchain security
- Transaction confirmation speed, trust in the main network nodes, and much more

The first blockchain platform with codes specifically designed for dApp development was created by Ethereum. Numerous other platforms have emerged as a result of their appearance, including Aeternity, Cardano, Qtum, Stellar, and Waves.

Building Blocks of Blockchain

As previously mentioned, a blockchain is made up of a series of secure data blocks that are linked to each other in a sequential fashion. When combined, they create an unchangeable ledger that is shared among the involved nodes. These nodes are platforms for computing that communicate with customers. Sharing information among all parties who access it through an application is the goal of the blockchain. There are two options for reading and writing this ledger: (1) unrestricted (also known as "permissionless"), or (2) restricted (also known as "permissioned").

Main Building Blocks

We have already learned about what is the basic block in blockchain technology earlier in this chapter. The main building blocks of a Blockchain system are its

- Data structure (that is, the Blockchain) and
- Its nodes, where the logic and computations take place.

  There are two types of nodes:

  - Full-function nodes and
  - Partial nodes

The full-function node maintains a complete copy of the blockchain and is capable of executing transactions and contributes to extending the chain. All full-function nodes are equivalent in terms of functionality and are connected in a peer-to-peer network. As such, there's no hierarchy among nodes, and all nodes can communicate with one another.

A partial node is also connected to the network in a peer-to-peer fashion, but doesn't contain a full copy of the blockchain. It needs the services of a full-function node to execute transactions, and it doesn't extend the chain. Partial nodes are also called **lightweight nodes**. They do not store a complete ledger. They only download the part of the blockchain that they require using Simplified Payment Verification (SPV) mode.

A blockchain starts from its genesis block and new blocks are appended periodically. Each block records executed transactions. The nodes collaborate to connect the blocks into a blockchain, creating a ledger that cannot be changed backward without redoing a PoW.

An Ethereum system's primary components are its data structure, that is the blockchain and its nodes, which house the computations and logic. Full-function nodes and partial nodes are the two different kinds of nodes. In addition to keeping an entire copy of the blockchain up to date, the full-function node can carry out transactions and add nodes to the chain. Every full-function node in a peer-to-peer network has the same functionality and is connected. Nodes can thus communicate with one another and there is no hierarchy among them. Although it lacks a complete copy of the Blockchain, a partial node is still peer-to-peer connected to the network. It does not add to the chain; rather, it executes transactions through the assistance of a full-function node. Another name for partial nodes is lightweight nodes. They do not keep an entire ledger on file. They utilize SPV mode to download only the portion of the blockchain that they need. A blockchain begins with its genesis block, to which new blocks are periodically added. All executed transactions are recorded in each block. Working together, the nodes join the blocks to form a blockchain, which is a ledger that cannot be altered in the past without resolving a PoW.

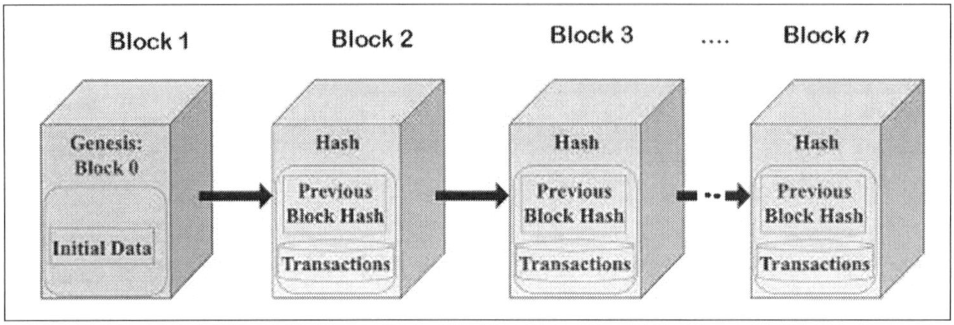

Figure 1.6: *Formation of Blockchain*

Every block has two types of information: internal information that describes how the block is chained to other blocks and provides security, and application-specific information (also known as the "payload") that logs transactions or smart contracts (which are composed of a mix of data and code that can be executed by the nodes). Blocks are automatically shared throughout the network, validated, and connected by hash values. This is something we will discuss in *Chapter 2, Cryptographic Hash Function* (CHF), of the book.

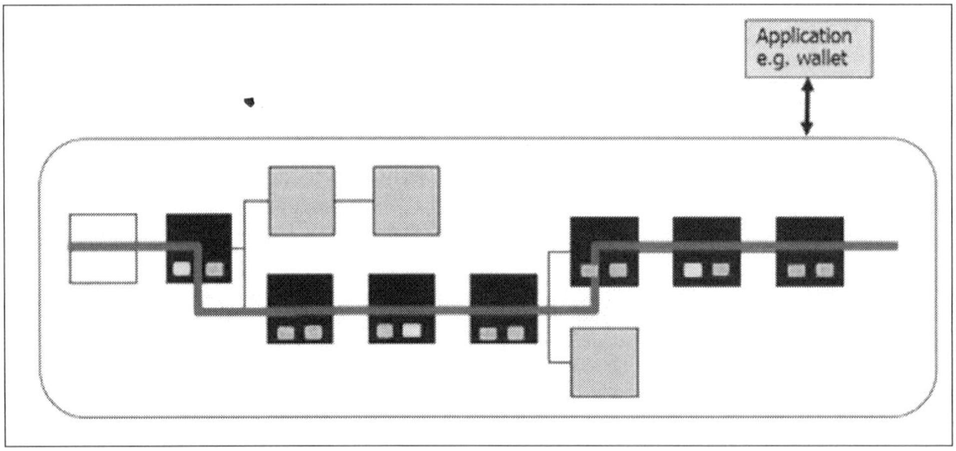

Figure 1.7: *Chain of Successful Blocks in a Set of Transactions*

Every blockchain has two built-in security features and an additional optional third. The first lesson teaches you to link every block to its predecessor in a way that makes it difficult to undo computationally. The first method involves using a hash tree to calculate a hash for each block, which includes the hash value of the previous block (this is done for every new block created, except for the first block, known as the "genesis" block, which has no predecessor); the second method involves adding a unique number, known as the block's "nonce", to each block. It is possible to determine a specific hash value for the entire block by inserting the correct nonce. Since calculating a nonce is computationally difficult, it is also known as a PoW. When the nonce is inserted in the proper location, calculating the hash function over the block yields a specific hash value (one that starts with a specified number of zeroes). We will read about PoW in *Chapter* 4 of this book.

In short, the PoW is the original consensus algorithm in a blockchain network. The algorithm is used to confirm the transaction and create a new block to the chain. In this algorithm, minors (a group of people) compete against each other to complete the transaction on the network.

Changing a block would require recalculating the nonce for every block that was subsequently linked to it because the nonce is difficult to calculate. It is generally accepted that after the chain has been extended by roughly six blocks, it is not feasible to alter it given the state of algorithms and computing power at this time. The second protection mechanism, which requires a majority of nodes to agree on the next block that extends the chain, is provided by a peer-to-peer built-in consensus mechanism. This implies that there isn't a single point of control that could be attacked. A blockchain operates in a peer-to-peer model, where all nodes are equal, and does not rely on a central and trustworthy entity. Nodes rely on a consensus process to validate transactions in the absence of trust between them. The consensus mechanism relies on each node verifying that the data it has received complies with a set of rules and on each node verifying the nonce. The application functionality is specific to the application, and the inbuilt rules verify that the proposed transaction conforms with it. In the case of virtual currency, for instance, it is first confirmed that the payer has ownership of the coins they wish to spend (as shown by a signature signed with the private key of a Public Key Infrastructure (PKI) key pair, where the signature can be successfully verified), and that the transaction follows the necessary structure. The Proof of Work Verification process then needs to show that a node made the necessary computational investment.

Taking the case in which two nodes broadcast different versions of the next block at the same time, some nodes may receive one or the other first. In such case, each node would work on the first block received, but save the other branch in case it becomes longer. The tie will be broken when the next nonce is found and one branch becomes longer; the nodes that were working on the other branch will then switch to the longer one.

The third (optional) protection mechanism stems from the fact that blockchains come in two different flavors: permissionless and permissioned. The public and Bitcoin-like systems where every node can participate (read, add entries, or extend the blockchain by finalizing a candidate block with the correct nonce) are denoted as permissionless.

The permissioned blockchains allow only a limited set of known and accepted nodes to process transactions and extend the chain. As this type of chain is typically set by known and consenting organizations with an assumed level of trust, the consensus mechanism can be based on a less intensive computational process (they don't need to prove to each other that they have invested a sufficient amount of computational power in confirming the transactions)

Currently, most active Blockchain and pioneer technologies include the **Bitcoin, Ethereum**, and **Ripple**, as well as Ethereum-based follow-ups that apply new approaches for scalability, such as **Tendermint, Hydrachain**, **and Hyperledger**. Ripple is a clearing and settlement technology. There is also a broad category of more scalable designs such as the **Lightning Network, Raiden, BigchainDB, RChain**, and **Aeternity**. There are also Superchains, which connect multiple blockchains together. These include Interledger and Cosmos, and there are others, such as Cord, which come with separated 'fact' databases, where the data is kept consistent, but not everyone has a copy of everything.

Transactions

Before a transaction is added to the blockchain, it must be authenticated and authorized.

Key Steps of Blockchain Transaction

There are several key steps a transaction must go through before it is added to the blockchain (see *Figure* 1.8)[5]. We have to understand the process of authentication using cryptographic keys and authorization via proof of work, together with the role of mining, and the more recent adoption of proof of stake protocols in later blockchain networks.

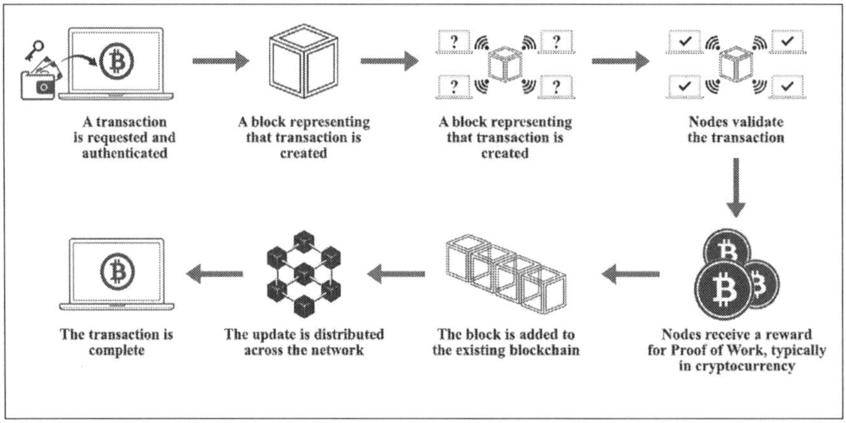

Figure 1.8: *Steps in Blockchain Transactions (Courtesy: Euromoney Learning 2020)*

Authentication

Although the original blockchain was designed to operate without a central authority (that is, with no bank or regulator controlling who transacts), transactions still have to be authenticated.

Authentication is done using cryptographic keys, a string of data (like a password) that identifies a user and gives access to their "**account**" or "**wallet**" of value on the system.

For this, each user has to have their own *private key* and a *public key* that everyone can see. Using them, both create a secure digital identity to authenticate the user via digital signatures and to 'unlock' the transaction they want to perform.

Authorization

Once the transaction is agreed upon by the users mutually, it needs to be *approved*, or *authorized*, before it is added to a block in the chain.

For a *public* blockchain, the decision to add a transaction to the chain is made by arriving at **consensus**. This means that the majority of "nodes" (on different computers in the network) must agree that the transaction is valid. The people who own the computers in the network are most of the time incentivized to verify transactions through rewards. This process is known as 'Proof of Work'.

Proof of Work (PoW)

The process of Proof of Work (POW) requires the people who own the computers in the network to solve a complex mathematical problem (by mining) to be able to add a block to the chain.

Miners

This process of solving the problem is known as **mining**, and '**miner**s' are usually rewarded for their work in cryptocurrency.

The mathematical problem can only be solved by trial and error and the odds of solving the problem are about 1 in 5.9 trillion, so mining is very cumbersome and not at all easy. It requires substantial computing power and involves considerable amounts of energy. This means the rewards for undertaking the mining must outweigh the cost of the computers and the electricity cost of running them, as one computer alone would take years to find a solution to the mathematical problem.

The Energy Consumption in the Process of Mining

The process of creating Bitcoin to spend or trade consumes around 91 terawatt-hours of electricity annually worldwide, more than is used by Finland, a nation of about 5.5 million persons. The Cambridge Bitcoin Electricity Consumption Index estimates the bitcoin mining network consumes almost 70 terawatt-hours (TWh) of electricity per year, ranking it the 40th largest consumer of electricity by 'country'. By way of comparison, Ireland (ranked 68th) uses just over a third of Bitcoin's consumption, or 25 TWh, and Austria at number 42 consumes 64.6 TWh of electricity per year, according to 2016 data compiled by the CIA.

The Problem with Proof of Work

To create economies of scale, miners often pool their resources together through companies that aggregate a large group of miners. These prospective miners then share the rewards and fees offered by the blockchain network.

The problem gets harder and the network gets larger, theoretically distributing the chain further due to blockchain growth. More and more computers join to try and solve the problem, making it ever more difficult to sabotage or hack. In practice though, mining power has become concentrated in the hands of a few mining pools. These large organizations have the vast computing and electrical power now needed to maintain and grow a blockchain network based around Proof of Work validation.

Proof of Stake

To combat this problem, later blockchain networks have evolved and adopted the process of "Proof of Stake" validation consensus protocols, where participants must have a stake in the blockchain - usually by owning some of the cryptocurrency - to be in with a chance of selecting, verifying, and validating transactions. This saves substantial computing power resources because no mining is required.

In addition, blockchain technologies have evolved to include "Smart Contracts", which automatically execute transactions when certain conditions have been met.

The Process of Transaction

One of blockchain technology's fundamental (rather cardinal) features is the way it confirms and authorizes transactions. For example, if two individuals wish to perform a transaction with a *private and public* key, respectively, the first person party would attach the transaction information to the public key of the second party. This total information is gathered together into a block.

Distributed Consensus

A distributed consensus ensures a consensus of data among nodes in a distributed system or reaches an agreement on a proposal[6].

A fundamental problem in distributed computing and multi-agent systems is to achieve overall system reliability in the presence of a number of faulty processes. This often requires coordinating processes to reach **consensus** or agree on some data value that is needed during computation. Example applications of consensus include agreeing on what transactions to commit to a database in which order, state machine replication, and atomic broadcasts. Real-world applications often requiring consensus include cloud computing, clock synchronization, PageRank, opinion formation, smart power grids, state estimation, control of UAVs (and multiple robots/agents in general), load balancing, blockchain, and others.

The process of achieving consensus requires agreement among a number of **processes** (or agents) for a single data value. Some of the processes (agents) may fail or be unreliable in other ways, so consensus protocols must be fault-tolerant or resilient. The processes must somehow put forth their candidate values, communicate with one another, and agree on a single consensus value.

In the control of multi-agent systems, the consensus problem is fundamental. One approach to generating consensus is for all processes (agents) to agree on a majority value. In this context, a majority requires at least one more than half of the available votes (where each process is given a vote). However, one or more faulty processes may skew the resultant outcome, such that consensus may not be reached or may be reached incorrectly.

Protocols that solve consensus problems are designed to deal with a limited number of faulty processes. These protocols must satisfy a number of requirements to be useful. For instance, a trivial protocol could have all processes output binary value 1. This is not useful and thus the requirement is modified such that the output must somehow depend on the input. That is, the output value of a consensus protocol must be the input value of some process. Another requirement is that a process may decide upon an output value only once and this decision is irrevocable. A process is called correct in an execution if it does not experience a failure. A consensus protocol tolerating halting failures must satisfy the following properties[7]:

1. **Agreement:** Every correct process must agree on the same value.
2. **Integrity: If all correct processes propose the same value, then any correct process must decide on that value.**
3. **Termination**: Eventually, every correct process decides on some value.
4. A consensus algorithm may be defined as the mechanism through which a blockchain network reaches consensus.

Agreement, a safety property, means that all correct processes select the same value and these values are valid within the dictates of the protocol. In other words, the state of being "correct" is determined by how many other processes share your value (all, some quorum, or even one).

Integrity addresses the ability to recover from the failure of a participating node. Variations on the definition of integrity may be appropriate, according to the application. For example, a weaker type of integrity would be for the decision value to equal a value that some correct process proposed – not necessarily all of them[7]. The integrity condition is also known as validity in the literature.

Termination is a liveness property, which means that agreement ceases if all correct (non-faulty) processes eventually do not produce a value.

Public (decentralized) blockchains are built as distributed systems and, since they do not rely on a central authority, the distributed nodes need to agree on the validity of transactions. This is where consensus algorithms come into play. They assure that the protocol rules are being followed and guarantee that all transactions occur in a trustless way, so the coins are only able to be spent once.

Properties of Blockchain

A blockchain exhibits several properties that make it a suitable candidate for several application domains[8]. The properties are as follows:

- **Distributed consensus on the chain state**: One of the crucial properties of any blockchain is its capability to achieve a distributed consensus on the state of the chain without being reliant on any trusted third party. This opens up the door of opportunities to build and utilize a system where states and interactions are verifiable by the miners in public blockchain systems or by the

  Authorized entities in private blockchain systems.

- **Immutability and irreversibility of chain state**: Achieving a distributed consensus with the participation of a large number of nodes ensures that the chain state becomes practically immutable and irreversible after a certain period of time. This also applies to smart contracts, hence enabling the deployment and execution of immutable computer programs.
- **Data (transaction) persistence**: Data in a blockchain is stored in a distributed fashion, ensuring data persistence as long as there are participating nodes in the P2P network.
- **Data provenance**: The data storage process in any blockchain is facilitated by means of a mechanism called the transaction. Every transaction needs to be digitally signed using public key cryptography, which ensures the authenticity of the source of data. Combining this with the immutability and irreversibility of a blockchain provides a strong non-repudiation instrument for any data in the blockchain.
- **Distributed data control**: A blockchain ensures that data stored in the chain or retrieved from the chain can be carried out in a distributed manner that exhibits no single point of failure.

- **Accountability and transparency**: Since the state of the chain, along with every single interaction among participating entities, can be verified by any authorized entity, a blockchain promotes accountability and transparency.

Blockchain Layers

There are several components in a blockchain system whose functionalities range from collecting transactions, propagating blocks, mining, achieving consensus, and maintaining the ledger for its underlying crypto-currencies[9].

The aforementioned components can be grouped together according to their functionalities using different layers, similar to the well-known TCP/IP layer. In fact, there have been a few suggestions to design a blockchain system using a layered approach. The motivation is that a layered design will be much more modular and easier to maintain. For example, in case a bug is found in a component of a layer in a blockchain system, it will only affect the functionalities of that corresponding layer while other layers remain unaffected.

For example, David et al.[10] suggest four layers:

1. Consensus
2. Mining
3. Propagation
4. Semantic

However, it is believed that the proposed layers do not reflect the proper grouping of functionalities. For example, consensus and mining should be part of the same layer as mining can be considered an inherent part of achieving consensus. In addition to this, some blockchain systems might not have any mining algorithms associated with it.

However, Md Sadek Ferdous et al.[9] suggested four layers (see *Figure* 1.9): network, consensus, application, and meta-application. The functionalities of these layers are briefly presented as follows:

- **Meta-Application Layer:** The functionalities of the meta-application layer in a blockchain system (see *Figure* 1.9) are to provide an overlay on top of the application layer to exploit the semantic interpretation of a blockchain system for other purposes in various application domains. For example, Bitcoin has been experimented to adopt in multiple application domains, such as DNS-like decentralized naming systems, decentralized immutable time-stamped hashed records, and decentralized Public Key Infrastructure (PKI) like Certcoin.

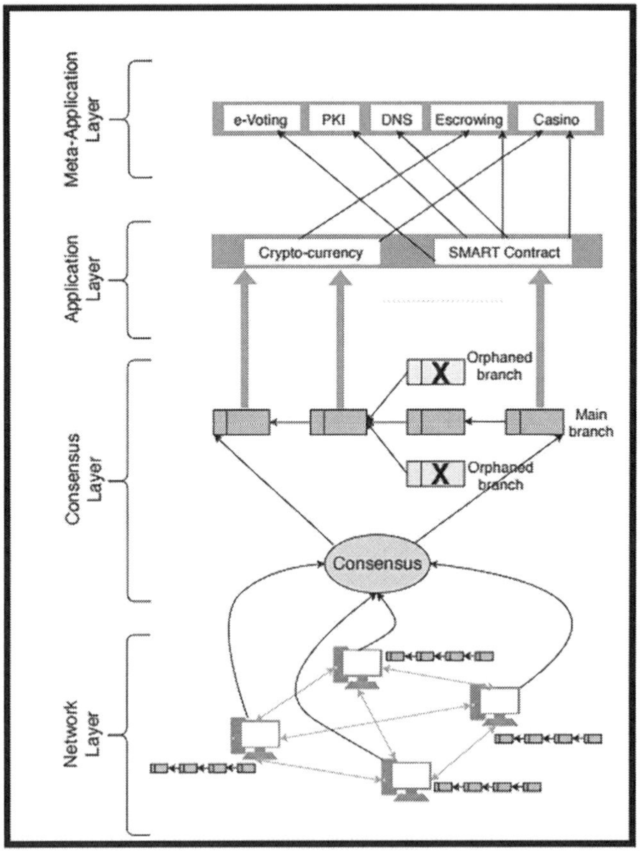

Figure 1.9: *Blockchain Layers*

- **Application Layer:** The application layer (see *Figure* 1.9) defines the semantic interpretation of a blockchain system. Semantic interpretation would be to define a crypto-currency and then set up protocols for how such a currency can be exchanged between different entities.

  Another example is to establish protocols to maintain a state machine embodying programming capabilities within the blockchain, which can be exploited to create and deploy immutable code (the so-called smart contract). The application also defines the rewarding mechanism, if any, in the blockchain system.

- **Consensus Layer:** The consensus layer, as presented in *Figure* 1.9, is responsible for providing the distributed consensus mechanism in the blockchain that essentially governs the order of the blocks. A critical component of this layer is the proof protocol (for example, PoW and PoS), which is often used to verify every single block, which ultimately is used to achieve the required consensus in the system.

- **Network Layer:** The components in the network layer are responsible for handling network functionalities, which include joining in the underlying P2P network, the remaining Network Layer. The components in the network layer are responsible for handling network functionalities, which include joining in the underlying P2P network, remaining in the network by following the underlying networking protocol, disseminating the current state of the blockchain to newly joined nodes, propagating and receiving transactions and blocks, and so on.

Consensus Taxonomy and Properties

With the introduction and advancement of different blockchain systems, there has been a renewed interest in distributed consensus with the consequent innovation of different types of consensus algorithms. These consensus algorithms have different characteristics and functionalities. In this section, we first distinguish between two major types of consensus and then present a taxonomy of their properties.

The mechanisms for establishing consensus by the various blockchain systems can be classified based on the reward mechanism that participating nodes might receive. Therefore, we first classify the consensus mechanisms in blockchain systems into two categories:

- Incentivized and
- Non-incentivized algorithms

Incentivized Consensus: The algorithms belonging to this category reward participating nodes for creating and adding a new block in the blockchain. Incentivized Consensus algorithms are exclusively used in public blockchain systems, and the reward provided acts as an incentive for participating nodes to behave accordingly and to follow the corresponding consensus protocol rigorously.

Non-incentivized Consensus: Private blockchain systems deploy a type of consensus algorithm that does not rely on any incentive mechanism for the participating nodes to create and add a new block in the blockchain. Such algorithms belong to this category. With the absence of any reward mechanism, these nodes are considered trusted as only authorized (allowed) nodes can participate in the block creation process of the consensus algorithm.

Consensus Properties

Various consensus algorithms have different characteristics and are meant to serve different purposes. To compare these disparate groups of consensus algorithms, we need to define evaluation criteria. In this section, we present this evaluation criteria in the form of taxonomies of consensus properties.

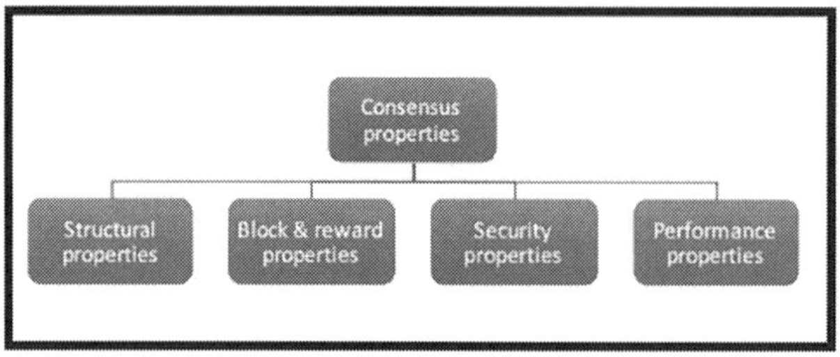

Figure 1.10: *Taxonomy of Consensus Properties*

The taxonomy of various consensus schemes is depicted in *Figure* 1.10. According to this taxonomy, a consensus mechanism has four major groups of properties:

- Structural
- Block and reward
- Security
- Performance properties

Structural properties

Structural properties define how different nodes within a blockchain network are structured to participate in a consensus algorithm. These properties can be sub-divided into different categories, as illustrated in *Figure* 1.11. We briefly describe each of these categories as follows:

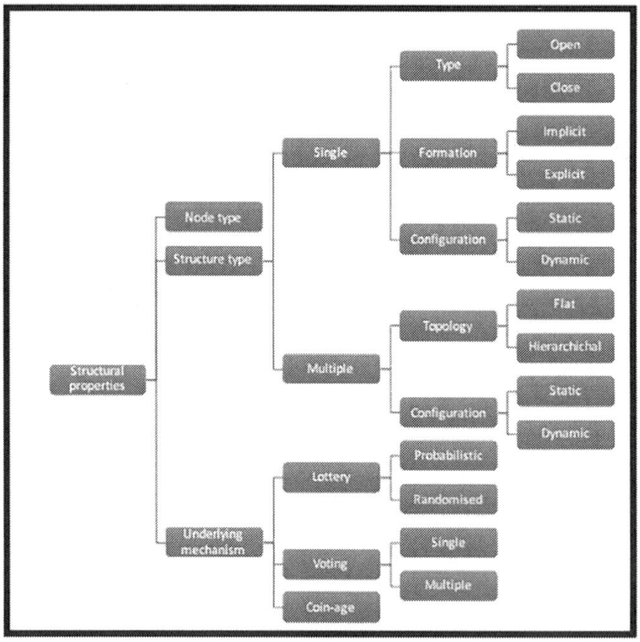

Figure 1.11: *Taxonomy of Structural Properties*

- **Node types**: It refers to different types of nodes that a consensus algorithm is required to engage with to achieve its consensus.
- **Structure type**: It refers to the ways different nodes are structured within the consensus algorithm using the concept of a committee. The committee itself can be of two types: single and multiple committees.
- **Underlying mechanism**: This refers to the specific mechanism that a consensus algorithm deploys to select a particular node. The mechanism can utilize a lottery, either a cryptography-based probabilistic mechanism or other randomized mechanisms. In a voting mechanism, **voting** can be carried out either in a single or multiple rounds. The **coinage**, on the other hand, utilizes a special property, which depends on how long a particular coin has been owned by its owner.

Types of Transactions

Now, let's explore the different types of blockchain networks.

Types of Blockchain

There are four different types of blockchain. They are as follows:

- **Private Blockchain Networks**

  Private blockchain operates on closed networks and tends to work well for private businesses and organizations. Firms can use a private blockchain to customize their accessibility and authorization preferences, parameters to the network, and other important security options. Only one authority manages a private blockchain network.

- **Public Blockchain Networks**

  Bitcoin and other cryptocurrencies originated from public blockchain, which also played a role in popularizing DLT. Public blockchain also helps to eliminate certain challenges and issues, such as security flaws and centralization. With DLT, data is distributed across a peer-to-peer network, rather than being stored in a single location. A **consensus algorithm** is used for verifying information authenticity; PoS and PoW are two frequently used consensus methods.

- **Permissioned Blockchain Networks**

  Also sometimes known as hybrid blockchain, permissioned blockchain networks are private blockchains that allow special access for authorized individuals. Organizations typically set up these types of blockchain to get the best of both worlds, and it enables better structure when assigning who can participate in the network and in what transactions.

- **Consortium Blockchain**

  Similar to permissioned blockchains, consortium blockchains have both public and private components, except multiple organizations will manage a single consortium blockchain network. Although these types of blockchains can initially be more complex to set up, once they are running, they can offer better security. Additionally, consortium blockchains are optimal for collaboration with multiple organizations.

Private Transactions

Many blockchain networks operate as public databases, meaning that anyone with an Internet connection can view a list of the network's transaction history. Although users can access details about transactions, they cannot access identifying information about the users making those transactions. It is a common misperception that blockchain networks like bitcoin are anonymous, when in fact they are only confidential.

When a user makes a public transaction, their unique code – called a public key, as mentioned earlier – is recorded on the blockchain, while their personal information is not. If a person has made a Bitcoin purchase on an exchange that requires identification, then the person's identity is still linked to their blockchain address – but a transaction, even when tied to a person's name, does not reveal any personal information.

To see how a bank differs from blockchain, let's compare the banking system to Bitcoin's implementation of blockchain. *Table 1.2* provides other details.

Cryptocurrencies: The Beginning of Blockchain's Technological Rise

Blockchain's most well-known use (and maybe most controversial) is in cryptocurrencies. Cryptocurrencies are digital currencies (or tokens), such as Bitcoin, Ethereum, or Litecoin, that can be used to buy goods and services. Just like a digital form of cash, crypto can be used to buy everything from your lunch to your next home. Unlike cash, crypto uses blockchain to act as both a public ledger and an enhanced cryptographic security system, so online transactions are always recorded and secured.

A cryptocurrency is a digital or virtual currency that is secured by cryptography, which makes it nearly impossible to counterfeit or double-spend[11]. Many cryptocurrencies are decentralized networks based on blockchain technology – a distributed ledger enforced by a disparate network of computers. A defining feature of cryptocurrencies is that they are generally not issued by any central authority, rendering them theoretically immune to government interference or manipulation.

"Crypto" refers to the various encryption algorithms and cryptographic techniques that safeguard these entries, such as elliptical curve encryption, public-private key pairs, and hashing functions.

A cryptocurrency can be considered as a form of digital asset based on a network that is distributed across a large number of computers. This decentralized structure allows them to exist outside the control of governments and central authorities. Experts believe that blockchain and related technology will disrupt many industries, including finance and law.

Cryptocurrencies can be mined or purchased from *cryptocurrency exchanges*. Not all e-commerce sites allow purchases using cryptocurrencies. In fact, cryptocurrencies, even popular ones like Bitcoin, are hardly used for retail transactions. However, the skyrocketing value of cryptocurrencies has made them popular as trading instruments. To a limited extent, they are also used for cross-border transfers.

Cryptocurrencies as a Blockchain

Blockchain technology is central to Bitcoin's and other cryptocurrencies' usefulness and allure. A collection of linked blocks from an online ledger is what blockchain, as its name suggests, basically is. Every network participant has independently verified a set of transactions that make up each block. This makes it nearly impossible to fabricate transaction histories, as each node must validate each newly generated block before it is confirmed. Every machine on a node, or individual network, that keeps a copy of the ledger must concur on the information that goes into the online ledger. Blockchain technology is useful for a variety of industries and processes, including online voting and crowdfunding, according to industry experts. Companies involved in finance, such as JPMorgan Chase & Co., are testing the use of blockchain technology to reduce transaction costs by expediting payment processing.

Cryptocurrency: Procedure of Its Working

In practice, all cryptocurrencies ought to be digital currencies that use blockchain technology to record and secure every transaction. A cryptocurrency (for example, Bitcoin) ought to be used in a digital form of cash to pay for everything from everyday items to larger purchases like cars and homes. These items can be bought using one of several digital wallets issued by various trading platforms, then digitally transferred upon purchase of an item, with the blockchain recording the transaction and the new owner. The beauty of carrying transactions through cryptocurrencies is that everything is recorded in a public ledger and secured using cryptography, making an irrefutable, timestamped, and secure record of every payment.

At the time of writing this para (January 2022), there are roughly 6,700 cryptocurrencies in the world, which have a total market cap of around $1.6 trillion, with Bitcoin holding a majority of the value. These tokens have become incredibly popular over the last few years, with one Bitcoin equaling $60,000. Here are some of the main reasons why everyone is suddenly taking notice of cryptocurrencies:

- Blockchain's security makes theft much harder since each cryptocurrency has its own irrefutable identifiable number that is attached to one owner.
- Crypto reduces the need for individualized currencies and central banks. With blockchain, any of the cryptocurrencies can be sent to anywhere and anyone in the world without the need for their native currency exchange or without interference from central banks.
- Cryptocurrencies have made certain people rich, with early adopters becoming billionaires. Whether this is a positive feature remains to be seen, as some retractors believe that speculators do not have the long-term benefits of crypto in mind.
- More and more large corporations are fascinated around the idea of a blockchain-based payments using digital currency. In February 2021, Tesla famously announced that it would invest $1.5 billion into Bitcoin and accept it as payment for their electric cars.

Types of Cryptocurrency

There are thousands of cryptocurrencies present in the market today. Out of which, Bitcoin is the most popular and valuable cryptocurrency. An anonymous person, Satoshi Nakamoto, invented and introduced it to the world via a white paper in 2008.

Bitcoin, which was made available to the public in 2009, remains the most widely traded and covered cryptocurrency. As of November 2021, there were over 18.8 million bitcoins in circulation, with a total market cap of around $1.2 trillion. Only 21 million bitcoins will ever exist.

Most of the cryptocurrency providers claim to have a different specification and set of attractive functions. For example, Ethereum's ether markets itself as a booster device for the underlying smart contract platform. Ripple's XRP is used by banks to facilitate transfers between different geographies.

Bitcoin is by far the most popular cryptocurrency followed by other cryptocurrencies such as **Ethereum, Binance Coin, Solana,** and **Cardano.**

In the wake of Bitcoin's success, many other cryptocurrencies, known as "**altcoins** (short for alternative coins)," have been launched. Some of these are clones or forks of Bitcoin, while others are new currencies that were built from scratch. They include **Solana, Litecoin, Ethereum, Cardano,** and **EOS**. By November 2021, the aggregate value of all the cryptocurrencies in existence had reached over $2.1 trillion – Bitcoin represented approximately 41% of that total value.

Advantages and Disadvantages of Cryptocurrency

Cryptocurrencies were introduced and traded with the intent to revolutionize financial infrastructure. As with every revolution, however, there are tradeoffs involved. Some advantages and disadvantages of cryptocurrencies are as follows:

Advantages:

- A new and decentralized paradigm for money is represented by cryptocurrencies. This system eliminates the need for centralized middlemen, such as banks and other financial institutions, to uphold trust and oversee interparty transactions. So, a cryptocurrency-based system removes the chance that a single point of failure, like a Big Bank, could trigger a chain reaction of global financial crises similar to the one that happened in 2008 due to the failure of the US institutions.
- The goal of cryptocurrencies is to facilitate direct money transfers between two people without the involvement of a credit card issuer or bank, which is a reliable third party. These decentralized transfers are safeguarded by implanting the public and private keys as well as various incentive schemes, such as PoS or PoW.
- Compared to traditional money transfers, cryptocurrency transfers between two transacting parties are quicker because they do not involve third parties as middlemen. In decentralized finance, flash loans are an excellent illustration of this type of decentralized transfer. These loans are used for trading and can be completed in a matter of seconds without the need for collateral.
- Coin investments have the potential to yield profits. Over the last 10 years, cryptocurrency markets have experienced a sharp increase in value, reaching nearly $2 trillion by 1st December. As of 2021, the value of Bitcoin in cryptocurrency markets exceeded $862 billion.
- An experiment is being conducted by the remittance economy.

Disadvantages:

- Though they claim to be an anonymous form of transaction, cryptocurrencies are actually pseudonymous. They leave a digital trail that agencies such as the Federal Bureau of Investigation (FBI) or CBI in India can decipher. This opened up possibilities for governments or federal/central authorities to track the financial transactions of ordinary citizens.
- Cryptocurrencies have become a popular tool with criminals for nefarious activities such as money laundering and illicit purchases. The case of Dread Pirate Roberts, who ran a marketplace to sell drugs on the dark web, is already

well known. Cryptocurrencies have also become a favorite of hackers who use them for ransomware activities.

- In theory, cryptocurrencies are meant to remain decentralized in operation, their wealth distributed between many parties on a blockchain. In real life, ownership is highly concentrated. For example, an MIT study found that just 11,000 investors held roughly 45% of Bitcoin's surging value.
- One of the conceits of cryptocurrencies is that anyone can mine them using a computer with an Internet connection. However, mining popular cryptocurrencies requires considerable energy, sometimes as much energy as entire countries consume. The expensive energy costs coupled with the unpredictability of mining have concentrated mining among large firms whose revenues run into billions of dollars. According to an MIT study, 10% of miners account for 90% of its mining capacity.
- Though cryptocurrency blockchains are highly secure, other crypto repositories, such as exchanges and wallets, can be hacked. Many cryptocurrency exchanges and wallets have been hacked over the years, sometimes resulting in millions of dollars worth of "coins" stolen.
- Cryptocurrencies traded in public markets suffer from price volatility. Bitcoin has experienced rapid surges and crashes in its value, climbing to as high as $17,738 in December 2017 before dropping to $7,575 in the following months. Some economists thus consider cryptocurrencies to be a short-lived fad or speculative bubble.
- Cryptocurrencies are a new paradigm for **money**. Their promise is to streamline existing financial architecture to make it faster and cheaper. Their technology and architecture decentralize existing monetary systems and make it possible for transacting parties to exchange value and money independently of intermediary institutions such as banks.
- Cryptocurrencies are generated by mining. For example, Bitcoin is generated using Bitcoin mining. The process involves downloading software that contains a partial or full history of transactions that have occurred in its network. Though anyone with a computer and an Internet connection can mine cryptocurrency, the energy- and resource-intensive nature of mining means that large firms dominate the industry. The process of creating Bitcoin to spend or trade consumes around 91 terawatt-hours of electricity annually, more than is used by Finland or Norway a nation of about 5.5 million.

Permissioned Model of BlockChain

It is now needless to say that blockchain technology works on principles of Decentralized Ledger Technology (DLT). DLT has opened up a multitude of opportunities for companies that are looking to innovate. It is not new; blockchain technology is one of those technologies that have radically changed how industries work.

Permissioned Blockchains

A permissioned blockchain is a blockchain network that requires access to the chain[12]. In this blockchain type, a control layer runs on top of the blockchain that governs the actions performed by the allowed participants. As you can see, permissioned blockchains work entirely different than that of private and public blockchains. They are crafted to take advantage of blockchains without sacrificing the authority aspect of a centralized system.

Basically, there is one big difference between a *permissioned* and a *permissionless blockchain in the manner* the participants are going to interact with the network. A permissioned system is also known to have a restriction on the consensus participants, making permissioned networks highly configured and controlled by the owners. However, it is not a bad thing, but it is all about building a suitable blockchain network.

There are many popular permissioned blockchain frameworks available in the market. The list includes ***Hyperledger*, *Quorum*, *Corda***, and *others*.

Benefits of Permissioned Blockchains

Let's understand the beneficial features of permissioned blockchains.

There are many benefits of permissioned blockchains, which makes it the most preferable to use as compared with permissionless blockchains:

- Permissioned blockchains offer superior performance compared to permissionless blockchains due to a limited number of nodes, eliminating unnecessary computations for reaching consensus and enhancing overall performance. Additionally, permissioned networks have pre-determined nodes for validating transactions.
- Permissioned networks have a structured governance system that allows for quicker rule updates compared to public blockchains. Public blockchains face consensus problems as not all nodes collaborate for implementing updates, leading to slower network updates. In contrast, permissioned blockchains have nodes that work together for faster updates.
- Permissioned networks effectively utilize blockchain for decentralized data storage.
- Permissioned blockchain technology offers cost-effective solutions for various industries.

Consequences of Permissioned Blockchains

Permissioned blockchains have the following drawbacks:

- **Compromised security**: Because all nodes correctly participate in the consensus process, permissionless public or private blockchains have better security. However, this might not apply to permissioned blockchains. A permissioned network's security is only as strong as the integrity of its members. This implies that a limited group within a permissioned system may collaborate to alter network-stored data. The network's integrity may be jeopardized in this way. The system should have the right permissions set in order to prevent those bad actors from combining to produce the intended effect.
- **Control, Censorship, and Regulation**: In a perfect world, permissioned blockchains would function similarly to public blockchains under strict guidelines. Regulating bodies have the ability to impose restrictions on transactions or prevent them altogether, thereby introducing censorship into the network. Any company or organization using the permissioned network is at risk from these. Additionally, this strategy prevents the permissioned network from maximizing the benefits of the entire blockchain ecosystem.

Difference Between Permissioned and Permissionless Blockchain

When we take a stock of the working of these two types of blockchain technology, there are many differences. *Table 1.2* gives you a quick insight into the permissioned blockchain vs. permissionless blockchain:

Criteria	**Permissioned Blockchain**	**Permissionless Blockchain**
General Description	A user has to be permitted by the blockchain authority before she or he could access the network. The user might join only if she or he gets an invitation	An open network system where all the devices can freely access without any type of permission. The ledger is shared and transparent
Speed	Faster	Slower
Privacy	A Private membership holder can also become a member	Transparent and open to anyone
Legitimacy	Legal	Illegal
Ownership	Nodes pre-defined the network	Managed by a group of Public ownership - no one owns

Decentralization	Partially decentralized	Truly decentralized
Cost	Cost-effective	Not so cost-effective
Security	Less secure	More secure

Table 1.2: *Permissioned Blockchain vs. Permissionless Blockchain*

Figure 1.12 shows the distributed network of Public (permissionless) vs. Private (Permissioned) Blockchain.

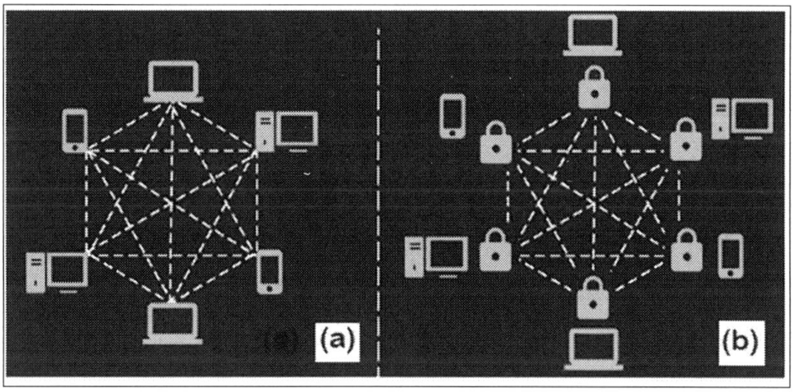

Figure 1.12: *Public (Permissionless) vs. Private (Permissioned) Blockchain Network*

Blockchain Security

Decentralized security and trust have been accomplished via Blockchain technology in a number of ways. New blocks are initially always kept both chronologically and linearly. Put differently, they are continuously appended to the blockchain's "end". Unless the majority of the network has come to a consensus to do so, it is very difficult to go back and change the contents of a block once it has been added to the end of the blockchain. This is so that each block has its own hash, which is also accompanied by the hash of the block that came before it and the time stamp that was previously mentioned. Digital information is converted into a string of numbers and letters by a mathematical function to create hash codes. Should that data be modified in any manner, the hash code will also be altered. Imagine that a hacker who is also a node operator on a blockchain network aims to change a blockchain and pilfer cryptocurrency from other users. Imagine if they changed the one copy they had, it would no longer match the copies of everyone else. The hacker's version of the chain would be rejected as illegitimate when the other copies are compared to each other, and they notice that this one copy stands out. For the hack to be successful, at least 51 percent of the blockchain copies would need to be controlled and altered concurrently by the hacker in order for their new copy to become the majority copy and the agreed-upon chain. Additionally, a massive amount of funding and resources would be needed for such an attack.

Benefits and Drawbacks of Blockchain

Despite its intricacy, blockchain technology offers virtually infinite possibilities for decentralized data storage. Beyond the aforementioned uses, blockchain technology may find use in areas such as increased security, reduced processing costs, and reduced user privacy.

Benefits:

- Increased accuracy through the elimination of human verification
- Lower costs through the elimination of third-party verification
- Decentralization increases the difficulty of tampering with transactions
- Secure, private, and efficient transactions
- Transparent technology
- Offers a banking alternative and a means of protecting personal information for citizens of nations with unstable or underdeveloped governments

Drawbacks:

In addition to the aforementioned benefits, there are certain drawbacks associated with blockchain technology. These include:

- High technology costs involved in mining bitcoin
- Limited transactions per second
- Past associations with illicit activities on the dark web
- Uncertainty and variation in regulations across different jurisdictions
- Restrictions on data storage capacity
- Speed and Data Inefficiency

Unlawful Behavior

On the blockchain network, secrecy safeguards users' privacy and shields them from hackers, but it also permits illicit behavior and trading. The Silk Road, an online dark web bazaar for illegal drugs and money laundering that was operational from February 2011 until October 2013, when it was shut down by the US FBI, is likely the most frequently cited example of blockchain being used for criminal activities.

Using the Tor Browser, users can buy and sell illicit things without being detected on the dark web. They can also make illicit Bitcoin or other cryptocurrency purchases. Financial service providers are required by current U.S. rules to collect data about their clients when they open an account, authenticate each client, and ensure that clients do not appear on any list of recognized or suspected terrorist groups.

We can see the benefits and drawbacks of this arrangement. Financial accounts are accessible to anyone, but it also makes it easier for thieves to conduct business. Many have claimed that the benefits of cryptocurrencies, such as banking the unbanked, outweigh its drawbacks, particularly given that the majority of illicit activity is still carried out using untraceable cash.

Although Bitcoin was initially utilized for these kinds of things, its transparency and development as a financial tool have actually caused criminal behavior to shift to other cryptocurrencies like Dash and Monero. Nowadays, just a very small percentage of Bitcoin transactions are the result of illicit activities.

Business Benefits of Blockchain

Let's examine the two distinct financial systems side by side. All members of legacy business networks have their own ledgers, which are prone to duplication and inconsistencies that lead to disagreements, longer settlement periods, and the requirement for middlemen and their corresponding overhead expenses. However, organizations can save time and money while lowering risks by utilizing blockchain-based shared ledgers, where transactions cannot be changed once they are written to the ledger and certified by consensus.

Blockchain consensus techniques also offer near-real-time reference data, a consolidated, consistent dataset with fewer inaccuracies, and the ability for users to modify the descriptions of the assets they possess.

Because no participating member owns the source of origin for information stored in the shared ledger, blockchain technologies promote trust and integrity in the flow of transaction information among the participating members. Blockchain technologies' inherent immutability mechanisms reduce audit costs and increase regulatory compliance while improving transparency. Additionally, businesses gain from faster execution times, lower costs, and less risk due to contracts executed on business networks using blockchain technologies. These factors allow businesses to engage with clients and create new revenue streams.

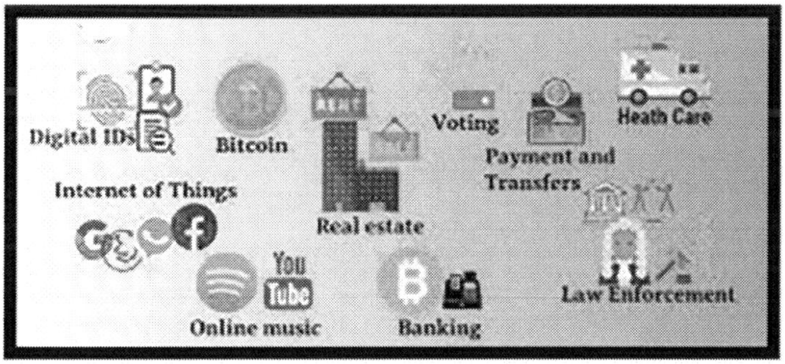

Figure 1.13: *Some Applications of Blockchain*

Evolution of Blockchain

Although blockchain is a very recent new technology, it already boasts a rich and interesting history. The following is a brief timeline of some of the most important and notable events in the development of blockchain.

To understand the type of data system the blockchain is, let's take a look at the kinds of data software and systems we deal with in everyday scenarios.

We have been dealing with the following database technologies in the past:

- A spreadsheet on the user's computer
- A spreadsheet in the user's company's data management system
- A remote cloud-based working model
- Blockchain: a distributed and public data management system

Let us explore the pros and cons of all the four systems.

1. **A spreadsheet on the user's computer**

When you create a new spreadsheet, you are essentially constructing an electronic version of information so you can store it on your computer's internal hard drive as data. The spreadsheet software, as well as your internal hard drive (the hardware), are designed for a single person to use at a time.

Benefits:

- As long as your computer remains secure, you will be the only one who has access to your data.
- The spreadsheet software allows you to use formulas to automatically calculate values based on data in another data cell or spreadsheet stored on your hard drive.

If your spreadsheet software is compatible with your database tool, you will be able to automate data interactions between the two.

Drawbacks:

- If your computer is stolen or your hard drive is corrupted, all of your data will begone.
- Your computer could get hacked, giving unauthorized parties access to your data.
- If you wanted someone else to work collaboratively on the same spreadsheet, you would have to send them the file. They would then have to return the latest version of the file. The file will pass to and from, resulting in many different versions of the same spreadsheet.

2. **A spreadsheet in your company's Data Management System**

When you create a spreadsheet on the computer system at work, the electronic data will be stored on powerful computers (the server) located downstairs in the IT department. Most likely, your company will have backup servers keeping a duplicate of the entire database - either on or off-premise.

Since the company's servers store all the data generated by each person and department, the entire database will be accessible to people with the correct permissions - if they know where to look.

Benefits:

- Anyone who has access to the server can be granted permission to read and/or write the same spreadsheet to improve collaboration.
- Depending on the sophistication of your company's software (ERP system), you will be able to automate data interactions between a number of your software tools. For example, should the projected profit margins calculated by one of your programs fall below a certain level, your email software would automatically send a notification to a relevant individual.

Drawbacks:

- Everyone with access to the data can write, rewrite, or erase data, with no record kept of the changes. Should an error slip in or a willful manipulation of data occur, it will be very difficult to detect and trace it back to its source to correct and hold accountable the person at fault.
- When audit time comes, you will need a team of auditors to sift through data stored in various locations on your server to combine it into a single, coherent report. Because they have to rely on the latest version of the file with no record of the changes (legitimate or illegitimate) that have occurred along the way, it will be impossible to guarantee the accuracy of the data they report. Failing an audit could result in fines and/or other penalties for the company.
- Other departments or regional offices might use different software systems that are incompatible with yours. This creates data silos that limit collaboration and prevent anyone from gaining a Big Picture overview of operations.
- The company is responsible for the entire cost of ownership of the system, including computers, servers, software, security, and the cost of employing IT personnel.
- Company servers can go down and cause operational downtime.
- Company servers are a prime target for cyber-attacks. If your server is hacked, sensitive data like client's personal information and corporate secrets might be compromised. A ransomware attack could encrypt your data and hold you ransom to get access to the decryption key.

- If a cyber-attack occurs, it will be essential to detect it early to isolate the affected machines. However, because your database allows people to read, write, and erase data, hackers can erase traces of their access. This will let them lurk in your servers until they can do maximal damage to your systems.

3. **A remote cloud-based working model**

In a remote working setup, you would create your spreadsheets via Cloud-based software that stores data on a Cloud server, such as Google Drive.

In a cloud computing model, the servers that run your software and store your data are made up of powerful computers located in special remote warehouses (data center). Hundreds or even thousands of computers combine their power and storage so many clients (that is, different companies) and users can access the database simultaneously. To access your data from this data center, you could use an Internet connection or a more secure direct line.

Benefits:

- If your server is hooked up to the Internet, you can collaborate with anyone, wherever they find themselves in the world.
- Depending on your software's sophistication (Cloud-based ERP system), you will be able to automate data interactions between your software tools.

Drawbacks:

- Everyone with access to the data can write, rewrite, or erase data, with no record kept of the changes. Should an error slip in or a willful manipulation of data occur, it will be very difficult to detect and trace it back to its source.
- Company auditors have to assume that the data in your system is accurate, even
- though changes could have occurred between the time the data was logged and the present.
- If your company needs to collaborate with other organizations, the other parties will have to use the same software. Alternatively, you would need a software integrations specialist to build a bridge to allow different programs to communicate with each other.
- Although the cloud provider bears the costs of the outlay, maintenance, and security of their infrastructure, you will have to pay a subscription fee to use it. There are different costs associated with different types of data. For example, a customer would pay ingress and egress fees for accessing their archival data. If it's a free product, the provider is probably selling your data to fund their business model.

- When your provider's servers go down, your data will become inaccessible.
- Cloud servers can get hacked or mistakenly share your data with unauthorized individuals.

4. **Blockchain: a distributed and public data management system**

The blockchain model is derived from the invention of Bitcoin. So, we consider the Bitcoin blockchain as the archetype for a blockchain system. Refer to *Chapter 4, Distributed Consensus in Open Environments*, for more information.

a. If your company operates on a public blockchain system, exact copies of your database will be stored on a computer network (the server) distributed across the globe.

b. Each time someone changes the data, a new record will be published to indicate the latest version. The latest version will not overwrite any of your data's previous versions but show the entire history of changes.

c. Additionally, the record will show which party was responsible for making each change and indicate the date and time.

d. The blockchain database is also publicly accessible. Unless data is encrypted before being recorded, anyone who accesses the database (via a blockchain explorer over the Internet) will be able to sift through the data. They won't be able to make sense of how the data relates to other data or who created or made changes to any particular data record. This is because the blockchain attributes pseudonyms to each person who interacts with it in the form of a blockchain address. And, unless they reveal their pseudonym to you, you would need incredibly sophisticated algorithms to decipher the identity behind a blockchain address.

Figure 1.14: *Isometric View of Universal Blockchain Technology*

History of Blockchain

- **1990**: In the late 1990s, cypherpunk Nick Szabo advocated securing a digital payments system called bit gold (which was never implemented) with a blockchain.
- **1991**: Mathematicians Stuart Haber and W. Scott Stornetta first proposed the concept of blockchain technology in 1991. They aimed to create a system in which document timestamps could not be altered.
- **2008**: "Bitcoin: A Peer to Peer Electronic Cash System" is published by an anonymous individual or group going by the handle Satoshi Nakamoto.
- **2009**: Computer scientist Hal Finney and the enigmatic Satoshi Nakamoto conduct the first Bitcoin (BTC) transaction that is successful.
- **2010**: Two Papa John's pizzas are the first items ever purchased with Bitcoin by Florida-based programmer Laszlo Hanycez. Hanycez sent 10,000 BTC, which at the time was equivalent to roughly $60. It is now valued at $80 million. Officially, Bitcoin's market capitalization surpasses $1 million.
- **2011**: The cryptocurrencies reach parity with the US dollar, with 1 Bitcoin equaling $1 USD.

  Wikileaks, the Electronic Frontier Foundation, and other organizations have begun to accept Bitcoin donations.
- **2012**: The introduction of blockchain and cryptocurrencies into popular culture with references to them in series like The Good Wife. Vitalik Buterin, one of the original Bitcoin developers, established Bitcoin Magazine.
- **2013**: The market value of bitcoin reached $1 billion. For the first time, Bitcoin reached $100/BTC.
- **2014**: Overstock.com, The D Las Vegas Hotel, and gaming company Zynga begin to accept Bitcoin as payment. Through an Initial Coin Offering (ICO), Buterin's Ethereum Project is crowdfunded, raising over $18 million in Bitcoin and creating new opportunities for blockchain technology. To find new applications for blockchain technology, a consortium of more than 200 blockchain companies, called R3, is established. PayPal announces the incorporation of Bitcoin.
- **2015**: There are more than 100,000 retailers that take Bitcoin. To test the technology for exchanging shares in private companies, the San Francisco blockchain startup Chain and the American stock market NASDAQ are collaborating.
- **2016**: The announcement by IBM of a blockchain strategy for cloud-based enterprise applications.

The legitimacy of cryptocurrency and blockchain technology is acknowledged by the Japanese government. Bitcoin crossed $1,000/BTC for the first time in 2017. The market value of cryptocurrencies hits $150 billion.

CEO of JP Morgan, Jamie Dimon, has expressed his belief in blockchain as a technology for the future, endorsing the ledger system with support from Wall Street. Bitcoin hits $19,783.21/BTC, its all-time high.

Dubai declares that by 2020, its government will run on blockchain technology.

- **2018**: Facebook says it will launch a group focused on blockchain technology and makes a suggestion that it might launch its own coin. IBM is creating a blockchain-based banking platform, and major institutions like Barclays and Citi are participating.
- **2019**: As China's central bank declares it is developing its own cryptocurrency, President Ji Xinping of China openly welcomes blockchain technology. CEO of Twitter and Square Jack Dorsey said that blockchain developers will be hired by Square to work on the company's next cryptocurrency initiatives. Additionally, the New York Stock Exchange (NYSE) has announced the founding of Bakkt, a cryptocurrency trading and digital wallet startup.
- **2020**: By the end of the year, Bitcoin nearly hits $30,000. PayPal declares that users will be able to purchase, sell, and hold cryptocurrency.

  The Bahamas, aptly dubbed the "Sand Dollar," introduced the world's first digital money from its central bank. Blockchain emerges as a major weapon in the fight against COVID-19, namely for the safe storage of patient data and research data.
- **2021**: The year 2021 was a roller coaster ride for crypto investors as bitcoin value surged to $64,829.14 (highest yet) and declined to $35,000 as well.

  In March, the world's richest man, Elon Musk, announced the acceptance of Bitcoins as payment for Tesla cars. Later, he withdrew his statement due to environmental hazards as bitcoin mining requires high computation power.

  El Salvador became the first country to accept Bitcoin as a legal currency.

  Afterward, a giant wave of (Non-fungible Token) NFTs came with great earning opportunities for creators. An NFT is a digital asset such as digital art, music records, videos, or collectibles that is unique and tradable. Platforms like OpenSea, one of the most popular NFT marketplaces, presented a stage for artists and traders. An intersection of Blockchain, AR/VR, and web3 gave rise to Metaverse. Several start-ups inspired by COVID-19 pandemic work from home culture started working on virtual world creation.

  On 28 October, Mark Zuckerberg CEO of social network giant Facebook, renamed the company, Meta. In contrast, the cryptocurrency bill in India banned the use of cryptocurrencies as a payment system. On the other hand, the idea of web3 was promoted worldwide.

- **2022**: The ongoing year 2022 started with more fame towards NFTs and Metaverse. That eventually led to more trading options and earning opportunities. Several rich apparel companies like Nike, Adidas, Walmart, Puma, Gucci, Ferrari, and even Disney got on Metaverse to create and promote their product NFT designs for avatars.

  In contrast, the Indian government announced 30% taxation on digital asset transfers. Yet, it doesn't mean that it's legal in the country.

  However, various other blockchain use cases are being explored, tested, and released, such as smart contracts for satellite communications in Space, the use of blockchain in the supply chain, entertainment, healthcare, transportation, real estate, automation, and many more industries.

  Meanwhile, due to recent war tension between Russia and Ukraine, the Bitcoin community showed financial help to Ukrainian injured soldiers and civilians.

- **2023**: The leading blockchains are Bitcoin, Ethereum, Solana, Avalanche, and BNB Chain. Each offers unique attributes and advancements, distinguishing them in the decentralized technology space.Former FTX CEO Sam Bankman-Fried, a notable figure in the cryptocurrency industry, was found guilty on 3 November 2023 by a New York jury. The charges included two counts of wire fraud, two counts of wire fraud conspiracy, and three additional conspiracy charges.

- **2024**: Blockchain technology, the force behind cryptocurrencies like Bitcoin, has moved far beyond its initial niche. Industries are rapidly recognizing the potential of this secure, decentralized ledger system to transform everything from finance to supply chain management.

Likely Future Trends

The blockchain technology is much more than a system for securely transferring cryptocurrencies. The industry has a staggering CAGR rate of over 69% between 2019 and 2025. During this period, blockchain is no longer only relevant to cryptocurrency, blockchain-based applications are emerging to support many other scenarios that require decentralized data storage and accessibility.

The fact that blockchain is ushering in major economic shifts. However, the cryptocurrency market is still a 'wild west' with little regulation. According to recent reports, it appears the U.S. Securities and Exchange Commission is gearing up to more closely regulate the cryptocurrency industry in 2022.

Also, with many practical applications for the technology already being implemented and explored, blockchain is finally making a name for itself in no small part because of bitcoin and cryptocurrency. As a buzzword on the tongue of every investor in the nation, blockchain stands to make business and government operations more accurate, efficient, secure, and cheap, with fewer middlemen.

As we prepare to head into the third decade of blockchain, it's no longer a question of if legacy companies will catch on to the technology – it's a question of when. Today, that is, in 2022 start, we see a proliferation of NFTs and the tokenization of assets. The next decades will prove to be an important period of growth for blockchain.

Additional Information

- **Numbers of Blockchains**

  As of 2022, there are more than 10,000 active cryptocurrencies based on blockchain, with several hundred more non-cryptocurrency blockchains.

- **Blockchain Platform**

  Nevertheless, the blockchain platform allows users and developers to create novel uses of an existing blockchain infrastructure. One example is Ethereum, which has a native cryptocurrency known as ether (ETH).

  However, the Ethereum blockchain alternative also allows the creation of smart contracts and programmable tokens used in initial coin offerings (ICOs), and non-fungible tokens (NFTs). These are all built up around the Ethereum infrastructure and secured by nodes on the Ethereum network.

Conclusion

In this chapter, we have learned in detail about block technology, its inception, and partial adoption. Its application is predominantly in the financial sector and in generating and earning cryptocurrencies like bitcoins and Ethereum. We have also learned that this technology is beyond the control of several governments and other political powers. It involves many complications and requires a lot of skills, time, and huge electrical power.

In the next chapter, we shall learn about its core part, such as cryptographic hash functions, which help in keeping the transactions confidential to avoid misuse by miscreants.

References

[1] IBM Developer Technology Sandbox preview, Start developing with the open source Hyperledger Fabric and IBM Blockchain, https://developer.ibm.com/blogs/ibm-previews-developer-technology

[2] An Overview of Blockchain Technology and its Functionality, https://www.datasciencecentral.com/an-overview-of-blockchain-technology-and-its-functionality

[3] Bitcoin creator is now the 15th richest person in the world". The Independent. 15 November 2021. Retrieved 1 December 2021

[4] Morris, David Z. (15 May 2016). "Leaderless, Blockchain-Based Venture Capital Fund Raises $100 Million, And Counting". Fortune. Archived from the original on 21 May 2016. Retrieved 23 May 2016.

[5] EUROMONEY.COM, Home Blockchain Explained How Transactions Get into the Blockchain?

[6] Distributed consensus, https://www.alibabacloud.com/blog/from-distributed-consensus-algorithms-to-the-blockchain-consensus-mechanism_595315

[7] Coulouris, George; Jean Dollimore; Tim Kindberg (2001), Distributed Systems: Concepts and Design (3rd Edition), Addison-Wesley, p. 452, ISBN 978-0201-61918-8

[8] M. J. M. Chowdhury and M. S. Ferdous and K. Biswas and N. Chowdhury and A. S. M. Kayes and M. Alazab and P. Watters "A Comparative Analysis of Distributed Ledger Technology Platforms". IEEE Access, 7:167930-167943, 2019.

[9] Blockchain Consensus Algorithms: A Survey, Md Sadek Ferdous, Member, IEEE, Mohammad Jabed Morshed Chowdhury, Mohammad A. Hoque, Member, IEEE, and Alan Colman

[10] Xiao, David "The Four Layers of the Blockchain", 2018 Available: https://medium.com/@coriacetic/the-four-layers-of-the-blockchain-dc1376efa10f. June 22, 2016.

[11] Cryptocurrency, By JAKE FRANKENFIELD, Updated January 11, 2022, Reviewed by ETHAN VERA, https://www.investopedia.com/terms/c/cryptocurrency.asp

[12] Introduction to Permissioned Blockchains, Gwyneth Iredale on June 02, 2019, https://101blockchains.com/permissioned-blockchain/

Chapter 2
Cryptographic Hash Function

Introduction

Cryptography is utilized in blockchain to make message transmission very secret and secure. For this purpose, hash functions are used, which make the scripting very complicated by using mathematical functions and random probability. We will learn all of this in this chapter.

Structure

In this chapter, we will cover the following topics:

- Cryptographic Hash Function (CHF)
- The Nonce
- An Introduction to One-Way Hash Functions
- Hash Pointer and Merkle tree (Hash Tree)
- Digital Signature
- Public Key cryptography or Asymmetric Cryptography

Introduction to Cryptographic Hash Function

The Greek term "cryptography" originally meant "secret writing." The history of cryptocurrencies can be traced back to academic and military use cases, which were eventually taken away for private communication.

It is noteworthy that symbol **#** (known as *hash in information technology*) is mostly used for showing the numbering or counts of any item, but in modern digital cryptography, it is used for encrypted messages and vice versa.

To form a chronological single source of truth for the data, blockchain stores encrypted blocks of data, which are then chained together in blockchain technology. As such digital assets are distributed instead of copied or transferred to create an immutable record, the assets so created are decentralized to allow full real-time access and thus are transparent to the public using it. This transparency of ledger of changes maintains and preserves the integrity of the document, creating trust for users in the asset.

The inherent security measures provided in the blockchain system, along with its quality of being a public ledger, make it a prime technology for almost every single sector. Thus, blockchain is a promising and undoubtedly revolutionary technology as it helps to (i) reduce risk, (ii) stamps out fraud, and (iii) bring transparency. Thus, it is scalable and utilized in many ways for myriad uses.

The purpose of a hash function is to turn a random input of data (keys) into a string of bytes with a fixed length and structure **(hash value)**. In *Figure* 2.1, the encrypted hash message contains 10 bytes in each case. Cryptographic hash functions generate a fixed-length character string from data records of any length (shown in left). A data record of any block can be a *word*, a *sentence*, a *longer text, or an entire file.*

The hash function has become the backbone of crypto security. The hash provides a manner in which it is easy to identify transactions on the blockchain.

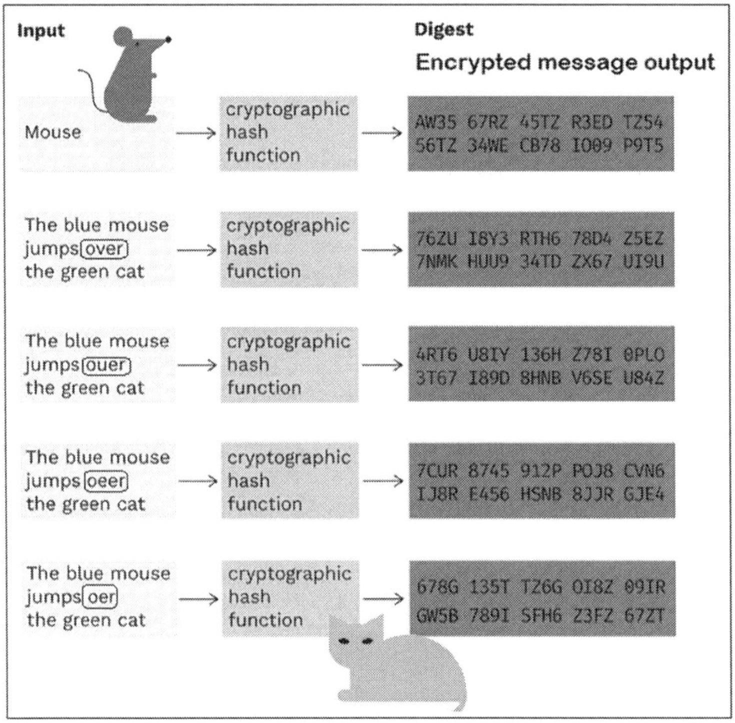

Figure 2.1: *Hash Function Generated for Similar but Different Text Strings (The crypted message is vastly different)*

It can be easily observed from *Figure* 2.1 that the output message so generated after hashing is vastly dissimilar if a slight change in the input message is done by the user. Always remember that a blockchain is a growing list of records, called blocks, that are linked together using cryptography.

Each block contains a:

- Cryptographic hash of the previous block,
- A timestamp, and
- Transaction data (generally represented as a Merkle tree, we shall read about this in the section *The Nonce*).

The **timestamp** is adopted to prove that the transaction data existed when the block was published (posted) in order to get into its hash. As each block contains information about the block previous to it, they form a continuous chain, with each additional block reinforcing the ones before it.

The data in any given block cannot be altered retroactively without altering all subsequent blocks as blockchains are resistant to modification.

"Although blockchain records are not unalterable as forks are possible, blockchains may be considered secure by design and exemplify a distributed computing system with high Byzantine fault tolerance"[1],[5].

Blockchain uses peer-to-peer network technology that is used as a publicly distributed ledger in which blockchains are transmitted as bonafide transactions.

Researchers and other people involved in this movement refer to themselves as "**cypherpunks**" and have been advocating a shift to greater privacy and control over our data since the late 1980s.

Hashing

Hashing simply means passing some data through a formula that produces a result, called a **hash**. Any hash (sentence) so created is usually a string of characters and the hashes generated by a formula are always the same *length*, regardless of how much data you feed into it.

The term hash rate is a measure of how many calculations can be performed per second and can be measured in *billions, trillions, quadrillions, and quintillions*. For example, a hash rate of 1ST/s means one trillion (10^9) hashed calculations can be performed every second. These calculations that are being measured are concerned with **mining**.

The cryptographic hashes are generated to secure data transferred on a public network.

Miners

Miners compete with their *peers to zero* in on a hash value generated by a crypto coin transaction, and the first miner to crack the code gets to add the block to the ledger and receive the *reward*.

Interested Bitcoin miners download the entire history of blockchain and assemble valid transactions into a block. If the block of assembled transactions is accepted and verified by other miners, then the miner receives a block reward.

Transaction fees provide another incentive for bitcoin miners to participate in the process.

Currently, Antminer S19 Pro-ASIC is one of the best Bitcoin mining hardware solutions. This hardware can also be used to mine other SHA-256 cryptocurrencies. The advantages of this hardware are as follows:

- Highest hash rate
- Efficiency and power consumption
- It is said to generate almost US$12 on a regular basis, with an electricity cost of US$0.1/kilowatt.

Ethereum at a mining hash rate of 750.00 MH/s consumes 1,350.00 watts of power at $0.10 per kWh, and a block reward of 2 ETH.

Before proceeding further, let us learn about some definitions:

- **Hash rate** is a measure of the computational power of a blockchain network, group, or individual. Hash rate is determined by how many guesses are made per second. The overall hash rate helps determine the mining difficulty of a blockchain network.
- **Hashing power** (otherwise known as Hash power) is the power that your computer or hardware uses to run and solve different hashing algorithms. These algorithms are used for generating new cryptocurrencies and allowing transactions between them. This process is also called mining.
- **Mining difficulty** is a unit of measurement used in the process of mining a cryptocurrency such as Bitcoin and refers to how difficult and time-consuming it is to find the right hash for each block.
- ETH is short for Ethereum.

Here is the list of the most popular (2022) Bitcoin miners:

1. Antminer S19 Pro
2. Antminer T9+

3. Minedollars
4. AvalonMiner A1166 Pro
5. WhatsMiner M30S++
6. AvalonMiner 1246
7. WhatsMiner M32-62T
8. Ebang EBIT E11++
9. Bitmain Antminer S5
10. DragonMint T1

Table 2.1 shows the list of the topmost six Bitcoin Mining Hardware and their hash power and algorithms used by them:

Bitcoin Mining Hardware	**Hash Power**	**Algorithm/Crypto to mine**	**Price**
Antminer S19 Pro	110 Th/s	SHA-256	$2,860
AvalonMiner A1166 Pro	81ST/s	SHA-256	$1,550
Minedollars	N/A	SHA-256, Ethereum, Bitcoin Cash, LTC, ETH, XRP, USDT, USDC, and DASH	$3,000
WhatsMiner M30S++	112TH/s±5%	SHA-256 Bitcoin mining and over 10 other crypto	$3,890
AvalonMiner 1246	90Th/s	SHA-256	$3,890
WhatsMiner M32-62T	62ND/s +/- 5	SHA-256	$1,100

Table 2.1: *The list of topmost six Bitcoin Mining Hardware and their hash power and algorithms used by them*

Non-Fungible tokens (NFTs)

Non-fungible tokens (NFTs) are blockchain-based tokens that may represent a unique asset like a piece of art, digital content, or media. NFT is assumed as an irrevocable digital certificate of ownership and authenticity for a given asset in both formats, either digital or physical.

Cryptographic Hash Function (CHF)

CHF is an acronym for **Cryptographic Hash Function** and is a mathematical algorithm that maps data of an arbitrary size to a bit array of a fixed size. It is a one-way function, that is, a function for which it is practically infeasible to invert or reverse the computation Brute force approach is an approach that finds all the possible solutions to find a satisfactory solution to a given problem. The brute force algorithm tries out all the possibilities till a satisfactory solution is found.

In an ideal situation, there is no other way to find a message that produces a given hash other than to attempt a brute-force search of possible inputs to see if they produce a match, or use a rainbow table of matched hashes.

We need the Rainbow tables for protecting passwords, which are actually tables of reversed hashes used to crack password hashes. In fact, computer systems require passwords typically to store the passwords as a hash value of the user's password. When a computer user enters a password, the system hashes the password and compares it to the stored hash. Normally, when you crack a password hash, your computer computes a word, generates the hash, and then compares it to see if there is a match. If there is a match, the password is correct; if not, it will keep guessing. Rainbow tables work on the principle of a time-memory trade-off. From a modern password cracking threat perspective though, rainbow tables are mostly obsolete. At the rate of 200,000 hashes per second, it would take 3 minutes to generate a four-character rainbow table.

The cryptographic hash functions are a basic tool of modern cryptography. Values returned by a hash function are called **message digest** or simply hash values. *Figure 2.2* illustrates the working of a hash function.

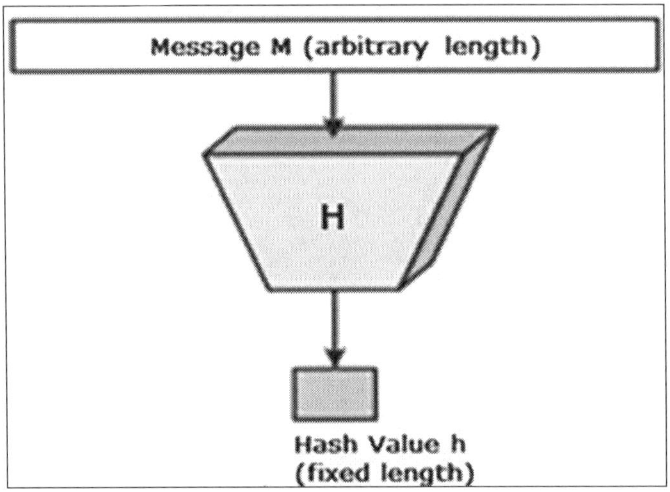

Figure 2.2: *Working of cryptologic hash function (Courtesy: Tutorial Point)*

A cryptographic hash function is devised as an algorithm that takes an arbitrary amount of data input (that is, a credential). This generates a fixed-size output in the form of enciphered text, which is called a hash value, or just "hash in short". The most important thing to note is that enciphered text can then be stored in place of the password itself, and later used to verify the user.

A hash algorithm (program) is designed to take an arbitrary-length data input and produce a fixed-length deterministic result, a digital fingerprint of the input. For any specific input, the resulting hash will always have to be the same and can be easily calculated and verified by any user implementing the same hash algorithm.

It is important to understand that the key characteristic of a cryptographic hash algorithm is that it is virtually impossible to find two different inputs that produce the same fingerprint. As a corollary, it is also virtually impossible to select an input in such a way as to produce a desired fingerprint, other than trying random inputs. Corollary to any theorem means forming a proposition that follows from one already proved in the concerned theorem.

As for Bitcoin is concerned, it uses the SHA-256 hash algorithm. The function of this algorithm is to generate verifiably random numbers in a way that requires a predictable amount of computer processing power. With the famous SHA256, the output is always 256 bits long, regardless of the size of the input. In Example 2.1, we will use the Python interpreter to calculate the SHA256 hash of the phrase, "I am Satoshi Nakamoto."[2].

Example 2.1: SHA256 Example

```
$ python
Python 2.7.1
>>> import hashlib
>>> print hashlib. sha256("I am Satoshi Nakamoto").hexdigest()
5d7c7ba21cbbcd75d14800b100252d5b428e5b1213d27c385bc141ca6b47989e
```

Example 2.1 shows the result of calculating the hash of **`"I am Satoshi Nakamoto"`**: **`5d7c7ba21cbbcd75d14800b100252d5b428e5b1213d27c385bc141ca6b47989e`**. This 256-bit number is the hash or digest of the phrase and depends on every part of the phrase. Adding a single letter, punctuation mark, or any other character will produce a different hash.

Now, if we change the phrase (part of the data/sentence inputted), we should expect to see completely different hashes. Let's try that by adding a number to the end of our phrase, using the simple Python scripting in *Example* 2.2.

Example 2.2: **SHA256:** A script for generating many hashes by iterating on a nonce

```
# example of iterating a nonce in a hashing algorithm's input
```

```
import hashlib
text = "I am Satoshi Nakamoto"
# iterate nonce from 0 to 19
for nonce in xrange(20):
    # add the nonce to the end of the text
    input = text + str(nonce)
    # calculate the SHA-256 hash of the input (text+nonce)
    hash = hashlib.sha256(input).hexdigest()
    # show the input and hash result
    print input, '=>', hash
```

Running this code snippet will produce the hashes of several phrases, made different by adding a number at the end of the text. By incrementing the number, you will get different hashes, as shown in *Example* 2.3.

Example 2.3: SHA256 output of a script for generating many hashes by iterating on a nonce

```
$ python hash_example.py
I am Satoshi Nakamoto0 => a80a81401765c8eddee25df36728d732...
I am Satoshi Nakamoto1 => f7bc9a6304a4647bb41241a677b5345f...
I am Satoshi Nakamoto2 => ea758a8134b115298a1583ffb80ae629...
I am Satoshi Nakamoto3 => bfa9779618ff072c903d773de30c99bd...
I am Satoshi Nakamoto4 => bce8564de9a83c18c31944a66bde992f...
I am Satoshi Nakamoto5 => eb362c3cf3479be0a97a20163589038e...
I am Satoshi Nakamoto6 => 4a2fd48e3be420d0d28e202360cfbaba...
I am Satoshi Nakamoto7 => 790b5a1349a5f2b909bf74d0d166b17a...
I am Satoshi Nakamoto8 => 702c45e5b15aa54b625d68dd947f1597...
I am Satoshi Nakamoto9 => 7007cf7dd40f5e933cd89fff5b791ff0...
I am Satoshi Nakamoto10 => c2f38c81992f4614206a21537bd634a...
I am Satoshi Nakamoto11 => 7045da6ed8a914690f087690e1e8d66...
I am Satoshi Nakamoto12 => 60f01db30c1a0d4cbce2b4b22e88b9b...
I am Satoshi Nakamoto13 => 0ebc56d59a34f5082aaef3d66b37a66...
I am Satoshi Nakamoto14 => 27ead1ca85da66981fd9da01a8c6816...
I am Satoshi Nakamoto15 => 394809fb809c5f83ce97ab554a2812c...
I am Satoshi Nakamoto16 => 8fa4992219df33f50834465d3047429...
I am Satoshi Nakamoto17 => dca9b8b4f8d8e1521fa4eaa46f4f0cd...
I am Satoshi Nakamoto18 => 9989a401b2a3a318b01e9ca9a22b0f3...
I am Satoshi Nakamoto19 => cda56022ecb5b67b2bc93a2d764e75f...
```

In this example, it can be seen clearly that each phrase produces a completely different hash result. Seemingly they are completely random, but to see the exact hashes, the user or his programming assistant can reproduce the exact results of this example on any computer with Python programming language.

This number used as a variable in such a scenario is called a nonce. In this case to vary the SHA256 fingerprint of the phrase, the nonce is used to vary the output of a cryptographic function,

To make a challenge out of this algorithm, let's set an arbitrary target: let us find a phrase that produces a hexadecimal hash that starts with a zero. Fortunately, this isn't difficult!

Example 2.3 shows that the phrase `"I am Satoshi Nakamoto13"` produces the hash **`0ebc56d59a34f5082aaef3d66b37a661696c2b618e62432727216ba9531041a5`**, which fits our criteria. The person trying to find out the result intimates that it took 13 attempts to find it. We would expect to find a result with a 0 as the hexadecimal prefix once every 16 hashes if the output of the hash function is evenly distributed (in terms of probabilities) (hexadecimal system means one out of 16 hexadecimal digits 0 through F). In numerical terms, that means finding a hash value that is less than 0x1 000000000000000000000000000000000000000000000000000000000000000 . This is called threshold target, and the goal is to find a hash that is numerically less than the target. If we decrease the target, the task of finding a hash that is less than the target becomes more and more difficult.

Trusted timestamping is the process of securely keeping track of the creation and modification time of a document. The security involved here means that no one – not even the owner of the document – should be able to change it once it has been recorded, provided that the times tamper's integrity is never compromised.

The Need and Purpose of Generating and Using Hash Functions

The idea of using hash functions originated from the need to make content uniform in length on one hand, and for using them as unique identifiers on the other hand. Typical uses for hash functions outside the cryptocurrency sphere include:

- The process of calculating a (short) checksum for an object, such as the checksum for an ISBN (International Standard Book Number):
- The process of Identifying any content almost without ambiguity but still "briefly", such that it does not disclose anything about the content in cryptographic applications.

Properties of Hash Functions[3]

The following are the characteristic properties of hash functions:

Property 1: Computationally Efficient: First and foremost, hash functions must be computationally efficient[3]. This is just a fancy way of saying that computers must be able to perform a hash function's mathematical labor in an extremely short period of time.

This property is probably somewhat obvious. If an ordinary computer needed several minutes to process a cryptographic hash function and receive the output, it would not be very practical. To be useful, hash functions must be computationally efficient.

In real life, this is not as large of a concern as it was 40 or 50 years ago. Nowadays, an average home computer can process an advanced hash function in just a small fraction of a second.

Property 2: Deterministic: Cryptographic hash functions must be deterministic. In other words, for any given input, a hash function must always give the same result. If you put in the same input ten million times in a row, a hash function must produce the same exact output ten million times over.

This may also be rather obvious. If a cryptographic hash function were to produce different outputs each time the same input was entered, the hash function would be random and therefore useless. It would be impossible to verify a specific input, which is the whole point of hash functions – to be able to verify that a private digital signature is authentic without ever having access to the private key.

Property 3: Pre-Image Resistant: The output of a cryptographic hash function must not reveal any information about the input. This is called pre-image resistance.

Note: *Cryptographic hashing algorithms can receive any kind of input. The input can be numbers, letters, words, or punctuation marks. It can be a single character, a sentence from a book, a page from a book, or an entire book.*

However, a hash function will always produce a fixed-length output. The output will be an alphanumeric code of fixed length, regardless of what the input is.

The importance of this is that if a longer input produced a longer output, then attackers would already have a seriously helpful clue when trying to discover someone's private input.

For example, if an input always produced an output 1.5 times its length, then the hash function would be giving away valuable information to hackers. In case, hackers saw an output of, say, 36 characters, they would immediately know that the input was 24 characters.

Instead, a useful hash function must conceal any clues about what the input may have looked like. It needs to be made impossible to determine whether the input was long or short, numbers or letters, even or odd, random characters, or a string of recognizable words. In addition, changing one character in a long string of text must result in a radically different digest.

Property 4: Collision Resistant[3]: The final property that all cryptographic hash functions must have is what's known as collision resistance, which means that it must be extremely unlikely – in other words, practically impossible – to find two different inputs that produce the same output.

As noted above, the inputs to a hash function can be of any length. This means there are infinite possible inputs that can be entered into a hash function.

However, outputs are of a fixed length. This means that there is a finite number – albeit an extremely large number – of outputs that a hash function can produce. A fixed length means a fixed number of possibilities.

If the number of inputs is essentially infinite, but the outputs are limited to a specific number, it is a mathematical certainty that more than one input will produce the same output.

The goal here is to make finding two inputs that produce the same output so astronomically improbable that the possibility can be practically dismissed outright. It should not pose a risk.

Property 5: Impossible to Reverse Engineer: The fifth and final property of a useful cryptographic hash function is that it must be impossible to reverse the mathematical process used to create the output. There is no inverse operation for a hash function.

You might be wondering up to this point what kind of incredible equations possess all five of these properties. The answer is probably far simpler than you think.

Other Miscellaneous Properties:

- It is infeasible to find two different messages with the same hash value.
- A small change to a message should change the hash value so extensively that a new hash value appears uncorrelated with the old hash value (avalanche effect)
- It should be quick to compute the hash value for any given message, the original password from the output or hash.
- Diffusion or avalanche effect. A change in just one bit of the original password should result in a change to half the bits of its hash. It can be said in other words that when a password is changed slightly, the output of enciphered text should change significantly and unpredictably

Certain properties of cryptographic hash functions impact the security of password storage[4].

The basic tool of modern cryptography is hash functions. CHF is defined as a mathematical algorithm that maps data of an arbitrary size (often called the "message") to a bit array of a fixed size (the "hash value", "hash", or "message digest"). This function is a one-way function. One-way function is a function for which it is practically infeasible to invert or reverse the computation[5]. Hash function is the backbone of entire cryptography. The only way to find a message that produces a given hash is to attempt a brute-force search of possible inputs to see if they produce a match, or use a rainbow table of matched hashes. Brute-force search is a general problem-solving technique and algorithmic paradigm that involves generating a list of all the possible candidates for a solution and then testing the validity of every single candidate. People use a rainbow table, which is a precomputed table for caching the outputs of a cryptographic hash function, usually for cracking password hashes.

Rainbow tables are "optimized lookup tables" that can be used to reverse one-way hash functions. Rainbow tables have been devised basically as a set of pre-computed set of plaintext strings and their corresponding hashes. Large rainbow tables are publicly available, and attackers can use one of these tables to retrieve cleartext data that has been hashed.

Bad Quality of Simple Cryptographic Hash

The bad quality of simple cryptographic hash is that it can slow down the efforts of non-bonafide attackers, but ultimately attackers will be able to overcome them. Attackers equipped with fast hardware can easily "crack" hashed credentials.

Good hash algorithms are designed to be collision-resistant, but it is impossible to eliminate them (that is, collisions) completely. Programmers know that MD5 and SHA-1 have been proven to contain known collisions – that is, produce the same hash value from different credentials.

Methods for Quick Production of Cryptographic Hashes

Following are the variations that can improve your hash function and provide a greater barrier against attacks:

- **Salted hashes**: This adds random data to each plaintext credential. As a result, two identical plaintext passwords are now differentiated in enciphered text form so that duplicates cannot be detected.
- **Keyed hash functions**: A keyed hash function (also known as Hash Message Authentication Code (HMAC)) is an algorithm that uses a cryptographic key AND a cryptographic hash function to produce a message authentication code that is keyed and hashed.
- **Adaptive hash functions**: This is an adaptive one-way function that is designed

to recursively iterate on its inner workings, feeding the output back as input, to take longer to execute. It is adaptive in a manner that allows the developer to adjust how many iterations occur. The designer architects of the Bitcoin software have applied the adaptive design to protect stored passwords. Hash functions such as PBKDF2 and bcrypt have the encryption schemes accordingly.

The Trade-Off of Design of Cryptographic Hash Functions

Cryptographic hash functions do provide barriers to attackers, in a similar way as speed breakers (bumps) are designed to slow down a speeding motorcycle. Note that, however, these barriers will slow down your defenders as well – normal users and your server. You have to set the speed bump too high, otherwise you run the risk of annoying your user – and resultantly overtaxing your server.

But no matter how high you build your speed bump, the irony is that an attacker WILL ultimately be able to overcome it. The best course of action is to slow down attackers while balancing the needs and satisfaction of your users.

Hash Functions for the Bitcoin Mining Process

A block is bundled so that it contains several transactions as well as information on the previous block. This is a part of the Bitcoin network validation process to avoid the chances of miscreants getting into the process of gaining an advantage. If someone wanted to change the ledger or double-spend a transaction, she or he would have to change the hash in all previous blocks.

The miners need to find a hash to add the bundled block to the blockchain, which meets the target difficulty. The requirement here is that each block should contain a block header with the number of the block, the hash of the previous block, and a "nonce", which includes a time stamp. The purpose of a nonce is to verify the input to a cryptographic hash function, that is increased randomness, in computation during the mining process. We are going to read about nonce in detail in the section "*The Nonce*".

The Process of Solving the Hash

The hash must start with the correct amount of zeroes. The concerned node then begins "hashing" the data by converting it into the hash value or "hash". The node checks whether a hash meets the criteria of difficulty. If the hash meets the criteria of difficulty, then it is broadcasted to the other prospective miners in the network. The first miner to find a valid hash validates the block into a new block and gets rewarded the block reward fees in Bitcoin.

Otherwise, if the hash does not meet the criteria of network difficulty, another nonce has to be selected and hashed. Miners probably have to generate many hashes with many nonces until they find a nonce that meets the difficulty. This process of Bitcoin mining is a repetitive and energy-intensive process that requires extensive computational power.

Hash functions are called the backbone of the Proof of Work process. The blockchain would not be tamper-proof and inalterable without confirmation and production of hash transactions, and it would not be possible to prove who owned which amount of Bitcoin at what time.

Protection by Providing Secured Hash Algorithms

The resilience provided in the algorithm of the SHA-256 restricts and thus prevents miners from being able to speed up and cheat the trial-and-error process. SHA is the acronym for Secure Hash Algorithm, SHA-256 belongs to the SHA-2 family of secure hash algorithms to overcome SHA -1 family and was released by the National Security Agency (NSA) of the USA in 2001. If this algorithm was broken, as happened to the SHA-1 class of cryptographic hash algorithms, then the Proof of Work (PoW) process would be undermined.

The characteristic feature of the SHA-2 family is that it consists of six hash functions with hash values (that is, digests) that are 224, 256, 384, or 512 bits long. These include SHA-224, SHA-256, SHA-384, SHA-512, SHA-512/224, SHA-512/256. SHA-256 and SHA-512 are novel hash functions computed with eight 32-bit and 64-bit words, respectively.

There are several ways to break a hash algorithm, which means being able to avoid (circumvent) the trial-and-error method and find correct nonces far quicker. One such method is collision attacks, which are the latest and most efficient way to do this.

Collision Attacks

The purpose of securing any hash algorithm is to ensure the uniqueness of a hash. The inputs should create a totally unique hash number whenever data is hashed. The only way the same number can be replicated with the exact same inputs is by using the nonce. Collision-resistant hash functions have been evolved to avoid collisions by cryptographers. A collision occurs when the same hash values is produced for two different inputs. It is easier to reach a collision in the case of simple hash functions. For example, assume a hash function h(text) is planned to get sums of all character codes in a text. We can try that it will produce the same hash value (collision) for texts holding the same letters in different order, that is, `h('xyz') == h('zxy') == h('yzx')`.

For example, assume a hash function h(text) sums all character codes in a text. It will produce the same hash value (collision) for texts holding the same letters in different order, that is, `h('xyz') == h('zxy') == h('yzx').`

Unfortunately, any malicious actor with sufficient computing resources can do this as such this completely undermines and overtakes the purpose of the secured hash algorithm.

Now since a collision attack has been shown to be effective against SHA-1 algorithms, they can no longer be relied upon. However, the attack was made possible in part because of the huge advances in computer power over the past decade.

With the advent of computing powers increased enough, it is hoped that SHA-256 will also be vulnerable to such attacks. However, Bitcoin developers knew this long before it happened.

It is also worth noting that most authentication protocols on the internet currently use SHA-2 algorithms. If they did become vulnerable overnight, then we would have major global problems far beyond Bitcoin's mining. SHA-3 (Secure Hash Algorithm 3) is the latest member of the Secure Hash Algorithm family of standards, released by NIST on August 5, 2015.

The Nonce

Pronounced as the "nons" in "nonsense", "nonce" is actually an English word that means "for the present occasion or time". However, nonces are random or pseudo-random numbers that authentication protocols attached to communications. The nonce is defined as a central part of the Proof of Work (PoW) mining algorithm for blockchains and other cryptocurrencies like Bitcoin. A perfect nonce is the time of day; for example, 36.19 seconds past 11:13 pm on 31st May 2024 can only occur once.

It is expected that Miners compete with each other to find a nonce that produces a hash with a value lower than or equal to that set by the network difficulty. An event is called a golden nonce if a miner happens to find such a nonce, as then they win the right to add that block to the blockchain and receive the block reward.

The nonce is a random, one-time, whole number. It is seen that the aspirating miners test and discard millions of nonces every second hoping to produce a hash value that meets the target and so win the block reward. In the case of PoW mining at the most basic level, this is what happens, although, there is a lot more to it. Here, we are going to explore the entire purpose of the nonce throughout the mining process.

Building Blocks with Nonces

The nonce is a 32-bit number that stays in the block header along with other key data, such as the difficulty target and timestamp. When miners build blocks, they have to randomly choose a nonce and try to input it into the block header, creating a new block header hash.

We know that the hash is a 256-bit number and has to start with a huge number of zeros, that is, have an incredibly small value. The miner discards if it does not have sufficient number of zeros, and tries a new nonce. This process is repeated until a miner discovers a nonce that produces a hash with a value less than or equal to that set by the difficulty.

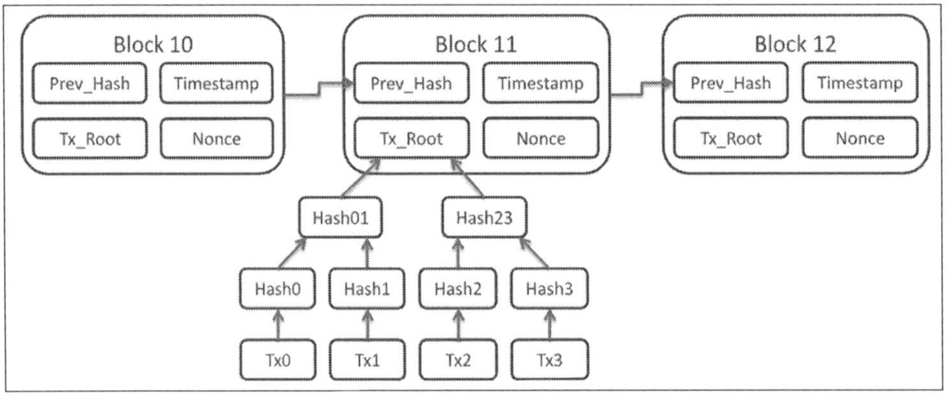

Figure 2.3: *The mining process of finding out the nearest block containing the required data*

Although in the 32-bit applications, nonce provides four billion possible combinations. A longer nonce can result in additional space having tens of billions of combinations.

The parameter that the miner can change is provided by the nonce (refer to *Chapter 1, Overview of Blockchain Technology*), all others remaining static. After hanging the parameter, if anyone out of the miners is successful in finding the golden nonce, she or he can add that block to the blockchain and receive the block reward. Note that, currently, there is no way to speed up the process of finding the correct nonce. As such miners are just operating in trial-and-error mode until they find a golden nonce. In the Proof of Work process, this portion is what constitutes the work.

Process of Reducing Mining Difficulty

As we explained earlier, the miner is trying to find a nonce that produces a hash below the value set by the network difficulty. The Bitcoin protocol is used to set this mining difficulty. In an effort to increase the difficulty level, the target value for the hash decreases, suggesting that there have to be more zeros at the start of the hash number. The miners have to test more nonces if they find a situation where the probability of finding a lower hash value is decreasing. In the process of miner hashing a block, the hash has to have a value equal to or less than the target number to be successful.

Note that while mining Bitcoin, the difficulty adjusts every 2016 block, which equates to the duration of every two weeks. Some other PoW blockchains have faster adjustments; for example, **Litecoin** adjusts its difficulty every three and a half days due to its shorter block time.

On the other hand, another application **Digibyte** adjusts its difficulty at every block in real time. People in the field of cryptocurrency know that Litecoin is a powerful, political, and economical tool that anyone, anywhere can use without permission to transact with anyone else in the world and partake in a genuinely global economy. Digibyte is a cryptocurrency project that aims to concentrate on increased transaction speed, decentralization, and security. In fact, Digibyte technology performs significantly better than most other cryptocurrencies.

Significance of the Adjustment

In case the difficulty did not adjust, there would be a linear relationship between the hashing power and the block rewards. As more miners join the network, resulting in an increase in hashing power, there would be a corresponding increase in the Bitcoin rewards. This would undermine the inflation controls on the Bitcoin protocol and with it, its sound money properties.

Fortunately, the block rewards can be kept relatively stable every two weeks by having a difficulty adjustment. In case the mining profitability disappears, then miners will cease their operations and the hash rate will falls. The difficulty automatically will get adjusted down appropriately.

It is seen that, in the case of Bitcoin, after every 2016 block, the Bitcoin client will compare the real-time for each block to be generated versus the goal time. As a result, it then adjusts the difficulty appropriately. The aim is to have miners producing blocks as close to exactly ten minutes as possible.

Introduction to One-Way Hash Functions

According to the aforementioned properties, hash functions are designed to be non-reversible, as such, they are often called one-way functions. Cryptography requires one-way hash functions; if an attacker could easily reverse a hash function, it would be totally useless.

Simple modular functions, also called modular arithmetic, provide the best way to demonstrate a one-way function. Modular arithmetic is a system of arithmetic for integers, which considers the remainder. In modular arithmetic, numbers "wrap around" upon reaching a given fixed quantity (this given quantity is known as the modulus) to leave a remainder.

So, for example, 10 mod 3 = 1. This is true because 10 divided by 3 is 3 with a remainder of 1. We ignore the number of times 3 goes into 10 (which is 3 in this case) and the only output is the remainder: 1.

Also, 3 mod 5 divides the first number by the second number and gives the remainder. It is an integer value. Since 5 does not divide by 3 (zero times), the answer is 3.

Let's use the equation X mod 5 = Y as our function. *Table* 2.2 provides help to get the point across:

Input(X)		**Output(Y)**
1		1
2		2
3		3
4		4
5		0
6		1
7		2
8		3
9		4
10		0
11		1
12		2
13		3
14		4
15		0

Table 2.2: *One-way hash function*

It's easy to spot and guess the pattern. There are only five possible outputs for this function. They rotate in this order to infinity. Modular functions are sometimes called "clock math" because the results go around in circles forever.

From the procedure, it can be stated that the underlying fact is significant because we know that both the hash function and the output can be made public but no one will ever be able to estimate the input. It's impossible for an attacker to figure it out as long as you keep the number you chose to use as X a secret.

For example, let's say that the user's input is 27. This gives an output of 2.

It becomes impossible to determine the inputs if much bigger numbers are incorporated. Users can apply this trick to make a cryptographic hash function much more secure and useful.

Hash Pointer and Merkle Tree (Hash Tree)

Hash Pointer is comprised of two parts (see *Figure 2.4(a)*):

- Pointer to where some information is stored
- Cryptographic hash of that information

The pointer can be used to get the information, and the hash can be used to verify that information hasn't been changed[6].

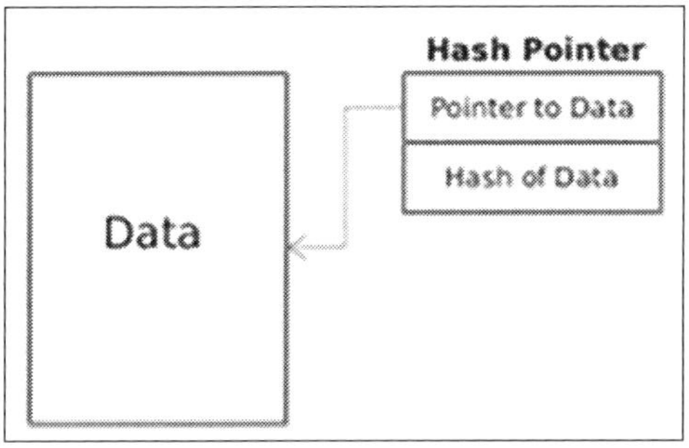

Figure 2.4(a) : *Hash Pointer*

Data Structures Built with Hash Pointers

Hash pointers can be used to build a *linked list*, which is also called a *blockchain* (see *Figure 2.4(b)*):

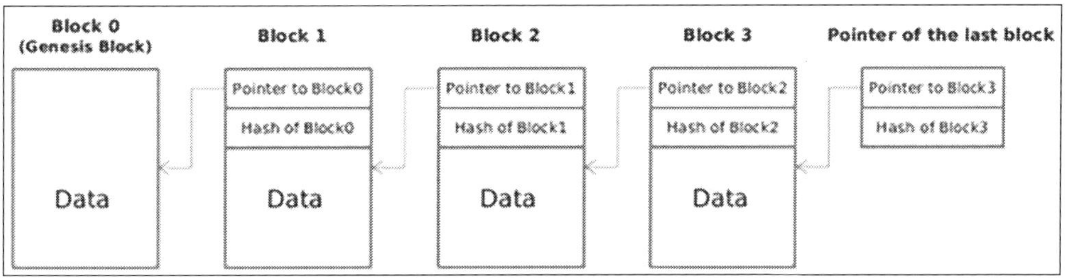

Figure 2.4(b): *Blockchain as a Linked List*

As far as the contents of the hash are concerned, it is noteworthy that the hash stored in the hash pointer is the hash of the whole data of the previous block, which also includes the hash pointer to the block before that one. This makes the procedure confidential, and now it's impossible to tamper a block in the blockchain without letting others know.

Tamper-Evident Property of Blockchain

The miner/user only needs to keep the hash pointer to the last block of the blockchain. As such when somebody shows the whole blockchain later and claims the data in it is not modified, miner/user can tell if any block in the chain is tampered with by traversing the blocks backward and verifying the hashes one by one.

Explanation of Procedure:

1. An attacker wants to tamper with one block of the chain, let's say, block x (say block 1).

   The attacker changed the content of block X, because of "collision-free" property of the hash function, she or he is not able to find another data that has the same hash as the old one. So, now the hash of this modified block is also changed.

2. To avoid others noticing the inconsistency, she/he also needs to change the hash pointer of that block in the next block, which is block x+1 (say in our case 2).

3. Now the content of block 2 is changed, so to make this story consistent, the hash pointer in block 3 must be changed.

4. Finally, the attacker goes to the hash pointer to the last block of the blockchain, which is a roadblock for her/him, because we keep and remember that hash pointer (see *Figure* 2.4(c)).

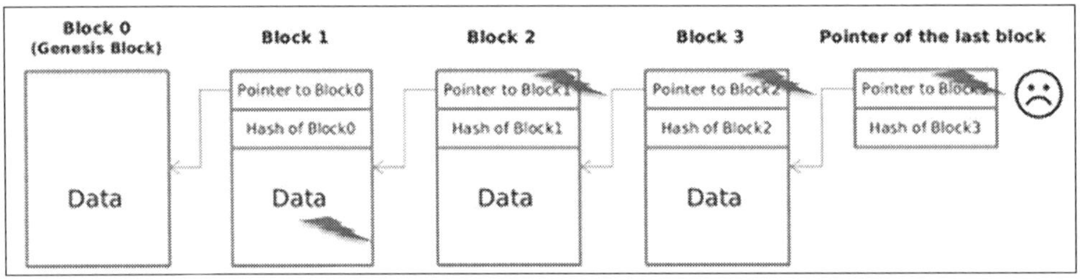

***Figure* 2.4(c):** *Hash Pointer as Additional Safety*

Merkle (Hash Tree)

A Merkle tree in cryptography is a device (pictorial representation chart) in which every "leaf" (node) is labeled with the cryptographic hash of a data block, and every node that is not a leaf is labeled with the cryptographic hash of the labels of its child nodes. A hash tree allows efficient and secure verification of the contents of a large data structure in blockchain. A hash tree is a generalization chart of a hash list and a hash chain, as shown in *Figure* 2.5.

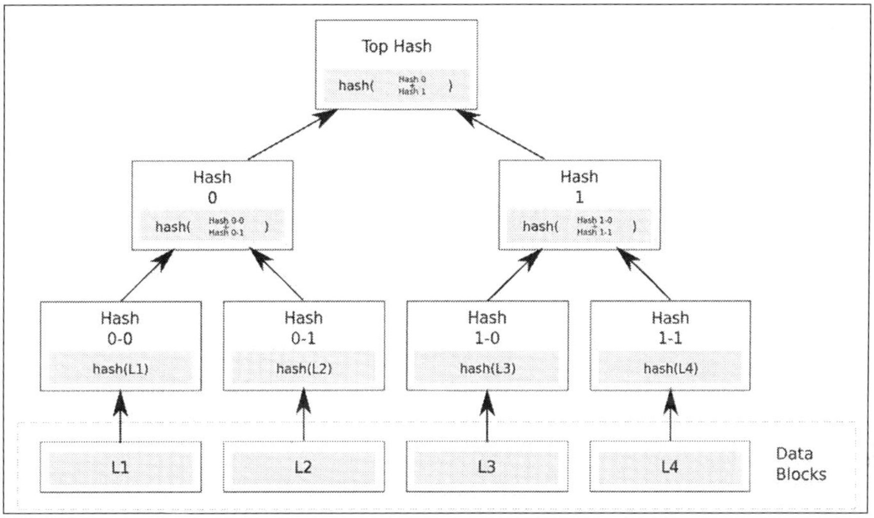

Figure 2.5: *Merkel Tree*

Electronic signatures have legal significance in some countries, including *Canada, South Africa, the United States, Algeria, Turkey, India, Brazil, Indonesia, Mexico, Saudi Arabia, Uruguay, Switzerland, Chile, and the countries of the European Union.*

In the physical world, it is common to use handwritten signatures on handwritten or typed messages[7]. Mostly used in documents and agreements, digital message authentication is done by signatures that are the public-key primitives. They are used to bind the signatory to the message. Similarly, a digital signature is a technique that binds a person/entity to the digital data. This binding can be independently verified by the receiver as well as any third party.

Cryptocurrency

Cryptocurrency also known as crypto-currency, or simply crypto is a digital currency designed to work as a medium of exchange through a computer network that is not reliant on any central authority, such as a government or bank, to uphold or maintain it.

For recording their valuable transactions ,most of the cryptocurrencies use blockchain technology. The Bitcoin network and Ethereum network are both based on blockchain for example. Facebook confirmed on 8th May 2018 that it would open a new blockchain group which would be headed by David Marcus, who previously was in charge of Messenger. Formally announced on 18th June 2019, Libra (now known as Diem) will be adopted as their planned cryptocurrency platform.

Some criminal enterprises known as Silk Road, operating on Tor, utilized cryptocurrency for payments. The United States federal government has seized some portion of these through research on the blockchain and forfeiture.

Governments have mixed policies all over the world regarding the legality of their citizens or banks owning cryptocurrencies. For example, the Chinese government implements blockchain technology in several industries including a national digital currency that launched in 2020. Most of the Western governments, including the European Union and the United States, have initiated similar projects to strengthen their respective currencies.

Advantages of Cryptocurrencies

The advantages of cryptocurrencies are as follows:

- Cheaper and faster money transfers.
- Decentralized systems that do not collapse at a single point of failure.
- Cryptocurrencies not only share many similarities with conventional fiat money but also offer some interesting advantages such as:
  - Both can be used for payments and as a store of value.
  - Both rely on widespread consumer trust in order to function as a means of exchange.
  - Fiat money is issued and controlled by (central) banks and governments.
  - Bitcoin is produced and distributed through a process called mining and is not controlled by a centralized authority.
  - Bitcoin can be trusted because it is tamper-proof and cannot be spent twice.
  - A Bitcoin transaction cannot be reversed, canceled, or charged back.

Disadvantages of Cryptocurrencies

The following are the disadvantages of cryptocurrencies:

- Their prices are volatile, that is, they keep on changing.
- Requirement of high energy consumption for mining activities.
- Possibility of their use in criminal activities.

Asymmetric cryptography is the main portion of vital aspects of a blockchain using two different keys (a public and a private key). These two keys are connected to each other utilizing mathematical terms.

The unique public key involves its origins as the private key. This interconnection allows users to create unforgeable signatures, which can only be validated by other participants of the network who have knowledge of the corresponding public key.

The following are reasons for cryptocurrencies such as Bitcoin employing a two-key system:

- The public key allows the intenders/users to receive transactions, while the private key is necessary to send transactions.
- It gets a little bit more complicated when we take a look at how this ingenious system actually works.

First Cryptocurrency Bitcoin

Now, it is no longer confidential that the blockchain was the brainchild of a person, Satoshi Nakamoto, in 2008 to serve as the public transaction ledger of the cryptocurrency Bitcoin, based on work by Stuart Haber. As such, it seems that there may be a group of people, including W. Scott Stornetta and Dave Bayer, involved. The identity of Satoshi Nakamoto remains unknown to date. The implementation of the blockchain of Bitcoin made it the first digital currency to solve the double-spending problem without the need for a trusted authority or central server. The idea of Bitcoin design has inspired other applications and blockchains that are readable by the public and are widely used by cryptocurrencies.

The following are the salient features of procuring and utilizing Bitcoins:

- **Tamper-evident**: Bitcoin is a case of blockchain system, and as such, its system is tamper-evident. As with other blockchains, we only need to remember the hash pointer in the root (top-level node). We can then traverse down to any leaf data block to check if a node is in the tree or has if it has been tampered with.
- **Efficiency of Traversal**: To verify a data block, we only need to traverse the path from the top to the leaf where the data is located. So, here the complexity is O(log n), which is much more efficient compared with O(n) of a linked list blockchain.
- **None-membership Proof**: To sort the Merkel tree, we can prove a given data is not in the tree. If the data before and after the given data are both in the tree and they are consecutive, so there is no space between them, this proves that the given data is not in the tree.

Digital Signature

Digital signature is a unique mathematical scheme devised for verifying the authenticity of digital messages, documents, or software. A valid digital signature, where the prerequisites are satisfied, gives a recipient very strong reason to believe that the message was created and signed in proof of acceptance, by a known sender (authenticity), and that the message was not altered in transit (integrity).

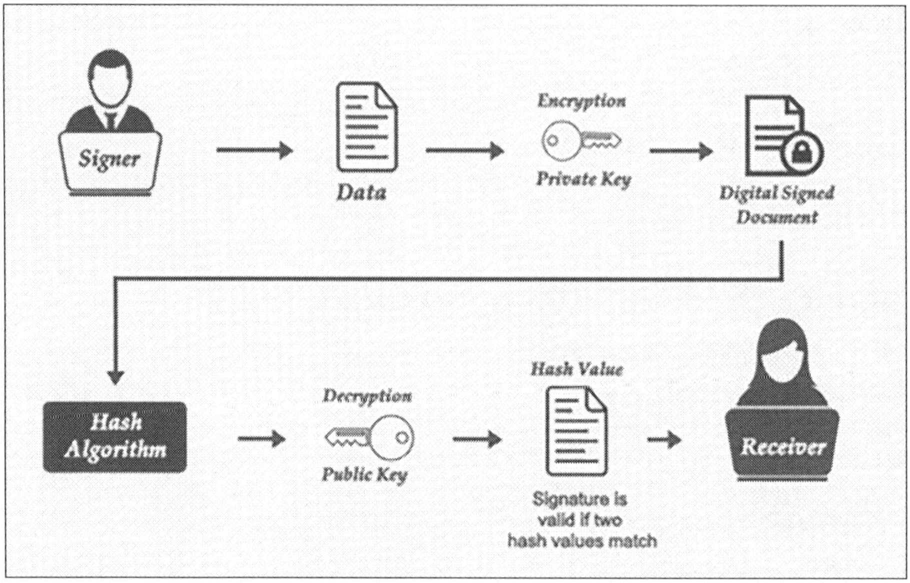

Figure 2.6: *Creation and Utilization of Digital Signatures*

Digital signatures are a standard element of most cryptographic protocol suites and are commonly used for the following:

- Software distribution
- Financial transactions
- Agreements/Contract management
- Detect forgery or tampering

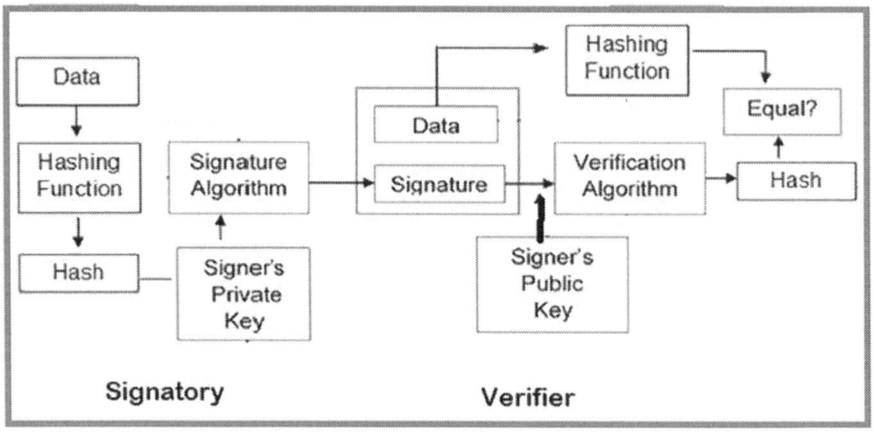

Figure 2.7: *Public Key Cryptography: A Digital Signature Scheme*

Two types of signatures are widely encountered in digital transactions. One is **digital signature** and another an **electronic signature**. Digital signatures always employ a secret key that has a cryptographic value and is calculated from the data and secret key is known only by the signer. Digital signatures are often used to implement electronic signatures. Electronic signatures may include any electronic data that carries the intent of a signature, but not all electronic signatures use digital signatures.

The receiver of a message needs assurance that the message belongs to the sender and he should not be able to repudiate the origination of that message, as it happens in the real world. As such, this requirement is very crucial in business applications since the likelihood of a dispute over exchanged data is very high.

The digital signature scheme is devised based on public key cryptography. The model of the digital signature scheme is depicted in *Figure* 2.7.

Encryption with Digital Signature

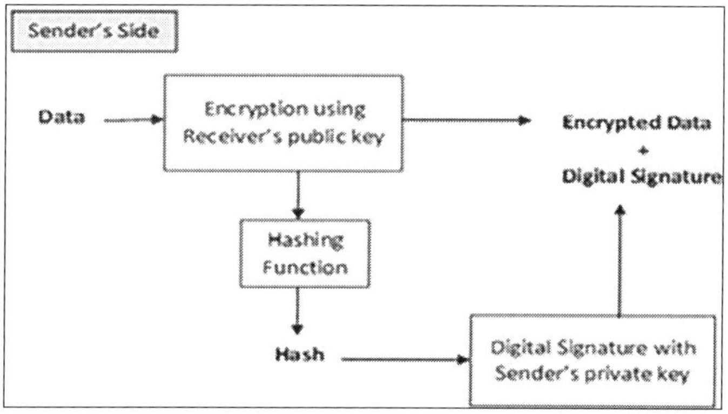

Figure 2.8: *Encryption with Digital Signature*

To achieve confidentiality in many digital communications, it is desirable to exchange encrypted messages rather than plain text. Anyone can spoof her or his identity and send an encrypted message to the receiver using the public key encryption scheme, as the public (encryption) key of the sender is available in the open domain. It is therefore essential for users employing PKC for encryption to seek digital signatures along with encrypted data to be assured of message authentication and non-repudiation.

This is possible to achieve by combining digital signatures with an encryption scheme. There are two possibilities: sign-then-encrypt and encrypt-then-sign.

However, the cryptosystem based on sign-then-encrypt can be exploited by the receiver to spoof the identity of the sender and send that data to a third party. Hence, this method is not preferred. The process of encrypt-then-sign is more reliable and widely adopted. This is depicted in *Figure* 2.8:

Encryption and decryption techniques are used to assure data security, especially for messages that are to be kept secure such as username, password, and more.

Encryption is the process of converting electronic data into another form, called ciphertext, which cannot be easily understood by anyone except the authorized parties. This assures data security.

Decryption is the process of translating code into data.

After ensuring the validity of the signature, she or he then retrieves the data through decryption using his private key. The receiver first verifies the signature using the sender's public key, after receiving the encrypted data and signature on it.

The message needs to be encrypted at the sender's side using various encryption algorithms and then the process is to be reversed, that is, decrypted at the receiver's end with the help of the decryption algorithms.

Types of Encryption Process

Here are some terms and types:

- **Public key:** It is the key that is known to everyone. For example, the ex-public key of A is 7, and this information is known to everyone.
- **Private key**: Key that is only known to the person using the transaction.

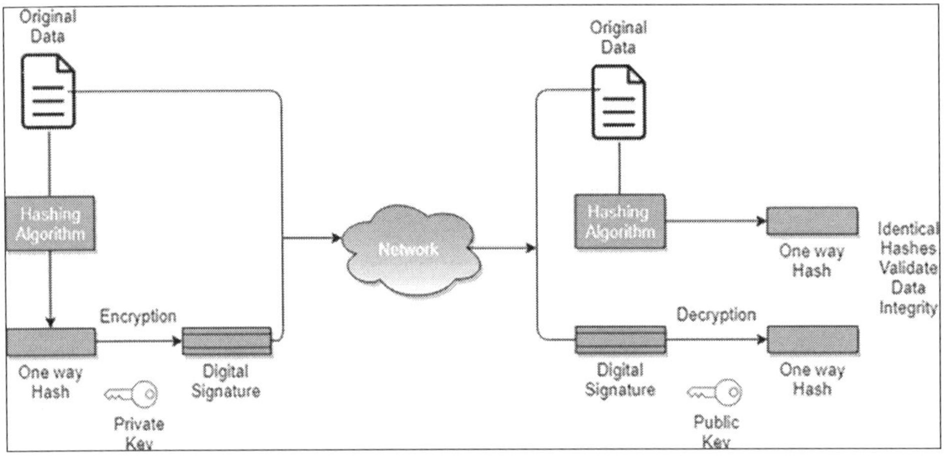

Figure 2.9: *Steps Followed in Creating Digital Signature*

Encryption procedure is of two types:

- **Symmetric Encryption**: Here data is encrypted using a key and the decryption is also done using the same key.
- **Asymmetric Encryption**: The encryption procedure in which either of the keys can be used to encrypt a message; the opposite key from the one used to encrypt the message is used for decryption. It is also known as public key cryptography, which uses public and private keys (secret) to encrypt and decrypt data. One key in the pair which can be shared with everyone is called

the public key. The other key in the pair which is kept secret and is only known by the owner is called the private key.

Here are some more procedures:

- **Authentication**: In cryptology, any process by which a system verifies the identity of a user who wishes to access it.
- **Non-repudiation** : Non-repudiation means to ensure that a transferred message has been sent and received by the parties claiming to have sent and received the message. Non-repudiation is a way to guarantee that the sender of a message cannot later deny having sent the message and that the recipient cannot deny having received the message.
- **Key Generation Algorithms**: While performing digital transactions, two factors - authenticity and integrity - should be assured. Otherwise, the data can be altered or someone can also act as if they were the sender and expect a reply.
- **Digital Signature:** Digital signature is an electronic signature method that is assigned to assure that the message was sent by a particular sender. This digital signature is appended with the data and sent to the verifier. The reason for encrypting the hash instead of the entire message or document is that a hash function converts any arbitrary input into a much shorter fixed-length value. This saves time, as now, instead of signing a long message, a shorter hash value has to be signed. Moreover, hashing is much faster than signing.
- **Integrity:** The integrity of any message-sending system is a process to ensure that the message is not altered during the transmission.
- **Signing Algorithms**: An important part of the process of creating a digital signature is the use of signing algorithms, which are like email programs, to create a one-way hash of the electronic data to be signed. The signing algorithm then encrypts the hash value using the private key (signature key). This encrypted hash along with other information, like the hashing algorithm, forms the digital signature.
- **Signature Verification Algorithms**: As per this algorithm, the verifier receives a digital Signature along with the data. The complete process is as follows:
    - The verification procedure first uses the verification algorithm to process the digital signature and the public key (verification key) and generates some value.
    - It then applies the same hash function on the received data and generates a hash value.
    - Then, the hash value and the output of the verification algorithm are compared. If they both are equal, then the digital signature is valid, otherwise, it is invalid.

The steps followed in creating a digital signature are as follows:

1. Message Digest: The representation of text in the form of a single string of digits, which is created using a formula called a one-way hash function. Encrypting a message digest with a private key creates a digital signature, which is an electronic means of authentication.
   Message digest is computed by applying the hash function on the message, and then message digest is encrypted using the private key of the sender to form the digital signature (digital signature = encryption (private key of sender, message digest) and message digest = message digest algorithm(message)).
2. Digital Signature is then transmitted with the message (message + digital signature is transmitted).
3. Receiver decrypts the digital signature using the public key of the sender (this assures authenticity, as only the sender has his private key, so only the sender can encrypt using his private key, which can thus be decrypted by the sender's public key).
4. The receiver now has the message digest. The receiver can compute the message digest from the message (the actual message is sent with the digital signature).
   The message digest computed by the receiver and the message digest (got by decryption on digital signature) need to be the same for ensuring integrity.
5. Message digest is computed using a one-way hash function, that is, a hash function in which computation of the hash value of a message is easy but computation of the message from the hash value of the message is very difficult.

Digital Certificate Authority

Digital certificate is issued by a trusted third party, which proves the sender's identity to the receiver and the receiver's identity to the sender[8].

Note that a digital certificate can only be issued by a Certificate Authority (CA) to verify the identity of the certificate holder. The CA issues an encrypted digital certificate containing the applicant's public key and a variety of other identification information. Digital certificate is used to attach a public key to a particular individual or an entity.

Components of Digital Certificate

Following are the essential components of Digital Certificate:

- Name of the certificate holder

- Serial number to be used to uniquely identify a certificate, the individual, or the entity identified by the certificate
- Expiry dates
- Copy of certificate holder's public key (to be used for decrypting messages and digital signatures)
- Digital signature of the certificate issuing authority

Note: *Digital certificate is also sent along with the digital signature and the message.*

Comparing Digital Certificate with Digital Signature

Digital signatures are used to verify three things: authenticity, integrity, and non-repudiation. To be in non-repudiation state, means that it assures that the message is sent by the known user and not modified, while digital certificate is used to verify the identity of the user, maybe the sender or receiver. As such, the digital signature and a certificate are two different kinds of things, but both are used for security. Digital certificates are used to enhance the trust of their users on most websites.

Rules for Working of Digital Signature

Digital signatures are based on Public Key infrastructure. According to this mechanism, two keys are generated, a Private Key and a Public Key. The private key is kept by the signer and it should be kept securely. On the other hand, the receiver must have the public key to decrypt the message.

For example, suppose a person named Murlidharan, resident of India, wants to send an encrypted message to Dubai. As mentioned earlier, Murlidharan must have a private key to sign the message digitally.

An algorithm, named `'MD algorithm'`, encrypts the message to be sent by Murlidharan into a 128/256-bit format, known as a hash value, before encrypting the message using the private key, After this, Murlidharan's private key encrypts this hash value. On completion of both processes, Murlidharan's message is said to be digitally signed.

Looking from the side of Dubai, the digitally signed message is decrypted with the help of the signer's public key. The public key has decrypted the message and converted it into another hash value. Then, the program that is used to open the message (for example, MS Word, Adobe Reader, and more) compares this hash value to the original hash value, which was generated on Murlidharan's side. If the hash value on Dubai's side matches with the hash value generated on Murlidharan's side, then the program will allow the message to open up and display the message: "The document has not been modified since this signature was applied." The program will not allow the document to open if both the hash values don't match.

Note: *The process of making digital signatures need employing asymmetric cryptography.*

In many instances, they provide a layer of validation and security to messages sent through a non-secure channel. Properly implemented, a digital signature gives the receiver the reason to believe that the message was sent by the claimed sender.

We can compare and see that digital signatures are equivalent to traditional handwritten signatures in many respects. However, they are quite different in the following sense:

- Properly implemented digital signatures are more difficult to forge than the handwritten type.
- Digital signature schemes, in the sense used here, are cryptographically based and must be implemented properly to be effective.
- They can also provide non-repudiation, meaning that the signer cannot successfully claim they did not sign a message, while also claiming their private key remains secret.
- Furthermore, some non-repudiation schemes offer a timestamp for the digital signature, so that even if the private key is exposed, the signature is valid.

Digitally signed messages may be anything like electronic mail, contracts, or a message sent via some other cryptographic protocol and should be representable as a bitstring.

Main Features of the Digital Signature

Here are the key features of the digital signature:

- It plays a primary role in identity verification.
- A digital signature is a unique property in digital form, something like a fingerprint embedded in a document. The signer must have a digital certificate to be associated with the document.
- The certification authority issues the digital signature.
- It is comparable to a driver's license or passport.
- A digital certificate helps to verify the document's authenticity to determine if it has been tampered with.
- Another significant feature of a digital signature is that it is used for protecting digital documents. Miscreants can forge documents to submit online using an electronic signature, but with a digital signature, it is nearly impossible.

When a digital signature is applied to a specific document, the digital certificate is bound to the signed data in a single and unique fingerprint. These two components of a digital signature are unique, and it makes them more practical than wet signatures because it is possible to authenticate their origin.

This cryptographic operation helps to perform the following actions:

- Proving the authenticity of the document and its source.
- Ensuring that there were no changes in the document after signing.
- Confirming the identity of the signer.

Electronic Signature

As per the United States law, an electronic signature is any electronic *symbol, process, or sound* associated with a record or contract that the interested party intends to sign. Thus, the main feature of an electronic signature is the intention to sign a document or agreement. Another noteworthy and distinguishing feature that distinguishes an electronic signature from a digital signature is that an electronic signature can be oral, a simple mouse click, or any electronic authorization.

Following are the characteristic features of an electronic signature:

- By putting the electronic signature, the person agrees to the term and conditions stated in the document. It usually complies with contracts or other agreements that are entered into by two parties. As mentioned earlier, there are different types of electronic signatures. They are legally binding once all parties have demonstrated their commitment and intention to enter into a particular contract.
- The important aspect of an electronic signature is that it helps to verify the authenticity of the document.

  Once it has been signed, the parties involved should be able to be identified. However, an electronic document can be hard to verify because there is no digital certificate, making the process secure.
- Yet, another notable feature of an electronic signature is that it is used to execute an agreement. For example, in a contract, two people usually agree to perform certain obligations. This agreement becomes legally binding if both parties sign it. In this case, you can use an electronic signature. In addition, electronic signatures are often used in contracts because they are easy to use.

Differences Between Digital Signature and Electronic Signature

The main difference between the two is that while an electronic signature is often associated with a contract that the signer agrees to, whereas a digital signature is primarily used to protect documents and is certified by certification authorities. *Figure* 2.10 shows the differences between Digital Signature and Electronic Signature:

Feature	Digital signature	Electronic signature
Purpose	Used to protect the document	Used mainly to verify the document
Regulation and third parties' participation	A digital signature is authorized and regulated by certification authorities	It is usually not regulated
Use of cryptographic algorithms	A digital signature is created using cryptographic algorithms	Significantly less protected. No cryptographic algorithms are used
Verification	A digital signature can be verified. To obtain a digital signature, a person has to produce proof of identity	An electronic signature cannot be verified
Advantages	Preferred over an electronic signature because of its higher level of authenticity	Easy to use, but the degree of evidential value is lower
The intention of the signer	The signer is particularly concerned about the security of the document	The signer indicates the intention to agree to the contract terms and conditions
Visual mark	The "fingerprint" of the signature is embedded in a document signed using a digital certificate	An electronic signature is considered to be not only a handwritten signature but also a password, a PIN code, or any other expression of consent

Figure 2.10: *Differences between Digital Signature and Electronic Signature*

Thus, although both electronic and digital signatures are legally binding, it is preferable to use the latter because they are more secure than the former.

Digital Certification in India

The IT Act, 2000 of India (vide Amendment Act, 2008) introduced the concept of Electronic Signatures. Electronic Signature means 'authentication' of any electronic record by a subscriber by means of the electronic technique specified in the Second Schedule of the Act and includes digital signature.

The term Digital Signature has been there in the Information Technology Act, 2000, since its inception, whereas the term Electronic Signature was inserted in the Information Technology Act, 2000, by the Information Technology (Amendment) Act, 2008.

A digital signature is a "secure" electronic signature, but an electronic signature is not necessarily a digital signature. *Table* 2.3 presents the difference between Digital Signature and Electronic Signature as enumerated by the IT Act 2009 of India.

Basis	Digital Signature	Electronic Signature
Scope	A digital signature is an electronic signature. Digital signatures are actually a subset of electronic signatures because they are also in electronic form	The term electronic signature is broader than digital signatures
Genesis	It uses an asymmetric cryptosystem (key pair)	It uses an electronic technique specified in the Second Schedule and includes a digital signature
Technology	It is technology-specific (public key cryptography). It is based on cryptography codes	It is 'Technology neutral'. It may be created by different technologies, such as the secret code or PIN used with ATM, retinal scans, and more
Security	Due to the technology used, digital signature offers more security	It is less secure as compared to digital signatures when it adopts methods other than digital signature

Table 2.3: *Difference between Digital Signature and Electronic Signature*

Public Key Cryptography or Asymmetric Cryptography

Let us have a look at public key and asymmetric cryptography.

Cryptographic Hashing

In cryptographic hashing, the hashed data is modified in a way that makes it completely unreadable.

Asymmetric cryptography is also known as public key cryptography and is a cryptographic system that uses pairs of keys (that is, the secret word). Each pair consists of a public key (which may be known to others) and a private key (which may not be known by anyone except the owner). The generation of such key pairs depends on cryptographic algorithms to make them secret. Cryptographic algorithms are based on mathematical features termed one-way functions. Effective security requires keeping the private key private but the public key can be openly distributed without compromising security[9].

In effect, in such a system, any person can encrypt a message using the intended receiver's public key, but that encrypted message can only be decrypted with the receiver's private key. As such it allows, for instance, a server program to generate a cryptographic key intended for a suitable symmetric-key cryptography, then to use a client's openly-shared public key to encrypt that newly generated symmetric key. In turn, the server can then send this encrypted symmetric key over an insecure channel to the client, only the client can decrypt it using the client's private key (which pairs with the public key used by the server to encrypt the message). In the client and server environment, both have the same symmetric key, and they can safely use symmetric key encryption (likely much faster) to communicate over otherwise insecure channels. This scheme has the advantage of not having to manually pre-share symmetric keys (a fundamentally difficult problem) while gaining the higher data throughput advantage of symmetric-key cryptography.

The acronym "RSA" has been derived from the three surnames of algorithm creator trio 'Ron Rivest, Adi Shamir, and Leonard Adleman', who publicly described the algorithm in 1977. RSA is a public key cryptosystem that is widely used for secure data transmission. It is also one of the oldest.

In a public key cryptosystem, the encryption key is public and distinct from the decryption key. They are purposely intended to be kept secret (private). An RSA user creates and publishes a public key based on two large prime numbers, along with an auxiliary value. The prime numbers ought to be kept secret. Messages can be encrypted by anyone, via the public key, but can only be decoded by someone who knows the prime numbers.

The security of RSA relies on the practical difficulty of factoring the product of two large prime numbers, known as the "factoring problem". Breaking RSA encryption is known as the RSA problem.

Classes of Cryptographic Hash Functions

There are several different classes of hash functions, of which some of the most commonly used currently are as follows:

- Secure Hashing Algorithm (SHA-2 and SHA-3)
- RACE Integrity Primitives Evaluation Message Digest (RIPEMD)

- Message Digest Algorithm 5 (MD5)
- BLAKE2

Each of these classes of hash functions may contain several different algorithms. For example, SHA-2 is a family of hash functions that includes SHA-224, SHA-256, SHA-384, SHA-512, SHA-512/224, and SHA-512/256."

These hash functions are similar in many ways; they differ slightly in the way the algorithm creates a digest, or output, from a given input. They may also differ in the fixed length of the digest they produce.

SHA-256 is perhaps the most famous of all cryptographic hash functions as it is extensively used in Satoshi Nakamoto's original Bitcoin protocol technology.

Compared to it, RSA is a relatively slow algorithm, as such it is not commonly used to directly encrypt user data. Also, RSA is used to transmit shared keys for symmetric-key cryptography that are then used for bulk encryption–decryption.

SHA-256 is a patented cryptographic hash function having a 256-bit long output value. For example, through SHA-256 hashing, a 512-bit string of data would be transformed into a 256-bit string.

Conclusion

In this chapter, we have learned that the Blockchain is an especially promising and revolutionary technology because it helps reduce risk, stamps out fraud, and brings transparency in a scalable way for myriad uses.

We have also learned that a cryptocurrency, crypto-currency, or crypto is a digital currency designed to work as a medium of exchange through a computer network that is not reliant on any central authority, such as a government or bank, to uphold or maintain it. In the process of learning cryptocurrency, we learned about a cryptographic hash function that is used for security purposes and constitutes the backbone of crypto security.

We also learned a new term known as Non-fungible tokens (NFTs), which are blockchain-based tokens, and each represent a unique asset like a piece of art, digital content, or media.

A digital signature is a mathematical scheme for verifying the authenticity of digital messages, documents, or software. A digital signature is a "secure" electronic signature, but an electronic signature is not necessarily a digital signature.

The term Digital Signature has been there in the Information Technology Act, 2000, since its inception, whereas the term Electronic Signature was inserted in the Information Technology Act, 2000, by the Information Technology (Amendment) Act, 2008.

In the next chapter, we are going to learn more about Bitcoin. Almost everybody knows that Bitcoin is a cryptocurrency, a digital asset designed to work as a store of value that uses cryptography to control its creation and management, rather than relying on any central authorities. Bitcoin was created to function as peer-to-peer electronic cash. Whether you are spending or accepting Bitcoin as payment, it is prudent to understand how a transaction works.

References

[1] What is a hash function in a blockchain transaction?, Bitpanda, https://www.bitpanda.com/academy/en/lessons/what-is-a-hash-function-in-a-blockchain-transaction

[2] Chapter 8. Mining and Consensus, https://www.oreilly.com/library/view/mastering-bitcoin/9781491902639/ch08.html

[3] Cryptographic Hash Functions Explained: A Beginner's Guide, Delton Rhodes, Last Updated: Dec 16, 2021

[4] What are cryptographic hash functions? Posted by Synopsys Editorial Team on Thursday, December 10, https://www.synopsys.com/blogs/software-security/cryptographic-hash-functions/2015

[5] Shai Halevi and Hugo Krawczyk, Randomized Hashing and Digital Signatures

[6] Hash Pointers and Data Structures, Huaabing Zhao, May 21, 2018, https://medium.com/@zhaohuabing/hash-pointers-and-data-structures

[7] Cryptography Digital Signatures, https://www.tutorialspoint.com/cryptography/cryptography_digital_signatures.htm

[8] Digital Signatures and Certificates, Shashank, Last Updated: 31 Aug, 2021, https://www.geeksforgeeks.org/digital-signatures-certificates/

[9] Stallings, William (3 May 1990). Cryptography and Network Security: Principles and Practice. Prentice Hall. p. 165. ISBN 9780138690175.

CHAPTER 3
Understanding Blockchain with Cryptocurrency

Introduction

When you buy, sell, or exchange cryptocurrency, information is gathered and stored in a blockchain. The cryptocurrency market is not supervised or regulated by a single government, so this information is kept private. To understand this chapter, you have to first revise *Chapter 2* on cryptocurrency. Then, we will explore one of the first and most popular cryptocurrencies, Bitcoin. You can transfer your money by keeping it in your wallet and when you become a bonafide user and allowed to transact, you can transfer the money.

Structure

In this chapter, we will discuss the following topics:

- Creation of Bitcoins
- Cryptocurrency Mining Reward (Using Bitcoin)
- User's Ideal Basic Requirements for New Payment System
- Pricing Cryptocurrencies
- Miners and Mining Process
- Preventing Double Spending
- Bitcoin Scripts and Objective of Creating Script Language
- Bitcoin's P2P (Peer-to-Peer) Network
- Block Processing - Mining
- Cryptocurrency Transactions

- Transactions - Public and Private Keys
- Bitcoin Transaction Fees
- Legality of Cryptocurrency
- Blockchain Data Structure
- Blockchain Relay Networks

Blockchain in Business

Two researchers, Stuart Haber and W. Scott Stornetta, in an attempt to implement a system where document timestamps could not be tampered with, outlined blockchain technology in 1991. However, it wasn't until almost two decades later that someone was able to launch its first real-world application, 'Bitcoin', in January 2009.

The protocol of Bitcoin was based on blockchain technology. Bitcoin's pseudonymous creator, Satoshi Nakamoto, had mentioned in his research paper introducing the digital currency as 'a new electronic cash system that's fully peer-to-peer, with no trusted third party.'

It is to be mentioned that the number of Bitcoins processed in a single day reached its highest value at the beginning of 2021, as more people displayed interest in cryptocurrency.

Also, there will never be more than 21 million Bitcoin, a limit known as the **hard cap**, which is encoded in Bitcoin's source code and enforced by nodes on the network. This limit was imposed by the inventor himself. Bitcoin's hard cap is central to its value proposition, both as money and as an investment.

While Bitcoin is regarded as the king of cryptocurrency, it doesn't surpass Ethereum in every quality comparison metric prepared by expert users. With a robust ecosystem of *decentralized finance (DeFi) protocols, play-to-earn blockchain games, and* NFTs, Ethereum's blockchain handles about five times the daily volume of Bitcoin.

The number of transactions per month for Bitcoin is shown in *Figure* 3.1:

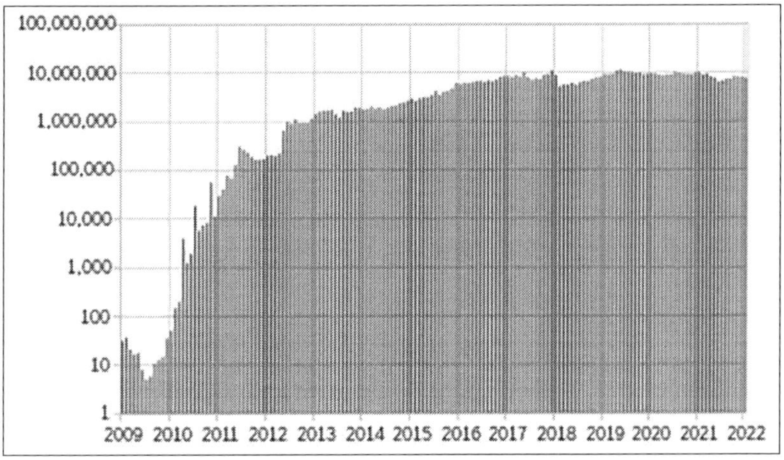

Figure 3.1: *Number of Bitcoin transactions per month (logarithmic scale)*

Creation of Bitcoins

Almost everybody knows that Bitcoin is a **cryptocurrency**, a *digital asset* designed to work as a store of value that uses cryptography to control its creation and management, rather than relying on any central authorities[1].

Procedure for Investment in Bitcoin

The following steps are suggested for purchasing Bitcoins and making investments:

Step 1: Inform yourself: Bitcoin is different than what you know and use every day. There are a few things that you need to know before you start using Bitcoin to use it securely and avoid common pitfalls.

Step 2: Choose your wallet: Free Bitcoin **wallets** are available for all major operating systems and devices to serve a variety of your needs. The term digital wallet may refer to *software, an electronic device*, or *an online service* that enables individuals or businesses to make transactions electronically. It stores the payment information of users for different payment modes on various websites, along with other items such as gift coupons and driver's licenses.

Anybody can install an app on a mobile device and have a wallet only for online payments on the desired computer. In any case, choosing a wallet is easy and can be done in minutes.

According to *due.com*, the following are the world's best eight digital wallets[2]:

- Cash App
- Google Wallet
- Android Pay

- Samsung Pay
- PayPal
- Venmo
- Alipay
- Walmart Pay

Step 3: Securing your wallet: Your wallet must be secured and protected as people do with a real-life wallet. Bitcoin makes it possible:

- To transfer value anywhere in a very easy way and
- Allows you to be in control of your money.

Such useful applications/features are available with great security concerns. If used correctly and securely, Bitcoin can provide very high levels of security. Always remember that it is your responsibility to adopt good practices in order to protect your money. You should be wary of any service designed to store your money online.

Note: *It may be noted that many exchanges and online wallets suffered from security breaches in the past, and such services generally still do not provide enough insurance and security to be used to store money like a bank.*

A Bitcoin wallet is very much similar to a wallet (so-called purse) with **cash**. If you don't keep a thousand dollars in your pocket, you might want to have the same consideration for your Bitcoin wallet. In general, it is a good practice to keep only small amounts of bitcoins on your *computer, mobile*, or *server* for everyday uses and to keep the remaining part of your funds in a safer environment.

If properly stored in a safe place, a backup of your wallet can protect you against computer failures and many human mistakes. It can also allow you to recover your wallet after your mobile or computer is stolen, provided you keep your wallet encrypted.

Safety Requirements

Following cares are required while dealing with bitcoin transactions:

- **Backup your entire wallet:** Some wallets use many hidden private keys internally. If you only have a backup of the private keys for your visible Bitcoin addresses, you might not be able to recover a great part of your funds with your backup.
- **Encrypt online backups:** Any backup that is stored online is highly vulnerable to theft. Even any computer that is connected to the Internet is vulnerable to malicious software. As such, encrypting any backup that is exposed to the network is a good security practice.
- **Use many secure locations:** Single points of failure are bad for security. In case

your backup is not dependent on a single location, it is less likely that any bad event will prevent you from recovering your wallet. You might also want to consider using different media such as USB keys, papers, and CDs.

- **Make regular backups:** You need to back up your wallet on a regular basis to make sure that all recent Bitcoin change addresses and all new Bitcoin addresses you created are included in your backup. However, all applications will be soon using wallets that only need to be backed up once.
- **Encrypt your wallet:** Encrypting your wallet or your smartphone allows you to set a password for anyone trying to withdraw any funds. This helps protect against thieves, though it cannot protect against keylogging hardware or software.
- **Never forget your password:** You should make sure you never forget the password, or your funds will be permanently lost. There are very limited password recovery options with Bitcoin as compared to your bank account. In fact, you should be able to remember your password even after many years without using it. In doubt, you might want to keep a paper copy of your password in a safe place like a vault.
- **Strong password:** Any password that contains only letters or recognizable words can be considered very weak and easy to break. A strong password must contain letters, numbers, and punctuation marks, and must be at least 16 characters long. The most secure passwords are those generated by programs designed specifically for that purpose. Strong passwords are usually harder to remember, so you should take care in memorizing them.

Step 1: Getting Bitcoin

You can obtain Bitcoin by accepting it as a payment for goods and services. There are also several ways you can buy Bitcoin as follows:

1. Purchase bitcoins at a Bitcoin exchange
2. Exchange bitcoins with someone near you
3. As payment for goods or services
4. Earn bitcoins through competitive mining

1. **Purchase bitcoins at a Bitcoin exchange**

Bitcoin payments are easier to make than debit or credit card purchases and can be received without a merchant account. In all cases, payments are made from a wallet application, either on your computer or smartphone, by entering the recipient's address, payment amount, and pressing send. To make it easier to enter a recipient's address, many wallets can obtain the address by scanning a QR code or touching two phones together with NFC technology.

2. **Exchange bitcoins with someone near you**

While it may be possible to find individuals who wish to sell bitcoins in exchange for a credit card or PayPal payment, most exchanges do not allow funding via these payment methods. This is due to cases where someone buys bitcoins with PayPal, and then reverses their half of the transaction. This is commonly referred to as a chargeback.

3. **As payment for goods or services**

There are a growing number of services and merchants accepting Bitcoin all over the world. It is advised to learn the method of using Bitcoin to pay them and rate your experience to help them gain more visibility. Template, as shown in *Figure* 3.2, makes it very easy to make payments in easy steps.

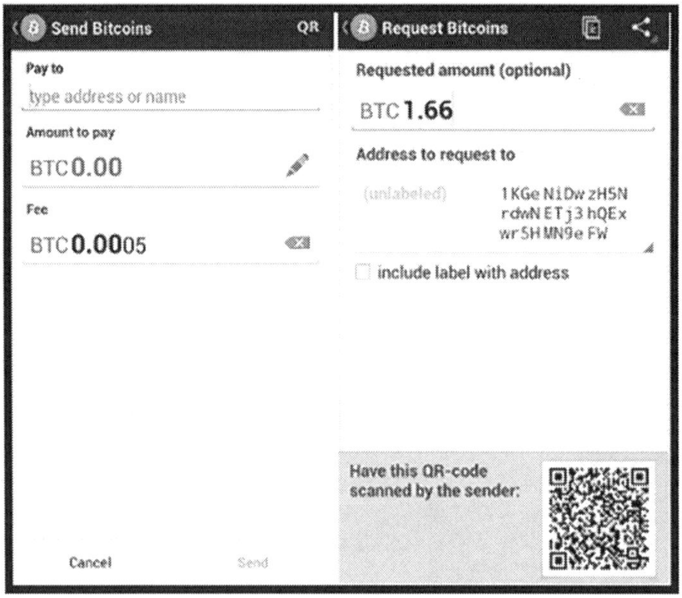

Figure 3.2: *Template for acquiring Bitcoins*

4. **Earn bitcoins through competitive mining**

Occasionally, you can earn cryptocurrency through mining without having to put down money for it.

The Bitcoin miners receive bitcoin as a reward for completing "blocks" of verified transactions, which are added to the blockchain. However, you have to be very skilled, and the process is time-consuming and cumbersome.

The probable mining rewards are paid to the miner who discovers a solution to a complex hashing puzzle first, and the probability that a participant will be the one to discover the solution is related to the portion of the network's total mining power. You need either a Graphics Processing Unit (GPU) or an application-specific integrated circuit (ASIC) to set up a **mining rig**. A mining rig is obtained with an arrangement of hardware elements, either CPU, GPU, FPGA, or ASIC, that have been arranged to perform cryptocurrency mining.

Creation of Coins

Cryptocurrencies are actually 'mined'. The 'Mining' process requires massive amounts of powerful computer hardware and, therefore, a very high amount of electric power and very sophisticated and resilient software. Mining is defined as a process through which cryptocurrency transactions are verified online and new units of cryptocurrency are created.

Cryptocurrency miner tries to decrypt the block containing the transaction information. This also serves as a node on the blockchain on which these transactions are taking place, For example, if Person Y wants to send 0.2 Bitcoins to Person Z, and then miners on the Bitcoin blockchain try and compete to be able to become the first to decrypt the block that contains the transaction information.

The miner must do the following in the process of decrypting the block:

1. Not only authenticates the transaction but also provides the information about:
   a. Who sent how many Bitcoins
   b. To whom and
   c. At what time and date

The block is then added to the blockchain.

2. Once the block has been decrypted and has been accepted by most of the nodes on the blockchain as being authentic. The verification process is highly energy and time-resource-intensive in terms of the computational power required. As such, individual miners often find the process too expensive and so they join pools to collectively use computing power.

Cryptocurrency Mining Reward (Using Bitcoin)

One question often arises in the mind of amateurs if the mining process is so expensive, why do miners compete to decrypt blocks? We have to understand reward mechanisms to get the answer to this question. In return for their services, the cryptocurrency miner is rewarded with a fraction of new units of the cryptocurrency. In easy-to-understand words, the miners are paid in the cryptocurrency that they choose to mine. So, if a miner chooses to decrypt a Bitcoin block, then they will be paid in Bitcoin.

Also, in the process of pooling their resources, miners increase their chances of success and spread out the costs, but they also then get only a share of the rewards.

Coins Versus Tokens

Cryptocurrencies are largely divided into two groups:

- Coins
- Tokens

For different types of businesses, coins and tokens are to be chosen distinctly, which may be vastly different from each other, and each has potential advantages.

A **coin** is an application of cryptocurrencies that runs on its own blockchain, which is where all the transactions take place. Some of the larger examples of coins are Bitcoin, Ethereum, Dogecoin, and more. These are the assets that people can invest in and exchange. If somebody wants to create a new coin, they would have to create a new blockchain.

On the other hand, a **token** functions on top of an existing blockchain infrastructure and is often used like smart contracts, which can be used for physical objects as well as services, physical and digital. One of the main reasons companies consider issuing a token is for a security token offering, which various projects and start-ups use to raise funds.

Figure 3.3 provides the comparison of Coin vs. Token:

Coin	Token
Needs a new blockchain to be created	Can use an existing blockchain
Requires in-depth knowledge of how blockchains work, and also coding skills	Tokens are relatively easier to create, using open-source code
Due to the creation of a new blockchain, the investment can be significant	Creating a token is faster and much more cost-efficient

Figure 3.3: *Comparison of Coin versus Token*

User's Ideal Basic Requirements for New Payment System

All users want the new payment system should have the following facilities:

- All transactions should be made over the Internet.
- There should not be a central authority that will process transactions and intervene in them, including blocking them on order from any investigating authority.
- The member users should be anonymous and identified only by their virtual identity.
- A single user can have as many virtual identities as she or he likes. Even the third gender should be able to join.

- Value supply (new virtual bills) must be added in a controlled way and without any other hidden charges and burdens.

Fulfilling the first two requirements from our list is already achieved by the rules of Bitcoin, as there is no central authority for information exchange over the Internet. What is needed is a peer-to-peer (P2P) network.

Information sharing in P2P networks is similar to information sharing among friends and family. If you share information with at least one member of the network, eventually this information will reach every other member of the network. The only difference is that in digital networks, this information will not be altered in any way.

You have probably heard of BitTorrent, one of the most popular P2P file-sharing (content delivery) systems. Another popular application for P2P sharing is Skype, as well as other chat systems.

The bottom line is that you can implement or use one of the existing open-source P2P protocols to support your new cryptocurrency, which we will call Topcoin.

Pricing Cryptocurrencies

In order to understand the method of pricing of cryptocurrencies, let's take the example of the most famous cryptocurrency – Bitcoin[2]. As with most other commodities in the market, the price of Bitcoin is determined by the interplay of existing supply and demand in the marketplace, and also by the expected future prices. In the case of cryptocurrencies, the pricing is done solely through market dynamics.

However, the supply of Bitcoin is still growing, but at a slow rate, due to (i) an artificial limit set by the creator on the number of Bitcoins that can be mined, and (ii) mining the cryptocurrency is expensive and resource-intensive.

The demand for Bitcoin, however, seems to be much more volatile. However, the demand for Bitcoin grew exponentially in the past as cryptocurrency became famous and stories of people investing early and earning a fortune spread across the world.

The other aspect that affects Bitcoin prices is the hope or expectation of the price rise in the future. Since the people in this market feel that the price of Bitcoin is set to grow in the future, they will be more willing to pay more for it now. The flip side of this expectation is that if the market believes that the price will fall in the future, more people will sell cryptocurrency now while the price is higher than what it could be in the future. While selling, they will accept a lower price than they otherwise would, as they expect the future price to be even lower.

Additionally, individual influencers can exert a huge influence on the price of a cryptocurrency. For example, as of early 2022, Elon Musk's various tweets about Bitcoin have each led to historic price swings in cryptocurrency.

Why Bitcoin Needs Miners

The process of Blockchain "mining" is a metaphor for the computational work that nodes in the network undertake in hopes of earning new tokens. In reality, miners are essentially getting paid for their work as auditors. They are doing the work of verifying the legitimacy of Bitcoin transactions. This convention/ restriction is meant to keep Bitcoin users honest and was conceived by Bitcoin's founder, Satoshi Nakamoto. By verifying transactions, miners are helping to prevent the "double-spending problem".

Reasons for Mining

In addition to prospering the pockets of miners and supporting the Bitcoin ecosystem, mining serves another vital purpose. It is the only way to release new cryptocurrency into circulation. In other words, miners are basically "minting" currency. For information of all bitcoin lovers, as of February 2022, there were just under 19 million bitcoins in circulation, out of an ultimate total of 21 million.

Apart from the coins minted via the genesis block (the very first block, which founder Satoshi Nakamoto created), every single one of those bitcoins came into being because of miners. In the absence of miners, Bitcoin as a network would still exist and be usable, but there would never be any additional bitcoin. However, because the rate of bitcoin "mined" is reduced over time, the final bitcoin won't be circulated until around the year 2140. This does not mean that transactions will cease to be verified. Miners will continue to verify transactions and will be paid fees for doing so to keep the integrity of Bitcoin's network.

You need to be the first miner to arrive at the right answer, or closest answer, to a numeric problem to earn new bitcoins. This process is also known as Proof of Work (PoW). To begin mining is to start engaging in this proof-of-work activity to find the answer to the puzzle. This does not need any advanced math or complex computations.

Bitcoin Versus Blockchain

The blockchain model is derived from the invention of Bitcoin.

To achieve the greatest efficiency, a certain blockchain model was devised that can operate as the integrated sole data management system to serve billions of applications globally. Due to this interoperability between all parts of business and society is maximal, keeping the infrastructure costs to a minimum as it replaces all other data systems.

Though there are blockchain projects that have established different versions of the model, they will not deliver the same efficiency.

Although the key thing to understand here is that Bitcoin merely uses blockchain as a means to transparently record a ledger of payments, blockchain can, in theory, be used to immutably record any number of data points. As discussed earlier, this could be in the form of transactions, votes in an election, product inventories, state identifications, deeds to homes, and much more.

In the previous decade, tens of thousands of projects were looking to implement blockchains in a variety of ways to help society other than just recording transactions –for example, as a way to vote securely in democratic elections. The nature of blockchain's immutability is designed such that fraudulent voting would become far more difficult to occur. For example, a voting system is designed in a manner so that each citizen of a country would be issued a single cryptocurrency or token. This requires that each candidate would then be given a specific wallet address, and the voters would send their token or crypto to the address of whichever candidate for whom they wish to vote. The transparent and traceable nature of blockchain may eliminate both the need for human vote counting and the ability of bad actors to tamper with physical ballots. It will be free from political inference.

Payments and Double Spending

The double spending of the same bitcoin is a scenario in which a Bitcoin owner illicitly spends the same bitcoin twice. With physical currency, this isn't an issue. When you hand someone a $40 bill to buy a bottle of vodka, you no longer have it, so there's no danger you could use that same $40 bill to buy lotto tickets next door. Although counterfeit cash is possible, it is not exactly the same as literally spending the same dollar twice. With digital currency, however, as the Investopedia dictionary explains, *"there is a risk that the holder could make a copy of the digital token and send it to a merchant or another party while retaining the original."*

Let's say, you had one legitimate $40 bill and one counterfeit of that same $40. If you were to try to spend both the real bill and the fake one, someone who took the trouble of looking at both of the bills' serial numbers would see that they were the same number, and thus one of them had to be false. What a blockchain miner does is analogous to that – they check transactions to make sure that users have not illegitimately tried to spend the same bitcoin twice. We will provide a more detailed explanation below.

Double-spending occurs when someone alters a blockchain network and inserts a special one that allows them to re-acquire a cryptocurrency. Double-spending can happen, but it is more likely that a cryptocurrency is stolen from a wallet that wasn't adequately protected and secured.

You go to restaurants and order a cappuccino worth $5. You pay in cash. The service provider at restaurants would instantly confirm that you have paid, and that you received your coffee in exchange for the money. Now, is it possible to spend the same $5 somewhere else to make another purchase? The answer is NO. But what if the answer is YES? This means the same person can use the same cash more than one times. This type of problem is known as the Double Spending Problem. In a physical currency, the double-spending problem can never arise. However, in digital cash like bitcoin, the double-spending problem can arise. Hence, bitcoin transactions have a possibility of being copied and rebroadcasted. It opens up the possibility that the same BTC could be spent twice by its owner.

To understand the problem of double-spending, it helps to review how the blockchain works first. When a block is created, it receives a hash – or encrypted number – that includes a *timestamp, information from the previous block, and transaction data.* The information so created is encrypted using a security protocol like the SHA-256 algorithm used by Bitcoin.

Once that block's information is verified by miners (in proof-of-work consensus), it is closed, and a new one is created with the timestamp, transaction information, and previous block's hash. A Bitcoin is awarded to the miner whose machine verified the hash.

If someone is interested in double-spending, a secret block has to be mined that outpaces the creation of the real blockchain. They would then need to introduce that chain to the network before it caught up – if this happened, then the network would recognize it as the latest set of blocks and add it to the chain. The person who did this could then give themselves back any cryptocurrency they had spent and use it again.

Preventing Double Spending

Double-spending remains a risk during blockchain transactions; however, it ought to be minimized in the case of the blockchain. The likelihood of a secret block being inserted into the blockchain is very rare because it has to be accepted and verified by the network of miners.

The only chance a miner with undesirable illicit intentions of inserting an altered block is to attempt to get another user to accept a transaction using their secret block and cryptocurrency. However, even then, the likelihood of the modified block getting accepted is very rare. The consensus mechanism of blockchain is so dynamic and moves so quickly that the modified block would be outdated before it was accepted. Even if it was accepted, the network would still have passed up the information in the block and would reject it.

Cryptocurrency transactions take some time to verify as the process involves randomly selecting numbers to solve the complex hash. This process also takes up a great deal of computational power. This renders it exceedingly difficult to duplicate or falsify the blockchain because of the immense amount of computing power needed to stay ahead of all of the other miners on the network.

Double-Spending Attacks

The most significant and dangerous risk for blockchains comes in the form of a 51% attack, which can occur if a miner controls more than 50% of the computing power that validates the transactions, creates blocks, and awards cryptocurrency.

If this user – or for that reason a group of users – controls a majority of the hashing in the blockchain, they will be able to dictate transaction consensus and control the award of currency. In more popular cryptocurrencies, such as Bitcoin, this is very unlikely due to the number of miners and hashing difficulty it has reached; however, new or forked cryptocurrencies with smaller networks are susceptible to this attack.

The unconfirmed transaction attack is used to fool cryptocurrency users most commonly. If you see one of these transactions, you should not accept it because it can cause an attempted double-spend attack.

Did Double-Spending Happen?

Rarely there have been occasions where double-spending attempts have been reported and stopped. The attacks where it could happen generally lead to theft rather than double-spending.

Bitcoin Scripts

Bitcoin Script is the language Bitcoin uses to do everything it can do, from sending funds from a wallet to allowing the creation of multi-user accounts[3].

Bitcoin Script C-based programming language is used in Bitcoin for the processing of transactions that are read from left to right.

This is based on a series of linear structures, known as stack, which contain existing data in order LIFO (Last In - First Out). Each instruction in this language is executed one after the other consecutively.

This language is not fully Turing type because its functionality is limited and cannot handle loops. So, it is not capable of solving any type of problem such as Turing machines. However, this limitation is intentional as this prevents infinite or endless looping and error execution, where malicious parts of the program can be free to create complicated operations to consume the rate of hash and slow down the Bitcoin system through infinite loops.

Note: *The concept of a Turing machine is an abstract computational model that performs computations by reading and writing to an infinite tape. Turing machines provide a powerful computational model for solving problems in computer science and testing the limits of computation. The sole advantage of a Turing machine is that it can model all the computable functions as well as the languages for which the algorithm is possible.*

Remember that Turing's machine is not a real machine, but it is a mathematical model, a concept, just like state machines, automata, or combinational logic.

In Bitcoin, we use opcodes (OP CODES) to communicate our wishes, which serve various functions such as memory manipulation, math, loops, function calls, and more.

Therefore, Bitcoin Script is essentially a set of programmed instructions that are recorded with every transaction made. These instructions describe how users can access and make use of the bitcoins available on the network.

Understanding an OP_CODE or Operation Code

An OP_CODE (Operation Code, in English) is a portion of a machine language instruction that specifies the operation to be performed. Its specification and format will be determined by the instruction set architecture (ISA) of the component that processes the instruction. Generally, this processing is done by the computer hardware (usually a CPU).

However, it can also be software specially prepared to emulate the operation of a CPU and process these instructions. In general, a complete machine language instruction contains an OP_CODE, and, optionally, the specification of one or more operands on which the operation code must act. Some operations have implicit operands or none at all.

In Bitcoin and many other cryptocurrencies, OP_CODES are the backbone of the system that allows you to program transaction instructions. Let's remember that Bitcoin (and other cryptocurrencies derived from it) are programmable money. The keyword here is "programmable", as Bitcoin Script is actually a programming language where instructions are given in OP_CODES that the Bitcoin network has defined beforehand for its operation. In fact, due to the structure in which Bitcoin has been created, there is the possibility of defining a total of 256 OP_CODES, which start from number 0 to 255. Of these 256 OP_CODES, a total of 116 are currently active.

These OP_CODES are the ones that allow you to carry out the different operations in Bitcoin and its transaction scheduling, such as data flow control, constant management, stack management, logical management, arithmetic, time lock, pseudo-words, cryptographic operations, and reserved words. You can see a complete and updated list of the different OP_CODES directly in the Bitcoin code.

- In the Bitcoin network, each Bitcoin Script is divided into two types of scripts: (1) the **`scriptSig`** and (2) **`scriptPubKey`**.

First, **`scriptSig`** is the unlock script, which requires a public key and a digital signature. Signature checks were included after detecting various problems in the early versions of the Bitcoin software. Therefore, the system only accepts to carry out transactions if the signatures and their verification comply with a series of established rules that guarantee proper behavior on the network.

The second, the **`scriptPubKey`**, is the blocking script, which contains a public key hash, also called a Bitcoin address. Some Bitcoin scripts require multi-signatures, that is, the authorization of several users to carry out the transaction. In this case, the script is more complicated because it is a much larger operation than the standard peer-to-peer operation. In fact, the scheduling of Bitcoin transactions as such is stored in this part of the script.

Objective of Creating Script Language

The purpose of creating a Script language in Bitcoin is to provide a series of easy and flexible parameters to enable a transaction. So, when Satoshi Nakamoto developed Bitcoin, it disabled various functions, including multiplication. So, the script is kept simple in terms of programming. So, it is this programming language that determines whether or not an operation can be performed, that is, if said operation is authorized for the transfer of funds.

Simply put, the creation of the Bitcoin Script is what gives the programmable nature of Bitcoin. This is what allows us, for example, to send a transaction that is validated only if certain conditions are met. This property is something unique to Bitcoin and cryptocurrencies, something that today's digital money cannot reach, let alone archaic physical money. It is the evolution of money reached a point where even money can act independently and decentralized simply by attending to the programming embedded in it.

At the same time, the Bitcoin script also prevents the creation of errors in the system and the unnecessary use of very complex transactions. In fact, the script makes transactions relatively easy to calculate. Also, infinite loops require a lot more computing power and slow down networks, as mentioned in the beginning.

Example of a Bitcoin Script

Before continuing to delve further into what it is and the different elements that make up a Bitcoin Script, let's see a small example of it. Next, we will see a small Bitcoin Script widely used today for Bitcoin transactions. We will explain its behavior and operation as well as the different parts of it, and then go deeper into its properties.

Bitcoin Script is present in all Bitcoin actions. The truth is that each operation in Bitcoin is carried out by a specific script that defines what is going to be done. Outside of what that script says nothing can happen.

For example, if we want to make a transaction, a script for it would be the following:

SECCIONES	CONTENIDO DEL BITCOIN SCRIPT
scriptPubKey	OP_DUP OP_HASH160 340cfcffe029e6935f4e4e5839a2ff5f29c7a571 OP_EQUALVERIFY OP_CHECKSIG
scriptSig (Signature)	30440220694ff325724a4f4b0f3f0c36bf8e94cac58ad7c9b4d5bd8c7286c0da623f0b 2c02206ae94680a8f31f30cd846da258e919c94afe2dd629b4f4ce11bbe8165ff99a5f01
scriptSig (Pub Key)	04fc60372d27b067ca306ba812ced9c8cd69296b83a40b9b57c593258c1b9e0 ee1c0c621ca558b878395f9645a4b67a96e51843e9c060d43a3833fdd29a91f4f31

Figure 3.4: *Example of a Bitcoin Script: Transactions in Bitcoin Using the P2PKH Script*

All the preceding content is a simple Bitcoin transaction of the type P2PKH (Pay to Public Key Hash). This type of script is a standard script and is the most used way to send bitcoins. At first glance, it is shown as something very cryptic and difficult to understand. The truth is that behind such complexity, there is a simple system, which we will explain now.

The previous Bitcoin Script is delimited into two parts: **`scriptPubKey`** and **`scriptSig`**. In the first, there are the actions to be performed, while the second contains the signature and public key to verify the authenticity of such actions. This ensures that only those who have access to the funds can carry out any operation with them. On the other hand, there are the OP_CODES that in the operation are the following:

1. **`OP_DUP`**: Duplicate the item on the top stack.
2. **`OP_HASH160`**: The input is encoded twice: first with SHA-256 and then with RIPEMD-160.
3. **`OP_EQUALVERIFY`**: Verify that the data entered is correct and valid.
4. **`OP_CHECKSIG`**: The outputs, inputs, and script of the entire transaction are summarized in a hash. The signature used must be a valid signature for this hash and must be next to the public key.

Now what happens during script execution is as follows:

1. First, the original public key of the owner (which is in the **`scriptSig`**) of the funds is duplicated.
2. The duplicate public key then goes through a hashing process. In this process, it is first hashed with SHA-256 and then RIPEMD-160 hash is applied to the result.
3. The result of the hashes is compared with the hash of the public key that is in the **`scriptPubKey`** to make sure it is **`EQUALVERIFY`** (that is, it is the same key and is verified as valid).

4. If it matches, the script continues to run and **CHECKSIG** is performed to verify the signature with the public key.

In this way, everything indicated in the script is carried out in a safe and scheduled way.

Bitcoin Script serves as the smart contract language of Bitcoin

Many people argue that Bitcoin is unable to execute smart contracts. However, the truth is that this is not true, as Bitcoin Script itself enables smart contracts. While its capabilities are more limited compared to platforms like Ethereum, Bitcoin Script does have the ability to create smart contracts. Let's explain this in a simpler and more detailed manner.

First of all, as mentioned, Bitcoin Script is not a fully Turing language. This is because it does not require greater complexity to perform its intended functions. However, one of the main reasons for this is the absence of loops, ensuring that you can know for sure when and how a certain program will end. There is no possibility for the execution of errors, which gives you greater security. Also, there is no possibility that the programs are blocked or their executor is blocked, which in this case is Bitcoin.

A good example of the importance of these protections is that with Bitcoin Script, it is impossible to create scripts that run forever. In fact, the risk of a script that runs forever is that it would open doors to attack on the network, such as denial-of-service attack (DoS).

However, the fact that Bitcoin Script limits these types of operations protects the network from such attacks. So, there is no chance that a Script program with a continuous loop could prevent Bitcoin from working properly. Simply put, Bitcoin Script is much more secure than its more complex counterparts, such as those featured by Ethereum or NEO.

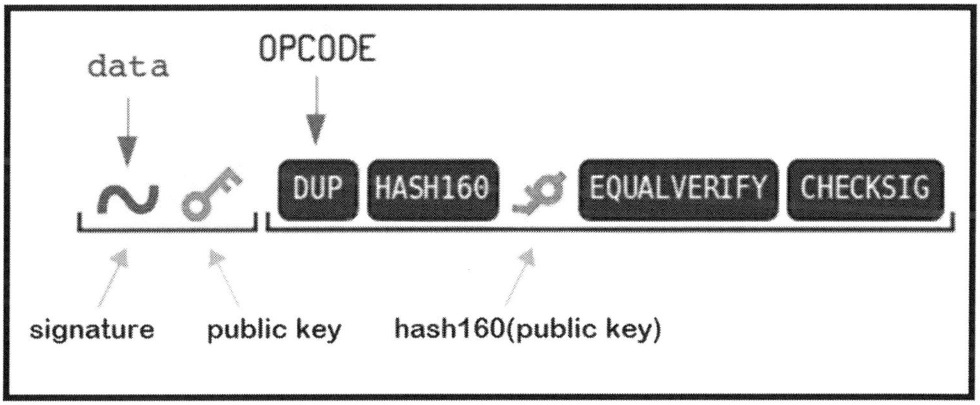

Figure 3.5: OPCODE *for encrypting and decrypting*

Bitcoin's P2P (Peer-to-Peer) Network

The Bitcoin network consists of nodes within a P2P (peer-to-peer) network. There is a need for each node to download the Bitcoin software to connect to the network. There are different types of nodes in the network, with miner nodes and general nodes being the major ones. A general node is always used by users to transfer bitcoin in the network, whereas a miner node is a special node used for mining bitcoins.

Each user within a node needs to utilize wallet software to create identities. An identity needed in the Bitcoin network consists of a private/public key pair, and a Bitcoin address is derived from the corresponding public key. A sender needs to know the address of the receiver to transfer any bitcoin. Bitcoin is transferred between two entities using the notion of a transaction where the sender utilizes wallet software for this purpose. This transaction is propagated to the network, which is collected by all miner nodes.

Each miner node combines these transactions into a block and then engages in solving a cryptographic puzzle, with other miners, in which it tries to generate a random number that satisfies the required condition (the random number must be less than a target value called the difficult target). When a miner successfully solves the puzzle, that miner is said to have generated a valid block, which is then propagated in the network. The Bitcoin protocol generates a certain amount of new Bitcoins for each new valid block and rewards the miner for their effort in creating the block. Other miners try to validate this newly mined block and then add it to the blockchain. Each new block refers to the last block in the chain, which in turn refers to its previous block, and so on.

The very first block in the chain, known as the genesis block, however, has no such reference.

The decentralized nature of this mining process might result in multiple valid blocks generated by different miners and propagated at the same time in the network. All of them are added to the blockchain, and they refer to the same last block in the chain. Consequently, *multiple branches* emerge from the same blockchain. This is a natural phenomenon in blockchain and is aptly known as **fork.**

The fundamental goal of the corresponding consensus protocol is to resolve this fork (branch) so that only one branch remains and other branches are discarded. The consensus algorithm utilized in Bitcoin follows a simple rule of allowing the branches to grow. As soon as one branch grows longer than the others (more specifically, the total cumulative computational effort of one branch exceeds the others), all miners select the longest branch (or the branch with the highest computational effort), discarding all other branches. Such a branch is known as the main branch and other branches are known as orphan branches. It is noteworthy that only the miners in the main branch are entitled to receive their Bitcoin rewards. When a fork is resolved across the network, a distributed consensus emerges in the network.

The frequency of the Bitcoin block generation depends on the **difficulty** parameter, which is adjusted after the 2016 blocks.

The protocol adjusts the difficulty parameter in such a way that a block is generated every 10 minutes on average.

However, the Bitcoin reward is halved after every 210, 000 blocks, or approximately after every 4 years. At the initial stage, the reward for generating a valid block had been 50 Bitcoins, which was halved to 25 Bitcoins in 2012 and 12.5 Bitcoins in 2016. The next halving will occur in 2020 when the reward will be reduced to 6.25 bitcoins per block.

Bitcoin allows this geometric reduction every 4 years, underlining a maximum total supply of 21 million Bitcoins. It is expected that this supply will be exhausted by the year 2140, when the rewarded bitcoin will be infinitesimally small for each block.

The Bitcoin protocol process is presented in *Table* 3.1:

Stage	Block Generation Process of Bitcoin
A	Each miner collects transactions that are broadcast in the network and uses her hash power to try to generate a block via repeated invocation of a hash function on data. The data consists of the transactions that the miner chose fit to include, the hash of the previous block, their public key address, and a nonce.
B	When a miner succeeds in generating a block, meaning that the hash of her block data is smaller than the current difficulty target, she broadcasts her block to the network.
C	The other miners continue to extend the blockchain from this new block, only if they find that this block is valid, that is, it refers to the hash of the previous block of the longest chain and meets the current difficulty target.
D	The block reward (as newly minted coins) and the fees from the transactions go to the miner's public address. This means that only the miner can spend those by signing with her/his corresponding private key.
E	The difficulty level readjusts according to the mining power of the participants, updating the hash target value every 2016 blocks (≈2 weeks), so that blocks get generated once every 10 minutes on average.
F	The block reward starts at 50 coins and halves in every 210, 000 blocks, that is, about every 4 years.

Table 3.1: *The process of Bitcoin protocol*

Transactions in Bitcoin Network

Bitcoin was created to function as peer-to-peer electronic cash. Whether you are spending or accepting bitcoin as payment, it is prudent to understand how a transaction works.

Bitcoin transactions are messages, like email, which are digitally signed using cryptography and sent to the entire Bitcoin network for verification[4]. Transaction information is public and can be found on the digital ledger known as the 'blockchain.' The history of each and every Bitcoin transaction leads back to the point where the bitcoins were first produced or 'mined.'

Satoshi Nakamoto, in the Historic Whitepaper, stated: "*We define a bitcoin as a chain of digital signatures. Each owner transfers bitcoin to the next by digitally signing a hash of the previous transaction and the public key of the next owner and adding these to the end of the coin. A payee can verify the signatures to verify the chain of ownership.*"

Don't be surprised to know that Bitcoins do not "exist" per se. There are no physical bitcoins, nor do Bitcoin owners have an "account." Instead, there is a 'blockchain,' which you can think of as a ledger, or a record, of all the transactions that have ever taken place between Bitcoin addresses. These transaction records are updated by the Bitcoin network participants (nodes) and shared across each of its nodes as balances increase and decrease. You can use a 'block explorer' if you want to see the history, as well as the current balance, of any given Bitcoin address.

Transactions - Private Keys

A Bitcoin transaction is a transfer of value between Bitcoin wallets that is included in the blockchain. Bitcoin wallets keep a secret piece of data called a private key or seed, which is used to sign transactions, providing mathematical proof that they have come from the owner of the wallet. The signature also prevents the transaction from being altered by anybody once it has been issued. All transactions are broadcast to the network and usually begin to be confirmed within 10-20 minutes through a process called mining.

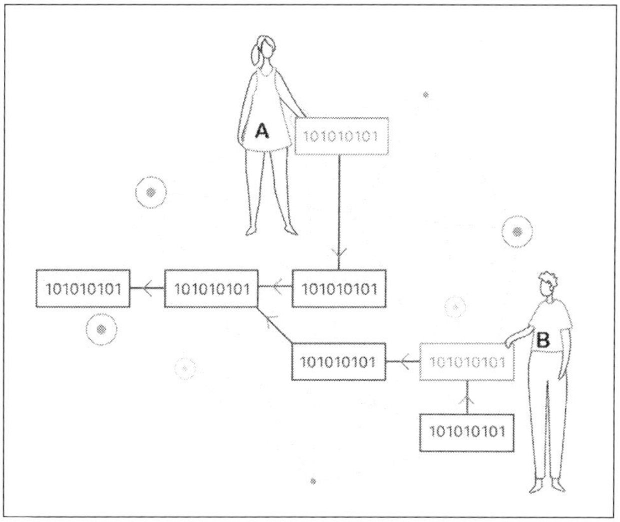

Figure 3.6: *Transferring secret message from A to B*

Public and Private keys

To send Bitcoin, you must have access to both the *public and private* keys associated with the amount of bitcoin you want to send. When we talk of someone "owning" bitcoins, this statement actually means that person has access to a 'key pair' comprised of:

- A public key (an address) to which some of the amount bitcoin was previously sent.
- The corresponding unique private key (a password), which authorizes the bitcoin previously sent to the above public key (address) to be sent elsewhere.

Public keys, also called *bitcoin addresses*, are randomly generated sequences of letters and numbers that function similarly to an email address or a social-media site username. They are public, so you are safe sharing them with others. In fact, you must give your Bitcoin address to others when you want them to send your bitcoin. The private key is another sequence of letters and numbers, also generated randomly. However, private keys, like passwords to email or other accounts, are to be kept secret. Never share your private key with anyone that you do not 100% trust to not steal from you.

Suppose Mark wants to send 1 BTC to Jessica. To do this, he uses his private key to 'sign' a message with the transaction-specific details. This message, which must be broadcast to the network, will contain the following:

- **Inputs:** It contains information about the bitcoin previously sent to Mark's address. For example, imagine Mark previously received 0.6 BTC from Alice and 0.6 BTC from Bob. Now, in order to send 1 BTC to Jessica, there might be two inputs: one input of 0.6 BTC previously from Alice and one input of 0.6 BTC previously from Bob.

- **Amount:** In this case, the amount Mark wants to send is 1 BTC.
- **Outputs:** There are two outputs. The first is 1.2 BTC (0.6 BTC + 0.6 BTC) to Jessica's public address. The second is 0.2 BTC returned as 'change' to Mark.

This sequence might seem confusing, but it's done this way to improve efficiency - and the good news is that knowing the behind-the-scenes details of Bitcoin transactions is not required to send or receive bitcoin. Your Bitcoin Wallet takes care of that!

Broadcasting and Confirmations

To explain the above example, Mark (via his wallet software) will broadcast his proposed transaction to the Bitcoin network. A special group of participants in the network known as 'miners' verify that Mark's keys are able to access the inputs (that is, the address(s) from where he previously received the bitcoin he claims to control). Miners also gather together a list of other transactions that were broadcast to the network around the same time as Mark's and form them into a block. Any miner who has completed the 'Proof of Work' is permitted to propose a new block that will be added or 'attached' to the chain by referencing the last block. That new block is then broadcast to the network. If other network participants (nodes) agree it's a valid block (that is, the transactions it contains follows all the rules of the protocol and properly references the previous block), they will pass it along. Eventually, another miner will build on top of it by referencing it as the previous block when proposing the next block. Any transactions that were in the previous block will now have been 'confirmed' by the next miner. As blocks are added to the chain, the number of confirmations of Mark's transaction increases.

Variable Duration of Bitcoin Transaction Confirmations

Each block in any transaction can only contain a certain number of transactions, and that number is determined largely by the space available in each block, or the 'block size,' which is 1MB. The limited space gives rise to the free market where miners, who collect fees, choose to include in the next block only those transactions that have included a high enough fee. Thus, higher fees act as an incentive for miners to prioritize your transactions.

Note that the block size is an arbitrary limit, but the Bitcoin community has chosen to keep the block size as small as possible to make it easier for people to operate Bitcoin nodes. Bitcoin Cash, which is a fork of Bitcoin, has a larger block size and therefore requires (much) lower fees for transactions.

Bitcoin Transaction Fees

Regarding the expenses, fees for sending bitcoin could be anywhere from a few cents to all the way up to $100. The reason for the big variation is that Bitcoin fees depend on both supply and demand (that is, how congested the network is at a given time) and the "size" of your transaction. Size is affected primarily by inputs, so if your transaction has many inputs, it will take up more block space, and demand a higher fee. For example, if you want to send 10 BTC, there is a good chance your transaction will require more inputs than if you want to send 1 BTC. The 10 BTC transaction might consist of 5+2+1+1+1 (so a total of 5 inputs), while the 1 BTC transaction might be just two inputs, as in our Mark/Jessica example mentioned earlier.

Many wallets allow users to manually set transaction fees, including the Bitcoin.com Wallet. This helps you to avoid overpaying. For example, if you are not in a rush, you can set the fee the lower such that it will be picked up by a miner when the network is less congested. You can also ensure your transactions are processed immediately by increasing your fee.

Is Creating a Cryptocurrency Legal?

Creating a cryptocurrency is generally legal as far as the local rules allow, although some countries and jurisdictions have partially or fully banned cryptocurrency. In India, you have to pay income tax on income from bitcoins or any other cryptocurrency gained by any Indian. In China, for example, raising money through virtual currencies has been illegal since 2017, and all cryptocurrency transactions have since been banned[4],[5]. Even where cryptocurrency is legal, it's possible to run afoul of existing securities regulations when launching and promoting a new cryptocurrency.

Block Processing - Mining

The concept of mining is a distributed consensus system that is used to confirm pending transactions by including them in the blockchain. It enforces a chronological order in the blockchain, protects the neutrality of the network, and allows different computers to agree on the state of the system. To be confirmed, transactions must be packed in a block that fits very strict cryptographic rules, which will be verified by the network. These rules prevent previous blocks from being modified because doing so would invalidate all the subsequent blocks. Mining also creates the equivalent of a competitive lottery that prevents any individual from easily adding new blocks consecutively to the blockchain. In this way, no group or individuals can control what is included in the blockchain or replace parts of the blockchain to roll back their own spending.

A rough overview of the process of mining bitcoins involves[5]:

1. New transactions are broadcast to all nodes.

2. Each miner node collects new transactions into a block.
3. Each miner node works on finding a proof-of-work code for its block.
4. When a node finds a proof-of-work, it broadcasts the block to all nodes.
5. Receiving nodes validate the transactions they hold and accept only if all are valid.
6. Nodes express their acceptance by moving to work on the next block, incorporating the hash of the accepted block.

Transactions[7] are the atomic units of information of any blockchain system, which are then grouped into blocks to be entered into the distributed ledger. *Figure* 3.7 provides an overview of the different concepts related to Bitcoin architecture:

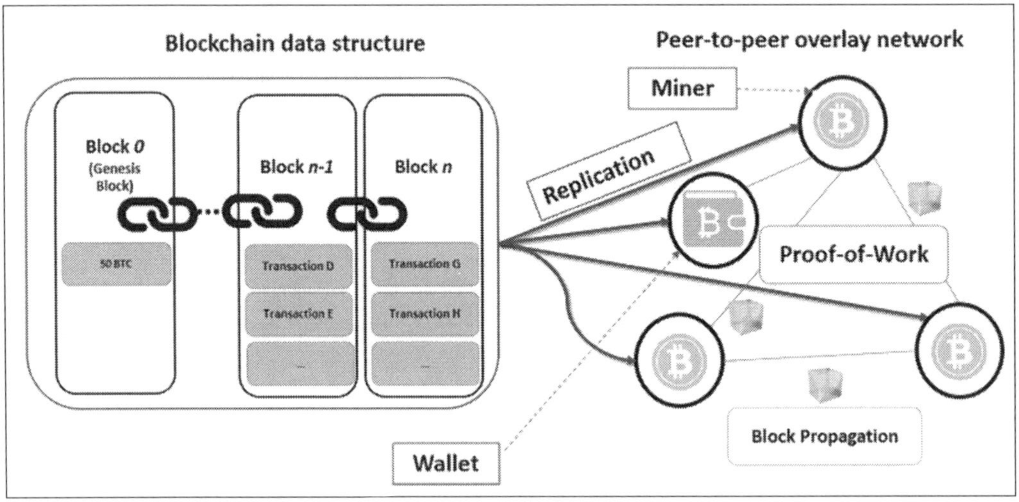

Figure 3.7: *Overview of the Bitcoin network*[6]

Blockchain Data Structure

Figure 3.8 illustrates the blockchain data structure. Blocks are linked together using the hash pointer of the previous block, starting from the root block (genesis block). In Bitcoin, the genesis block is hard-coded into the clients. These series of blocks are distributed, replicated, and stored in a ledger, which is located in all participating nodes. This ledger is necessary for the verification of transactions embedded in each block. Participating nodes run over a peer-to-peer network and there is no intermediary node between them. Any node with access to this distributed ledger can read it and be notified about new data stored in the nodes.

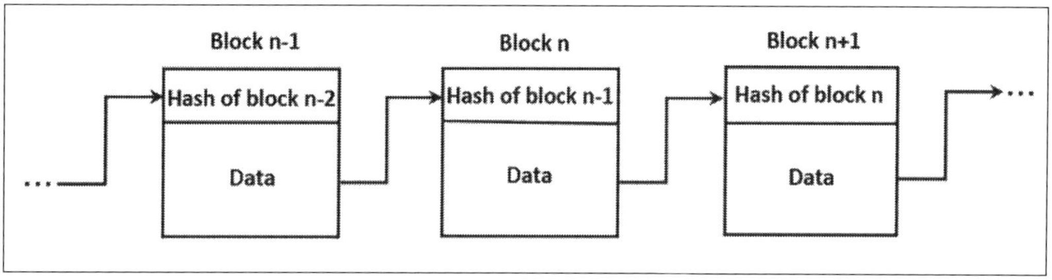

Figure 3.8: *Blockchain data structure*

Cryptocurrency Transactions

Transactions describe the transfer of digital coins between users in the Bitcoin system. Each transaction consists of several input and output records. Each input indicates funds to be spent from previous transactions and output records indicate the amount transferred to the specified addresses (which are generated from the public key of the recipient). To be valid, each transaction should be digitally signed by the private key of the sender.

In each transaction, the sum of inputs should be equal to or greater than the sum of outputs. There exists also special transactions (called coinbase), which have no input and grant a reward to the miner who successfully added the block.

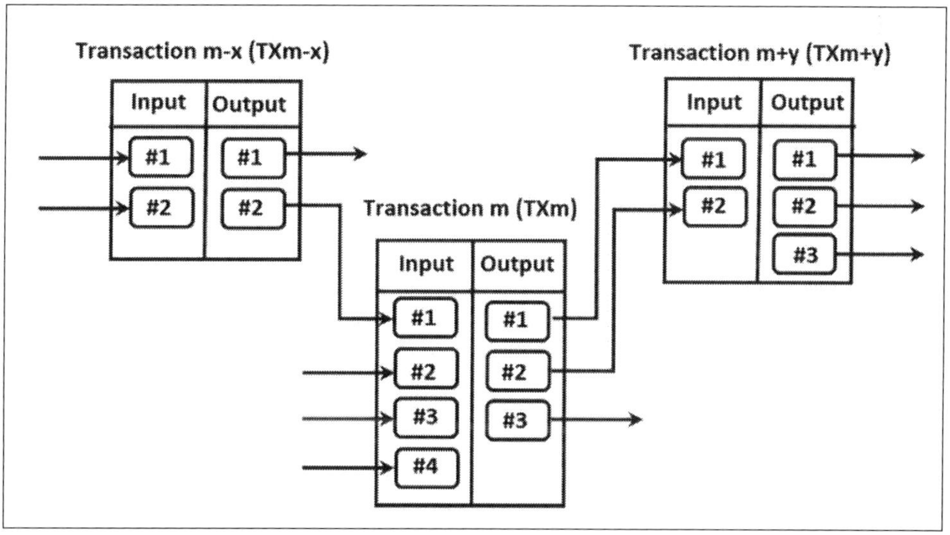

Figure 3.9: *Structure of a Transaction*

For example, transaction *TXm*, in *Figure* 3.9, takes as input #1 and the output #2 from transaction *Tm−x* and sends part of the funds to transaction *TXm + y*.

Blocks

As depicted in *Figure* 3.10, each block consists of several components:

- Hash of the previous block
- A timestamp
- Transactions arranged to form a Merkle tree[7]

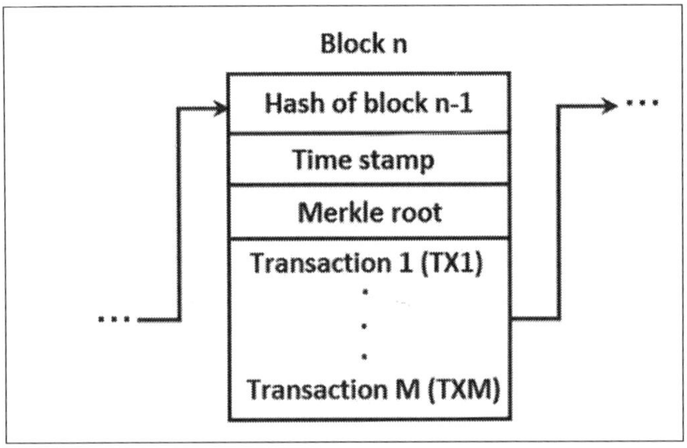

Figure 3.10: *Internal structure of a block*

To be recorded in the distributed ledger, individual transactions have to be embedded in the blocks. A subset of nodes in a Bitcoin network, called miners, gather transactions already propagated by users and group them into blocks to be added to the blockchain. Grouping the transactions in the blocks is an optimization, as a hash chain of blocks is significantly shorter than a hash chain of transactions.

To be eligible to propagate a proposed block as the next block in the chain, each miner has to show a PoW. To accomplish this, miners have to find a number called nonce. The hash of the nonce, combined with the hash of the previous block and the Merkle root of the tree containing the transactions proposed by the miner, should be below a certain target threshold.

In other words:

$$H(\text{nonce} \| \text{H(prev\_block)} \| \text{Root}\{TX_1 \|$$

Where *H(prev_block)* is the hash of the previous block. This means that the result of equation (1) should start with a certain number of leading zeros.

The difficulty of the mentioned puzzle is adjusted periodically. Say for a given block, the miner who first solves the PoW will broadcast his block over the network. The nodes that receive the block must verify the incoming block and add it to the local copy of the blockchain, thus becoming the new blockchain head. Since Bitcoin has a very wide peer-to-peer network, inconsistencies in this network are unavoidable. When multiple valid blocks are solved and disseminated at the same time, we say that a fork has occurred in the network, which is likely to be resolved by the following block mined[8].

In order to reduce the block propagation delay in the Bitcoin network, the compact block proposal was introduced in BIP 152. According to this proposal, compact blocks have the same metadata as legacy blocks. The main difference is that the hash of the block transactions is disseminated instead of a full copy of the transactions.

Block Propagation and Block Relay

There is no defined scalability in the whole game of bitcoin. The lack of scalability is known to be the foremost obstacle standing in the way of mass adoption of blockchain technology. All existing blockchain projects look for solutions that could improve the performance of their network[9]. Many emerging projects claim that they have a magic bullet that could solve the problem. However, such assertions are not always valid. Unfortunately, many business observers and investors do not realize the core and root of this problem.

Block Propagation Time or Block Propagation Delay

The well-known bottleneck that prevents Bitcoin from scaling is Block Propagation Problem in Blockchains. Block propagation time is the average time needed for the new block to reach the majority of nodes in the network.

The block propagation time or block propagation delay is the average time that is needed for the new block to reach the majority of nodes in the network. In a large decentralized network like Bitcoin, whenever a new block is generated, it is broadcasted according to the Gossip **proBlock** propagation time or block propagation **delaytocol.** In case, some node has got the new valid block, it informs nodes to connect block propagation time or block propagation delayed to it about its new possession.

Blockchain throughput is measured by the number of transactions per second that it can support and is measured as follows:

Throughput = Transactions/Block x Blocks/second (Inverse of Block interval),

Where:

- *Transactions/Block* is a factor of Bitcoin's current block capacity and average transaction size
- *Transactions/Block = Bitcoin capacity /average Transaction size*

The current Block capacity for Bitcoin is 1MB for a Block interval of 10 minutes, and given the average transaction size of nearly 540 bytes, the Bitcoin network currently processes ~1950 transactions per Block, which translates to ~3 transactions per second (TPS).

To increase the throughput, one can either increase the Transactions/Block or Blocks/second.

Then, the node transfers this block to those nodes that asked it to do that. Before the block reaches each full node in the network, it passes through seven intermediary nodes. It's important that every honest node verifies the block before relaying it to other peers.

The whole thing takes a while. Every new block shakes the network and makes nodes and ethernet connections between them work at full power.

One might argue that since the launch of the network, there have been many improvements to the Gossip protocol. For example, the Bitcoin improvement proposal BIP 0152 introduced the option to transfer only short transaction IDs, instead of the whole list of transactions, in the block body.

However, if the node doesn't have that transaction in its mempool, it has to ask its peers to transfer it in a separate message. If there is a large number of such transactions in the block, then improvement from BIP 0152 disappears.

Another approach to reducing the information propagation delay in blockchain networks is to deploy a central backbone of high-speed servers with a high degree called a relay network.

Relay Network

Generally speaking, a relay network is a set of global gateways with high-velocity links, which form the backbone of the P2P network and connect to a large proportion of the network.

Relay networks can propagate blocks and transactions much faster than the regular P2P network, and thus increase the efficiency of information propagation. Relay networks can also be leveraged as a scalability solution for increasing the transaction throughput. Analytically, relay networks can have a centralized or decentralized architecture. In a centralized architecture, the relay gateways interact with each other via a central orchestrator entity. However, in decentralized architecture, the gateways are connected to each other in a P2P manner. *Figure* 3.11 illustrates a typical blockchain network with and without relay networks. However, relay networks are accused of decreasing decentralization since they can censor certain nodes, wallets, and miners or discriminate among different nodes by filtering the information they spread.

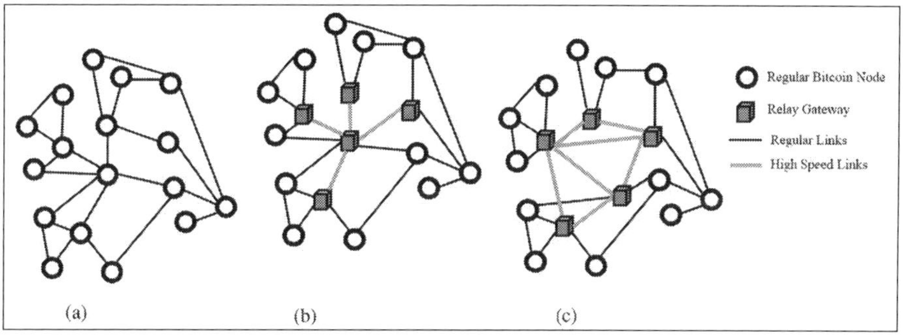

Figure 3.11: *Typical blockchain network with and without relay networks: (a) Regular Bitcoin overlay network; (b) Relay network with a centralized topology in a Bitcoin network; (c) Relay network with a decentralized topology in a Bitcoin network*

Compact block relay is a protocol that allows two nodes with roughly similar sets of unconfirmed transactions to minimize both the bandwidth and the latency required to transfer a block that confirms many of those same transactions[10].

Blockchain Relay Networks

There are three different types of nodes:

- Full Nodes
- Lightweight Nodes
- Mining Nodes

Although all nodes in the blockchain network are equal, the nodes could opt to perform a variety of roles. A few nodes might function as **full nodes**, maintaining the entire blockchain, whereas a few others function as **lightweight nodes** by maintaining only the required transactions. In addition to this, the nodes that are willing to create new blocks will perform mining operations. When all these nodes communicate with each other in a P2P fashion, there will be a network latency involved.

Since mining nodes are involved in time-sensitive operations, they need to keep latency to a minimum. Even during a critical financial transaction, a decentralized system needs to keep latency as minimal as possible for its clients.

Latency denotes and also indicates how long it takes for packets to reach their destination. Throughput is the term given to the number of packets that are processed within a specific period of time.

The Bitcoin network handles an average of 1.58 TB of data globally daily. Obtaining this data is simple:

First of all, we must bear in mind that on average about 144 blocks are produced each day, with 1 MB per block. This totals to an average of 144 MB of data per day. However, these must be replicated across the 11000 nodes that make up the network. In other words, all the blocks and their data travel through the network so that each node can have an exact copy of it. Therefore, we have: 11000 (nodes) * 144 (MB) = 1584000 MB (data replicated across all nodes).

If we take this data to TB, we obtain: 1584000/1000000 = 1.58 TB Thus, we can know the approximate data mobilized throughout the Bitcoin network. This involves a huge amount of bandwidth-consuming information. Moreover, this generates two problems: it slows down the network in terms of network performance and complicates the creation of a consensus throughout the network and the nodes that comprise it.

If we add that the problems can only increase in scale with a greater number of nodes and people using the network, then we understand why it is urgent to solve this problem. In fact, developers like Greg Maxwell have been very emphatic in this regard, stating:

"The decentralized Bitcoin blockchain that is a globally shared medium of transmission, and therefore is probably the most incredibly inefficient mode of communication ever devised by man."

Gregory Maxwell is a renowned developer of cryptographic systems, streams, and coding in the world of free software. Many may believe that Maxwell's words attack the decentralization of the network. However, in reality, they attack a problem known to all, P2P networks are a rather inefficient means to send information in networks that must always be synchronized. Faced with this situation, it is best to make the transmission medium more efficient, and for this, there are several proposals such as Relay Network, Erlay, and, of course, Compact Blocks.

The three advantages that compact blocks offer us are as follows:

- It does not modify the Bitcoin protocol.
- It doesn't break the scheme P2P of the current network, protecting its decentralization.
- It considerably reduces bandwidth needs and the amount of data transmitted within the network.

Without a doubt, these are not arguments of little weight, and they keep Bitcoin in line with its philosophical line: decentralized money available to everyone.

How do Compact Blocks work?

What the Compact Blocks seek is to divide the information of the mined blocks in the network into two processes, as follows:

Generating a valid block on the network

The first process is the generation of the block, where the miners will create a valid block within the consensus rules of the network. At this point, the miners include all the information that this block would normally have, that is, your block hash or Block ID, its Merkle Root, the complete information of the header of the block, and the whole set of transactions that have been validated by it. At this point, there is no modification of any kind in the process, it remains the same block generation process without any changes.

This means that the miners do their work, generate the block, and send it to the network. At this point, the first node to receive said block verifies it and begins to send the compact blocks following the solution described below.

Sending the information to the rest of the network

Now, the second process begins, which involves the transmission of this information, and it's crucial because this is where the innovation of compact blocks lies. As we know, each node in the blockchain has a space called **mempool,** where the transactions that are waiting to be processed are stored. This mempool is present in all nodes without exception. From this situation, we can deduce the following: many of the transactions of the recently generated block are present in the mempool of each and every nodes of the network.

This deduction is very important because the current process of transmission of the blocks involves sending the said block with all this set of transactions in duplicate. It is precisely this duplication that makes the process of transmitting data on the network less efficient. Faced with this, the following question is valid: Can't we take advantage of the fact that the nodes already have many of these transactions in their mempool and thus reduce the amount of data sent to the nodes and allow them to consolidate the new block by themselves? The answer is yes, it can be done. In fact, this is precisely what happens in the second compact block process.

The nodes that make use of the compact blocks propagate the block by means of a "minimum block" of the mined block. This "minimum block" actually contains vital information, among which we can find the following:

The 80-byte header of the new block contains information such as the Block ID or block hash, the Merkel root, the nounce, the number of transactions, and the date and time it was mined.

It also includes transaction identifiers or TXID (without data from the scripts of those transactions); and some complete transactions (with all the information from the scripts of those transactions) such that the sending node predicts that the receiving node does not have in its mempool yet.

In total, these minimum blocks occupy a maximum of 20 KB of data. This represents a drastic reduction of information compared to 1 MB of data that on average occupies a block.

Rebuilding the block

As we can see, the amount of information in this "minimum block" is much less than what a complete block normally has. However, this information would perfectly allow the rest of the nodes to accurately reconstruct the mined block. For this, you should only use the information received in that minimum block and its mempool. In this way, the node uses this data to completely recreate the final block, which can be verified without problems.

Even if it is not possible to rebuild the block locally, the node will make the information requests to achieve this. To do this, the node will require said transaction (or transactions) to another full node to rebuild the index and form the block unequivocally. This prevents, for example, the nodes build disparate blocks and thus break the consensus of the network.

This process of sending information piecemeal and using local data to fill in the information in the validated blocks drastically reduce the size of network messages. You can see it as sending small signals that you can completely rebuild. This is possible, thanks to the fact that you possess the elements used to build these signals. Also, thanks to the use of cryptography, you can be sure that your reconstructed message will be identical to the original.

Impact of Compact Blocks on Bitcoin

Here are some of the pros of compact blocks:

- It greatly reduces the need for network bandwidth to transmit information to all nodes. In fact, on average, the network's data consumption reaches 1.4 TB of data per day. This is a reduction of more than 90% in the data consumption of the entire network.
- It allows the propagation of data over the network to be faster. In fact, it takes about 15 seconds for all the nodes of the network to have the information of the new block.
- Another point in favor of compact blocks is that it reduces data consumption for those who have a limited connection. In this way, they can participate in the network without major problems or excessive costs.
- Additionally, it improves network security, since the rapid transmission of information prevents attackers from sending false information.

Conclusion

In this chapter we learned that Bitcoin is a cryptocurrency, a digital asset designed to work as a store of value that uses cryptography to control its creation and management, rather than relying on any central authorities.

We learned the procedure for investment in Bitcoin. We have also learned the names of the world's eight best digital wallets. There are neither physical bitcoins nor do Bitcoin owners have an "account". Instead, there is a 'blockchain,' which you can think of as a ledger, or a record, of all the transactions that have ever taken place between Bitcoin addresses.

We have learned about the process of mining. Transactions describe the transfer of digital coins between users in the Bitcoin system. To be recorded in the distributed ledger, individual transactions have to be embedded in the blocks. A subset of nodes in a Bitcoin network, called miners, gather transactions already propagated by users and group them into blocks to be added to the blockchain.

To be eligible to propagate a proposed block as the next block in the chain, each miner has to show a PoW. To accomplish this, miners have to find a number called nonce. The hash of the nonce, combined with the hash of the previous block and the Merkle root of the tree containing the transactions proposed by the miner, should be below a certain target threshold.

In next chapter, we will learn about distributed consensus in open environments, and in *Chapter* 6, we will learn about distributed consensus in closed environment.

References

[1] Jerry Brito; Andrea Castillo (2013). "Bitcoin: A Primer for Policymakers" (PDF). Mercatus Center. George Mason University. Retrieved 22 October 2013

[2] The Best Digital Wallets, https://due.com/blog/best-digital-wallets/

[3] What is Bitcoin Script? https://academy.bit2me.com/en/what-is-bitcoin-script/

[4] How do Bitcoin transactions work? https://www.bitcoin.com/get-started/how-bitcoin-transactions-work/

[5] Barber, Simon; Boyen, Xavier; Shi, Elaine & Uzun, Ersin (2012). "Bitter to Better - how to make Bitcoin a better currency" (PDF). Financial Cryptography and Data Security. Lecture Notes in Computer Science. Springer Publishing. 7397: 399–414. doi:10.1007/978-3-642-32946-3_29. ISBN 978-3-642-32945-6

[6] A Theoretical Model for Block Propagation Analysis in Bitcoin Network by Yahya Shahsavari, Kaiwen Zhang, Member, IEEE, and Chamseddine Talhi, IEEE Transactions on Engineering Management

[7] A. Narayanan, J. Bonneau, E. Felten, A. Miller, and S. Goldfeder, Bitcoin and Cryptocurrency Technologies: A Comprehensive Introduction. Princeton, NJ, USA: Princeton Univ. Press, 2016.

[8] I. Eyal, A. E. Gencer, E. G. Sirer, and R. Van Renesse, "Bitcoin-ng: A scalable blockchain protocol," in Proc. Usenix Conf. Netw. Syst. Des. Implementation, 2016, pp. 45–59.

[9] Understanding the Block Propagation Problem in Blockchains, Vinod Manoharan, CEO and Founder at Jax.Network, http://jax.network, https://hackernoon.com › understanding-the-block-propagation-problem-in-blockchains-1t2s3x9b

[10] What is a Compact Block? https://academy.bit2me.com/en/what-are-compact-block/

CHAPTER 4

Distributed Consensus in Open Environments

Introduction

Consensus is the process by which a group of peers (competitor's or their authorized agents) – known as 'nodes' – on a network determine which blockchain transactions are valid and which are not. Consensus mechanisms are the methodologies used to achieve this agreement. By ensuring most users on the network agree on the state of the ledger, consensus mechanisms maintain the security and integrity of the blockchain. The consensus mechanism maintains the security of the blockchain by keeping a record of all legitimate transactions. Since crypto trading is a decentralized process, this becomes important to stop sellers from deliberately cheating a buyer.

This chapter delves into the world of distributed systems, where data and tasks are spread across multiple devices or computers. We'll also explore different types of consensus mechanisms such as Proof of Work (PoW), Proof of Stake (PoS), and more, used in cryptocurrencies including Bitcoin. We will also understand how they contribute to reliable and secure data management in decentralized environments.

Structure

In this chapter, we will discuss the following topics:

- Consensus in a Bitcoin Network
- Public Blockchains Function
- HashCash Protocol for PoW
- Bitcoin and PoW
- The Proof of Stake (PoS)
- Attacks on PoW and the Monopoly
- Proof of Burn (PoB)
- Proof of Elapsed Time (PoET) Blockchain

- Proof of History (PoH)
- The Hardness of Mining and Mining Difficulty
- Mining Pool

Consensus in a Bitcoin Network

Shared databases were created when computers and networks became popular in the 1980s and 90s. They were created so that multiple users could access the data they stored. Most of them had a centralized database with permissions that people could access from various workstations. This arrangement grew into centralized networks with administrators who gave user rights and ensured data integrity.

Programming for some of these shared databases spread processing and storage power across a network of storage devices located in multiple places. Preventing data tampering and unauthorized access – whether malicious or not – was one of the most important issues that needed to be addressed. To ensure that the information was not altered, a method was needed to automate distributed database management.

Distributed autonomous consensus refers to a method where network programs agree on state of a shared database using cryptographic techniques. This agreement was intended to be accomplished by using encryption algorithms to generate long strings of alphanumeric numbers, known as hashes, which were then validated by programs running on the network. Hashes only change if the hashing algorithm's input is changed, so programs are designed to compare hashes to make sure they are similar in distributed systems.

Distributed consensus is a process to reach a common agreement in a distributed or decentralized multi-agent platform. It is crucial for the message transmission system.

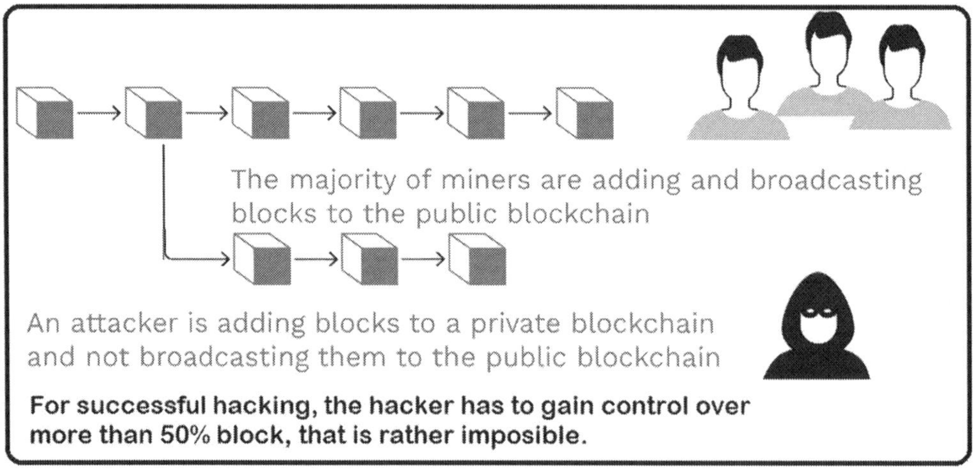

Figure 4.1: *Blockchain Process and Attackers*

An attack on a blockchain that uses a PoW algorithm for consensus is possible if the attackers have over 50 percent control of the network hash rate.

If this is the case, the controlling CPU power will allow an attacker to create a separate chain from any previous block in the blockchain. Given that it has the majority of computing power, its new chain will eventually overtake the accepted chain by the network, thereby defining a new transaction history.

In this new chain, the attackers are able to double spend virtual currency, meaning that the funds that have already been spent on the network's chain could be spent again on the attackers' chain.

With Bitcoin, staging a 51% attack on the network is seemingly unlikely, simply due to the size of the network and its hash rate. One estimate puts the cost of running a 51% attack on Bitcoin at just over 15 billion USD. Many altcoins, however, are much more at risk.

Numerous 51% attacks have taken place in recent years. In August 2021, Bitcoin SV (BSV) slid about 5%value after an attack. Another Bitcoin fork, Bitcoin Gold (BTG), suffered a 51% attack in 2019.

Because there is a central server in a typical software architecture, consensus is rarely an issue; instead, the other nodes just need to line up with the server. To reach a consensus, each node in a distributed network like blockchain serves as both a host and a server and must communicate with other nodes. The consensus process may occasionally be severely hampered or destroyed by malevolent nodes in addition to downed or unavailable nodes. As a result, a good consensus protocol can reduce the harm and accept the occurrence of these phenomena without affecting the consensus's ultimate outcome.

Generally speaking, every new block that is added to the Blockchain is guaranteed by the consensus protocol to be the only version of the truth that is accepted by every node in the Blockchain.

Let's reiterate: Blockchain is an immutable, private, secure, and transparent distributed decentralized network. Despite the lack of a central authority to validate and verify the transactions, each and every transaction on the Blockchain is thought to be totally secure. Only the consensus mechanism, an essential component of every Blockchain network, makes this feasible.

The process by which all of the peers in the Blockchain network come to a consensus regarding the current state of the distributed ledger is known as the algorithm (of consensus). Consensus algorithms accomplish this by building trust amongst strangers in a distributed computing environment and ensuring reliability in the Blockchain network. In essence, the consensus mechanism ensures that each new block added to the Blockchain represents the singular, accepted version of the truth accepted by all of the nodes in the Blockchain.

Consensus-Building Process

In computer and blockchain systems, a consensus mechanism should essentially be a fault-tolerant method that is used to get the required agreement on a single data value or a single state of the network across distributed processes or multi-agent systems, like with cryptocurrencies[1]. This ensures that record-keeping benefits from its utilization. For example, the Proof-of-Work (PoW) consensus process in the Bitcoin blockchain necessitates the use of computer power to solve a challenging but arbitrary problem in order to maintain network integrity for all nodes.

The Mechanism of Consensus

A central administrator has the power to maintain and update any conventional centralized system, such as a database containing important data regarding driver's licenses in a nation. Any adjustments, such as adding, removing, or amending the names of individuals who meet the requirements for a particular license, are carried out by a central authority that is still the only one responsible for keeping accurate records.

Public Blockchains Function

Public blockchains function as globally distributed, autonomous, decentralized networks that are not governed by a single entity. They are made possible by the participation of hundreds of thousands of users who work on block mining and the verification and validation of transactions that take place on the blockchain.

Due to the dynamic nature of blockchain technology, publicly accessible ledgers require a mechanism that is efficient, equitable, real-time, functional, dependable, and secure to guarantee that all network transactions are authentic and that all participants reach a consensus regarding the ledger's status. The consensus mechanism, a collection of guidelines that determines the validity of contributions made by the various blockchain participants (that is, nodes or transactors), carries out this crucial duty.

An open Blockchain is a public network that keeps an unchangeable record of all transactions. By following specified regulations, anyone can publish a transaction and take part in the network. Examples of open blockchains are Litecoin and Bitcoin. In simpler words, it's a shared digital event ledger accessible to all system members.

Open Blockchain is a shared record of digital events, or transactions, among many users who have an interest in the system. Information entered into the ledger cannot be removed after it has been recorded and may only be changed by consensus among the participants. Every event that is recorded can be cryptographically verified by providing evidence of participant agreement.

Technically speaking, Open Blockchain is a fabric architecture that enables companies to use the strength of distributed, peer-to-peer, immutable (append-only), cryptographically secure databases. These characteristics, pioneered by Ethereum and Bitcoin, make blockchains secure and reliable for recording transactions.

Blockchain is a distributed ledger system that operates on a peer-to-peer basis, catering to a new breed of transaction applications. It streamlines corporate procedures while establishing transparency, accountability, and trust. In contrast to public blockchains, some systems use a modular private blockchain architecture.

This approach is used to store and retrieve transactions on a private ledger. In this context, the term "transaction" can refer to many different things, including data, assets, identities, and instructions. For various domains, a system that integrates the information storage and the transactional processing protocol is quite beneficial. A key advantage of this modular design is that network administrators can specify their own limitations and then configure the protocol to meet those needs. This approach is beneficial for creating permissioned networks.

An endless number of distinct actors can build their own networks with the help of this open-source fabric. Communities establish a permissioned network in which known whitelisted entities run both validating and non-validating nodes. A network issuing authority grants access to these identities. This concept differs greatly from blockchains that are in use today. Traditional blockchain technology are expanded upon by Open Blockchain through the following:

- **Logic (Chain Code):** Chain code is an extension of conventional smart-contracts, which are generally understood to be self-executing contracts expressed in code that can interact with one another and trigger other smart-contracts. Chain-code can communicate with other hlp-fabric-golang networks or the outside world while running in sandboxed Docker containers. Additionally, chain-code inherits confidentiality and privacy and the ability to store persistent data.
- **Variable Confidentiality**: Networks have the ability to control who can see and engage with the environment at various levels. This extends to transactions, where specific privacy standard can be applied.
- **Verifiable Identification:** Although the network has the ability to obfuscate identities, it is nevertheless feasible to have peers that are 100% anonymous and whose identities can be independently verified using safe cryptography techniques. An auditor can de-anonymize users and transactions on a network if the users provide authorization. This transparency is crucial for regulatory analysis and inspections.
- **Private Transactions:** All transaction information is encrypted, including but not limited to peers, assets, volumes, and chain-code. This removes the possibility of identifying patterns or of private information being disclosed

to unauthorized users on the network. Exclusive actors possess the ability to decode, observe, interact, and execute (using chain-code).

- **Customizable Consensus Protocols:** Almost any consensus mechanism, like proof-of-work or proof-of-stake, can be used with the fabric to operate with ease. There are many applications for Open Blockchain, owing to its adaptable architectural architecture. For example, the Proof-of-Work (PoW) consensus process used in the Bitcoin blockchain demands the application of computational resources to solve a challenging but arbitrary puzzle in order to maintain the integrity of all nodes in the network

PoS mechanism is covered in length in section *Attacks on PoW and the Monopoly*.

Workproofing

In 2009, Satoshi Nakamoto, creator of Bitcoin, intended for it to be a decentralized, distributed consensus form of money. This innovation aimed to achieve decentralization in both the financial and technological aspects of money. For example, when you use a trusted system to transact money, the debit and credit transactions are handled by a third party (think banks, credit/debit cards, PayPal, and more).

The bank act as intermediaries, debiting the sender's account (for example, Mark) and crediting the recipient's account (for example, Sally) with the corresponding amount.

Until the transaction is complete, none of the transacted funds belong to Mark or Sally because they are all managed by and within the unidentified third party.

Bitcoin, on the other hand, disrupts this centralized model. It operates on a peer-to-peer network, eliminating the need for a trusted intermediary. This approach aims to empower users with greater control over their finances and potentially fosters transparency and trust in the financial system.

The Proof of Work (PoW)

Several consensus mechanism algorithms exist, each based on a distinct set of principles. These include:

- Proof of Work (PoW)
- Proof of Stake (PoS)

For example, the Proof-of-Work (PoW) consensus process used in the Bitcoin blockchain demands the application of computational resources to solve a challenging but arbitrary puzzle in order to maintain the integrity of all nodes in the network. PoS mechanism is covered in length in section *Attacks on PoW and the Monopoly* .

In Proof-of-Work, participating nodes must demonstrate that the work they have completed and submitted qualifies them to be granted permission to add new transactions to the blockchain. However, entire bitcoin mining process requires a lot of energy and takes a long time to process.

Cryptocurrencies like Ethereum and Bitcoin have embraced the PoW. In every round of consensus, PoW uses a competition between compute power to choose one node to produce a new block. The participating nodes in the challenge have to figure out a cryptographic riddle. The ability to add a new block may belong to the node that solves the puzzle first. *Figure* 4.1 shows the block formation process in PoW flow.

It is very difficult to solve a PoW puzzle. Nodes need to constantly adjust the random value (nonce) to get the correct answer, which requires much computational power. It is feasible for a malicious attacker to overthrow one block in a chain, but this amounts to increase the number of valid blocks in the chain. The workload gets accumulated, therefore overthrowing a long chain requires a huge amount of computational power. PoW belongs to the probabilistic-finality consensus protocols since it guarantees eventual consistency. In Blockchain, all nodes maintain and work on the same distributed ledger.

The following table illustrates the properties of atomic broadcast in distributed consensus:

Properties	**Note**
Validity	This validity guarantees that if a message is broadcast by a valid node, it will be correctly included within the consensus protocol.
Agreement	Agreement provides the guarantee that if a message is delivered to a valid node, it will ultimately be delivered to all valid nodes.
Integrity	It is to ensure that a message is broadcast only once by a valid node.
Total Order	It is to ensure that all nodes agree to the order of all delivered messages.

Table 4.1: *Atomic broadcast Properties of Distributed Consensus Protocols*

A consensus protocol should have the following three properties; namely consistency, availability, and fault tolerance[2]. These properties are elaborated in *Table 4.2*:

Properties	**Note**
Safety/ Consistency	A consensus protocol is considered safe (or consistent) only when all nodes produce the same valid output, according to the protocol rules, for the same atomic broadcast

Liveness/ availability	If all non-faulty participating nodes produce an output (indicating the termination of the protocol), the protocol is considered live.
Fault Tolerance	It exhibits the network's capability to perform as intended in the midst of node failures

Table 4.2: *Properties of Distributed Consensus Protocols*

Open and Closed Types of Blockchains

Unlike traditional financial institutions that rely on trust, Bitcoin operates as a trustless system. This might seem counterintuitive, but it actually allows for secure peer-to-peer transactions without the need for a middleman.

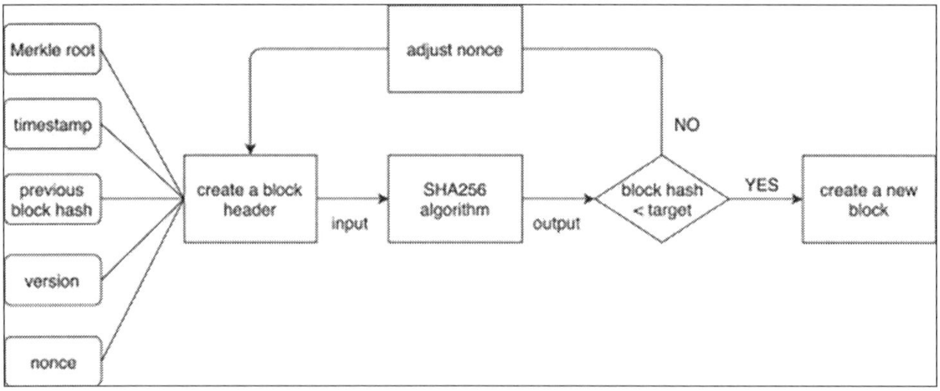

Figure 4.2: *Creation of a new block after getting verified by consensus algorithm*

Here, miners take the position of the traditional mediators, and their job is to ensure that transactions involving Bitcoin are successfully completed on behalf of the cryptocurrency's owners. Miners use the computing power of their computers to decipher the encrypted algorithms contained in each transaction in order to ensure that it is accepted. In a Proof of Work system, miners compete to confirm the validity of each and every transaction in the candidate block, or the block that is presently being constructed[3]. They need to solve the encrypted puzzles that confirm the coins' integrity in order to accomplish this. Block rewards, or a portion of the transacted currency, are given to the fortunate first miner who solves these problems. When the issue is resolved, the transactions form a block that is kept on the blockchain as a public record, and the miner notifies everyone on the network of the resolution.

PoW is determined by computational output and competition. Imagine there is an international math tournament, and the competitors (the miners) are handed a proof (the block) that has never been solved. The first person to solve this proof will receive a reward (a block reward), and once it is, it will be made public online, establishing a new blockchain block.

Advantages of Proof of Work

A Proof of Work system, as previously mentioned, requires computers to perform a small amount of additional work before carrying out a requested operation. After this additional work is completed, a solution is produced and shared with the other computers connected to the network. The accuracy of the answer and the approval of any action may be simply verified by the other computers.

One essential feature of a Proof of Work system is that solving a problem should be rather challenging, while confirming that a given solution actually solves the problem should be very simple. Cryptographic hash functions are essential to contemporary Proof of Work systems. Proof of Work systems are comparable to Merkle trees in this sense. With relatively little computational work, every other machine can confirm that a hash is a valid result after it has been formed.

Some key advantages of Proof of Work systems are elaborated as follows:

- They work wonders in discouraging spammers. If sending one email requires a considerable amount of work, most spammers wouldn't have access to enough computing power to send a significant volume of unsolicited emails.
- Alternatively, even if a spammer were to possess the computational power to send a large volume of emails, the expenses associated with this processing power – such as purchasing hardware and paying for electricity – would probably outweigh the money gained from spamming. A Proof of Work system works in a way to deter spam and other harmful activity.
- It's noteworthy to mention that Proof of Work systems can also be utilized to secure a whole network. A single bad actor or even a small group of bad actors cannot get the computational power necessary to dominate and influence a network if enough nodes (computers or specialized mining equipment) are fighting to find a particular solution.

Technical Specifics of Blockchain Proof of Work

Proof of Work blockchains involve nodes on the network discovering a block hash that is less than or equal to a predefined number, called the "target." This is the "work" or mathematical problem the nodes are attempting to solve. The block header data combined with a cryptographic hash algorithm is the block hash. Six pieces of information make up the block header itself, including:

- The blockchain codebase version number that is in effect when a block is mined
- The desired number in compressed form, or bits
- The timestamp corresponding to the precise moment the block is mined

- The Merkle Root, which is the hashed set of all transaction IDs in the block using a Merkle Tree
- A cryptographic hash of the block hash from the previous block
- The nonce

Thus, the header of a block is composed of these six pieces of data. The hash that results from hashing these six pieces of information collectively is referred to as the "block hash." A block must have a block hash that is less than or equal to the goal in order for a miner to begin mining it.

It's crucial to understand that the quantity targeted and what's usually called the challenge are not the same. The difficulty and the target are really inversely correlated. As the target is reduced, the difficulty of finding a block increases.

This is true because miners are trying to find a block hash that is less than or equal to the target. If the target is extremely high, the chances that a miner can find a block hash less than the target are comparatively high. If the targeted amount is low, then there is a much more limited set of numbers that are less than or equal to that target. This makes it harder to find a block hash beneath the threshold.

Every Proof of Work blockchain has a target that is frequently changed to guarantee a block time that is comparatively constant. For example, the goal for Bitcoin is changed every two weeks. The goal of Bitcoin is to maintain block time at ten minutes. If blocks are discovered too quickly (less than ten minutes on average), the difficulty increases, making it harder for miners to find new blocks and slowing down block creation. Conversely, if block times consistently exceed ten minutes, the difficulty decreases, allowing miners to find blocks faster and restore the target block time.

Now remember that the cryptographic hash of the header of a block in a Proof of Work blockchain, which consists of six pieces of data, is the block hash of any block in the blockchain. You'll see that five of the six data points are static, which means they can't be changed and must stay the same.

The nonce is the only integer that is modifiable. Because it is a single-use number, the nonce is known as such. Every block is unique in its nonce.

As previously said, the goal of mining cryptocurrencies is to locate a block hash that is either less than or equal to the target. Miners attempt to mine blocks by repeatedly and incrementally changing the nonce because it is the sole number that is modifiable. Finding a nonce that, when combined with the other five pieces of information that comprise the block header, results in a block hash that is less than or equal to the target is the aim.

A miner broadcasts a nonce and its associated block hash to all other nodes on the network once it discovers one that meets these requirements. Every node confirms that the hash generated by the nonce is accurate and either less than or equal to the target. That block is added to the chain if the network reaches consensus. After the miner obtains their block reward, the competition recommences with a fresh block.

Disadvantages of Proof of Work Blockchains

There are two primary disadvantages to Proof of Work systems:

- The first is that they waste energy, which is bad for the environment. As computers perform extra computational work, additional electricity is used. This can add up to an extremely large amount of excess electricity consumption. This has led to the rise of Proof of Stake chains as a greener alternative.

  However, the simple statistic of how much energy the Bitcoin network consumes doesn't tell the whole story. Environmentally speaking, Bitcoin mining isn't as bad as you might think. A report on crypto mining released in November 2018 estimates that around 80% of the electricity used in mining is green energy. In some cases, Bitcoin mining operations are making use of excess electricity that a country's power grid would be unable to store and distribute anyway.

- The second major drawback to Proof of Work blockchains is about security. Proof of Work blockchains provide adequate security only if there is a large network of miners competing for block rewards. If the network is small, the possibility remains that a hacker could gain a simple majority of the network's computational power and stage what is known as a 51% attack.

In today's circumstances, manipulating the Bitcoin blockchain is practically impossible. However, there are dozens of smaller Proof of Work blockchains that remain extremely vulnerable to 51% attacks.

In fact, many of these small Proof of Work chains can be successfully attacked for just several hundred dollars an hour on NiceHash, a website that allows users to rent hash power to enable mining of cryptocurrencies. For more details, check out Crypto51, a website that lists in real time how much money it would cost to 51% attack every Proof of Work blockchain in existence.

While these two disadvantages of Proof of Work blockchains are serious concerns, Komodo's Blockchain Security Service provides a solution to both.

As far as environmental issues are concerned, Komodo's innovative delayed Proof of Work security mechanism recycles the incredible hash rate of the Bitcoin network to provide BTC-level security to all integrated blockchains. It leverages the gargantuan amount of electricity already being consumed to protect small Proof of Work blockchains.

As for the concern about 51% attacks and other types of blockchain manipulation, they are no longer an issue once a chain is secured with the power of the BTC network. A potential hacker would need to overpower both the KMD network and the BTC network at the same time in order to successfully attack a chain integrated to Komodo's Blockchain security service.

HashCash Protocol for POW

In 1997, a member of the cypherpunk movement named Adam Back founded a protocol called HashCash, which laid the foundation of "Proof of Work" mechanisms. HashCash even included "*Double Spending Protection*," a foundational concept in blockchain for keeping networks secure from double spend attacks.

Moreover, Satoshi Nakamoto cited HashCash as an influence in Bitcoin, writing that in order "*to implement a distributed timestamp server on a peer-to-peer basis, we will need to use a proof-of-work system similar to Adam Back's Hashcash.*" The connection is not just assumed but made explicit by the founder of Bitcoin themself.

HashCash was a solution designed to combat spam by generating a proof of work that allowed verifying that a certain email was not spam. It introduced Proof of Work (PoW) that was used to minimize spam and denial of service attacks (known as DoS or DDoS). This technology gained wide popularity, thanks to its implementation in the Bitcoin and many others cryptocurrencies.

Bitcoin and PoW

Bitcoin makes use of the Hashcash function as part of its mining core. All bitcoin miners use GPU rather than CPU. The GPUs are graphics processing units that have a higher computing power than those of conventional central processing units (CPUs). Like many cryptographic algorithms, HashCash uses a hash function as a building block. Solving these puzzles creates new blocks and validates transactions on the Bitcoin network. Without this software, the current Bitcoin mining and security structure would not be possible.

The Proof of Stake (PoS)

Another popular consensus method that developed as a low-cost, low-energy substitute for the proof of work (PoW) algorithm is the proof of stake (PoS). It includes assigning a participant node a certain amount of tokens representing virtual currency in proportion to how many tokens it holds, which is the public ledger. One potential disadvantage of PoS is that it encourages storing cryptocurrency rather than spending it, which could affect overall circulation.

In this method, the age of a forger's stake within the blockchain network determines which forgers—the proof-of-work equivalent of a miner—are selected to produce blocks. Let's take an example where you own 500,000 QTUM. Let me begin by speculatively congratulating you on your fat stacks. Returning to the example, you would have a higher chance of creating the candidate block under the Proof of Stake mechanism than someone with 100,000 QTUM. Furthermore, you would be more likely to generate the following block if you had been holding your 500,000 QTUM in the same address for a year as opposed to someone who had the same amount of QTUM but had been storing it in a network address for half that time.

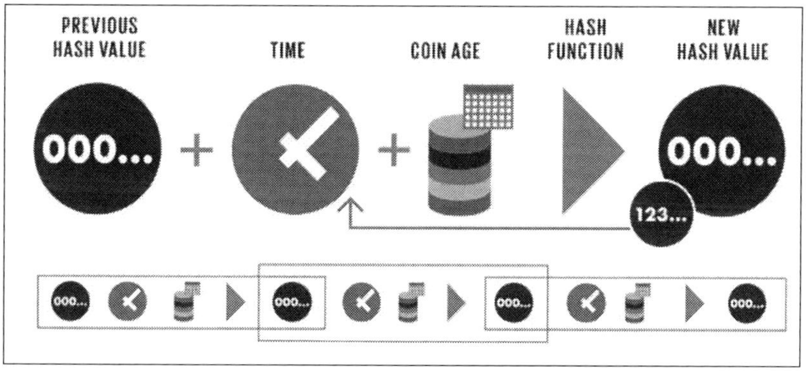

Figure 4.3: *Age of a forger's stake within the blockchain network*

Another way to think about it would be if your chances of winning the lottery were dependent on two things:

- How much money you invested, and
- How long you had been purchasing tickets.

Staking your preferred PoS currency won't make you millions of dollars, but you can still increase the value of your investments and generate some nice passive income.

It is significant to remember that a stake can only be selected if it is kept on an address connected to the coin's network.

Thus, you would have to keep your QTUM in the QTUM core wallet if you were holding it like in the preceding example. The PoS mechanism does not have any block rewards either. Forgers only receive transaction fees because there is no motivation to outcompete other miners based on their effort.

Additionally, there is a significant distinction between ordinary Proof of Stake and Delegated Proof of Stake, which will be discussed later. The list of coins utilizing the various technologies is as follows:

- **PoW Coins**: Bitcoin, Ethereum, Litecoin, Monero
- **PoW/PoS Hybrids**: Dash, Stratis, HShare, Pivx
- **PoS Coins:** Cardano, OmiseGo, QTUM, Ardor

While PoW and PoS are by far the most prevalent in the blockchain space, there are other consensus algorithms like Proof of Capacity (PoC) which allow sharing of memory space of the contributing nodes on the blockchain network. The more memory or hard disk space a node has, the more rights it is granted for maintaining the public ledger.

Proof of Activity (PoA), used on the Decred blockchain, is a hybrid that makes use of aspects of both PoW and PoS.

Attacks on PoW and the Monopoly

A 51% attack, also known as a majority attack, occurs when a single person or group gains control of over 50% of a blockchain's hashing power. That is usually achieved by renting mining hash power from a third party. The attackers consume enough power to control most events in the network. The term 51 is just symbolic, it means more than 50% control. They can monopolize generating new blocks and receive rewards since they are able to prevent other miners from completing blocks and can reverse transactions.

Proof of Burn (PoB)

Proof-of-burn (PoB) is another blockchain consensus process that uses less energy than proof-of-work (PoW). By burning currencies, decentralized platforms using the Proof-of-Battle technique make sure miners come to a consensus. The procedure of burning cryptocurrency is to remove it from use forever. Blockchains backed by Proof of Bases (PoBs) use this technique to validate transactions even though it lowers inflation[4].

In contrast to Proof-of-Work decentralized networks like Bitcoin, Proof-of-Burn verifies transactions using virtual mining machines rather than real ones. In simpler terms, PoB miners start coin burns to demonstrate their network participation and gain mining permission.

The fact that a miner can burn bitcoin demonstrates the strength of virtual mining. As a result, power increases with coin quantity and vice versa. Keep in mind that more mining power accelerates the process of discovering new blocks, exactly like in PoW systems. The miner receives greater payouts as a result.

Using proof-of-burn (PoB) networks, the coins are sent to an "*eater address*" as part of the coin burn procedure.

This address is unreachable but can be verified by the public. It is noteworthy that eater addresses are not secret keys; instead, they are randomized.

Proof-of-stake (PoS) and proof-of-burn (PoB) consensus procedures are comparable in that they both rely on currency interactions to safeguard the network. In contrast to PoB, coins held in PoS systems can still be accessed and sold by their owners should they wish to quit the network. Conversely, PoB causes a coin shortage as opposed to PoS.

Because the PoB method is a novel kind of consensus algorithm, its applicability to big networks has not yet been established. The PoB technique has a number of benefits, including a fully decentralized mining process and sustainability.

Proof of Elapsed Time (PoET) Blockchain

Another network consensus technique that avoids excessive resource and energy consumption is the Proof of Elapsed Time (PoET) blockchain, which maintains process efficiency by employing a random lottery system.

Permissioned blockchain networks can choose who writes the next block thanks to Intel Corporation's PoET consensus algorithm[5].

On a blockchain network, the PoET algorithm determines mining rights and block winners using a randomly generated elapsed time. Additionally, the PoET method increases transparency by guaranteeing that lottery outcomes may be independently verified by other parties by executing a trusted code in a safe environment.

One of PoET's interesting features is that it uses a lottery approach to distribute winnings evenly among network users, providing each node an equal chance of winning. Every node in the blockchain network is assigned a random wait time by the PoET algorithm, and it is necessary for every node to sleep for that period.

Understanding Proof of Elapsed Time (PoET)

Blockchain networks employ consensus mechanisms to confirm transactions and add new blocks. On permissioned blockchain networks, the consensus method known as PoET is frequently employed to determine who has the right to mine or who wins a block. Blockchain networks that need identity verification before allowing anyone to join are known as permissioned networks.

Following two essential components were supposed to be guaranteed by the PoET network consensus mechanism:

- In the first place, it guarantees that the nodes taking part actually choose a random time, rather than picking a shorter period of time on purpose to win.
- It also certifies that the winner has served out their waiting period.

Evidence of a failing consensus process time consumes a lot less energy than proof of work since it chooses a node at random rather than pitting all of the miners on a network against one another.

The massive chip manufacturer Intel Corporation (INTC) came up with the PoET concept at the beginning of 2016. It provides a ready-made, cutting-edge solution to the computational issue of "random leader election." Applications can run trusted code in a secure environment due to the embedded mechanism. This ensures that the two requirements are met: all participating nodes' waiting times must be randomly selected, and the winning participant must actually finish the waiting period. The open-source Hyperledger Sawtooth project, which employs the PoET consensus mechanism, was supported by Intel in collaboration with other groups like the Linux Project and IBM. A distributed ledger system that is both scalable and flexible for a wide range of business applications is called Hyperledger Sawtooth.

Operation of PoET

By distributing the odds of winning across the greatest number of network users, the PoET mechanism follows the idea of a fair lottery system in which each node has an equal chance of being selected. Every node in the network that takes part in the PoET scheme has to wait for a predetermined amount of time; the first node to finish the waiting period wins the next block. In the blockchain network, every node creates a random wait time and goes to sleep for that amount of time.

It is simple to understand that the person who wakes up first, or who has the lowest wait time, broadcasts the required information to the whole peer network when they wake up and commit a new block to the blockchain. The next block is then discovered by repeating the same procedure.

Distinguishing PoET from PoW

The proof of work (PoW) algorithm's workflow is essentially the same as the consensus method used by Bitcoin, although it doesn't require as much power. It improves the efficiency of the network by enabling a node to sleep and transition to other duties for the predetermined amount of time.

As a result, unlike Proof-of-Work, which encourages decentralization and transparency, Proof-of-Elapsed Time necessitates the issuance of certificates to all network participants.

Numerous other network requirements are met in this case by the trusted code execution mechanism operating inside a secure environment. It guarantees that the trusted code operates in a secure setting and cannot be changed by any party involved. Additionally, it makes sure that the outcomes can be independently verified by users or other authorized parties, which increases the network consensus's transparency.

PoET also maintains the consensus process's vitality, or nimbleness, in order to keep the cost under control and proportionate to the value generated by the process–a crucial need for the cryptocurrency economy to keep growing. Hyperledger Sawtooth is an enterprise-focused distributed ledger, akin to a blockchain, intended for supply chain and logistics applications. It might even be used to bookkeeping, inventory control, and other time-consuming and error-prone company operations.

PoET is mostly utilized in Sawtooth Hyperledger. There isn't a cryptocurrency that uses Proof of Elapsed Time (PoET) as of January 2022, hence there isn't a Proof of Elapsed Time Coin yet.

Proof-of-Work and Proof-of-Elapsed Time differ significantly. PoW is a competitive work method, while PoET relies on random selection.

Proof of History (PoH)

Similar to Proof-of- Elapsed Time (PoET), another consensus technique known as Proof of History (PoH) was created by the Solana Project. It achieves consensus without requiring a lot of resources by cryptographically encoding the passage of time. In order to reach the required consensus across distributed processes or multi-agent systems, like cryptocurrency systems, on a single data value or a single state of the network, any consensus method used in computer and blockchain systems must be fault-tolerant[6]. Among other aspects, record-keeping benefits from its utilization.

The Hardness of Mining and Mining Difficulty

A cryptocurrency like Bitcoin grows in popularity in proportion to the number of computers involved in its peer-to-peer network. Miners fight for the few benefits offered by each block. The so-called "hashpower" of the entire network rises as the number of users and computer power do[7].

This process of competition is referred to as the **mining difficulty** or in simple words **difficulty** (felt in competing), which is easier to understand once you grasp the basics of Bitcoin mining. It refers to the effort required to solve a complex cryptographic puzzle. Since Bitcoin transactions are stored in blocks, they are added to the blockchain every 10 minutes (= 600 seconds). To maintain the time, it takes to process one block at around 10 minutes, difficulty has to be adjusted periodically.

Mining difficulty is a measurement unit used in the process of Bitcoin mining.

The mining difficulty of a cryptocurrency such as Bitcoin indicates how difficult and time-consuming it is to find the right hash for each block.

The difficulty of mining new units increases or decreases over time, depending on the number of miners in the network.

It is noteworthy that the mining difficulty in the Bitcoin network is adjusted automatically after 2,016 blocks have been mined in the network. An adjustment of difficulty upwards or downwards depends on the number of participants in the mining network and their combined hashpower.

Evolution of Mining Equipment

Mining equipment has evolved considerably since the beginnings of Bitcoin. In the early days, the first miners used the CPUs of their PCs to mine Bitcoin. Miners eventually realized that graphics cards are better suited for mining Bitcoin. However, graphics cards also need more energy.

In recent years, special "ASICs" (application-specific integrated circuit chips) have been developed specifically for Bitcoin mining.

Presently, Bitcoin and other digital currencies are mined via **mining pools**, where lots of miners join forces and combine their hash rates in the quest for block rewards. Solving the mathematical puzzles for valid block creation requires huge amounts of computational power. Because the difficulty is rising continually, miners join forces in Bitcoin mining pools and solve the mathematical puzzles together. The first individual miner or the mining pool that finds the right hash gets the block reward.

Usually, block rewards consist of new coins or tokens native to a blockchain network such as Bitcoin. In a mining pool, block rewards are split among participants in proportion to their share of computing power in the mining pool. This way each participant is adequately invested in the process.

Mining Pool

A mining pool is the pooling of resources by miners, who share their processing power over a network, to split the reward equally, according to the amount of work they contributed to the probability of finding a block[8].

A "share" is awarded to members of the mining pool who present a valid partial proof-of-work. Mining in pools began when the difficulty for mining increased to the point where it could take centuries for slower miners to generate a block[9]. The solution to this problem was for miners to pool their resources so they could generate blocks more quickly and therefore receive a portion of the block reward on a consistent basis, rather than randomly once every few years[9].

Usually, the blocks in the cryptocurrency network contain transactions. Transaction fees are paid to the miner (mining pool). Different mining pools could share these fees between their miners or not.

Every cryptocurrency pool will require you to pay mining fees, hence it is best to opt for pools that have a high payout and low fees.

Mining pools are groups of cooperating miners who agree to share block rewards in proportion to their contributed mining hash power.

While mining pools are desirable to the average miner as they smooth out rewards and make them more predictable, they unfortunately concentrate power to the mining pool's owner. It's important to note that most mining pools are in China. Many only have Chinese websites and support. One of Bitcoin's biggest concerns currently is mining centralization in China. With roughly 20 major mining pools, estimates suggest Chinese pools control a whopping 65% of the network's hash rate. Other major players include Malta (10%), USA (3%), Czech Republic (3%), and Japan (0.5%).

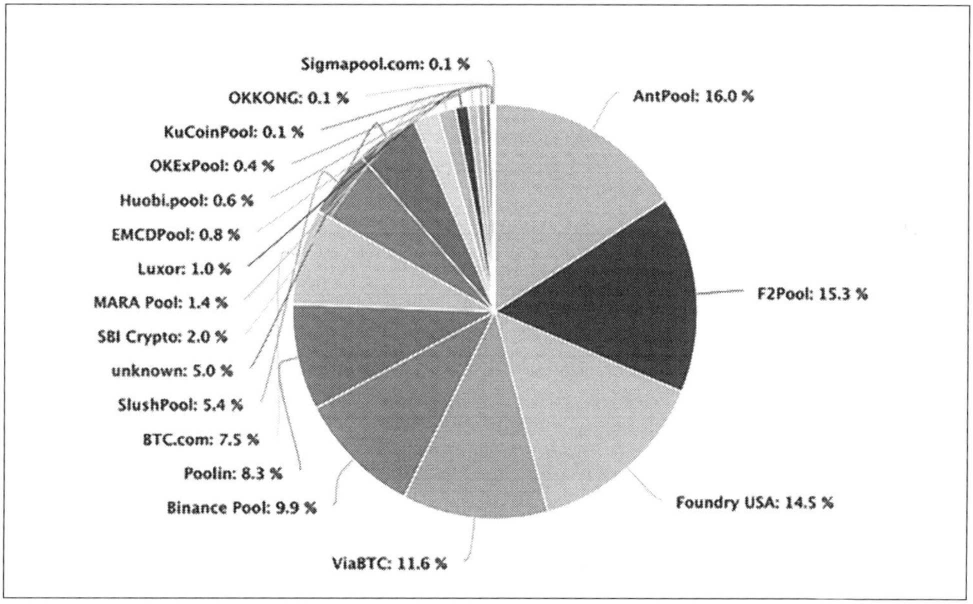

Figure 4.4: *Share of World's Mining Pools [Courtesy reference 9]*

Miners can, however, choose to redirect their hashing power to a different mining pool anytime. Here is a look at some popular options:

- **Slush Pool**: It is the oldest mining pool currently in use, operational since 2010. This current mining pool is accessible to the public and is known for its accuracy and stability. It offers a simple registration process, and to learn how the dashboard functions, you can even build a demo miner. There are two options on the website: one for novice miners and another for seasoned ones.
- **AntPool**: The largest mining pool globally is AntPool. About 11% of all blocks are mined by it, and its servers are located all over the world. During setup, AntPool's novel peer-to-peer mining mechanism can connect your device to the closest one for a dependable connection.
- **BTC.com**: If you are acquainted with Bitcoin.com, the same business also owns BTC.com. Before launching the mining section, BTC.com was well-known for its cutting-edge blockchain explorer and Bitcoin wallet. Litecoin, Ether, and other cryptocurrencies are supported by its medium-sized mining pool, which is located in multiple countries including the US and Germany.

- **KanoPool:** This pool, which has been operational since 2014, is smaller than the others but offers inexpensive mining costs and a simple startup procedure. The only prerequisites are a username and a Bitcoin wallet address; registration is completely voluntary. There is a comprehensive help page with all the necessary FAQ answers, and the interface is straightforward and easy to use.
- **Binance Pool**: One of the biggest cryptocurrency exchanges in the world, Binance, powers Binance Pool. Binance Pool is an up-and-coming, well-liked platform that presently mining roughly 9% of all blocks, following the success of its exchange platform and native currency, Binance coin.

Conclusion

This chapter explored various mechanisms that underpin the operation of secure and decentralized blockchains. We started by examining the concept of consensus in a Bitcoin network, highlighting the crucial role it plays in maintaining network integrity. We then delved into the inner workings of public blockchains, followed by a deep dive into the Proof-of-Work (PoW) system utilized by Bitcoin and its reliance on the HashCash protocol. The chapter further explored alternative consensus mechanisms like Proof-of-Stake (PoS), Proof-of-Burn (PoB), and Proof-of-Elapsed Time (PoET), each offering advantages and disadvantages compared to PoW. Finally, we discussed potential vulnerabilities and centralization concerns associated with Proof-of-Work. By understanding these core concepts, you gain valuable insights into the foundation of various blockchain technologies.

The next chapter is solely devoted to the deployment of Blockchain technology for different types of enterprises all over the world.

References

[1] Consensus Mechanism (Cryptocurrency), CRYPTOCURRENCY BLOCKCHAIN By JAKE FRANKENFIELD Updated November 30,https://www.investopedia.com/terms/c/consensus-mechanism-cryptocurrency.asp

[2] Baliga, A. "Understanding Blockchain Consensus Models". April, 2017. [Online] Available: https: //www.persistent.com/wp-content/uploads/2017/04/WP-Understanding-Blockchain-Consensus-Models.pdf.

[3] Making Sense of Proof of Work vs. Proof of Stake by COLIN HARPER,24 JANUARY 2018,https://coincentral.com/making-sense-of-proof-of-work-vs-proof-of-stake/

[4] Proof-of-Burn (PoB), Alexandria Web site, https://coinmarketcap.com/alexandria/glossary/proof-of-burn/-pob/

[5] Sawtooth Hyperledger. "Intel Corporation, PoET 1.0 Specification." Accessed

Jan. 13, 2022,https://www.investopedia.com/terms/p/proof-elapsed-time-cryptocurrency.asp

[6] Consensus Mechanism (Cryptocurrency),CRYPTOCURRENCY BLOCKCHAIN By JAKE FRANKENFIELD Updated November 30,https://www.investopedia.com/terms/c/consensus-mechanism-cryptocurrency.asp

[7] What does mining difficulty mean?, https://www.bitpanda.com/academy/en/lessons/what-does-mining-difficulty-mean/

[8] "A Complete Guide to Mining Pools", Amir Adabi, Full stack Developer, https://miradabi.ir/

[9] Eyal, Ittay. "The Miner's Dilemma" (PDF). Cornell University, In the IEEE Symposium on Security and Privacy (Oakland), 2015.

CHAPTER 5
Understanding Blockchain for Enterprises

Introduction

This chapter is solely devoted to deployment of Blockchain technology for different types of enterprises all over the world. We will discuss about permissioned blockchain model, its use cases and permissioned blockchain platforms. Readers will also learn about the challenges of permissioned solutions and state machine replication in detail.

Structure

In this chapter, we will cover the following topics:

- Permissioned Blockchain Model and Their Use Cases
- List of Best Permissioned Blockchain Platforms
- Challenges of Permissioned Solutions
- State Machine Replication

Permissioned Blockchain Model and Use Cases

A blockchain is a distributed ledger that is based on cryptographic protocols that allow data transmission and storage on a peer-to-peer basis. Network consensus protocol maintains this distributed ledger and provides notable security features. Blockchain is designed to eliminate the need for a third-party intermediary for the transfer of value, assets, or data between two parties.

Although in it is nascent development stages, blockchain offered significant promise. But considering the diverse needs of businesses and individual users, blockchain is forced to devise several models that have emerged in due course.

Over the past several years, blockchains have rapidly evolved in several ways, offering a diverse range depending upon their build and configuration. The contents stored on the blocks of the blockchain as well as the activities performed by the various participants on the blockchain networks depends on two key factors:

- How the blockchain is configured and
- How it is expected to fulfill the desired business purpose.

Types of Blockchains

Generally, two types of blockchain models are used as follows:

- Permissionless Blockchains which can be further divided into two types:
  - Public blockchains
  - Private blockchains
- Permissioned blockchains are also known as private blockchains or permissioned sandboxes have also gained attention and momentum.

In the next section, we will discuss in detail about these two categories of blockchains.

Permissionless Blockchains

A permissionless blockchain is devised to be a type of blockchain network (as the name suggests) that allows anyone to become a part of the network and to contribute to its upkeep. In other words, a permissionless blockchain is a decentralized ledger that is open to the public. The vast majority of cryptocurrencies, including Bitcoin, are using this type powered by permissionless blockchain networks. The key characteristics of permissionless blockchains are enumerated as follows:

- **Transparent**: The permissionless blockchains transactions are transparent, allowing users to access all information except private keys. Users have access to view all transactions in the network. Because blockchain networks must incentivize users to trust the network, the transparency is necessary.
- **Anonymous**: Most permissionless blockchains do not ask users to provide any personal information when creating an address. Anonymous means that the whereabouts of the concerned person is unknown to the public. Let us understand this in another way sighting an example, as in the case of an alcoholics group takes its name from the fact that it's a confidential group - people use only their first names and do not identify one another as members of the group.

- **Decentralized**: Permissionless networks tend to be fully decentralized. This means that:
  - No single entity can change the network protocols,
  - Shut down the network, or
  - Edit the ledger in a permissionless blockchain.

Note: *This blockchain model is based on a 'majority' consensus protocol, having a requirement that a change to the blockchain must have a "consensus" among more than 50% of the users.*

Permissioned blockchains have enabled new applications that depend on *privacy and security*, including:

- Supply chain provenance tracking;
- Claims settlement; and
- Identity verification.

In case of supply chain, **provenance** is the validated history of ownership, custody and origin of a specific product instance such as a lot, a batch, or a serial number. It also applies to a pallet that may contain more than one product as well.

To illustrate, let's consider a scenario and the key considerations that ensue from it.

In case of any large healthcare organization, with many subsidiaries and ecosystem partners need to evaluate their system using Distributed Ledger Technology (DLT). Decentralizing health records contains its several value propositions for the organization including its employees, patients, partners and)medical research. By distribution of this information the organization achieves the following:

- Lowers the risk of data tampering, fraud, human error and singular attack-point vulnerability; Improves records integrity, access, privacy and auditability; and
- Streamlines information portability across service providers, compliance adherence, insurance settlement, latency, cost reductions, even medical research efficiencies.

However, the organization ought to be aware of following risk factors:

- Diverse risks involved in still-immature blockchain technology,
- Unclear regulatory requirements,
- Cultural and political objections involving sensitive information, business models and stakeholder adoption,
- Risk of failure.

In spite of having a broad grasp of potential applications as detailed here, most of the organizations may not be able to choose correct architecture.

Difference Between Permissioned Blockchain and Permissionless Blockchain

Table 5.1 summarizes the difference between permissoned blockchain systems and permissionless blockchain systems:

Permissioned Blockchain versus Permissionless Blockchain		
Category	**Permissioned**	**Permissionless**
Speed	Faster	Slower
Privacy	Private membership	Transparent and open - anyone can become a member
Legitimacy	Legal	Illegal
Ownership	Managed by a group of pre-defined nodes	Public ownership - no one owns the network
Decentralization	Partially decentralized	Truly decentralized
Cost	Cost-effective	Not so cost-effective
Security	Less secure	More secure

Table 5.1: *Permissoned blockchain systems as compared to permissionless*[1]

Permissioned Blockchains and Tokens

The permissioned blockchains are also known as private blockchains or permissioned sandboxes and are closed networks in which previously designated parties, which may be sometimes members of a consortium, interact and participate in consensus and data validation. They are required to be partially decentralized in the sense of being distributed across known participants rather than unknown participants, as in permissionless blockchains. Generally, here also tokens and digital assets are possible but less common as compared to permissionless.

Characteristic features of permissioned blockchains and tokens are:

- Permissioned blockchains allow for a mixed implication bag between the public and private blockchains and support many customization options. These include allowing anyone to join the permissioned network after suitable verification of their identity, and allocation of select and designated permissions to perform only certain activities on the network. For example, Ripple's XRP, one of the largest cryptocurrencies, supports permission-based roles for participants. This is detailed in the section titled *Permissioned blockchains and Tokens.*
- In such scheme of blockchains are built in a manner so that they grant special permissions to each participant. At the same time this allows participants the

ability to perform specific functions such as read, access, and write information on the blockchains. People in different businesses are increasingly opting for permissioned blockchain networks, because it allows them to:

- Selectively place restrictions while configuring the networks, and
- Control the activities of the various participants in the desired roles.

For example, if a blockchain network is used for managing dealings, the process involves multiple entities, that is the dealing with the farm produce from its origin (the farm) to the end customer (the market). Say a farmer cultivates a medicinal plant that he/she ships to multiple markets across the world. In this case, multiple parties are involved:

- The customs authorities which clear the produce to enter their respective nation,
- The shipping companies who move the produce, and
- The warehouse operators that are supposed to maintain the product within a specified temperature range, all serve a vital but specific function in the farmer's transaction. In this case, permissioned networks may offer the best fit.
- The farmers may finalize a particular price and quantity for selling her/his or their produce to a buyer in America and another price and quantity to another buyer in India. The other involved entities such as the warehouse operator may not necessarily need information about the agreed prices between the farmer and his various buyers. They may simply need access to limited information—like quantity and quality specifications—to perform their function in supporting such deals.

Note: *Most permissionless blockchains allow for the use of utility known as monetary tokens, depending on the purpose that they serve. These tokens or digital assets are intended to incentivize users to become a part of the network. The value of the tokens can increase or decrease in value depending on the relevancy and state of the blockchain in the market.*

Advantages and Disadvantages of Permissioned Blockchain

Being closed to outsiders gives permissioned blockchains clear advantages, but there are downsides as well.

Advantages can be enumerated as:

- Decentralization can be incremental, which allows multiple businesses to participate without all the risks of highly centralized models
- Strong privacy, because permission is needed to access transaction information

- Customizability for specific uses, because it allows diverse configurations, modular components and hybrid integrations
- Performance and scalability because fewer nodes manage transaction verification and consensus

Disadvantages can be enumerated as:

- Increased risk of corruption and collusion because there are fewer participants than in a permissionless blockchain
- Consensus is more easily overridden because the owners and operators can change the rules of consensus, immutability and mining
- Less transparency to outside oversight because the number of participants is limited and the network's operators determine privacy requirements

Characteristics Associated with Permissioned (or Private Blockchain Networks)

The characteristics features associated with permissioned or private blockchain networks are set explained as follows:

- **Well-Defined Governance Structures**: Unlike permissionless blockchain networks, permissioned blockchains are not governed on consensus-based protocols. Needless to say, that decisions are made on a central, pre-defined level by members of the network.
- **Possessing Varying Degree of Decentralization**: Permissioned blockchains can have varying degrees of decentralization. Permissioned blockchains can be partially decentralized or fully centralized. Usually, members of the blockchain decide the level of decentralization that the network should have as well as the consensus algorithms it should deploy.
- **Being Non-Transparent**: In contrast to their permissionless counterparts, permissioned blockchains do not have to provide transparency. They can be transparent if they choose to, but most are not intended to be.

The Ripple and XRP

A technology to process international money transfers is known as Ripple, a payment protocol that uses blockchain. It has extremely fast processing times, and offers low transaction fees. It has partnered with hundreds of financial institutions that use this technology.

There's a common misconception that Ripple is a cryptocurrency. Although Ripple itself is not a cryptocurrency, but it does have a native cryptocurrency called XRP (CRYPTO:XRP).

The purpose of RippleNet is to provide fast, cheap, and convenient cross-border transactions for banks[2]. That makes it an alternative to SWIFT, the current international payments system that most banks use.

There are several advantages Ripple offers for international transactions, including:

- The average transaction processes in five seconds.
- The transaction fee is 0.00001 XRP, which was much less than a fraction of a cent even at the token's all-time high in price.
- The XRP cryptocurrency can be used as a bridge currency. This gives financial institutions a cheaper way to trade currencies. They can hold XRP instead of various types of fiat money

The main pros and cons of Ripple and its XRP cryptocurrency are given in *Table 5.2*:

XRP transactions are fast and cheap.	Ripple's consensus protocol is arguably less secure than other methods of processing crypto transactions.
Ripple's payment network is already being used by many financial institutions.	Most of Ripple's banking partners only use RippleNet and not its XRP cryptocurrency.
XRP can be used by small business owners and consumers for secure money transfers.	Ripple has attracted controversy because it's run by a private company and because of the SEC lawsuit.
XRP can be used as a bridge currency for international currency transfers.	XRP is difficult to purchase in the U.S.

***Table 5.2**: The main pros and cons of Ripple and its XRP cryptocurrency*

Layers of Blockchains

Blockchains can be abstracted into three different layers[3], as illustrated in *Figure 5.1*. At the core of blockchain is layer 1.

Layer 1 of Blockchain: BFT Consensus

BFT consensus – also known as *state machine replication* – which is a generic approach to tolerate failures. BFT consensus has different forms, ranging from conventional BFT protocols to PoW-based consensus. Despite fundamental differences in how consensus is achieved, any form must solve the same problem: how to enable nodes to reach consensus on the total order (that is, consistency) of transactions submitted by clients in the form of requests. After nodes reach a consensus about the order, the data/operations of the transactions are then processed according to the order of the transactions. As a result, distributed nodes functionally behave as if there were one centralized node. This ensures that there is only one sequence of client transactions, known as "*the longest chain.*"

Layer 2 of Blockchain: Smart Contracts

Layer 2 of blockchain is the smart contract, which is essentially software code. A smart contract provides an interface for blockchain developers to implement new functions. Smart contracts can then facilitate, verify, or enforce the execution of business transactions. A smart contract can be viewed as a program that connects the underlying consensus protocols with layer 3, applications and use cases.

Layer 3 of Blockchain: Applications and Use Cases

Figure 5.1 illustrates the various features of three layers of three different types of blockchain:

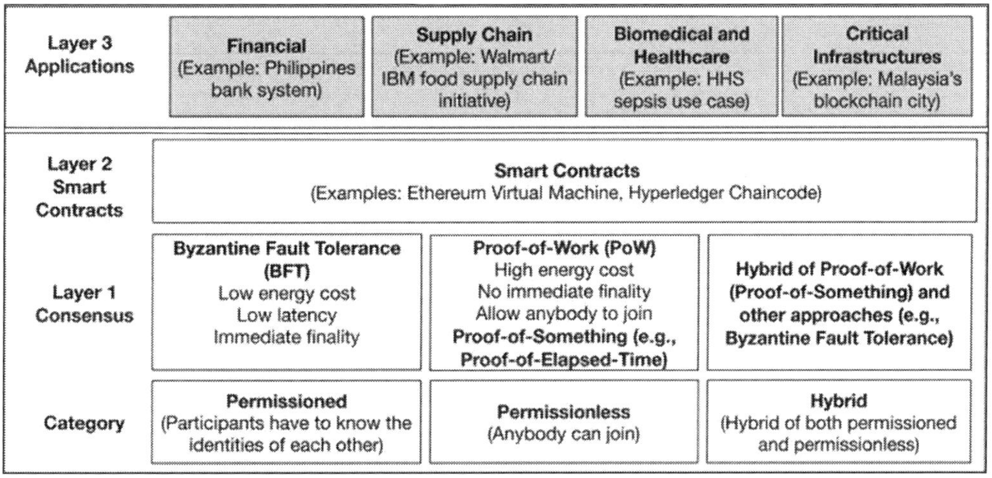

Figure 5.1: *Three layers of three different types of blockchain*

The following figure illustrates the system model of permissioned-blockchain where BC and BA refer to blockchain and blockchain authority, respectively:

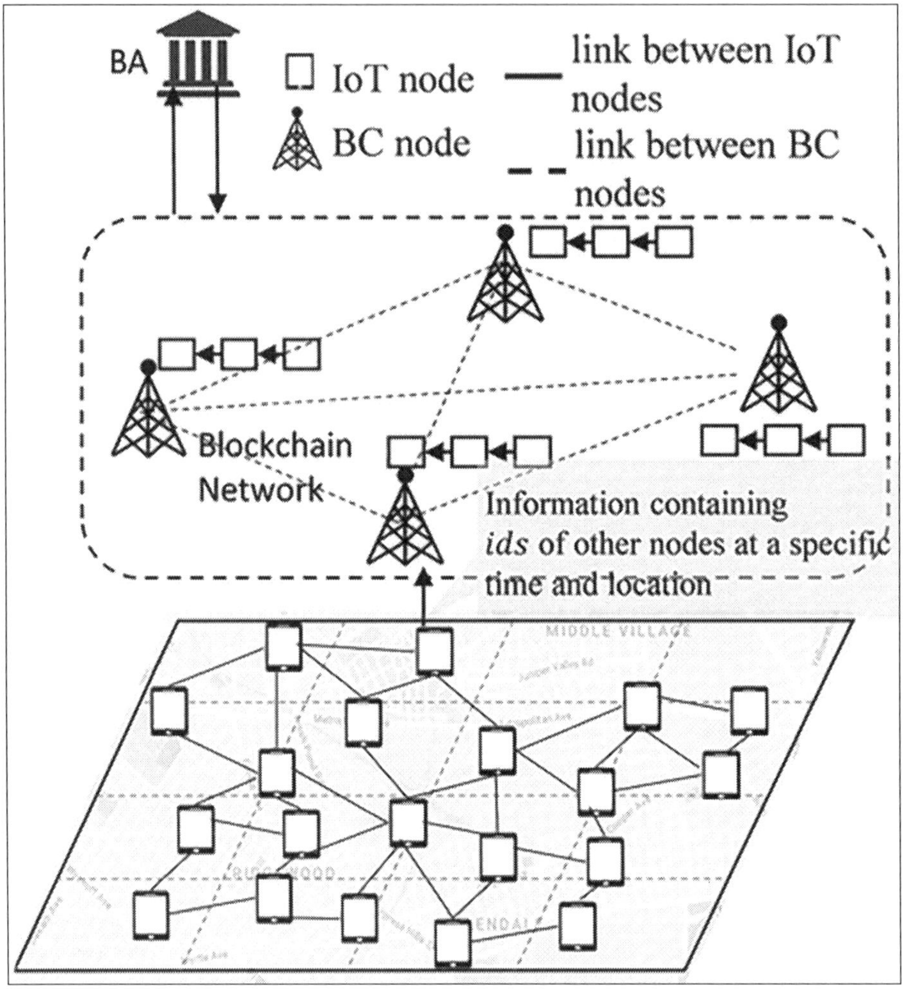

***Figure* 5.2:** *System model of permissioned-blockchain where BC and BA refer to blockchain and blockchain authority, respectively. The BA also acts as certificate authority and trace manager*

In *Figure* 5.2, the mobile IoT nodes are connected with each other in a P2P network using a short-range communication technology. These nodes make transactions with each other and send information on the transactions (for example, rating about other mobile nodes at a specific location and time) to the nearest blockchain node. Here, each grid refers to a specific location.

List of Best Permissioned Blockchain Platforms

The Blockchain platforms allow the development of blockchain-based applications. The permissioned networks are crucial to the different industries out there. Industries such as the finance industry, supply chain, and more can benefit immensely through permissioned networks.

The key permissioned blockchains include:

- Ethereum
- Quorum
- Parity
- MultiChain
- Hyperledger Fabric 1.0
- BigchainDB
- InterPlanetary File System
- Corda

Quorum, *Corda*, and *Hyperledger Fabric* are the top-notch solutions when it comes to permissioned solutions. Let's look briefly into each of the permissioned blockchains that falls in the "best permissioned blockchain" category.

Ethereum

Ethereum is one of the oldest and most established blockchain platforms that was introduced as early as in 2013. One interesting fact about Ethereum is that it provides a truly decentralized blockchain almost comparable to the that of Bitcoin blockchain network. Ethereum possess a key strength which enables it to be truly decentralized having support for smart contracts. Low processing times and higher transaction processing costs as compared to other platforms are the key weakness points. It has its own cryptocurrency called ether, along with its role of being a blockchain platform that underpins enterprise applications[4].

The Ethereum platform is getting very popular and getting widespread adoption by technologists developing decentralized applications (dApps) based on the Ethereum network. Ethereum has a mature ecosystem of tools for writing smart contracts using the solidity programming environment. Solidity programming environment runs on the Ethereum Virtual Machine. However, some more alternative blockchain networks can process transactions much faster at a potentially lower cost than Ethereum. It is correct to say that many observers expect (April 2022) this ought to change after Ethereum adopts a more efficient security mechanism.

Nevertheless, it also has an active developer community orchestrated by the Enterprise Ethereum Alliance. This Alliance which has more than 250 members, including Intel, JPMorgan and Microsoft.

The Ethereum community is in the process of migrating from the existing proof of work (PoW) consensus mechanism to proof of stake (PoS), which is more energy-friendly. This migration process requires an elaborate process to flourish up a separate, new type of blockchain called a Beacon chain. Beacon chain seems getting merged into the existing, main Ethereum blockchain. By adopting this change the Ethereum Foundation estimated to reduce energy use by 99.95%.

IBM Blockchain

IBM had developed Blockchain tool, a private, decentralized blockchain network that has been the most successful with enterprise clients who are less risk-averse. IBM thus sees the biggest opportunities in using it to link into enterprise cloud and legacy technologies more seamlessly than is possible in other decentralized networks.

This is a Blockchain developer tool introduced by IBM and was designed to be flexible, functional and customizable. Also, by this venture, IBM has invested in creating a user-friendly interface to simplify critical tasks, such as setting up, testing and rapidly deploying smart contracts. It is noteworthy that Alex-Paul Manders is a prominent industry thought leader on blockchain with hands-on technology experience and is sought out as a subject-matter expert presenter.

Hyperledger Fabric

Hyperledger Fabric championed by the Linux Foundation, is a set of tools that help in creating blockchain applications (refer to Chapter 6: *Distributed Consensus in Closed Environment* for more details). Hyperledger Fabric is designed with rich ecosystem of components that can be plugged to your system in modular architecture fashion. Working well in closed blockchain deployments, it can improve security and speed and also supports an open smart contract model that can support various data models, such as account and unspent transaction output, or UTXO, models.

Hyperledger Fabric improves data privacy by two methods, one by isolating transactions in channels and another by enabling the sharing of private data on a need-to-know basis in private data collections. According to its proponents, it also enables high-speed transactions at the same time, with low latency of finality and confirmation.

Hyperledger Sawtooth

Launched by the Linux Foundation and contributed by IBM and Digital Asset, this technology is an enterprise-grade and modular platform, designed for creating, deploying, and executing distributed ledgers which enable digital records to be maintained without a central authority.

Hosted by Hyperledger and the Linux Foundation, this application is another open source blockchain initiative. Hyperledger Sawtooth uses a novel consensus mechanism called Proof of Elapsed Time (PoET) that can integrate with hardware-based security technologies to enable "trusted execution environments" of program code to run in secure enclaves, which are protected areas of computer memory. We covered PoET in the previous chapter.

Its mechanism enables Hyperledger Sawtooth to integrate with hardware security solutions, known as "*trusted execution environments*". Intel's newly launched Xeon processor is one of its applications.

Sawtooth is Hyperledger's second open-source blockchain platform to integrate with an enterprise-ready 1.0 version. The launch of 1.0 software solutions is essential for every software developer. This version indicates that the maintainers are still dedicated to the core features and it gives blockchain companies a sense of confidence that whatever they build, won't be disrupted by future upgrades.

R3 Corda

It is debatable that R3 Corda is technically a blockchain or an alternative type of distributed ledger. The official Corda site describes it as "*both a blockchain and not a blockchain.*" Corda uses a novel innovative consensus mechanism in which transactions are cryptographically linked but does not periodically batch multiple transactions into a block. However, one of the key benefits of this approach is that all transactions are processed in real time, which can improve performance compared to other types of blockchains.

R3 consortium has a strong following in the financial industry as Corda provides an attractive approach for financial transactions and smart contracts with strong security. Leading proponents of R3 Corda include Bank of America, HSBC, Intel and Microsoft. It supports tools that automate business logic that can execute across company boundaries.

Tezos

Although a very old application, Tezos is still in development stage since 2014. Tezos is a decentralized blockchain platform that is self-governing and establishes a true digital commonwealth. Just like Ethereum, Neo, Waves and QTUM, Tezos is a platform for smart contracts and dApp applications. However, its self-amending cryptographic mechanism makes it unique from other platforms. It is a platform linked to a digital token, called a Tezzie or Tez. But the platform is not based on the mining of Tez. Rather, token holders get a reward for participating in the proof-of-stake consensus mechanism. Its noteworthy that Tezos supports decentralized applications, smart contracts and novel financial instruments, such as NFTs. NFT can be thought of as a modern variation on trading cards that are tied to digital assets. This platform supports a dynamically upgradable protocol and modular software clients that facilitates its adaption to new uses.

Since then, Tezos has improved performance and increased the size limit on smart contracts. It has also developed tools to help automate the process of weaving NFTs into enterprise supply chains.

EOSIO Blockchain Platform

This blockchain platform was first launched as an open-source project in 2018. It is optimized for developing decentralized applications and smart contracts. According to its proponents it uses a complex consensus mechanism based on PoS that provides better performance than older mechanisms, such as Ethereum. Main difference is that it also includes support for a governance feature for voting on changes to the platform.

Let us understand first that EOS (Enterprise Operating System) – the first (of many) deployed network running EOSIO software. EOS is a global digital cryptocurrency that enables the exchange of value across the EOS Network's ecosystem of dApps and smart contracts. It facilitates many functions, including transacting on decentralized finance (DeFi) protocols, buying and selling of verifiably owned digital art through NFTs. EOSIO is said to be a highly performant open-source blockchain platform, built to support and operate safe, compliant, and predictable digital infrastructures. EOSIO is an open-source platform that provides industry-leading transaction speeds and a sub-second block time latency rate, allowing developers to perform transactions at a lower cost through efficient resource management.

Needless to say, EOSIO and EOS both are part of the same ecosystem, but have different functionalities. EOSIO enables cryptographically secured transaction-layer infrastructure through programmable smart contracts.

The redesigned structure permits EOS to dispense with the requirement for transaction expenses and offers the capacity to more transactions per second (TPS). The most elevated recorded TPS of EOS is 3,996 contrasted with 15 TPS of Ethereum. The concept of Decentralized Finance (DeFi) has appeared as people are looking for ways to explore their possibilities in finance. Decentralization has entered into a new trustless and transparent financial services domain.

EOS may replace Ethereum as the dominant smart contract platform. Although, EOS has improved many of Ethereum's issues such as transaction fees and scalability but remains controversial due to its more centralized model.

In 2021, Google Cloud joined the EOS community, a leading open-source platform for blockchain innovation and performance, and is taking steps to support the EOS public blockchain by becoming a block producer (BP).

Its noteworthy that the blockchain technology behind the EOS.IO protocol has the potential to drastically change the future of computer resources and applications, and improve upon several businesses and industries. Due to the powerful impact EOS could have, it's long-term value could increase exponentially.

Not to forget, EOS was initially built on Ethereum as an ERC20 token, but has since split off onto its own mainnet. Now, like Ethereum, other dApps can live on the EOS protocol.

Ethereum (ETH) and EOS are two altcoins (acronym for alternative coins) that provide benefits beyond what Bitcoin provides and among the most popular cryptocurrencies today. Decentralized applications (dApps) can run on these blockchain "*supercomputers*" and power the next generation of decentralized internet. EOS in essence replicates all of the elements of a supercomputer, emulating computer processing hardware, storage, and more.

Key strengths of EOS include fast transactions and advanced account permission features for deploying applications. Over 400 applications have been developed on the platform, including identity management, supply chain management and gaming. The community also provides various tools for customizing blockchain implementations for various decentralized use cases in supply chain management, healthcare and DeFi.

Stellar

Stellar is a newer blockchain platform optimized for various kinds of DeFi applications evolved around two years back. Its protocol is Stellar Consensus, which purportedly can speed the time required to process and finalize transactions on a public blockchain network. The menace of shutting out bad or questionable actors in a financial transaction is also handled by Stellar that also includes security mechanisms for dealing with. It is being used by several companies for international trade and exchanging money across borders. The following are the examples of applications built on the Stellar blockchain and adopted as enterprise applications:

- MoneyGram for money transfer,
- Circle for payments and treasury infrastructure, and
- Flutterwave for integrating payment processing

ConsenSys Quorum

Developed by financial services company JPMorgan, the Quorum is a customized version of Ethereum. Taking and utilizing the advantage of the core work on the Ethereum blockchain platform and repackages it into a hardened environment suitable for banks. It has been then optimized to support high-speed transactions between institutions such as insurance companies and banks on a private network. Various privacy enhancements to Ethereum are also added to improve support for regulations such as CCPA in California and GDPR in Europe.

The California Consumer Privacy Act (CCPA) is a piece of data privacy legislation that applies to most businesses that process the personal data of California residents.

The General Data Protection Regulation (GDPR) is the toughest privacy and security law in the world. Though it was drafted and passed by the European Union (EU), it imposes obligations onto organizations anywhere, so long as they target or collect data related to people in the EU. The regulation was put into effect on May 25, 2018.

In contrast to the above, Central Consumer Protection Authority has the following powers:

If the commission finds violations of rights of consumers or in notice of trade practices which is unfair, it can inquire or cause an inquiry, either on receipt of complaint or suo moto or as directed by the Central Government.

In late 2021, ConsenSys acquired the intellectual property rights to the Quorum platform from JPMorgan. They then integrated these assets into their existing offerings, creating the ConsenSys Quorum open-source protocol layer. This layer aims to accelerate enterprise development of applications compatible with other Ethereum-based tools. ConsenSys offers development services for the combined platform, catering to enterprise customers like JPMorgan and the South African Reserve Bank.

Hedera Hashgraph

Another Blockchain Platform, Hedera Hashgraph provides a new form of distributed consensus, and is lightning secure, fast and fair platform that does not need to compute a heavy proof of work algorithm. Following changes have been made:

- Hedera Platform empowers and enables developers to build an entirely new class of decentralized applications that are scalable.
- Smart contracts in the Hedera Hashgraph platform can be made dynamic just like any other software component. Since it offers an optional mechanism which allows "*binding arbitration*", the smart contracts deployed with a list of the public key of arbitrators can be edited to fix bugs or add new features.
- If a designated arbitrator agrees on the amendment of a smart contract, the transaction having a new bytecode is approved by the arbitrator's keys and the change is implemented.
- The Hedera Hashgraph Council, the platform's governing body, ensures no single member or small group can exert undue control through its governance structure.

Emergence of OpenChain

Coinprism, a company behind the colored coins standard Open Assets, developed OpenChain. This system is an open-source distributed ledger technology, highly suited for organizations willing to manage the digital assets in a secure and scalable manner. ,

Unlike the consensus mechanism used in Bitcoin, it uses Partitioned Consensus where one instance will only have a single authority for validation of transactions.

There are three obvious advantages of using OpenChain:

- **Eliminates Mining Competition:** OpenChain removes the need for miners, eliminating competition associated with proof-of-work systems.
- **Free Transactions:** Transactions on OpenChain incur no fees, making it a cost-effective option.
- **Efficient Validation:** Asset administrators can validate transactions on OpenChain, streamlining the process compared to other platforms.

Challenges of Permissioned Solutions

Implementing permissioned blockchain solutions can be a tough task. Permissioned blockchains are not free from operational challenges. These challenges encompass data storage, messaging and integration, identity, smart contracts management, and more.

For new startups considering a permissioned network, several key decisions need to be taken. Here are two crucial initial questions:

- It needs to decide which blockchain platform to use.
- It needs to determine the blockchain runtime to use.

Needless to say, the answers to these two questions will provide them the development stack to build the permissioned network.

Let's have a detailed look at the challenges that one might come across while developing permissioned solutions:

- **Integration:** Biggest challenges that a business or organization encounter are integration challenges, especially when using APIs for communication. To make it easy, company can use Rhombus, Chain Link, and Oraclize. These are great tools that will help you connect and integrate services more efficiently.
- **Data Privacy:** In cases of regulated industries, privacy becomes a big concern. To ensure proper privacy, they are required to meet specific requirements. It is indicated by industry experts that Quorum and Aztec are a good pick when it comes to developing permissioned blockchains that offer great privacy.
- **Data Access**: Accessing information in a permissioned blockchain can be rather a slow process. The right solution is to use the Graph which can expose data to the Application Programming Interface (APIs) and smart contracts for easy access.
- **Data Storage:** It is possible to store data in many ways and formats on a blockchain. However, not all solutions are optimal, considering that a huge

amount of data is stored on the blockchain. To ensure proper storage, it is advised to use data storage solutions such as IPFS Private Network, Big chain DB, and AWS Quantum Ledger.

- **Identity:** The participant's identity is also a problem. Being permissioned network, the identity of the peers is already known, this may cause issues during the consensus computations. To simplify the issue, it is advised to use Azure BaaS or uPort that will help the businesses to better leverage their identity protocols and solutions for decentralized applications.

State Machine Replication

A state machine is a mathematical abstraction used to design algorithms. A state machine reads a set of inputs and changes to a different state based on those inputs.

A state is a description of the status of a system waiting to execute a transition. A transition is a set of actions to execute when a condition is fulfilled or an event received.

One state is marked as the initial state; this is where the execution of the machine starts. A state transition defines for which input a state is changed from one to another. Depending on the state machine type, states and/or transitions produce outputs.

The initial state is not a separate state, but more like an indication of which state that the machine should start in by default. A transition from a different state can target a substate of a compound state, thereby bypassing the state's initial state.

A state machine is a concept storing a state of the system at the moment[5]. As per this concept, it receives a set of inputs (also referred to as commands). The state machine concept apply these inputs in a sequential order using a transition function to generate an output and an updated state. A brief description of the state machine is as follows:

```
state = init
log = []
while true:
  on receiving cmd from a client:
    log.append(cmd)
    state, output = apply(cmd, state)
    send output to the client
```

The **state** machine is initialized to an initial state **init**. On receipt of an input **cmd** from a client, it first adds the input to a log. It then execute the **cmd** by applying the transition function **apply** to the state. As a result, it obtains an updated state and a resultant **output**. The **output** is then sent back to the client as a response. For the subsequent discussion, a State Machine will be defined as the following tuple of values:

- A set of States
- A set of Inputs
- A set of Outputs
- A transition function (Input × State → State)
- An output function (Input × State → Output)

The State Machine Approach

The state machine approach is a powerful technique for ensuring consistency in distributed systems. It relies on two key properties:

- **Safety**: This property guarantees that if any two non-faulty replicas (copies) of the system store the same sequence of commands in their logs, they will always be in the same state. This ensures consistency across the system.
- **Liveness:** This property ensures that honest server replicas will eventually execute any command proposed by a client. This guarantees that the system makes progress and doesn't stall indefinitely.

Consensus on a Sequence of Values

Our preceding discussion provided the simple technique for implementing a fault-tolerant service in terms of a state machine. The user/programmer is required to:

- Place copies of the state machine on multiple, independent servers.
- Receive client requests, interpreted as inputs to the state machine.
- Choose an ordering for the inputs.
- Execute inputs in the chosen order on each server.
- Respond to clients with the output from the state machine.
- Monitor replicas for differences in state or output.

We have seen that the Bitcoin ledger is the most prominent example of state machine. The state consists of the set of public keys along with the associated Bitcoins. The input (or **cmd**) to the state machine is a transaction between parties corresponds to the Bitcoin ledger. And the transition function is the function that determines whether a transaction is valid, and if it performs the desired bitcoin script operation.

Fault Tolerant State Machine Replication (FT-SMR)

While using a client-server network setting, the servers simulate a state machine in a fault tolerant manner. In such situation, clients send commands as if there is a single state machine. But alternatively maintaining a single server is prone to crashes or Byzantine faults. A Byzantine fault is any fault presenting different symptoms to different observers. Instead of maintaining a single server, a state machine replication (SMR) system uses multiple server replicas, some of which can be faulty. The group of servers presents the same interface as that of a single server to the client.

In continuing process, the server responds and replicates all initially start with the same state. As such honest replicas first need to agree on the sequence of client commands received by them when they receive concurrent requests from a client. This problem called log replication is a multi-shot version of consensus. The replicas apply the commands in the log in case the sequence is agreed upon, one by one, using the apply transition. Suppose that the transition is deterministic, all honest server replicas maintain an identical state at all times.

Thus, a Fault Tolerant SMR system needs to perform log replication efficiently and then execute the commands received on the log. Specifically, it needs to guarantee the following:

It is indicated here that FT-SMR needs log replication, or multi-shot consensus. One can sequentially compose single-shot consensus protocols conceptually. As per available practice, SMR protocols may optimize without necessarily relying on a sequential composition.

Who are the learners?

According to dictionary, Byzantine is a system or situation excessively complicated, and typically involving a great deal of administrative detail. In the so-called Byzantine Broadcast (BB) and Byzantine Agreement (BA), the parties executing the protocol are the ones learning the result. In FT-SMR, application, the replicas engage in the consensus protocol but eventually need to convince clients of the result. In the presence of Byzantine faults, in an FT-SMR protocol, the clients may communicate with multiple replicas before learning about the committed value. If there are of Byzantine faults, the client needs to communicate with at least f+1 replicas, where f represents the maximum number of Byzantine faults the system can tolerate. This is done to ensure that it has communicated with at least one honest replica.to obligate or pledge oneself

Fault tolerance means an essential consequence of clients not participating in the protocol is the fault tolerance one can obtain. The two terms Byzantine agreement (BA) and Byzantine broadcast (BB) are fundamental problems in distributed computing, and one of the most important practical applications of BA and BB is to implement Byzantine fault tolerant (BFT) state machine replication (SMR). With BB, we know of protocols such as Dolev-Strong that can tolerate $f<n-1$ faults among n replicas. SMR protocols that obtain safety and liveness cannot tolerate more than a minority corruption.

Finally, the definition does not explicitly state a validity property as in BB and BA. Fault Tolerant SMR protocols generally satisfy external validity, that is, a command is said to be valid so far as the client signs the value.

Optimizing for a Sequence of Values

Since FT-SMR protocols need to agree on a sequence of values, practical approaches for SMR (such as PBFT, Paxos, and more) use a steady-state-and-view-change approach to architect log replication. There is a designated leader that drives consensus in the steady-state. Typically, the leader does not change until it fails (for example, due to network delays) or Byzantine behavior is detected. In case when the leader fails, the replicas vote to de-throne the leader and elect a new one. This process of choosing a new leader is called view-change. The presence of a single leader for more extended periods yields simplicity and efficiency when the leader is honest. But however, it also reduces the amount of decentralization and can cause delays if Byzantine replicas are elected as leaders.

Example of State Machine: Smart Contract – Crowdfunding

This section explores the concept of representing algorithms using finite state machines. We'll use a crowdfunding platform implemented as a smart contract as an example.

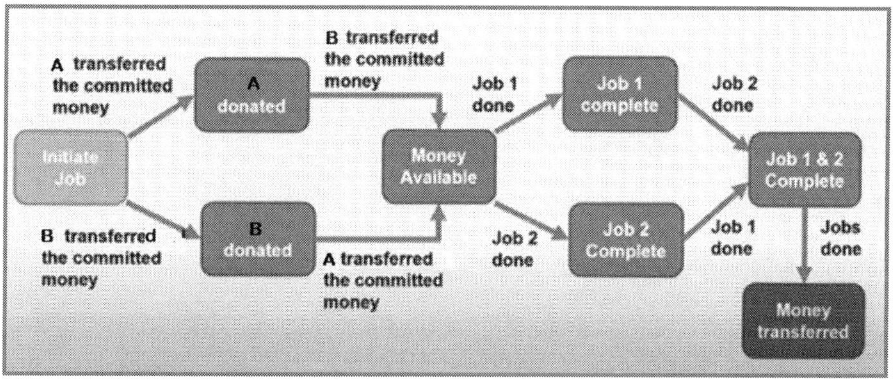

Figure 5.3: *Transaction in the smart contract state machine*

In case of the crowdfunding platform, there are mainly two parties which include the project proposes and project funders. The project proposers propose the project to the funders, and if they are interested, they will invest money in their project. The funders will release funds after the completion of a certain job. In *Figure* 5.3, party **B** and party **A** are the two funders, and they are transferring money after completing the proposed jobs by the proposers. In this case once the entire job is completed, money will be transferred to them.

Conclusion

This chapter explored permissioned blockchains, a powerful technology for controlled and secure data sharing within a defined group of participants. We examined various use cases where permissioned blockchains offer significant advantages, such as supply chain management, financial transactions, and identity verification. We then delved into a curated list of leading permissioned blockchain platforms, highlighting their unique features. However, the chapter also acknowledged the challenges associated with implementing permissioned solutions, including decisions around platform selection and operational hurdles. Finally, we introduced the concept of state machine replication, a fundamental technique used to ensure consistency in distributed systems like permissioned blockchains. By understanding these core concepts, you gain valuable insights into the potential and practical considerations of permissioned blockchain technology.

In the next chapter, we will learn about distributed consensus in blockchain transactions.

References

[1] Permissioned vs. permissionless blockchains: Key differences, By Jessica Groopman, Kaleido Insights, https://www.techtarget.com/searchcio/tip/Permissioned-vs-permissionless-blockchains-Key-differences

[2] What is Ripple? Lyle Daly, https://www.fool.com/investing/stock-market/market-sectors/financials/cryptocurrency-stocks/ripple/

[3] Ittai Abraham and Dahlia Malkhi. 2017. The blockchain consensus layer and BFT. Bulletin of EATCS 3, 123 (2017), 1–22.

[4] Top 9 blockchain platforms to consider in 2022, George Lawton, https://www.techtarget.com/searchcio/feature/Top-9-blockchain-platforms-to-consider

[5] Consensus for State Machine Replication, Written by Kartik Nayak, Ittai Abraham, https://decentralizedthoughts.github.io/2019-10-15-consensus-for-state-machine-replication/

CHAPTER 6

Distributed Consensus in Closed Environment

Introduction

In the previous chapter, we explored distributed consensus in open environments. This chapter delves into its counterpart: closed environment. Open blockchains allow large audiences or the public to consume all the ledger data. Closed blockchains attempt to restrict read access. Bitcoin is an open source that relies on the community to maintain and develop its underlying code. Any user can review the Bitcoin protocol and verify whether all processes are running correctly. The blockchain technology prevents a user from changing the code to benefit from it. Public blockchains allow unrestricted access; private blockchains are available to selected or authorized users; permissioned blockchains have different levels of user permissions or roles. Many cryptocurrencies are built on open-source, public blockchains. Ether is open-source software, among cryptocurrencies.

Structure

In this chapter, we will cover the following topics:

- Distributed Consensus
- Consortium Blockchain
- Consensus Models for Permissioned Blockchain
- Types of Distributed Consensus Algorithm
- The Paxos Algorithm
- The Raft Consensus Algorithm
- Byzantine Fault Tolerance (BFT)
- Practical Byzantine Fault Tolerance (PBFT, often written as pBFT)
- Asynchronous Byzantine Fault Tolerance (ABFT)

- Lamport-Shostak-Pease BFT Algorithm
- Working Style of pBFT

Distributed Consensus

The consensus is a general agreement on a decision made by the majority of those involved. For example, the problem may be as simple as some friends trying to decide which restaurant has multiple options to choose from or complex as decisions on distributed systems.

In blockchain technology, a distributed consensus ensures a consensus of data among nodes in a distributed system or reaches an agreement on a proposal.

The consensus may be reached in two ways:

- Open systems
- Closed Blockchain

The Open systems refer to systems that interact with other systems or the outside environment, whereas closed systems refer to systems having relatively little interaction with other systems or the outside environment.

Also, an open blockchain is a public network that maintains an immutable record of transactions. Anyone can publish a transaction and participate in the network by adhering to a set of published rules. Examples include Bitcoin and Litecoin.

In effect an open blockchain is a ledger of digital events, called transactions, shared among different participants, each having a stake in the system. The ledger can only be updated by consensus of the participants, and, once recorded, information can never be altered. Each recorded event is cryptographically verifiable with proof of agreement from the participants.

Closed Blockchain is defined as a private network that maintains a shared record of transactions. Here, the network is accessible only to those who have permission and transactions can be edited by administrators. Examples include: Hyperledger, Ripple and Eris.

The balance between public and private blockchains is essentially established based on which participants on the network are able to write data onto the blockchain or ledger. The distinction between the open and closed blockchain models takes into consideration who's able to read that data.

An open virtual currency can be substituted for real money using online exchange systems or ATMs that are designed for virtual to real currency exchanges. An example of an open virtual currency is Bitcoin, the most popular decentralized cryptocurrency online and peer-to-peer databases.

As there is a role for both the Internet and Intranets, there's probably a role for both open and closed blockchains. We know the fact that blockchain is decentralized, the network as such cannot be shut down by one government. Consortium blockchain is a hybrid system in which all better qualities of both the open and closed systems have been recognized and utilized but it can be controlled.

Consortium Blockchain

Consortium blockchain or Federated blockchain is a hybrid blockchain that combines private and public characteristics. However, it is different because several organizational members work together on a decentralized network. Basically, a consortium blockchain is a private blockchain that is only accessible to a group. This eliminates the risks associated with having a single entity controlling the network on a private blockchain.

The consensus processes in a consortium blockchain are managed by specific nodes. It has a node that is responsible for initiating, receiving, and validating transactions. Member nodes are able to accept or initiate transactions.

- **Advantages**: A consortium blockchain tends to be more efficient, secure, and scalable than public blockchain networks. It also provides access controls such as private and hybrid blockchains.
- **Disadvantages**: Compared to public blockchains, consortium blockchains are more transparent. Still, it can be compromised if a member node is breached; the blockchain's own rules can make it difficult for the network to work properly.
- **Examples:** This kind of blockchain is used in two areas: banking and payments. Different banks can band together and form a consortium, deciding which nodes will validate transactions. Similar models can be developed by research organizations or food tracking organizations. It is perfect for supply chains, especially for food and medicine applications.

In simpler terms, blockchain consensus algorithm is a procedure via which all the peers of a blockchain network reach a common acceptance or consensus about the real-time state of the distributed ledger.

Moreover, a consensus mechanism enables the blockchain network to attain reliability and build a level of trust between different nodes, while ensuring security in the environment.

There are some conditions that need to be followed in order to achieve distributed consensus every non-faulty process must eventually decide. The final decision of every non-faulty process must be identical, and every non-faulty process must begin and end with the same value.

Overview of Consensus Models for Permissioned Blockchain

Not everyone is able to join a permissioned blockchain. To join the network, each person will require specific authorization from the owner or network administrator. For businesses, banks, and other establishments that would rather follow the law and have total control over their data, this is helpful. Each participating node in a permissioned blockchain is selected and known in advance. We still need consensus, though, as we cannot take it for granted that every node is reliable.

Permissioned blockchains cannot use the same type of consensus models that are seen in permission less blockchains. There are numerous variants of such consensus algorithms that are available today for permissioned blockchains.

By using a blockchain consensus mechanism, all participants in the network can reach a consensus on the current data state of the ledger. This fosters confidence in a distributed computing environment amongst strangers. Before any update is permanently added to the blockchain, it is essential that the distributed peers of the blockchain evaluate and approve it. This applies to everyone wishing to add information to the blockchain.

To preserve fairness and transparency on a blockchain, several consensus mechanisms are employed. For blockchains that are permissionless or permissioned, these models differ.

Every consensus model is constructed with a set of goals in mind. Among them are:

- **Reaching a consensus**: Every model seeks to gather as many group agreements as it can.
- **Cooperation:** Every blockchain participant strives to reach a consensus that takes the group's interests into account as a whole.
- **Equal Rights**: Each group member's vote will be worth the same amount. This implies that each person's vote counts.
- **Engagement**: Every user on the blockchain is required to take part in the voting process.
- **Activity**: Every blockchain user needs to continue being as active as possible. There won't be any hierarchy of authority within the network.
- **Cooperation**: Each member will set aside their personal interests in order to function as a team.

Types of Distributed Consensus Algorithm

Here are some common Distributed Consensus Algorithms:

- The Paxos Algorithm
- The Raft Consensus Algorithm
- Byzantine Fault Tolerance (BFT)
  - Practical Byzantine Fault Tolerance (PBFT, often written as pBFT)
  - Asynchronous Byzantine Fault Tolerance (ABFT)
- Lamport-Shostak-Pease BFT Algorithm

Paxos Algorithm

Although it is also "notorious" in terms of complexity, Lamport's Paxos algorithm is one of the most well-known distributed consensus methods. Lamport put out this inventive approach, which is workable, engineering-implementable, and capable of providing the highest-level of consistency for distributed systems. Many distributed systems, such as Chubby and ZooKeeper, employ Paxos extensively. The applications for big data are the latter two.

- A Proposer can handle a client request and actively suggest a proposal value in the event that a Basic Paxos has a single decree, meaning that it only agrees on a value once.
- An Acceptor casts votes on proposals made by Proposers, quietly replies to the information they receive, and upholds the states' principles.

If we are to simplify the model, then the Learner role can be ignored. This does not affect the decision-making in the model.

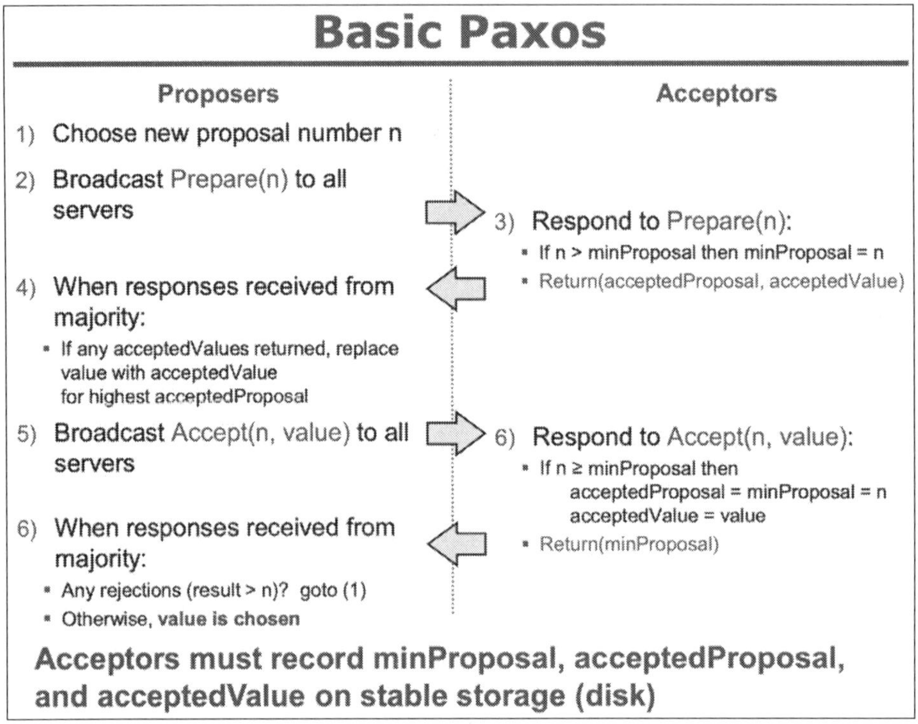

Figure 6.1: *Basic Paxos RPC communication and decision-making process*

As shown in the *Figure* 6.1, the consensus decision-making process uses the two-phase commit protocol:

- • In the first stage, broadcast the Prepare RPC command to block incomplete previous proposals and determine the final value determined by the protocol.
- • In order to force Acceptors to accept a predetermined value, broadcast the Accept RPC command during the first phase of the second phase.

Multiple instances of Basic Paxos combine to form Multi-Paxos, which can choose from a range of values.

The practical implementation of Paxos is likewise contingent upon numerous presumptions and limitations. Byzantine failures cannot be processed by Paxos; it can only handle Crash Fault Tolerance (CFT). It is not a Byzantine fault tolerance method as a result.

From the standpoint of FLP, Paxos gives up on liveness and implements fault tolerance and safety (safe but not live). That is to say, although it is quite rare, this algorithm might never finish or come to an agreement. From CAP's point of view, Paxos reduces availability while just guaranteeing C (consistency) and P (partition tolerance). In order to enhance Paxos system availability, we might augment the Learner count.

The reason Paxos works so well in reality is that most of the situations that could compromise the availability and liveness of Paxos systems are difficult to trigger. Even if those circumstances materialize, the result is not very unsatisfactory.

Followers

- Respond to RPCs from candidates and leaders.
- Convert to candidate if election timeout elapses without either:
  - Receiving valid AppendEntries RPC, or
  - Granting vote to candidate

Candidates

- Increment currentTerm, vote for self
- Reset election timeout
- Send RequestVote RPCs to all other servers, wait for either:
  - Votes received from majority of servers: become leader
  - AppendEntries RPC received from new leader: step down
  - Election timeout elapses without election resolution: increment term, start new election
  - Discover higher term: step down

Leaders

- Initialize nextIndex for each to last log index + 1
- Send initial empty AppendEntries RPCs (heartbeat) to each follower; repeat during idle periods to prevent election timeouts
- Accept commands from clients, append new entries to local log
- Whenever last log index ≥ nextIndex for a follower, send AppendEntries RPC with log entries starting at nextIndex, update nextIndex if successful
- If AppendEntries fails because of log inconsistency, decrement nextIndex and retry
- Mark log entries committed if stored on a majority of servers and at least one entry from current term is stored on a majority of servers
- Step down if currentTerm changes

Persistent State

Each server persists the following to stable storage synchronously before responding to RPCs:

currentTerm	latest term server has seen (initialized to 0 on first boot)
votedFor	candidateId that received vote in current term (or null if none)
log[]	log entries

Log Entry

term	term when entry was received by leader
index	position of entry in the log
command	command for state machine

RequestVote RPC

Invoked by candidates to gather votes.

Arguments:

candidateId	candidate requesting vote
term	candidate's term
lastLogIndex	index of candidate's last log entry
lastLogTerm	term of candidate's last log entry

Results:

term	currentTerm, for candidate to update itself
voteGranted	true means candidate received vote

Implementation:

1. If term > currentTerm, currentTerm ← term (step down if leader or candidate)
2. If term == currentTerm, votedFor is null or candidateId, and candidate's log is at least as complete as local log, grant vote and reset election timeout

AppendEntries RPC

Invoked by leader to replicate log entries and discover inconsistencies; also used as heartbeat.

Arguments:

term	leader's term
leaderId	so follower can redirect clients
prevLogIndex	index of log entry immediately preceding new ones
prevLogTerm	term of prevLogIndex entry
entries[]	log entries to store (empty for heartbeat)
commitIndex	last entry known to be committed

Results:

term	currentTerm, for leader to update itself
success	true if follower contained entry matching prevLogIndex and prevLogTerm

Implementation:

1. Return if term < currentTerm
2. If term > currentTerm, currentTerm ← term
3. If candidate or leader, step down
4. Reset election timeout
5. Return failure if log doesn't contain an entry at prevLogIndex whose term matches prevLogTerm
6. If existing entries conflict with new entries, delete all existing entries starting with first conflicting entry
7. Append any new entries not already in the log
8. Advance state machine with newly committed entries

***Figure 6.2**: RAFT protocol Summary*

Raft Consensus Algorithm

Owing to Paxos' complexity, Ongaro introduced Raft, a less complicated algorithm, in 2014. Raft is far simpler to comprehend and used in engineering. This is Raft's original goal as well. Many clear-cut design cues have been added, provided that functionality remains unaffected.

An asymmetric model based on leaders is the Raft algorithm. In a system, a node can only be in one of the following three states at any given time: candidate, follower, or leader. Every node is a follower in the early stages. A node, or follower, needs to run for office and start a round of electoral votes in order to take the lead. The node reverts to being a follower in the event that it does not collect enough votes. But the node becomes the leader if it gets the majority of the votes. The original leader immediately reverts to the follower state if it experiences setbacks and discovers that a new leader is chosen once it has recovered.

In order to quickly identify information that has expired, Raft additionally presents the Term notion. In Zookeeper, a term is comparable to an epoch file. A maximum of one leader may be elected in a given period, and the number of terms increases monotonically over time. The log containing the later phrase is more recent if the logs have a different last entry.

Raft additionally presents the timeout and heartbeat packet. An elected leader needs to deliver heartbeat packets to all other nodes in the cluster in order to stay in power. A follower considers the leader to have crashed and initiates a leader election if it does not receive the heartbeat packet within the allotted election timeout. In this case, the follower modifies its status to candidate.

The heartbeat and random timeout are used in Raft to conduct the leader election. Effective leadership is the key to implementing log replication. After receiving a client command, the leader adds it to their log and distributes the log to other followers. Raft limits the authority to commit logs to that of a leader, ensuring security.

Take note of how straightforward the leader election process and the leader's regular activities are. In Raft, the procedure of changing leaders is actually a little more intricate.

Though Raft and Paxos don't operate on precisely the same concept or mechanism, their approaches to solving issues and choosing trade-offs can be compared. In other words, Raft emphasizes fault tolerance but is limited to solving crash defects, emphasizing fault tolerance, safety, and consistency and weakens the level of liveness and availability.

Byzantine (Military) Generals Problem

The problem was discussed and explained aptly in a paper by Leslie Lamport, Robert Shostak, and Marshall Pease at Microsoft research in 1982.

Imagine that several divisions of the Byzantine army are camped outside an enemy city, each division commanded by its own general. The generals can communicate with one another only by messenger. After observing the enemy, they must decide upon a common plan of action. However, some of the generals may be traitors, trying to prevent the loyal generals from reaching an agreement. The generals must decide on when to attack the city, but they need a strong majority of their army to attack at the same time. The generals must have an algorithm to guarantee that:

- All loyal generals decide upon the same plan of action, and
- A small number of traitors cannot cause the loyal generals to adopt a bad plan.

The loyal generals will all do what the algorithm says they should, but the traitors may do anything they wish. The algorithm must guarantee the first condition regardless of what the traitors do. The loyal generals should not only reach agreement, but should agree upon a reasonable plan.

A Byzantine fault (also Byzantine Generals Problem, interactive consistency, source congruency, error avalanche, Byzantine agreement problem, and Byzantine failure) is a condition of a computer system, particularly distributed computing systems, where components may fail and there is imperfect information on whether a component has failed. The term takes its name from an allegory, the "Byzantine generals problem"[1], developed to describe a situation in which, in order to avoid catastrophic failure of the system, the system's actors must agree on a concerted strategy, but some of these actors are unreliable.

Satoshi devised a means to use cryptographic security and public-key encryption to answer the Byzantine general problem in a digital electronic network. To prevent data tampering, cryptographic security uses hashing, a process of encoding. The identity of a network user is verified via public key encryption.

Byzantine Generals Problem describes the difficulty decentralized systems have in agreeing on a single truth. The Byzantine Generals Problem plagued money for millennia, until the invention of Bitcoin. Bitcoin uses a Proof-of-Work mechanism and a blockchain to solve the Byzantine Generals Problem.

Note: *Byzantine Empire, the eastern half of the Roman Empire, which survived for a thousand years after the western half had crumbled into various feudal kingdoms and which finally fell to Ottoman Turkish onslaughts in 1453. But the Byzantine Romans differed from the Western Romans in two important ways: they spoke primarily Greek instead of Latin, and they were Eastern Orthodox Christians rather than Roman Catholic Christians. The Byzantines viewed the emperor not just as the head of the government but as the living representative of God and Jesus Christ. This meant that church and state were combined into one all-powerful body.*

In a Byzantine fault, a component such as a server can inconsistently appear both failed and functioning to failure-detection systems, presenting different symptoms to different observers. It is difficult for the other components to declare it failed and shut it out of the network, because they need to first reach a consensus regarding which component has failed in the first place.

Analogy

In its simplest form, a number of generals are attacking a fortress and must decide as a group only whether to attack or retreat. Some generals may prefer to attack, while others prefer to retreat. The important thing is that all generals agree on a common decision, for a halfhearted attack by a few generals would become a rout, and would be worse than either a coordinated attack or a coordinated retreat.

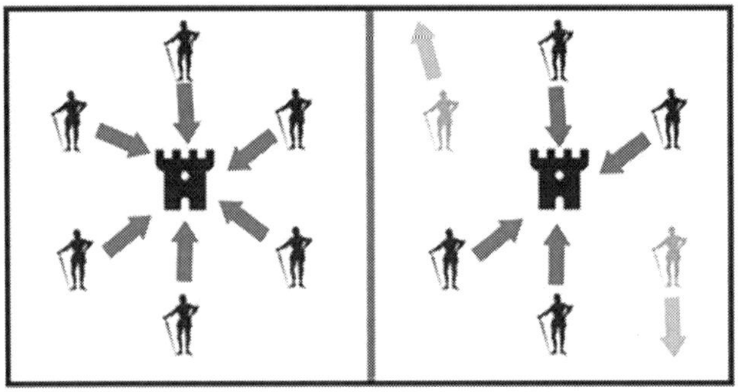

Figure 6.3: *Analogy Byzantine Generals Problem*

The problem is complicated by the presence of treacherous generals who may not only cast a vote for a suboptimal strategy, they may do so selectively. For instance, if nine generals are voting, four of whom support attacking while four others are in favor of retreat, the ninth general may send a vote of retreat to those generals in favor of retreat, and a vote of attack to the rest. Those who received a retreat vote from the ninth general will retreat, while the rest will attack (which may not go well for the attackers). The problem is complicated further by the generals being physically separated and having to send their votes via messengers who may fail to deliver votes or may forge false votes.

Resolution

Byzantine fault tolerance can be achieved if the loyal (non-faulty) generals have a majority agreement on their strategy. There can be a default vote value given to missing messages. For example, missing messages can be given a "null" value. Further, if the agreement is that the null votes are in the majority, a pre-assigned default strategy can be used (for example, retreat).

The typical mapping of this story onto computer systems is that the computers are the generals and their digital communication system links are the messengers. Although the problem is formulated in the analogy as a decision-making and security problem, in electronics, it cannot be solved simply by cryptographic digital signatures, because failures such as incorrect voltages can propagate through the encryption process. Thus, a component may appear functioning to one component and faulty to another, which prevents forming a consensus as to whether the component is faulty or not.

Byzantine Fault Tolerance (BFT)

Byzantine Fault Tolerance (BFT) is the feature of a distributed network to reach consensus (agreement on the same value) even when some of the nodes in the network fail to respond or respond with incorrect information. The objective of a BFT mechanism is to safeguard against the system failures by employing collective decision making (both – correct and faulty nodes) which aims to reduce to influence of the faulty nodes. BFT is derived from Byzantine Generals Problem.

Byzantine fault tolerance can be achieved if the correctly working nodes in the network reach an agreement on their values. There can be a default vote value given to missing messages, that is, we can assume that the message from a particular node is 'faulty' if the message is not received within a certain time limit. Furthermore, we can also assign a default response if the majority of nodes respond with a correct value.

Leslie Lamport proved that if we have 3m+1 correctly working processors, a consensus (agreement on same state) can be reached if at most m processors are faulty. This means that strictly more than two-thirds of the total number of processors should be honest.

Characteristics/Objective of Byzantine Fault Tolerance

A Byzantine fault is any fault presenting different symptoms to different observers. A Byzantine failure is the loss of a system service due to a Byzantine fault in systems that require consensus.

The objective of Byzantine fault tolerance is to be able to defend against failures of system components with or without symptoms that prevent other components of the system from reaching an agreement among themselves, where such an agreement is needed for the correct operation of the system.

The remaining operationally correct components of a Byzantine fault tolerant system will be able to continue providing the system's service as originally intended, assuming there are a sufficient number of accurately operating components to maintain the service.

Byzantine failures are considered the most general and most difficult class of failures among the failure modes. The so-called fail-stop failure mode occupies the simplest end of the spectrum. Whereas fail-stop failure mode simply means that the only way to fail is a node crash, detected by other nodes, Byzantine failures imply no restrictions, which means that the failed node can generate arbitrary data, including data that makes it appear like a functioning node. Thus, Byzantine failures can confuse failure detection systems, which makes fault tolerance difficult. Despite the analogy, a Byzantine failure is not necessarily a security problem involving hostile human interference: it can arise purely from electrical or software faults.

Types of Byzantine Failures

There are two categories of failures that are considered:

- One is fail-stop (in which the node fails and stops operating) and
- Other is arbitrary-node failure.

Byzantine Fault Tolerance (BFT) is of two types:

- Practical Byzantine Fault Tolerance (PBFT, often written as pBFT)
- Asynchronous Byzantine Fault Tolerance (ABFT)

Practical Byzantine Fault Tolerance

Since Lamport first introduced the Byzantine Generals Problem in 1982, there have been several talks regarding BFT solutions; however, many of the solutions to these difficulties are laborious, slow, and inefficient. When Castro and Liskov introduced the Practical Byzantine Fault Tolerance (PBFT) method in 1999, things started to get better. The PBFT algorithm is the first of its kind to have its complexity lowered from an exponential to a polynomial level. Several thousands of transactions per second (TPS) and workable solutions to malicious nodes in practice are made possible by PBFT. It has been demonstrated that if there are no more than 1/3 of malicious nodes in a system, the PBFT algorithm will function as intended.

In a PBFT system, each node is arranged in a sequential order, with one node serving as the leader and the rest as backup nodes. In a system, every node talks to every other node and uses the majority principle to come to decisions. We refer to each PBFT consensus round as a perspective. Every view involves a change in the leading node, which can be substituted by a protocol known as a view change if a predetermined period of time elapses without the leading node broadcasting the request. This replica timeout technique makes sure that a new view begins by re-electing a new leader and that the crashed or malicious leader may be identified.

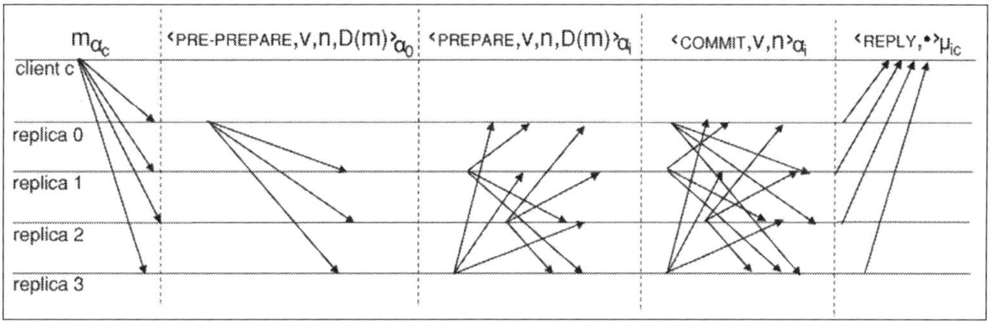

***Figure 6.4**: pBFT normal operations*

As shown in *Figure* 6.4, five phases are experienced from the client launching requests to receiving responses. The consensus process adopts the three-phase protocol. The following content briefly describes the five phases:

1. **Launch:** The client (**`client c`**) initiates the service request m to the cluster.
2. **Pre-prepare**: The leader node (**`replica 0`**) verifies the validity of the request message m, assigns the sequence number n to the request m in the view and broadcasts the assigned pre-prepare message to all the backup nodes (**`replica 1-3`**).
3. **Prepare:** The backup nodes verify the validity of the request message m and accept the sequence number n. If a backup node accepts the assignment scheme, it broadcasts the corresponding prepare message to the other nodes. In this phase, all the replicas are required to reach a globally consistent order.
4. **Commit:** Once the assignment agreement message is received from the cluster, all the nodes (primary and secondary nodes) broadcast the commit message to all the other nodes. In this phase, all the replicas have agreed on the order and confirmed the received request.
5. **Execute and Reply:** After receiving the commit message from the cluster, the nodes execute the request m and send replies to the client. The client awaits the same reply from **`f+1`** different nodes and considers that the request has been executed successfully. *f* represents the maximum number of potential faulty nodes in the clusters. All the nodes directly return messages to the client is also to prevent the primary node from having problems during the request.

PBFT implements safety based on an asynchronous network model, but it depends on message timeouts to perform periodic synchronization. Because the leader-plan solution is adopted, the message synchronization process is very fast and the sequential writing is also implemented. However, the leader re-election is difficult. A malicious leader may start to send a message when the time is very close to the timeout window, causing the system to be seriously slow. This disadvantage can be used to launch attacks against the network and make correctly running nodes look incorrect, causing endless leader election.

Compared with *Paxos and Raft*, *PBFT* can process more problems. In addition to crash faults, it can process Byzantine problems that may cause troubles and unauthorized changes. However, from the perspective of the trade-off policy adopted in PBFT, PBFT is still similar to Paxos and Raft. From the perspective of FLP, PBFT also emphasizes the fault tolerance and safety and weakens the level of liveness. From the perspective of CAP, PBFT emphasizes the tolerance to network partition faults and consistency and weakens the level of availability.

Despite these shortcomings, PBFT is still effective and feasible in practice if the number of faulty or malicious nodes is no more than 1/3 of the total nodes. PBFT is not the only BFT algorithm. Other BFT-like algorithms are also evolving, for example, Lamport once suggested BFT Paxos (an enhanced version of Paxos) to process Byzantine faults. Recently, the BFT Raft algorithm was presented based on the combination of PBFT and Raft. However, from the perspective of the problem scope and mechanism, these algorithms are still similar to previous ideas and frameworks.

We know that a permissioned blockchain is a secure distributed ledger maintained by a number of trusted validation nodes. However, if during operation a validator may become compromised then it may send inconsistent messages to different nodes. This problem can be countered by consensus protocols like Practical Byzantine Fault Tolerance can be used.

PBFT provide consensus mechanisms in permissioned blockchains. A BGP protocol allows the network to detect the behavior of malicious nodes, and all working nodes can reach a consensus if the number of compromised nodes is less than one-third of the total number of nodes, or ***n >= 3f +1***, where n is the number of nodes and *f* is the number of compromised nodes.

Border Gateway Protocol (BGP) is a standardized exterior gateway protocol designed to exchange routing and reachability information among autonomous systems. Partition Attack on Bitcoin Nodes[2].

The partition attack includes isolation of a victim Bitcoin node from the Bitcoin network. Traffic from/to the attacked Bitcoin nodes is deliberately blackholed by an attacker in a certain point of the Internet. The attacker effectively splits the Bitcoin network into two isolated components that have no connectivity between each other. As a result, the block is solved in both components (the new block is solved approximately every 10 minutes) and it is broadcasted toward other Bitcoin nodes within components. Afterwards, the attacker stops the attack and connectivity between components is regained. However, all blocks mined within the smaller component (with less mining power) will be discarded, along with all transactions and the miner's revenue. Therefore, the consequences of partition attacks are Denial of Service (DoS) for the

Bitcoin clients in a smaller component and the loss of revenue. Moreover, transactions in a smaller component can be reverted (double-spending).

In order to blackhole traffic of the targeted Bitcoin nodes, the attacker exploits the weakness of the BGP protocol. As a result, the attacker effectively hijacks IP prefixes where Bitcoin nodes are located. As we know, BGP does not validate whether an origin AS is eligible to announce a prefix. Therefore, an attacker who gains access to an ISP router can announce any prefix via BGP. Let's say that the attacker announces a prefix with the same length (partial BGP hijacking) as the owner of the prefix but AS_PATH attribute is shorter (fewer AS hops) than the AS_PATH in the original BGP announcement. As a result, the newer prefix, announced by the attacker AS, is installed into routing tables.

However, it is more effective for the attacker to announce a more specific prefix. In that case a complete BGP hijacking situation occurs, as BGP routers install more specific routes into their routing tables. As Maria Apostolaki in her paper claims, the vast majority of Bitcoin nodes are hosted in prefixes less than /24. Therefore, an attacker is announcing prefixes with length /24. Prefixes longer than /24 would be very likely filtered by upstream providers. Perfix length /24 means that the first 24 bits are the network address.

The *delay attack* is another type of network attack against the Bitcoin network using BGP hijacking. The attack effectively slows down propagation of blocks towards a victim. The goal is to delay a delivery of a new block to a victim, keeping the victim uninformed for almost 20 minutes about a new block. Contrary to the partition attack, the attacker does not blackhole a victim's connection. Instead, BGP hijacking is used to conduct a Man-in-the-Middle attack (MITM) between a victim and its peer. The attacker also needs to modify Bitcoin messages sent from the victim to the peer in order to perform a successful delay attack.

A Simplified Three-Phase pBFT Process

PBFT distributed consensus algorithm has three phases, and each node maintains its own view of the network. The protocol is initiated by a leader in the network. Even if the leader failed, other nodes take over the responsibility and resume the operation.

A simplified three-phase process is as follows:

1. A leader sends out pre-prepare message to all the nodes;
2. Each node receiving the message will produce a response, and send the response, that is, prepare, to every node;
3. After receiving sufficient such as 2/3 prepare messages from the nodes, each can commit to the agreement, and send out the commit message to everyone.

Thus, to reach a consensus, there will be three rounds of messaging, one for each pre-prepare, prepare, and commit message. The PBFT is more complicated as it also handles the case when a leader is crashed. In permissioned BCs, a Byzantine consensus will be needed only when a new block is to be created, and all working nodes need to agree with the contents of the new block.

However, for an enterprise system, due to asynchronous message arrival and large volume of data, each node may receive different messages since the previous block creation, and thus it can be difficult for all the nodes to agree with all the contents of the new block even if the nodes are working properly.

If the system has few transactions per second, this is not an issue, but this is an issue for an enterprise system. Thus, the goal of consensus protocol is modified as follows:

- Most of working nodes can reach a consensus on most of items in a new block;
- Detection of those failed nodes so that they can be safely ignored during consensus building;
- Detection of those compromised nodes that sent out different messages to different nodes to disrupt the operation;
- Those items that should be in the BC, but not voted in the current block, will be placed in the next block to be voted in the future;
- Those items that should not be in the BC should be clearly identified and should not be placed in a queue to be considered in the next block.

Issue 1 is a relaxed version of a common BC. Instead of having identical contents, one can allow each node to have slightly different contents in a new block yet to be voted on. This is to allow each node to receive different messages from different sources due to asynchronous messaging. However, as a part of the voting process, all working nodes must decide on the contents of the new block. In this way, after voting, all the nodes will have identical content in the newly created block.

Issue 2 is important in a permissioned BC as failed nodes should not be involved in future voting until they are fully recovered. The recovered node also needs to retrieve any missing data during the absent period.

Issue 3 is important as compromised nodes should not be involved as a compromised node can cause significant troubles for a BC. In fact, they should be excluded from the BC operation completely as soon as they are identified as the damage done by compromised nodes is far greater than the damage done by failed nodes.

Issue 4 is a new problem in a permissioned BC as each second numerous data may enter the BC, and those valid data must be stored to maintain the trust of the BC. For example, a lottery machine may send out ticket information to a permissioned BC. Due to message delays, some messages did not get into every node, and they were not included in the new block. As they are valid tickets, they should be stored in the next block. This scenario is considered as false negative as a valid message was excluded due to various reasons.

Issue 5 is a new problem due to Issue 4 as data not included in the previous block can be included in the next new block to be created, thus potentially an increasing number of data can be postponed and continued to be considered for inclusion. But some of these data may not be valid at all, and should be removed for good rather than to be re-considered in future blocks. This scenario is considered as false positive as invalid messages continued to be considered in block creation.

Applicable Scenarios

Distributed consensus algorithms have been developing, improving and evolving since the introduction of Paxos, Raft, and PBFT. Many big companies have also developed distributed consensus algorithms that meet their business scenarios. Although these algorithms are not very perfect, they play an important role in specific business practices.

Non-BFT algorithms such as Paxos and Raft can only process machine hardware faults and cannot handle situations where malicious nodes are present. These non-BFT algorithms can only run in very reliable network environments, for example, the internal network of a company. In such relatively closed networks, access requires strict authorization, ensuring that the identities of individual nodes are known and reliable. This serves to eliminate malicious nodes, and to allow the algorithms to run effectively.

BFT algorithms do have very strict requirements on the network environment. Even if malicious nodes are present, the entire system is still secure only if the malicious nodes are no more than one-third of the total nodes. However, this brings about new problems. How do you know exactly the number of malicious nodes in the network? What is the proportion of the malicious nodes to the total nodes? If access to the network requires permissions, it is relatively easy to solve this problem. For example, in a private network consisting of 10 affiliates, only the 10 authorized companies can access the network. Even if some companies (less than 3 companies) act maliciously and attempt to change data without authorization, the whole system is still reliable and secure. In such a permissioned network, the number of nodes that may act maliciously has been estimated. When some nodes do act maliciously, their real identities can be quickly located. This indirectly improves the safety of the network.

Limitations

However, BFT algorithms may cause problems in a permissionless (open permission, without permission control) open network. If a distributed network is open and can be accessed by anyone and the cost of the network access is low, it is unknown how many potentially malicious nodes may be in the network. Even when some nodes act maliciously, determining their identities is also a difficult issue. A typical attack scenario is a Sybil attack where attackers can forge identities to control a large number of nodes and then the entire distributed network.

In addition, the biggest limitation of BFT algorithms is that they can only coordinate a small number of nodes (for example, no more than 100 nodes). If the nodes are in the thousands, the system shows very poor performance or even fails to reach consensus, affecting the liveness and availability of the system. You may have noticed that multicast is required throughout the three-phase protocol of PBFT. In the pre-prepare phase, the primary node broadcasts the request to all the secondary nodes; in the prepare phase, the secondary nodes broadcast to all other nodes; in the commit phase, individual nodes (primary and secondary) broadcast to all other nodes. From this process, we can know that the number of communication times is the number of nodes squared. When a system has a large number of nodes, this broadcast mechanism will be a disaster. The system is almost unable to reach consensus in a short period of time.

From this explanation, we can draw a conclusion that traditional distributed consensus algorithms such as Paxos, Raft, and PBFT are generally applicable to reliable distributed networks that require permission control and have a small number of nodes.

Advantages of pBFT

The following are the advantages of using PBFT:

- **Energy Efficiency**: PBFT can achieve distributed consensus without carrying out complex mathematical computations (like in PoW). **Zilliqa** employs pBFT in combination with PoW-like complex computations round for every 100th block.
- **Transaction Finality**: The transactions do not require multiple confirmations (like in case of PoW mechanism in Bitcoin where every node individually verifies all the transactions before adding the new block to the blockchain; confirmations can take between 10-60 minutes depending upon how many entities confirm the new block) after they have been finalized and agreed upon.
- **Low Reward Variance**: Every node in the network takes part in responding to the request by the client and hence every node can be incentivized leading to low variance in rewarding the nodes that help in decision making.

Working Style of pBFT

pBFT tries to provide a practical Byzantine state machine replication that can work even when malicious nodes are operating in the system.

Nodes in a pBFT enabled distributed system are sequentially ordered and used with one node being the primary (or the leader node) and others referred to as secondary (or the backup nodes). Note here that any eligible node in the system can become the primary by transitioning from secondary to primary (typically, in the case of a primary node failure). The goal is that all honest nodes help in reaching a consensus regarding the state of the system using the majority rule.

A practical Byzantine Fault Tolerant system can function on the condition that the maximum number of malicious nodes must not be greater than or equal to one-third of all the nodes in the system. As the number of nodes increase, the system becomes more secure.

pBFT consensus rounds are broken into four phases: (refer to *Figure* 6.5):

1. The client sends a request to the primary (leader) node.
2. The primary (leader) node broadcasts the request to the all the secondary (backup) nodes.
3. The nodes (primary and secondaries) perform the service requested and then send back a reply to the client.
4. The request is served successfully when the client receives 'm+1' replies from different nodes in the network with the same result, where m is the maximum number of faulty nodes allowed.

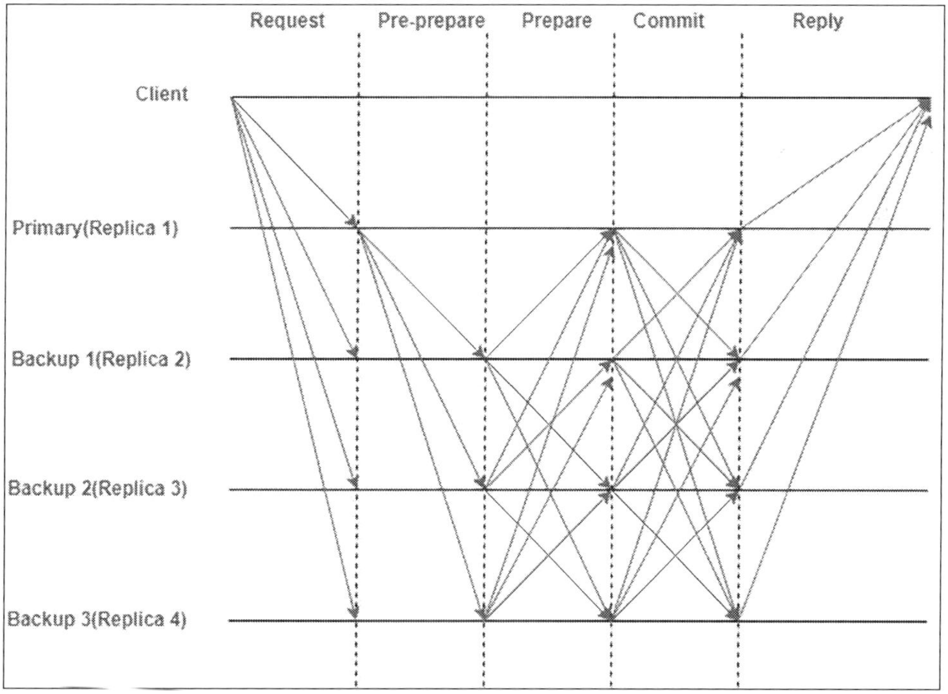

Figure 6.5: *pBFT consensus rounds*

The primary (leader) node is changed during every view (pBFT consensus rounds) and can be substituted by a view change protocol if a predefined quantity of time has passed without the leading node broadcasting a request to the backups (secondary). If needed, a majority of the honest nodes can vote on the legitimacy of the current leading node and replace it with the next leading node in line.

Limitations of pBFT

The pBFT consensus model works efficiently only when the number of nodes in the distributed network is small due to the high communication overhead that increases exponentially with every extra node in the network.

- **Sybil Attacks**: The pBFT mechanisms are susceptible to Sybil attacks, where one entity (party) controls many identities. A Sybil attack is a type of attack on a computer network service in which an attacker subverts the service's reputation system by creating a large number of pseudonymous identities and uses them to gain a disproportionately large influence. As the number of nodes in the network increase, sybil attacks become increasingly difficult to carry out. But as pBFT mechanisms have scalability issues too, the pBFT mechanism is used in combination with other mechanism(s).
- **Scaling**: pBFT does not scale well because of its communication (with all the other nodes at every step) overhead. As the number of nodes in the network increase, so does the time taken to respond to the request.

Platforms Using pBFT Variants

- **Zilliqa**: pBFT in combination with PoW consensus
- **Hyperledger Fabric**: permissioned version of pBFT
- **Tendermint**: pBFT + DPoS (Delegated Proof-of-Stake)

Asynchronous Byzantine Fault Tolerance (ABFT)

When a decentralized network is Byzantine fault tolerant, it means that the honest members, or nodes, of a network can be guaranteed to agree on the timing and order (consensus) of a set of transactions. Regardless as to whether there are some nodes maliciously trying to prevent that consensus – even if as many as one-third of nodes are trying to negatively affect consensus by delaying transactions or otherwise corrupting things. This is the 'fault tolerance' of the network, meaning how many nodes can the network tolerate acting maliciously, but still come to an honest consensus.

The 'asynchronous' property of Byzantine fault tolerance overcomes a challenge of fault tolerance, which is that of timing. Many forms of Byzantine fault tolerance assume there is a maximum threshold of message latency when coming to a consensus. An ABFT network eliminates this assumption and allows for some messages to be lost or indefinitely delayed.

An ABFT network allows for messages to be lost or indefinitely delayed and assumes only that at some point an honest node's messages will eventually get through. It is much more challenging for an honest node to assess whether another node is not following the rules, if that node's messages can be indeterminately delayed, but this scenario much better reflects that network reliability in the real world.

Lamport-Shostak-Pease BFT Algorithm

Practical Byzantine Fault Tolerance (pBFT) is a consensus algorithm introduced in the late 90s by Barbara Liskov and Miguel Castro. pBFT was designed to work efficiently in asynchronous (no upper bound on when the response to the request will be received) systems. It is optimized for low overhead time. Its goal was to solve many problems associated with already available Byzantine Fault Tolerance solutions. Application areas include distributed computing and blockchain.

Conclusion

This chapter delved into the fundamental concept of distributed consensus, the backbone of achieving agreement in permissioned blockchains. We explored various consensus models suitable for controlled environments, including the popular Paxos and Raft algorithms. We then contrasted these with Byzantine Fault Tolerance (BFT) algorithms like PBFT and ABFT, designed to handle malicious actors.

By understanding the strengths and limitations of different consensus algorithms, developers can choose the most appropriate approach for their specific consortium blockchain application. While PBFT offers robust fault tolerance, its communication overhead might limit scalability in large networks. On the other hand, Paxos and Raft provide efficient consensus but require a more controlled and trusted environment.

The ongoing evolution of consensus algorithms promises even more efficient and secure solutions for permissioned blockchains. As these technologies mature, they will continue to play a vital role in driving innovation and trust in distributed ledger systems.

In the next chapter, we will focus on the enterprise application of blockchain.

References

[1] Lamport, L.; Shostak, R.; Pease, M. (1982). "The Byzantine Generals Problem" (PDF). ACM Transactions on Programming Languages and Systems.

[2] BGP and Cryptocurrencies, Oct 19, 2017, https://www.noction.com/blog/bgp-and-cryptocurrencies

CHAPTER 7
Enterprise Application of Blockchain

Introduction

While blockchain technology gained initial recognition for powering cryptocurrencies like Bitcoin, its potential extends far beyond the realm of digital money. Businesses are increasingly recognizing the transformative potential of blockchain for streamlining operations, enhancing security, and fostering trust in a collaborative environment. Enterprise applications of blockchain leverage the core strengths of this technology to revolutionize various aspects of how organizations function. The potential applications of enterprise blockchain are vast and constantly evolving. As businesses seek greater efficiency, security, and transparency, blockchain technology is poised to play a transformative role in the future of enterprise operations.

Structure

In this chapter, the following topics will be covered:

- Cross-Border Payments
  - Blockchain and Cross-Border Money Transfer
  - Drawbacks of Cross Border Money Transfer
- Know Your Customer (KYC)
  - Steps Involved in KYC
  - KYC Registry for SWIFT
  - India: The Reserve Bank of India KYC guidelines for Banks in 2002
- Blockchains Applications
- Blockchain in Food industry
- Blockchain in Mortgage Processing
  - Conventional Loan Procedure

    - The Mortgage Process and Blockchain
    - A Blockchain Mortgage Process Example
    - Blockchain Mortgages' Advantages
- Blockchain Enabled Trade
    - Finance and Banking
    - The Use of blockchain Technology in Logistics
    - Blockchain in Real Estate Documents
- Blockchain in the Medical Field
- Blockchain in Elections and Voting
- Enterprise Blockchain Requirements
    - Currency
    - Property Records
    - Supply Chains
- How Blockchain Technology Can Disrupt Financial Services
- Application of Blockchain in the Legal Field
- The Use of Blockchain in Real Estate
- Logistics and Supply Chain Through Blockchain
- Trade
- International Trade
- Trade Finance
- we.trade: The Largest Blockchain-Enabled Trade Networks
- Supply Chain Finance
- Digital Identity in Blockchain
- Benefits of Blockchain

Cross-Border Payments

It is very much clear that safe transfers between an endless number of bank ledgers can be made possible by blockchain technology in cross-border payments. By doing this, we can avoid using financial middlemen, who act as go-betweens when transferring money between banks[1].

Since blockchain technology employs encrypted distributed ledgers to provide reliable real-time transaction verification without the need for middlemen like correspondent banks, it has a bright future for cross-border payments. It makes verification possible without relying on other sources. Since anyone can utilize the technology to integrate their product to their advantage, it also preserves the idea of banking. A few banks in Korea and Japan have already begun to use this technology for their payment processes.

- **AntPool**: The largest mining pool globally is AntPool. About 11% of all blocks are mined by it, and its servers are located all over the world. During setup, AntPool's novel peer-to-peer mining mechanism can connect your device to the closest one for a dependable connection.
- **BTC.com**: If you are acquainted with Bitcoin.com, the same business also owns BTC.com. Before launching the mining section, BTC.com was well-known for its cutting-edge blockchain explorer and Bitcoin wallet. Litecoin, Ether, and other cryptocurrencies are supported by BTC.com's medium-sized mining pool, which is located in multiple countries including the US and Germany.

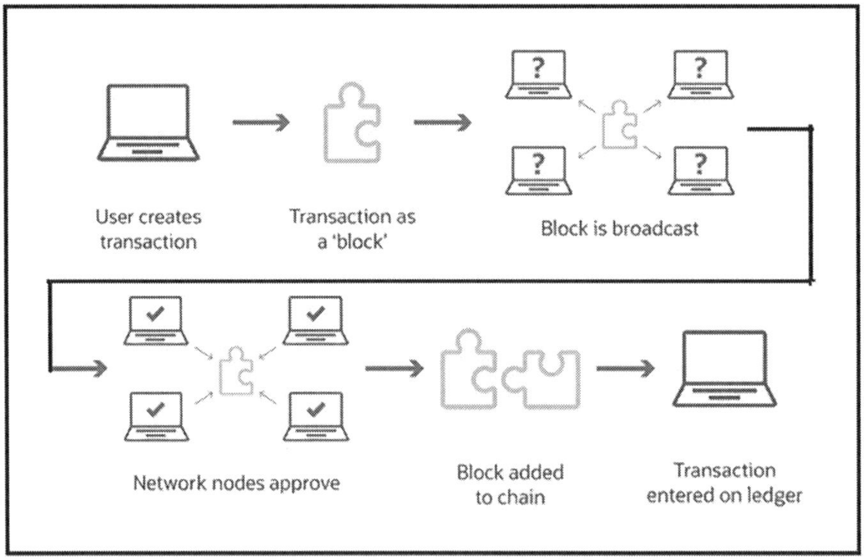

Figure 7.1: *Systematic diagram of Broadcasting of a transaction*

Figure 7.1 is to show a transaction created gets converted into a block for further processing and the same gets broadcasted. Immediately the network nodes approve the block, the same gets added to the chain and finally gets entered on the ledger.

One utility known as *Oracle's FLEXCUBE Blockchain adapter* enables users to interface Blockchain systems to transform data between traditional applications. Besides, this adapter can be used for any version and configured at the module level. The adapter helps to process information with minimal human intervention.

FLEXCUBE is a real-time, online, comprehensive universal banking solution which supports the changing landscape of retail, corporate, and investment banking needs with strong conventional banking and Islamic banking capabilities. FLEXCUBE is a microservices-based platform – developers can work with a single functionality without a significant impact on other modules. It provides fast integration with third-party applications to meet the needs of large banking ecosystems.

Oracle's FLEXCUBE Blockchain technology can be used for the following features:

- Automation of loan creation
- Automating the liquidation of bills and loan contract
- Reducing the cost of SWIFT transfer

To put the preceding scenario into clearer perspective, Blockchain technology can be utilized to make the disbursement of a buyer's credit loan much more accessible. The importer's bank generates a dummy import bill with all the information from the actual bill under a letter of credit, including shipment and goods details, when it accepts the offer for buyer's credit made by the foreign bank. The information will be sent to the Blockchain network for verification, and the Blockchain network will notify the foreign bank of the contract's specifics.

A Nostro Correspondent will receive an MT 202 shortly after the loan contract has been approved. The importer's bank will get the loan disbursement details via the Blockchain.

MT202 message informs each of the banks in the chain of the payment amount, currency and recipient bank. It is mentioned here that MT202 COV is a SWIFT message format for financial institution (FI) funds transfer between financial institutions. Prior to MT202 COV the message format, MT202, were used primarily for two purposes, bank-to-bank payments (that is, interest payments and settlement of FX trades) and cover payments.

Note: *SWIFT is an acronym for the Society for Worldwide Interbank Financial Telecommunication. It allows banks to relay information about financial transactions to one another. SWIFT is a cooperative company under Belgian law and is owned and controlled by its shareholders (financial institutions) representing approximately 3,500 firms from across the world except Russia. Just to mention here, Russia has already developed its own transaction system known as the System for Transfer of Financial Messages (SPFS), currently used only for domestic transactions.*

A SWIFT payment generally takes 1–4 working days. The transaction time taken varies based on the destination, time zones and different banking procedures. SWIFT transfers aren't instant. Before your funds are credited to the recipient, they will undergo anti-fraud and anti-money laundering checks, which takes time.

When the import bill is due for liquidation, the user will do so, and the Blockchain will notify the lending bank that the loan has been repaid. Here, FLEXCUBE can interface with Blockchain systems, owing to the Blockchain adaptor, making it simple to convert data between Blockchain datasets and standard applications. A blockchain's infrastructure is made up of nodes. They disseminate, store, and maintain the Blockchain data.

Through the adaptor, which serves as a messenger, the transaction recorded in the importer's bank's FLEXCUBE platform will be sent to the lending bank. Through the adapter's APIs (Application Programming Interface), the transaction details are translated into nodes. The same will be sent by the API principle to the lending bank via an additional adaptor, assisting in the creation of a record in FLEXCUBE between the lending bank and itself. The adapter and node will facilitate communication between the two parties.

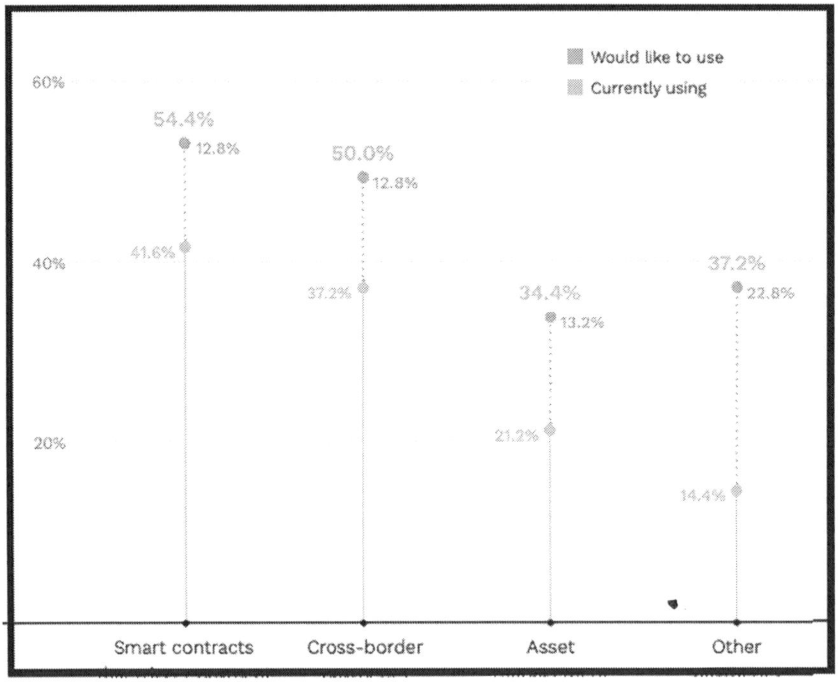

***Figure* 7.2**: *Business Uses of Blockchain*

The second most common use case for cryptocurrency and/or blockchain is cross-border payments, which 37% of businesses currently do and another 13% want to begin doing. Other common ways that multinational firms utilize cryptocurrency and blockchain include asset management and other payments.

Blockchain and Cross-Border Money Transfer

Given the current state of the art's deficiencies with regard to cross-border payments, blockchain technology and the notion of a distributed ledger have found favor with the banking and financial industry. Banks also frequently discuss the distributed ledger blockchain, which has been the subject of much discussion for some years now. Blockchain is an open ledger that exists in a distributed network and is available to all users.

As a result, every node in the network will have a complete copy of the entire database or ledger, and any changes made to it will require proper verification by other nodes or parties in order to confirm the changes made. As such, for the ledger to be considered genuine, all nodes must concur on its current status. This would imply that since there are no middlemen or correspondent banks involved, direct transfers can happen instantaneously, without concern about manipulation, even for cross-border payments. The settlement agency will decide on a bilateral, visible, and irreversible transfer of value between the banks thanks to the fundamental idea of distributed ledger.

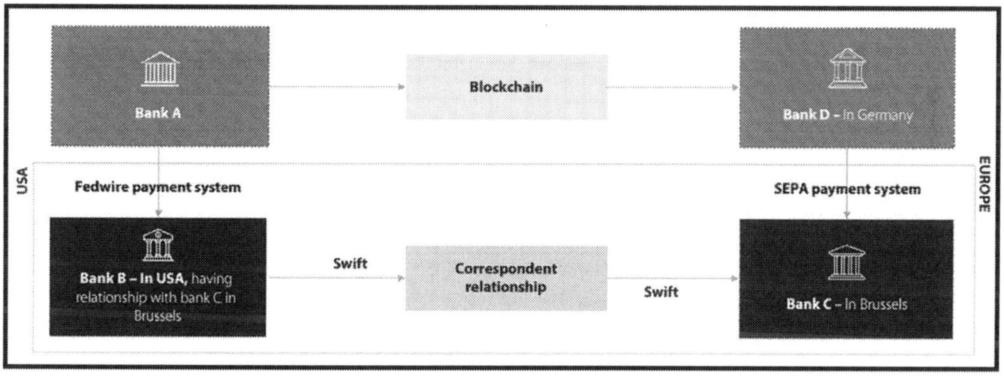

Figure 7.3: *Money transfer from bank A to bank D through blockchain eliminating the third party as highlighted*

The following are some advantages that blockchain offers, as seen in *Figure 7.3*:

- It stipulates that all intermediaries, central agencies, and correspondents will be excluded from the payment proceedings. Transactions can happen between parties that have signed a bilateral agreement, guaranteeing mutual trust.
- A lower total cost with little fees applied throughout the payment process. Furthermore, if the messages are routed through SWIFT, there is a processing fee. Due to these fees levied by the central agency and correspondent banks, processing payments becomes more expensive for tasks like receiving, compiling, and netting payment messages before retransmitting data and confirmations to the appropriate institutions. Since there is no need for central agencies or message movement, there is a possibility of a very short turnaround time for settlement.
- The nodes of the network maintain a copy of the balances because they are maintained in the settlement accounts with the other banks, so there is no need to ensure intra-day liquidity.
- Since the transaction details are encrypted and hashed, there is very little chance that the data will be modified.
- The challenges associated with standardization are also reduced.

- There is increased payment transparency with distributed ledger since sender and receiver are the nodes of the network or chain. A private or permissioned blockchain, in which users are unable to join the network anonymously and become nodes, may help to mitigate some of the privacy and data protection issues. In order to access transactions involving a private key among the network's trusted parties, the parties will need to register or sign a bilateral agreement. Everyone is also aware of how hard it is to hack the block's underlying hashed transactions.

About 11 banks have contracted on a private peer-to-peer distributed ledger supported by the R3 group in order to test the distributed ledger on a worldwide private network. Ethereum technology is housed on a virtual private network built on the public cloud platform Microsoft Azure.

But rather than working together, the R3 consortium is facing some issues in light of the recent announcement that some of the big companies are leaving the group. Blockchain is turning into a battlefield where rivalry is now the main focus.

This is evident from the fact that there are currently no established criteria or regulations for the game, yet the majority of the important aspects appear to be amenable to a just settlement. The regulatory reporting aspect presents the most obstacle. Numerous blockchain use cases advocate for the elimination of intermediaries, such as regulatory bodies. These proposals aim to foster collaboration to minimize disruption in this sector, given the known conservative stance taken by banks and other financial institutions. Every regulatory reporting and transaction monitoring activity seeks complete payment transparency and the specifics of the parties involved in order to perform customer due diligence, sanction screening checks, FATF, Dodd-Frank, AML/KYC, Basel III, and other requirements. An industry study has shown that the two main factors that are thought to contribute to internal resistance to blockchain adoption are regulatory and compliance issues, which must be appropriately addressed.

Drawbacks of Cross-Border Money Transfer

Transferring money from one account to another within the same financial institution or any other financial institution is known as remittance. All that SWIFT does in a cross-border payment is manage the flow of messages across the payment chain. On the other hand, the correspondent banks assist in passing the value to the final beneficiary by performing the real debits and credits between accounts in accordance with the message.

As an illustration, bank A is transferring money in euros to a German bank D account. The following is the workflow:

1. Bank A in the US receives an MT103 (a SWIFT message format) in $US.
2. Bank A uses Fedwire to transmit the payment request to Bank B, its

correspondent bank, along with a debit/credit instruction for further transmission.

3. Bank B makes the necessary modifications and uses the SWIFT network to communicate with Bank C, its correspondent bank in Brussels.
4. Bank D in Germany receives the value from Bank C via the Single Euro Payments Area (SEPA).
5. Bank D credits the supplier account in EUR.

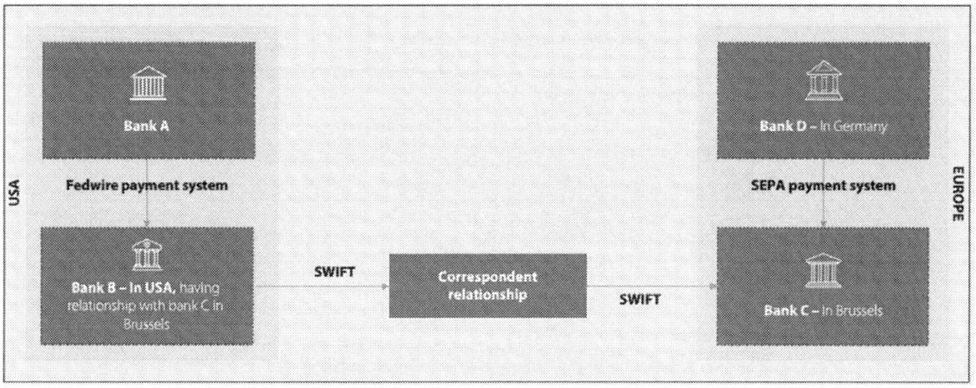

Figure 7.4: *Payment flow chart - Bank A sending euro amount to a euro account bank D in Germany*

As shown in the payment flow chart of *Figure* 7.4, the banks charge fees for processing of each transaction, thus increasing the costs involved for all parties concerned. The SWIFT bank charges for transmitting the messages and thus adds to the cost. Since the ledgers are local to the banks, the SWIFT messages ensure the debit entry of one bank's ledger is communicated to another bank so as to pass/post the corresponding credit entry in its ledger. Due to this increase in the number of payment messages in the chain, fees on SWIFT messages also increase.

The following drawbacks are observed in the current process of international payments transfer system with involvement of correspondent banks has:

- Each transaction is subject to processing fees levied by the banks, which raises the overall cost to all participants. The cost is increased by the SWIFT bank, which charges for message transmission. Due to the local nature of the bank ledgers, SWIFT messages make sure that a debit entry from one bank's ledger is shared with another bank so that the other bank can pass along or post the corresponding credit record in its ledger. Fees for SWIFT communications also rise as a result of this growth in the chain's payment messages.

The existing international funds transfer system, which involves correspondent banks, has the following observed drawbacks:

- SWIFT came into being to guarantee and confirm message transmission as no two banks can agree on a transaction based on their own ledger, Central banks operated as settlement agents to guarantee payments.
- Also SWIFT charges the bank for processing the payment orders irrespective of whether the bank is at both the receiving and sending end of the instruction.
- In case a single cross-border payment has to traverse through certain correspondent banks which are involved in activities like receiving, collating, and netting payment messages before retransmitting confirmations/denials to the respective banks. This increases the time to settle presence of a trusted third party with powers to overwrite and overturn ledger activities needed to have a unified view.
- It is expected that a Central bank typically may insist for banks to maintain sufficient liquidity in their settlement accounts or nostro accounts maintained with the Central banks.
- Note that in case of a cross-border payment for pooled account in certain banks, the originator of the message is modified and populated by an internal bank account number. This raises concern around the data protection and security in the receiving bank.

Know Your Customer (KYC)

Financial institutions are particularly susceptible to illegal criminal activity in an increasingly global economy. Financial institutions are shielded against fraud, corruption, money laundering, and terrorism financing by Know Your Customer (KYC) regulations.

KYC is the process of identification and verification of the identity of a client in which a series of controls are applied to avoid having commercial relations with people related to terrorism, corruption or money laundering, among others.

The KYC process is involved in verifying that the client is actually who she/he says she/he is and giving her/him access to the services or products he/she needs. This verification is carried out through different methods, although not all comply with legal requirements.

The KYC process takes place in such a way that the user who wants to become client of a company demonstrates with legal and binding evidence his identity. For this, methods such as video identification by streaming video and videoconferencing are used, in which the user shows and validates his identity documents, the authenticity of them, and their face, in addition to other biometric tests and security checks.

Know Your Customer process can be carried out both remotely online and in-person at a commercial office or store. When it is done remotely and online, or the process has been digitized, we talk about eKYC (electronic Know Your Customer) process.

Financial services professionals are required by KYC rules to attempt to confirm the identity, suitability, and risks associated with sustaining a business relationship. The protocols are under the larger purview of an institution's anti-money laundering (AML) guidelines. Businesses of all sizes also use KYC procedures to make sure that potential clients, representatives, advisers, or distributors follow anti-bribery laws and are who they say they are. Customers are being asked to submit more and more thorough due diligence information by banks, insurance, export creditors, and other financial organizations.

A reasonable firm or individual would often be required to do due diligence before engaging into a contract or agreement with another party, or before acting with a specific standard of care.

The purpose of the KYC guidelines is to stop criminal elements from using enterprises as a means of money laundering. Businesses can also gain a deeper understanding of their clients' financial transactions through related procedures. This enables them to prudently manage their risks. Nowadays, banks and various internet companies must adhere to KYC guidelines. Typically, they incorporate the following four essential components within their KYC policies:

- The policy for accepting customers;
- The processes for identifying customers;
- Transaction monitoring; and
- Risk control.

KYC is an essential and required process for both financial and non-financial companies due to the strict regulatory environment. Because it recognizes suspicious features early in the client-business interaction, it reduces the chance of fraud.

Steps Involved in KYC

KYC involves several steps:

1. For Establishing customer identity;
2. To understand the nature of customers' activities and qualify that the source of funds is legitimate; and
3. Assess money laundering risks associated with customers.

A customer/user may be defined as (for the purposes of a KYC policy):

- Entity or a person or that maintains an account or has a business relationship with the reporting entity;
- Agency on whose behalf the account is maintained (that is, the beneficial owner);

- Any or all Beneficiaries of transactions conducted by professional intermediaries such as stockbrokers, chartered accountants, or solicitors, as permitted under the law; or
- Any unknown person or entity connected with a financial transaction that can pose significant reputational or other risks to the bank, for example, a wire transfer or issue of a high-value demand draft as a single transaction.

Blockchain analytics and crypto compliance experts can help perfect the execution of your KYC lifecycle, allowing you to onboard more customers while feeling safe in the knowledge that you're meeting regulatory requirements.

This involves a unique combination of:

- Artificial intelligence,
- Optical character recognition,
- Natural language processing and automation,

This unique combination of technologies provide a single source of truth for compliance teams on all of their corporate, SME and individual clients.

KYC process includes:

1. ID card verification,
2. Face verification,
3. Documents for verification, such as utility bills as proof of address and biometric verification.

In addition, real-time cross-border payments depend heavily on KYC compliance, which reduces risk and promotes increased levels of trust, transparency, and cooperation. In order to expedite the compliance process and develop novel, cooperative strategies for addressing financial crime, a community approach is needed.

KYC Registry for SWIFT

Currently, around 6,000 financial institutions publish and receive KYC data from their correspondent banks via the SWIFT KYC registry. The acknowledged benchmark for correspondent banking due diligence is SWIFT KYC. In an effort to streamline the KYC procedure between banks and corporations, the registration has now been expanded to include corporate SWIFT clients. Customer due diligence and KYC are essential to protect the global financial system from money laundering and financing of illegal and criminal activities.

As of 2018, around half of all high-value cross-border payments worldwide used the SWIFT network, and in 2015, SWIFT linked more than 11,000 financial institutions in over 200 countries and territories, who were exchanging an average of over 32 million messages per day.

The SWIFT's KYC registry is a secure global platform providing predefined data fields and document types to standardize and streamline the data collection process.

To date, almost 6,000 financial institutions are using SWIFT's KYC Registry to both publish their KYC data and receive data from their counterparties. SWIFT's KYC is recognized as the accepted standard for correspondent banking due diligence. The registry has now been extended to corporate customers of SWIFT to help simplify the KYC process between banks and corporates.

India: The Reserve Bank of India KYC Guidelines for Banks in 2002

The goal of KYC guidelines is to stop criminal elements from using banks for money laundering activities, whether on purpose or accidentally. Banks can better know and comprehend their customers and their financial transactions thanks to these KYC procedures, which also help them manage their risks. The following essential components should be incorporated by banks into their KYC policies:

- Customer Acceptance Policy
- Customer Identification Procedures
- Monitoring of Transactions

Blockchains Applications

As far as we know, the blockchain of Bitcoin stores information about financial transactions in blocks. More than 10,000 other cryptocurrency systems are currently operating on blockchain technology. By 2022, a number of businesses, including Walmart, Pfizer, AIG, Siemens, Unilever, and many more, will have used blockchain technology. For instance, IBM developed the Food Trust blockchain to track the path taken by food goods as they are delivered to their destinations.

History tells us that Blockchain was first introduced in 2009 to the market as the technology underpinning Bitcoin exchanges, but its practical uses in the world of business extend far beyond cryptocurrency transactions. For example, in finance, blockchain networks allow securities trades to be settled in minutes rather than days. In supply chains, blockchain networks allow the flow of goods and payments to be tracked and logged in real time.

Following questions may be asked to determine whether your use case is a good fit for blockchain questions:

- Is a business network involved?
- Is consensus used to validate transactions?
- Is an audit trail, or provenance, required?
- Is the record of transactions be immutable, or tamper proof?
- Should dispute resolution be final?

Even if you answered yes to the first question and to at least one other, then your use case would benefit from blockchain technology. A network always needs to be involved for blockchain to be the right solution, but the network can take many forms. The network can be between organizations, such as a supply chain, or the network can be within an organization. Within an organization, a blockchain network could be used to share reference data between divisions or to create an audit or compliance network, for example. The network can also exist between individuals, who might need to store data, digital assets, or contracts on the blockchain, for example.

Blockchain in Food Industry

If a food is found to be contaminated, then it can be traced all the way back through each stop to its origin. Not only that, but these companies can also now see everything else it may have come in contact with, allowing the identification of the problem to occur far sooner and potentially saving lives. This is one example of blockchain in practice, but there are many other forms of blockchain implementation.

In the food industry, there have been several reports of E. *Coli* infections, salmonella outbreaks, and listeria outbreaks in addition to inadvertent exposure to dangerous substances in food. It has previously taken weeks to identify the cause of these outbreaks or the reason why people are getting sick from their meals. Blockchain technology allows brands to track a food product from the point of origin to every stop it makes, all the way to delivery.

Blockchain in Mortgage Processing

Loans against property are another term for mortgage loans, or just mortgages. One can refinance or purchase or build a home with a mortgage loan. Obtaining a new loan for a property while the previous loan is still being paid back is known as refinancing. Usually, the goal is to obtain a loan with favorable conditions.

Blockchain accelerators and blockchain technology are still relatively new in the mortgage market, but they have potential. Understanding every step of the standard mortgage process and how long it takes overall will help you fully appreciate the advantages of blockchain mortgages[2].

Conventional Loan Procedure

The length of time it takes to obtain a mortgage through the traditional route might range from 30 to around 60 days, depending on the time of year and the number of people looking to purchase a property at any particular moment. The normal stages in obtaining a mortgage are listed as follows:

- **Prequalification**: A mortgage lender evaluates your credit and provides you with an estimate throughout this process.
- **Application**: Submitting an application is the next action to take. A buyer of a house will often fill out the uniform residential loan application. The application includes all the pertinent information a mortgage lender would need to approve or reject your application, including your income, assets, and work history.
- **Processing**: The following action involves verifying all the information on the application or processing the loan. Appraising the house you want to buy to make sure its value is at least as much as what you're paying for it is another step in the loan approval process.
- **Underwriting**: A mortgage is not yet ready even after the loan processor has examined everything and approved it. The underwriter then receives the file, reviews it all, and determines whether to approve or reject the loan. In particular, the underwriter is assessing the degree of risk and figuring out if a certain applicant would be a problematic borrower.
- **Settlement**: The last stage is settlement, also known as closing, if the underwriter approves the mortgage. The buyer can move into their new house once the mortgage is finalized following the settlement.

The Mortgage Process and Blockchain

By increasing productivity and lowering costs associated with the mortgage process, blockchain technology can help simplify the mortgage sector.

The mortgage business can gain from blockchain technology in a number of ways. It may contribute to accelerating transaction times, resulting in quicker settlements. It can also result in more accurate documentation and lower costs for all parties participating in the process.

Blockchain accelerators and blockchain technology are still relatively new in the mortgage market, but they have potential. Understanding every step of the standard mortgage process and how long it takes overall will help you fully appreciate the advantages of blockchain mortgages. Gaining a rudimentary understanding of blockchain technology can assist you in seeing how it can simplify the mortgage application process.

A Blockchain Mortgage Process Example

A prospective homeowner is already pre-approved for a mortgage. They've located a house they wish to purchase.

After they finish the mortgage application, it turns into a block. All participants involved in the mortgage process have access to the block, and the information submitted in the application is validated almost immediately.

The buyer gets an encrypted key to sign the offer after the financing is approved. The buyer's signature record is added to the chain as a distinct block. Transferring the loan cash to the buyer is the next stage. Both the title transfer and the money transfer become into links in the chain. All things considered, utilizing blockchain technology reduces the time it takes to obtain approval for a mortgage and settle on a loan from several weeks to a few days.

Blockchain technology is still relevant after a mortgage is approved and closed. Blockchain technology can be used by mortgage servicers to monitor borrower payments. Blockchain can assist in proving property ownership for homeowners looking to sell or refinance their property. Blockchain can assist mortgage businesses in verifying that the original servicer has ownership rights to the loans in case one wishes to sell its loans to another mortgage company.

Blockchain Mortgages' Advantages

For all parties participating in the mortgage process, blockchain technology has advantages. The following are some possible benefits of the technology:

- **More precise record-keeping**: As everyone who has ever bought a house knows, the conventional mortgage application process requires an amazing volume of documentation. Buyers must substantiate their assets, income, and work history. Underwriters and loan processors may find themselves engulfed in piles of paperwork. Blockchain gathers all required papers and data into digital records that can be accessed at any time by simply clicking a button.
- **Lower closing costs for buyers**: Blockchain technology can help cut expenses by doing away with the requirement for third parties throughout the settlement process.
- **Easier to confirm the chain of title**: When purchasing a home through a traditional manner, purchasers are frequently required to acquire title insurance in case the property is subject to liens. Title insurance is no longer necessary because blockchain technology greatly simplifies the chain of title verification process.
- **Smart contract implementation**: Smart contracts are coded sets of instructions that start acting upon the occurrence of a predetermined event. For instance,

the mortgage procedure can proceed automatically to the next stage if the buyer purchases homeowner's insurance.

Blockchain-Enabled Trade

The value of the world's cryptocurrency industry peaked at $3 trillion at the end of 2021. Blockchain technology is the foundation of cryptocurrencies like Ethereum and Bitcoin. The use of blockchain technology and the products and services it enables will continue to have a significant impact on corporate operations.

However, blockchain technology[3] is much more than just a cryptocurrency transfer method that is safe. It can be applied in areas other than finance, such as voting, healthcare, insurance, welfare benefits, gaming, and artist royalties.

The blockchain revolution is coming, and the world economy is getting ready thanks to the way technology is already affecting society and business on many fronts. If you think the word "revolution" sounds dramatic, consider this: eight of the top ten corporations in the world are developing a range of blockchain-based products.

Blockchain in Finance and Banking

Blockchain helps banks and financial services firms to make loan applications and payment record-keeping more efficient.

The banking sector is one that may stand to gain the most from incorporating blockchain technology into its operations. Financial institutions are only open for business five days a week, during regular business hours. This implies that you will probably have to wait until Monday morning for the money to appear in your account if you try to deposit a check on Friday at 6 p.m.

Because banks have a large volume of transactions to settle, even if you make your deposit during business hours, it may still take one to three days for the transaction to be verified. Blockchain, however, is a 24/7 system.

Banking: Blockchain is being used by banks and other financial services organizations to automate payment record-keeping and loan processing. Regardless of holidays, the time of day, or the week, customers can get their transactions processed in as little as 10 minutes by integrating blockchain into banks. This is essentially the same amount of time it takes to add a block to the blockchain. Banks may now transfer money more swiftly and securely between organizations because of blockchain technology. For instance, in the stock trading industry, the money and shares are frozen for up to three days throughout the settlement and clearing procedure (or longer, if trading overseas). Even the few days that the money is in transit can be very costly and risky for banks because of the scale of the amounts involved.

Blockchain is most usually associated with cryptocurrencies like Bitcoin, although it has a wide range of other possible uses.

Currency: Without the assistance of a central bank, cryptocurrencies run independently. Like any other currency, they are used by people to make purchases–mostly online. While Bitcoin is among the most well-known cryptocurrencies, there exist other others as well.

The following are some of the existing and possible applications of blockchain technology.

The Use of Blockchain Technology in Logistics

Businesses can use blockchain to confirm the origin of materials they employ in their products or to reassure consumers that an item comes from a verified source.

Blockchain in Real Estate Documents

Blockchain technology can be used to confirm or establish the identity of a property's owner. It can also assist in lowering the price of title searches and property insurance.

Mortgages: There are various ways in which blockchain technology might help the mortgage sector. It may contribute to accelerating transaction times, resulting in quicker settlements. It can also result in more accurate documentation and lower costs for all parties participating in the process.

Blockchain in Medical Field

Blockchain technology can be used by healthcare professionals to safely preserve patient medical records. Patients can have the assurance that their medical records are unchangeable by writing them onto the blockchain after they are created and signed. To ensure privacy, these private health records might be encrypted and kept on the blockchain using a private key, making them available to only specific people.

Concerns about patient privacy and security are paramount when it comes to electronic patient data storage. Patient information can be kept secret thanks to blockchain technology's security. The procedure of exchanging patient data with other physicians and healthcare providers is also made easier by blockchain technology.

Other primary applications for blockchain in healthcare include:

- Protection of healthcare data
- Personal health record data management
- Point-of-care genomics management
- Electronics health records data management

These are some innovative blockchain applications in this space:

- **MedicalChain:** Offers a blockchain solution to create a user-centric digital health record that can be shared with doctors easily. All information is recorded in an auditable, secure, and transparent format.
- **Guardtime:** This company is helping healthcare organizations and governments implement blockchain in their cybersecurity systems to keep essential data secure.
- **Curisium:** This blockchain platform is designed to streamline rebate negotiation and contract management through the use of innovative digital contracts.
- **Robomed:** This platform uses telemedicine sessions, chatbots, and wearable devices to collect patient data, recording it on blockchain so it can be shared securely with healthcare professionals.
- **The MediLedger Project:** Initially launched by Chronicled in 2019, the MediLedger Project aims to improve the track-and-trace capabilities for prescription medicine. Built to meet the requirements set out by the U.S. Drug Supply Chain Security Act (DSCSA), the blockchain healthcare project meets the legal requirements as well as supporting the operational needs of the pharmaceutical supply industry.

Blockchain in Elections and Voting

Election officials can use blockchain technology to capture and count people's votes immediately. Since the technology is more secure than other options, it would also cut down on the risk of voter fraud and tampering.

As previously mentioned, blockchain could be used to facilitate a modern voting system. Voting with blockchain carries the potential to eliminate election fraud and boost voter turnout, as was tested in the November 2018 midterm elections in West Virginia. Using blockchain in this way would make votes nearly impossible to tamper with. The blockchain protocol would also maintain transparency in the electoral process, reducing the personnel needed to conduct an election and providing officials with nearly instant results. This would eliminate the need for recounts or any real concern that fraud might threaten the election.

Enterprise Blockchain Requirements

We believe that blockchain is a truly disruptive technology that can transform business networks. We also believe that this innovation has to happen in the open, collaborating with other technology companies and industries. To this end, IBM continues to contribute code to several active Hyperledger projects.

From IBM's perspective, industrial-grade blockchain technologies have the following characteristics:

- A shared, permissioned ledger is the append-only system of record (SOR) and single source of truth. It is visible to the authenticated members in the business network channels.
- A consensus protocol agreed to by all participating members of the business network ensures that the ledger is updated only with network-verified transactions.
- Cryptography ensures tamper-proof security, authentication, and integrity of transactions.
- Chaincode (also called smart contracts) encapsulates participant terms of agreement for the business that takes place on the network; chaincode is stored on the validating peer nodes in the blockchain.
- In addition to these attributes, enterprise blockchain technology needs to meet key industry requirements such as performance, verified identifies, and private and confidential transactions. Hyperledger Fabric has been architected to meet these needs. It is also designed with a pluggable consensus model, allowing businesses to select an optimal algorithm for their networks.

Currency

Blockchain forms the bedrock for cryptocurrencies like Bitcoin. The U.S. dollar is controlled by the Federal Reserve. Under this central authority system, a user's data and currency are technically at the whim of their bank or government. If a user's bank is hacked, the client's private information is at risk. If the client's bank collapses or the client lives in a country with an unstable government, the value of their currency may be at risk. In 2008, several failing banks were bailed out – partially using taxpayer money. These are the worries out of which Bitcoin was first conceived and developed.

By spreading its operations across a network of computers, blockchain allows Bitcoin and other cryptocurrencies to operate without the need for a central authority. This not only reduces risk but also eliminates many of the processing and transaction fees. It can also give those in countries with unstable currencies or financial infrastructures a more stable currency with more applications and a wider network of individuals and institutions with whom they can do business, both domestically and internationally.

Using cryptocurrency wallets for savings accounts or as a means of payment is especially profound for those who have no state identification. Some countries may be war-torn or have governments that lack any real infrastructure to provide identification. Citizens of such countries may not have access to savings or brokerage accounts – and, therefore, no way to safely store wealth.

Property Records

If you have ever spent time in your local recorder's office, you will know that the process of recording property rights is both burdensome and inefficient. Today, a physical deed must be delivered to a government employee at the local recording office, where it is manually entered into the county's central database and public index. In the case of a property dispute, claims to the property must be reconciled with the public index.

This process is not just costly and time-consuming – it is also prone to human error, where each inaccuracy makes tracking property ownership less efficient. Blockchain has the potential to eliminate the need for scanning documents and tracking down physical files in a local recording office. If property ownership is stored and verified on the blockchain, owners can trust that their deed is accurate and permanently recorded.

In war-torn countries or areas that have little to no government or financial infrastructure, and certainly no recorder's office, it can be nearly impossible to prove ownership of a property. If a group of people living in such an area is able to leverage blockchain, then transparent and clear timelines of property ownership could be established.

Supply Chains

As in the IBM Food Trust example, suppliers can use blockchain to record the origins of materials that they have purchased. This would allow companies to verify the authenticity of not only their products but also common labels such as "*Organic*," "*Local*," and "*Fair Trade*."

As reported by Forbes, the food industry is increasingly adopting the use of blockchain to track the path and safety of food throughout the farm-to-user journey.

Any industry or organization involved in the recording and overseeing of transactions of any kind stands to benefit from moving its operations onto a blockchain-based platform. Take a look at the following predictions of how blockchain technology will influence various sectors of the global landscape.

Blockchain Technology Disrupting Financial Services

One area predicted to continue evolving with blockchain technology is cross-border payments. These recent developments are leading transformation on this front:

- **IBM's Blockchain World Wire:** This blockchain-enabled conduit used the Stellar protocol and allowed for banks to clear and settle cross-border payments almost immediately. The World Wire API integrated into banks' payment systems, with World Wire then converting the digital asset into currency, completing the transaction. In light of the COVID-19 pandemic, IBM ceased running the network and made the code open source, inviting the development community to build on their learnings.

- **Paystack:** Paystack creates payment infrastructures and connects payment processors with each other with the goal of making it quicker and easier to facilitate online payments. In October 2020, financial services company Stripe acquired Pay stack for $200 million. The service expanded to South Africa in May 2021, by that point it was powering 50 percent of online payments in Nigeria, where it was founded. In September, it became the first Nigerian payment gateway to become an Apple Pay partner, opening it up to 380 million users across 60 countries.
- **Ripple and Pyypl:** San Francisco-based software vendor Ripple has been specializing in global real-time payments, based on blockchain technology, since 2014. They recently partnered with Dubai-based technology company Pyypl, which has created a blockchain-based platform offering non-bank financial services via smartphone. Because the platform doesn't require the pre-funding needed in traditional cross-border payments, where additional funds must be kept in the user's bank account, this should help increase the liquidity of companies that use it.
- **AZA Finance:** This company uses blockchain technology for small businesses to send and collect payments to and from Africa. By converting the relevant fiat currencies into stablecoins rather than US dollars when trading, AZA says it can reduce reliance on a dollar-dominated system, trade during banking holidays, and increase trade efficiency.

Blockchain technology has applications outside of payments too. Following are additional examples of fintech innovations using blockchain:

- **Securrency:** This is a trading platform for cryptocurrencies and any kind of asset. It is exchanged through Securrency tokens, which allows cryptos to be traded outside of their dedicated exchanges.
- **ABRA:** This global app and cryptocurrency wallet allows you to buy, invest, and store up to 100 cryptocurrencies. The company recently raised $55 million in funding to help develop a comprehensive product range to help people manage their money.
- **Numerai:** This company aims to build an open-source hedge fund by sending encrypted datasets to thousands of decentralized quantitative analysts, who build predictive models. The best are rewarded with Numerai's token and used to create a trading meta-model.

- **Bloom:** This startup is applying blockchain to credit scoring by building a protocol that manages risk, identity, and credit scoring.

If you want to learn more about cryptocurrencies, UCT offers the Blockchain and Digital Currency: The Future of Money online short course. This six-week program reveals how crypto assets are set to shape the future of the financial industry, while imparting a practical working knowledge of blockchain and cryptocurrency assets.

Also focusing on cryptocurrencies is the SDA Bocconi School of Management's Bitcoin and Blockchain Program. This five-week online course explores the technical pillars that underpin these technologies, and is ideally suited to individuals driven to remain relevant by upskilling to address this new business need.

Adopting Blockchain Technology in Business

Blockchain technology has huge implications for business, with the main drivers for adoption being higher revenue, lower costs, and more efficient use of time. Examples of how blockchain is being adopted by corporate companies include:

- **ConsenSys Quorum:** Originally developed by JP Morgan, Quorum is an enterprise-grade service that helps companies grow and manage large-scale blockchain networks.
- **LVMH:** The luxury goods company is tracking goods and fighting counterfeiting through blockchain. It has registered more than 10 million products on a platform created in conjunction with Prada and Cartier.
- **MediaChain:** This blockchain database was acquired by Spotify to manage copyrights and royalty payments, and resolve rights holder issues.

Application of Blockchain in Legal Field

In law, blockchain technology can be used to create smart contracts, as well as validate ownership documents such as title deeds. If used to validate, authenticate, and secure courtroom evidence, blockchain could improve efficiency in the criminal justice system.

Smart contracts are digital contracts that uphold the nature of a legal contract. The terms of the contract are written in code and automatically executed when the agreed conditions have been met, without the need for any involvement or intermediary. When this happens, the blockchain is updated, and only parties with permissions can see the results.

Some states in the U.S. have begun to permit the use of smart contracts in certain legal contexts. These include Arizona, where parties can create enforceable legal agreements through smart contracts, and California, where marriage licenses can be issued via blockchain.

Use of Blockchain in Real Estate

Real estate transactions are usually expensive, paperwork-heavy, and require the assistance of agents. Blockchain has the potential to ease the process of finding and buying real estate through tokenization, using digital real estate tokens to represent physical assets. This would:

- Ease transfer between buyer and seller by cutting out the need for a middleman.
- Provide irrefutable proof of ownership via a distributed digital ledger.
- Facilitate smaller real estate investments, as a token can be divided in the same way as a bitcoin.
- Improve market security and transparency because every transaction is processed and approved by others.

Examples of real estate using blockchain technology include Deedcoin, which connects real estate agents with home buyers and reduces commission to 1 percent, and Harbor, which enables the tokenization of private securities, REITs, land titles, and land registry records.

Logistics and Supply Chain Through Blockchain

Supply chains: The links between the creation and distribution of goods – have always been disrupted by innovation. Today's supply chains are extremely complex, threading multiple continents, including huge numbers of invoices and payments, involving myriad entities, and potentially extending over months.

Due to this complexity, blockchain is an attractive means to transform the supply chain and logistics industry. When goods are transferred to a new step in the supply chain, the process can be logged securely and permanently, creating an immutable, auditable history from its point of origin to that of sale.

Following are some examples of innovative logistics and supply chain-focused blockchain applications:

- **TradeLens:** Developed by IBM, this blockchain solution for logistics and supply chain provides transparency and improved efficiency through blockchain, offering a holistic view of shipment data and documents. More than half the world's container ships are registered on the platform, and in 2020 it processed 1 billion shipments.
- **Provenance:** Consumers are increasingly demanding transparency regarding the products they purchase to ensure the ethical sourcing and production of products. Provenance uses blockchain to prove chain-of-custody and certification of supply chains.

- **Honeywell:** The US conglomerate has partnered with iTRACE and SecureMarking to secure, track, and trace its aerospace parts throughout the world. It does so using laser-etching and invisible ink on the parts, encoding this information onto a blockchain ledger for digital authenticity.
- **De Beers:** De Beers mines, trades, and markets more than 30% of the world's supply of diamonds. The company uses a blockchain ledger to trace diamonds from the mine to the customer purchase, and helps confirm diamonds are free from conflict.

Impact of Blockchain Innovation on Business

The tools and platforms described are just a few examples of how blockchain technology has been applied in various industries. This highlights the implications this technology will have for businesses, trade, and entire economies and how important it is for business leaders, tradespeople, and decision-makers to become familiar with the technology.

Deloitte's 2021 Global Blockchain Survey found that 81 percent of business leaders believed blockchain was broadly scalable and had achieved mainstream adoption. Blockchain skills have become one of the most sought-after proficiencies in the world, with the demand increasing by 59 percent from the end of 2020 to the beginning of 2021.

Trade

Blockchain in financial trading means transparent pricing, new alternative markets, faster payment processing and immutable transaction recordkeeping. Blockchain's ledger techno Blockchain enables data to be recorded in a secure digital format by providing real-time information on transactions between different parties, be they corporations, supplier networks, investment pools, or an international supply chain. Technology is enabling people to trade for lower costs and at faster speeds than ever before.

It provides all parties with a record that is secure, encrypted, transparent, easy to access, and impossible to tamper with. Although blockchain emerged within the financial system with the launch of cryptocurrency Bitcoin, today it is used in a wide range of activities, including ones that are directly or indirectly related to foreign trade.

The long value chain tied to international trade includes vast, complex areas like logistics, transportation, customs administration, financing, and administrative procedures between firms, all of which could be streamlined by adopting this technology.

Blockchain optimizes processes, makes goods traceable, guarantees the security of payments and financing, facilitates the verification of digital quality and origin certifications, enables real-time sharing of information on the different stages of trade, and helps improve how related public and private services operate, among other benefits.

Blockchain provides solutions for trade operations by simplifying cross-border trade, contributing to competitive improvements, and reducing transaction costs. Although blockchain has been used within foreign trade for several years, its significance has increased since the start of the COVID-19 health crisis and it is expected to play an even more prominent role in the post-pandemic world.

A concrete example of how blockchain is being used today comes from French retailer Auchan, which has implemented an international food traceability system using blockchain throughout its supply chain. After piloting this solution in Vietnam, it has applied this technology to track goods and services originating in France, Italy, Spain, Portugal, and Senegal, working in partnership with Te-Food. The system enables the tracking of different products from farm to fork and the recording of food quality data (and related logistical information) via QR codes.

International Trade

International trade is a $16 trillion market that accounts for the exchange of capital, goods, and services across international borders or territories. It is broadly split into two categories:

- 75% various goods typically shipped by shipping containers or ground transportation
- 25% commodities

From a shipping and transportation viewpoint, the trade and financing industry primarily suffers from a lack of trust and coordination between exporters and importers, particularly within emerging to developed markets. Additionally, the industry maintains various operational inefficiencies due to the complex nature of operational processes in the international trade of goods and commodities. For instance, shipping and trading still heavily rely on human resources and are affected by manual and paper-based processes which are very costly, slow and error-prone.

Exporters and importers face challenges to finance or guarantee their transactions, which stymies growth and limits the benefits from globalization. Historically, this space has been very resistant to advances in technology and digitization although some technologies like Commodities Trading and Risk Management (CTRM) solutions have proved useful.

Benefits of Blockchain in Global Trade and Commerce

Over the past 10-15 years, many start-ups and technology companies have attempted to develop products with mixed success – until the emergence of blockchain technology for which international trade is identified as a primary use case[4]. The potential impact of blockchain technology on international trade finance has spurred many companies and consortiums to update their outdated technology. Beyond ushering in the era of digitization, blockchain enables the tokenization of existing documents, letters of credit, and more. Smart contracts will improve coordination between exporters and importers through the automation of agreements, business events, and other manually intensive processes. The global adoption of blockchain technology will create even greater benefits for cross-border coordination, trade settlement, and standardization.

Blockchains are effective in scenarios where a confirmed sequence of events is business critical. And they work very well where predetermined business logic needs to be respected by multiple nodes in a network, with no scope for tampering. So far, several startups have attempted to address trade finance issues with blockchain. However, we have found their approach to be defective in two key regards.

Firstly, they usually aim to map existing processes into a blockchain, rather than fundamentally rethinking the underlying business model and information flows.

This approach has led to multiple solutions providing a "digital letter of credit". What these solutions fail to do is a question whether such a letter is needed, when credit can be issued and confirmed and payment initiated instantly.

Secondly, they tend to map only a single, isolated piece of the value chain, focused usually on letters of credit or bills of lading. They are much less concerned with the issuance and advisory aspects that are part of the wider process. Importers and exporters today pay for services in these areas and they are expensive. Yet in practice, they are often neglected and the customer experience is poor. By contrast, along the total trade finance transaction, we foresee blockchain addressing two fundamental challenges:

- **Automating issuance:** Assume the various network players have adopted the proposed platform. Now they will record events such as issuance of credit, shipment of goods or the payment for a transaction in Realtime to the blockchain, which in turn broadcasts this out to the network. Given this public record of events, a paper-trail-chasing operations team is no longer required. And subsequent steps in the workflow can be reliably initiated on an automated basis.
- **Full audit transparency**: Shipments are prone to fraud or illegal activity. A

shipping container labelled as carrying bananas may in reality be freighting weapons. Effective control is clearly needed.

Blockchain can very effectively meet this need through a network-controlled mechanism, where a "*shared truth*" is established by participation of the majority. In addition, all salient events, such as term agreements, shipments or payments can be traced back and the likelihood of erroneous events is minimized. Access to this information can be limited if desired to approved network participants, resulting in a hybrid that shares traits of both private and public blockchains.

As well as addressing the areas referenced above, blockchain can enable cost-effective development of client endpoints across the globe. This gives key actors the physical ability to feed information directly into the system in real time. If we assume the platform champions decide to adopt open development, and to make the blockchain's logic accessible, we see much more than a workflow solution emerging. We witness the creation of an entire ecosystem of trade finance applications. These will all be backed by the same internal logic, but are closely tailored to the needs of different actors, such as a shipping coordinator, a bank employee or a buyer of goods.

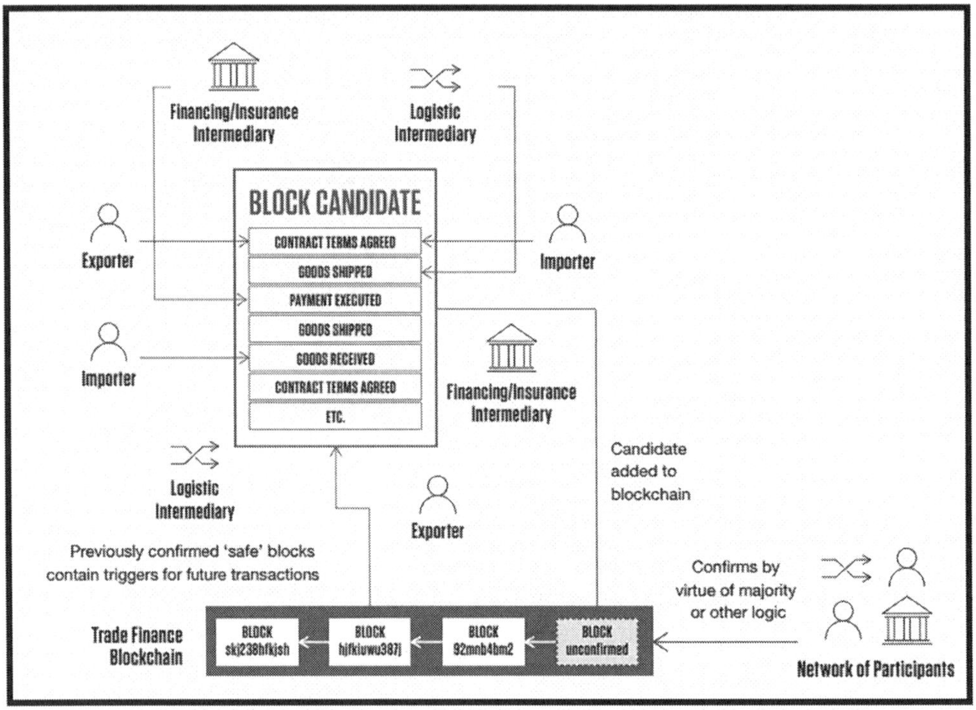

Figure 7.5: *The trade finance transactional environment workflow interpreted as a blockchain sequence*

Just as most of the protocols on internet like TCP/IP, HTML, and HTTP provide shared and open standards and protocols that enabled the internet to become what it is today, so too can blockchain and related technologies create a flatter, smarter, more connected, and overall better world for global trade and commerce.

Trade Finance

Trade Finance is the financing of goods or services in a trade or transaction, from a supplier through to the end buyer[5]. It accounts for 3% of global trade, worth some $3tn annually. The '*Trade Finance*' is an umbrella term, which includes a variety of financial instruments that can be used by an importer or exporter.

These include:

- Purchase Order Finance
- Stock Finance
- Structured Commodity Finance
- Invoice Finance (Discounting and Factoring)
- Supply Chain Finance
- Letters of Credit (LCs)
- Bonds and Guarantees

The two terms *Import Finance and Export Finance* are used interchangeably with **Trade Finance.**

Trade Finance Benefit to Business

In business trade finance facilitates the growth of a business by securing funds required to purchase *goods and stock*. Managing cash and working capital is critical to the success of any business. Trade finance is a tool which is used to unlock capital from a company's existing stock or receivables or add further finance facilities based on a company's trade cycles.

To sum up a trade finance facility may allow you to offer more competitive terms to both suppliers and customers, by reducing payment gaps in your trade cycle. It is beneficial for supply chain relationships and growth as follows:

- Small to medium-term working capital, using the underlying products or services being imported/exported as security/collateral. It increases the revenue potential of a company, and earlier payments may allow for higher margins.
- Trade finance allows companies to request higher volumes of stock or place larger orders with suppliers, leading to economies of scale and bulk discounts.
- Trade finance helps in strengthening the relationship between buyers and sellers, increasing profit margins. It allows a company to be more competitive.

- The work of managing the supply chain is critical for any business. Trade and supply chain finance helps ease out cash constraints or liquidity gaps – for suppliers, customers, third parties, employees or providers. Earlier payments also mitigate risk for suppliers.
- It is important to note that trade finance focuses more on the trade rather than the underlying borrower, that is, it is not balance sheet led. Therefore, small businesses with weaker balance sheets can use trade finance to trade significantly larger volumes of goods or services and work with stronger end customers.

Due to the factor of embedded risk mitigants that surround trade finance lending and instruments, it leads to the potential of a diversity of supplier base for trading companies. A more diverse supplier network increases competition and efficiency in markets and supply chains.

The trading companies can also mitigate business risks by using appropriate trade finance structures. Late payments from debtors, bad debts, excess stock and demanding creditors can have detrimental effects on a business. External financing or revolving credit facilities can ease this pressure by effectively financing trade flows.

Note : *The International Chamber of Commerce (ICC) is the world's largest business organization with a network of over 6 million members in more than 100 countries.*

we.trade: The Largest Blockchain-Enabled Trade Networks

Until the launch of we.trade, the universal solution for open account trading or documentary trading was to use paper. But the slow process led to a lot of replication, with business owners filling out the same documents for different trade partners and leaving themselves more susceptible to forgery and human error.

Luckily there is already a growing number of businesses looking for blockchain-based solutions like we.trade.

Already one of the largest blockchain-enabled trade networks in production, we.trade is designed to improve the trade finance lending process, supporting companies as they grow their business and expand into new markets. Starting in 2020, over the last few months we.trade has seen momentum continue to build as companies move to replace paper based trade finance processes with a digitized solution. Starting July 2020, we.trade had extended services to additional banks and clients across Europe before expanding the network globally, starting with Asia.

we.trade is a digital platform for securely managing, tracking and settling trade transactions between SMEs in one place. It aims are to make domestic and cross-border commerce easier for European companies by harnessing the power of distributed ledger technology.

The platform we.trade's is built on IBM's blockchain platform using the **open-source Hyperledger Fabric**.

we.trade is the world's first enterprise-grade, blockchain-enabled trade finance platform. It offers a safe and more reliable platform for buyers and sellers to Built on the latest version of the IBM Blockchain Platform. Itis backed by some of the world's top banks including ***CaixaBank, Deutsche Bank, Erste Group, HSBC, KBC, Nordea, Rabobank, Santander, Société Générale, UBS and UniCredit***. It is having facility to connect buyers, sellers, banks, insurers and logistics organizations in a network that simplifies cross-border trading.

we.trade also automate many of the processes around trade finance, as well as provide traders with access to *insurance, credit rating* and *logistics services*. Once on the network, traders can initiate orders, manage the order-to-payment process and attain financing. They can also search the network to discover new trading partners.trade globally using distributed ledger technology and smart contracts[6].

we.trade was established as an independent company based in Ireland in 2017 through a joint venture between seven European banks. Today the company is owned by 12 banks, technology leader IBM, and global commercial credit and business information provider CRIF with shareholders from institutions such as CaixaBank, Deutsche Bank, Erste Group, HSBC, KBC, Nordea, Rabobank, Santander, Societe Generale, UBS, and UniCredit. In 2019, the company brought we.trade technology to market under a SaaS model and has already onboarded 16 banks across 15 countries to join the platform.

Any company that is a customer of the European consortium of banks which supports the we.trade platform can easily sign up and begin trading. Abank *Flattered* – who is a client of *Nordea*, the leading bank in the Nordic region and a founding member of we.trade – was one of the early adopters to recognize how they could reap the benefits of we.trade to solve their cash flow problems and grow their business.

we.trade and Small and Medium-sized Enterprises (SMEs)

SMEs such as Flattered AB represent 90% of the businesses and 50% of the employment worldwide. According to the World Bank, SMEs traditionally do not have access to bank guarantees, invoice financing, or credit insurance to help maintain and scale their businesses. Instead, SME owners are left to navigate a laborious paper-based process to account for their international transactions with no protections against late invoice payments, fraud, or managing pre-payments.

Supply Chain Finance

By definition supply chain finance, also known as *supplier finance or reverse factoring*, is a set of solutions that optimizes cash flow by allowing businesses to lengthen their payment terms to their suppliers while providing the option for their large and SME suppliers to get paid early. The best part of Supply Chain Finance is a set of tech-based business and financing processes that lower costs and improve efficiency for the parties involved in a transaction. Supply chain finance works best when the buyer has a better credit rating than the seller and can thus access capital at a lower cost. Also, supply chain financing is a set of services available for medium-sized and big corporates. for example, loans, purchasing order finance, factoring and invoice discounting are the most common.

The difference between *trade finance and supply chain finance* is that while both trade finance and supply chain finance are designed to finance international and domestic supply chains, trade finance offers a broader set of solutions. In recent years, supply chain finance volumes have grown significantly, reaching a total value of $1.31 trillion in 2020, according to the latest World Supply Chain Finance Report.

Worldwide large manufacturers, such as airplane manufacturer Boeing Co., and other global companies, including soft drinks producer Keurig Dr Pepper Inc., are avid users of supply-chain financing to extend payment terms. But there tends to be a barrier to entry for some businesses, especially those with weaker credit ratings.

Digital Identity in Blockchain

Since the dawn of the Internet, identity management has been a key concern, with billions of dollars being spent on usability, security, and privacy[7]. Despite very huge investment, managing digital identities continues to be plagued by three Cs – Cumbersome, Costly, and Challenging.

With data driving the world today, digital identity is critical to most business and social transactions. But traditional identity systems continue to be highly vulnerable, with single points of failure, attracting continuous attempts to gain access to the complete repository of high-value data.

Blockchain can empower users to have greater control over their own identity.

Organizations can use the information only with customers' consent and no central entity would be able to compromise a consumer's identity.

Meaning of Identity

Blockchain has facilitated the so-called self-sovereign identity, which is inherently unalterable and more secure than traditional identity systems. As such this has the potential to completely change the way we use identities to connect to different online services. Individuals would use their self-sovereign ID to verify their identity, removing the need for passwords.

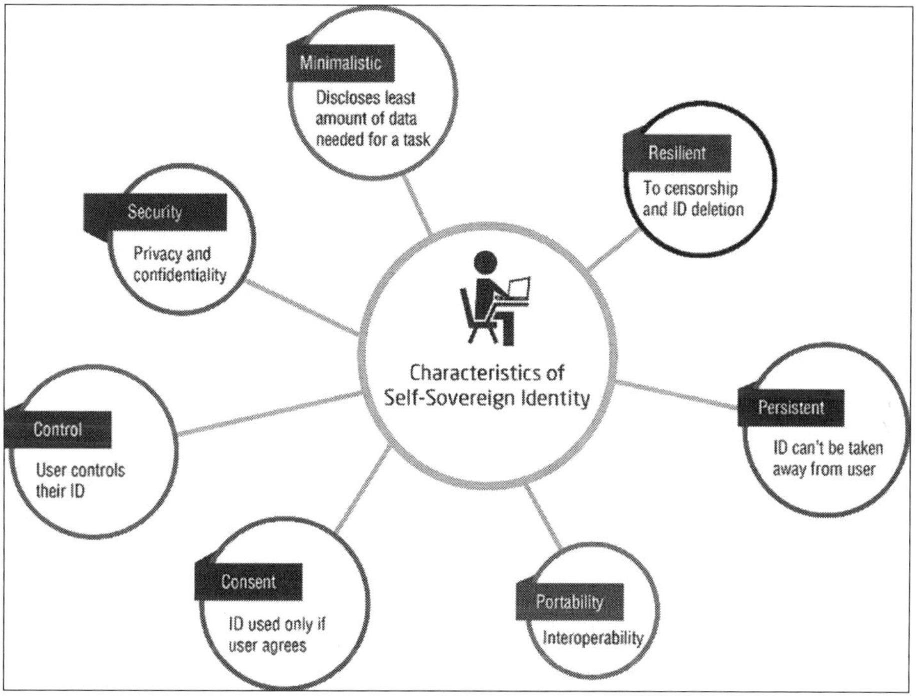

Figure 7.6: *Characteristics of Identity in Blockchain transactions*

As with every lifechanging innovation, there's been an extended period of evolution, with experts exchanging ideas and little consensus on what self-sovereign ID means! It's a concept that stems from the belief that an individual must have control over the administration of his identity.

The ID cannot be locked into one site and there needs to be interoperability of the ID across multiple platforms, with user consent.

Most experts have been contemplating the summation of various identifying information like demographic and employment related data and even information about the individual revealed by other people.

In principle, self-sovereign identity would allow users to control their identities in following manner:

1. Access and update information (though third-party verification may be required with some claims)
2. Choose the information that they prefer to keep private
3. Transporting the data (to another organization or even another jurisdiction if they relocate)
4. Delete the identity if that's what is wanted

Such a system would need to ensure certain things:

- Powerful algorithms to validate an identity and its claims
- Independent of a particular platform or architecture
- Identities to have a long shelf life (ideally forever)
- Interoperability (to make it widely available)
- Sharing of data only with the consent of the user
- Organizations should be able to access only what is needed and not the complete information
- Protection of user rights

Managing Multiple Identities

Use of multiple Identities: An individual may have one identity across multiple platforms or may want different identities supporting different 'personas' for the workplace, friends, family, and so on.

It is noteworthy that Blockchain can support this flexibility and offer a key for each of these identities, giving the user the power to decide which persona to use in a particular situation.

Anonymous Authentication

The solution deploys anonymous authentication to ensure maximum security. If a public key is needed to access one's digital identity, this key is prone to hacker attacks. Having anonymous authentication allows individuals to use unique attributes that identify them, eliminating the need for a public key.

Advantages of having digital identity:

- It puts control of your personal data back into your hands rather than being in the hands of industry giants.
- Addresses issues faced by refugees. They have no access to the country they belong to. They don't have proper documentation. They cannot borrow money, open an account, buy a house or start a business. They remain as non-entities and cannot participate in society.
- Removes the need to deal with bureaucratic processes for passport creation.
- Enhances security and privacy of medical records and intellectual property, while facilitating compliance with regulations protecting patient data.
- Simplifies KYC processes. Currently, every bank and financial institution individually performs the KYC process, validates the information and documents, and stores a digitized version. With digital identity being

maintained on a shared ledger, banks can access relevant parts of the stored data (with customer consent) and perform due diligence.

Blockchain: The Challenges Facing Governments

To make these benefits a reality, the governments of LAC countries need to tackle the challenges that implementing blockchain implies[6].

These challenges fall into three groups:

- The first concerns technical issues, which include the difficulties associated with developing technological infrastructure.
- The second relates to administration and governance, including the need for open standards and the creation of sector and business coalitions in different LAC countries to develop interoperability and economies of scale.
- The third issue is large-scale implementation, which includes data quality, the participation of all players involved in the transaction, the development of inclusive systems, and secure interfaces with legacy systems.

The IDB provides - through its Integration and Trade Sector, LAC countries with different technical and financial support programs to help spread blockchain technology and its use in international trade, drawing on the lessons learned from the development and implementation of the CADENA initiative.

For international trade this is a major new opportunity, one that is described in detail in "*Blockchain and International Trade: New Technologies for a Bigger and Better Latin America International Insertion*". LAC cannot remain on the sidelines when it comes to increasing the quantity and quality of trade flows between countries in the region and with the rest of the world.

Tata Steel has executed a blockchain enabled paperless export order with a metals major in Bangladesh. This makes it the first such deal executed between an India-based company and a counterparty in Bangladesh assisted by different banks at respective ends. This transaction was facilitated and expediated by Standard Chartered, India, and was conducted on Contour's blockchain trade platform, which enables banks, corporates, and other trade partners across the world to transact with each other.

Standard Chartered Bank advised and confirmed the letter of credit (LoC) favoring Tata Steel basis instructions received over Contour and was also able to present documents to the buyer's bank over the platform. This helped in early resolution of discrepancies and reducing the overall turn-around-time from weeks to days.

The seamless transmission of LoC and e-presentation of document between the two different banks at both ends via the platform under three hours is a testament to reduced paperwork and time, and increased operational efficiency brought about by this solution.

Rajeev Singhal, Vice President (Flat Products), Tata Steel, said: "*Tata Steel has made pioneering efforts this year to digitally transform its trade practices that are sustainable, efficient, and also saves time. We are glad and more confident now that we have executed the first multi-bank blockchain enabled trade. The technology along with the pivoting efforts of Tata Steel provides efficiency and agility in enabling a better customer interface. The Covid-19 pandemic has highlighted that technology will lead the way of doing business in future and experimentation using blockchain for better customer experience is one such step towards enabling this transformation.*"

This integrated solution using blockchain technology allows all parties involved in the transaction to communicate on a single platform in real time. It aims to reduce processing time by digitizing the entire LC process and eliminating the operational inefficiencies as compared to traditional paper-intensive process of LoCs. Further, this technology also enhances the safety of transactions. The information can be shared only with other authorized members on the network and is immutable, reducing the risk of data manipulation and fraud while increasing transparency for all parties involved in the transaction.

Earlier this year, Tata Steel executed its first blockchain enabled trade and this will be its first multi-bank transaction out of India. The Company is committed to move towards digitally enabled transactions which will help in seamless and efficient trading practices in the future.

About Tata Steel

Tata Steel group is among the top global steel companies with an annual crude steel capacity of 33 million tons per annum. It is one of the world's most geographically diversified steel producers, with operations and commercial presence across the world. The group recorded a consolidated turnover of US $21.06 billion in the financial year ending March 31, 2021.

Benefits of Blockchain

Blockchain can be used to[8]:

- Facilitate the traceability of traded goods, which helps reduce logistics costs and safeguard operations from start to finish;
- Contribute to the digitalization of the entire rules of origin process at every stage, which is key to streamlining certifications and customs clearance;
- Address the challenges of cross-border data exchanges between public agencies or authorities and private companies. Through the CADENA initiative,

which the IDB is facilitating as part of its LACChain program, eight customs authorities in LAC are now sharing data from firms that have been certified as Authorized Economic Operators (AEOs), as stipulated in their mutual recognition agreements;

- Modernize Single Windows for Foreign Trade (VUCEs) to streamline operations and reduce transaction costs by increasing interoperability between players and facilitating access to information for all parties involved ;
- Transfer payments more quickly and cheaply than is currently possible through the SWIFT network. As well as reducing transaction times, blockchain commissions are lower and without maximum limits, which is especially advantageous for exporting SMEs;
- Reduce the time needed to issue a letter of credit from 7 to 10 days to as little as 4 hours.

Conclusion

In this chapter, we learned how blockchain technology can streamline cross-border payments by facilitating faster, cheaper, and more transparent transactions. We gained knowledge about the KYC process and its importance in financial regulations. Additionally, we are able to identify key areas within an enterprise that could benefit from blockchain implementation, such as managing currency, property records, and supply chains. By studying this chapter, we gained a comprehensive understanding of how blockchain technology can be leveraged across various industries, potentially leading to a more efficient, transparent, and secure business landscape. In the next chapter, we will learn Hyperledger and Smart Contracts.

References

[1] How Blockchain works in cross-border payments, Murali Ramakrishnan, Senior Principal Consultant, May 25, 2021

[2] ASSURANCE FINANCIAL BLOG, How Blockchain Technology Is Impacting the Mortgage Industry, https://assurancemortgage.com/how-blockchain-technology-impacts-mortgage-industry/

[3] The Future of Blockchain Technology in 2022,7.1.22, https://www.getsmarter.com/blog/market-trends/the-future-of-blockchain-technology-in-2022/

[4] Blockchain for Global Trade and Commerce, https://consensys.net/blockchain-use-cases/global-trade-and-commerce/

[5] Trade Finance & International Trade, HTTPs://www.tradefinanceglobal.com/trade-finance/

[6] Case Study: How we.trade Helps Businesses Grow With Digital Smart Contracts Powered by Hyperledger fabric, https://www.hyperledger.org/learn/publications/wetrade-case-study

[7] What Blockchain can do for Digital Identity? https://www.nec.com/en/global/solutions/blockchain/blockchain-for-digital-identity.html

[8] Blockchain technology: a new opportunity for international trade, July 29, 2021, by Magdalena Barafani - Pablo M. Garcia - Ricardo Rozemberg

CHAPTER 8
Hyperledger and Smart Contracts

Introduction

Smart contracts and voting systems are extra facilities which have made Blockchain technology popular. We have learnt about distributed open environment in *Chapter* 4 titled *Distributed Consensus in Open Environments* and similarly closed environment in *Chapter* 6 titled *Distributed Consensus in Closed Environment*, which provides information about consensus models for permissioned blockchain. Fabric is the first completely expandable blockchain system for running distributed applications because it supports modular consensus protocols. This has later on become a part of Hyperledger. Launched in 2016, Hyperledger has more than 200 members from a variety of global industries including financial services, healthcare, supply chains, manufacturing, and the tech sector. Notable members include Walmart, Visa, FedEx, Huawei, Aetna, and Telefonica, among others.

We shall learn about various components of the Hyperledger Fabric Network.

Structure

In this chapter, we will discuss the following topics:

- Hyperledger Fabric
- Architecture of Hyperledger
- Writing a Blockchain Application
- Identity
- Policies in Hyperledger Fabric
- Access Control
- Membership Service Provider (MSP)
- Channels in Hyperledger System

- Transaction Validation
- Executing Contracts in Blockchain
- Smart Contract Platforms
- Benefits of Smart Contracts
- Challenges to Smart Contracts Technology

Hyperledger Fabric

Fabric is the first completely expandable blockchain system for running distributed applications because it supports modular consensus protocols. This means that the system can be customized to fit specific use cases and trust models. Additionally, Fabric is the first blockchain system that does not rely on a native cryptocurrency to execute distributed applications written in common, general-purpose programming languages. This is a stark contrast to current blockchain platforms, which demand that smart-contracts be cryptocurrency-dependent or written in domain-specific languages.

One of the Hyperledger projects housed by the Linux Foundation, the "Fabric" is a modular and expandable open-source architecture for implementing and running permissioned blockchains. This was later expanded as Hyperledger.

Using a portable idea of membership–which can be combined with industry-standard identity management–Fabric realizes the permissioned model. Fabric provides a whole new blockchain design and reworks how blockchains handle non-determinism, resource exhaustion, and performance threats in order to accommodate such flexibility.

Advantages of Hyperledger Fabric Architecture

The Hyperledger Fabric architecture delivers the following advantages[1]:

- **Permissioned blockchain framework:** Hyperledger Fabric is a permissioned blockchain framework with a modular architecture (plug-and-play). It utilizes container technology to host smart contract (Chaincode) which contains application logic. Before going to each component in detail, let us see a high-level transaction flow and basic components involved.
- **Open-source blockchain:** Hyperledger Fabric platform is an open-source blockchain framework hosted by the Linux Foundation. It has an active and growing community of developers. Hyperledger Fabric networks are permissioned, meaning all participating member's identities are known and authenticated.

- **Chaincode trust flexibility**: Hyperledger's architecture distinguishes between trust assumptions for ordering chaincodes, or blockchain applications. Put differently, one group of nodes (orderers) may provide the ordering service and accept some of them failing or misbehaving, and each chaincode may have a separate set of endorsers.
- **Capability to grow**: The system may scale better if these roles were performed by the same nodes since the endorser nodes in charge of a given chaincode are impertinent (orthogonal) to the orderers. Specifically, this happens when distinct chaincodes designate discontinuous endorsers, introducing a chaincode partitioning across endorsers and permitting simultaneous chaincode execution (endorsement). In addition, the ordering service's critical path is freed from the potentially expensive chaincode execution.
- **Propriety**: The architecture makes it easier to implement chaincodes with secrecy requirements for transaction, state updates, and content.
- **Modularity of consensus**: Because of its modular design, ordering services or pluggable consensus implementations are possible.

Architecture of Hyperledger

The blockchain is a decentralized network made up of numerous nodes that exchange messages with one another. The blockchain stores state and ledger data, performs transactions, and runs programs known as chaincode. Since transactions are operations performed on the chaincode, the chaincode serves as the focal point. All transactions on the Hyperledger network must be "endorsed," and only those that have been approved can be carried out and impact the state. System chaincodes are special chaincodes that are used for management functions and parameters. One or more of these code types may exist.

Transaction

There are two kinds of transactions:

- **Implement transactions** makes a new chaincode, and pass in a program. Upon successful execution of a deploy transaction, the chaincode is installed "on" the blockchain.
- Use transactions to carry out a task within the framework of previously implemented chaincode. A chaincode and one of its functionalities are referred to as **invoke transactions**. If the chaincode runs successfully, it performs the designated action, which could include changing the associated state and producing an output.

Invoke transactions are special cases of deploy transactions; an invoke transaction on a system chaincode corresponds to a deploy transaction that generates new chaincode.

Data Structures in Blockchain

An ordered set of back-linked transaction blocks makes up the blockchain data structure. It can be kept in a straightforward database or as a flat file. Every block can be uniquely identified by its hash, which is produced on the block header by the SHA256 cryptographic hash algorithm. Following are the various components of structure:

- **State**

A ledger state records a set of facts about a particular business object. In the context of blockchain and cryptocurrencies, a "state" is analogous to the contents of a database at one instant in time. For bitcoin, the "state" is the number of bitcoins that exist at that instant and what is necessary to transfer each one of them. For XRP, the "state" is how many XRP exist, which accounts hold them, the security settings of those accounts, what other assets exist, who holds them, what offers have been made to transfer one asset for another, and so on.

A "transition" is a discontinuous change, that is, a change that requires a jump. So, a "state transition" is a jump from one state to another. For bitcoin, a "state transition" occurs each time a block is accepted, causing the ownership of bitcoins to change. For XRP, a "state transition" occurs each time a new ledger is accepted, causing ownership of XRP, account settings, offers on the decentralized exchange, and other kinds of state to change.

One of the most important properties of almost all blockchains is that from minute to minute, every participant in that system can monitor each state transition as it happens and will refuse to accept that transition if it does not follow the system's rules. So, if you have one bitcoin now, the only way to convince bitcoin participants that you do not have that bitcoin anymore is to show them a transfer that you authorized.

Peers, not customers or orderers, are responsible for maintaining a state. Because only transactions within a specific chaincode are able to edit the keys associated with that code, keys in the KVS can be identified by their name as belonging to a specific chaincode. Any chaincode has the ability to read the keys of other chaincodes in theory.

The most recent state of the blockchain, also referred to as just "state," is represented as a versioned key-value store (KVS), in which values are random blobs and keys are names. Notably, the science fiction movie The Blob from the 1950s tells the story of an alien creature that falls on Earth and begins to devour everything in its path.

Cryptocurrency is the blob, the event horizon of today, the one-way door that has the potential to completely change the way we work, play, and live. Through put and get KVS-operations, the chaincodes (applications) operating on the blockchain manipulate these entries. Updates to the state are recorded and the state is kept around for future use. It should be noted that versioned KVS is used as the state model; actual KVSs, RDBMSs, or any other solution can be used in an implementation.

- **Ledger**

The ledger offers a verifiable history of all successful state modifications (here, valid transactions) and unsuccessful state change attempts (here, invalid transactions) that took place while the system was in operation.

Ledger is constructed by the *ordering service* as a *totally ordered hashchain of blocks* of (valid or invalid) transactions. The hashchain imposes the total order of blocks in a ledger and each block contains an array of *totally ordered transactions*, imposing total order across all transactions. Ledger is kept at all peers and, optionally, at a subset of orderers.

- **Nodes**

Nodes are the communication entities of the blockchain. A "node" is only a logical function in the sense that multiple nodes of different types can run on the same physical server. What counts is how nodes are grouped in "trust domains" and associated to logical entities that control them.

There are three types of nodes:

  - **Client** or **submitting-client**: A client that submits an actual transaction-invocation to the endorsers, and broadcasts transaction-proposals to the ordering service.
  - **Peer**: A node that commits transactions and maintains the state and a copy of the ledger. Besides, peers can have a special endorser role.
  - **Ordering-service-node** or **orderer**: A node running the communication service that implements a delivery guarantee, such as atomic or total order broadcast.

Client: The client represents the entity that acts on behalf of *an end-user*. It must connect to a peer for communicating with the blockchain. The client may connect to any peer of its choice. Clients create and thereby invoke transactions. They communicate with both peers and the ordering service.

Peer: A peer receives ordered state updates in the form of blocks from the ordering service and maintain the state and the ledger.

Peers can additionally take up a special role of an *endorsing peer*, or an *endorser*. The special function of an endorsing peer occurs with respect to a particular chaincode and consists in endorsing a transaction before it is committed. Every chaincode may specify an *endorsement policy* that may refer to a set of endorsing peers. The policy defines the necessary and sufficient conditions for a valid transaction endorsement (typically a set of endorsers' signatures). In the special case of deploy transactions that install new chaincode, the (deployment) endorsement policy is specified as an endorsement policy of the system chaincode.

Ordering-service-nodes (Orderers):

The **orderers** form the ordering service, that is, a communication fabric that provides delivery guarantees. The ordering service can be implemented in different ways: ranging from a centralized service (example, in development and testing) to distributed protocols that target different networks and node fault models.

Ordering service provides a shared communication channel to *clients* and *peers*, offering a *broadcast service* for messages containing transactions. Clients connect to the channel and may broadcast messages on *the channel* which are then delivered to all peers. The channel supports atomic delivery of all messages, that is, message communication with total-order delivery and (implementation specific) reliability. In other words, the channel outputs the same messages to all connected peers and it outputs them to all peers in the same logical order. This atomic communication guarantee is also called *total-order broadcast*, *atomic broadcast*, or *consensus* in the context of distributed systems. The communicated messages are the candidate transactions for inclusion in the blockchain state.

Partitioning (Ordering Service Channels)

Ordering service may support multiple channels similar to the topics of a publish/subscribe (pub/sub) messaging system. Clients can connect to a given channel, send messages, and obtain the messages that arrive. Channels can be thought of as partitions, clients connecting to one channel are unaware of the existence of other channels, but clients may connect to multiple channels. Some ordering service implementations included with Hyperledger Fabric support multiple channels for simplicity of presentation.

Ordering service API: Peers connect to the channel provided by the ordering service, via the interface provided by the latter. The ordering service API consists of two basic operations (more generally asynchronous events):

TODO add the part of the API for fetching particular blocks under client/peer specified sequence numbers.

Ledger and block formation: The ledger contains all data output by the ordering service. In a nutshell, it is a sequence of deliver (seqno, prevhash, blob) events, which forms a hash chain according to the computation of prevhash described before.

Most of the time, for efficiency reasons, instead of outputting individual transactions (blobs), the ordering service will group (batch) the blobs and output blocks within a single deliver event. In this case, the ordering service must impose and convey a deterministic ordering of the blobs within each block. The number of blobs in a block may be chosen dynamically by an ordering service implementation.

Hyperledger Fabric network has the following components:

- Assets
- Shared ledger
- Smart contract
- Peer nodes
- Channel
- Organizations
- Membership Services Provider (MSP)
- Ordering service

Hyperledger incubates and supports a range of blockchain business technologies, frameworks, libraries, and applications. The Hyperledger project hosts several blockchain frameworks, including Hyperledger Fabric.

Components of a Hyperledger Fabric Network

A Hyperledger Fabric network has these components:

- **Assets**: An asset is anything that has value. It has state and ownership. Assets are represented in Hyperledger Fabric as a collection of key-value pairs.
- **Shared Ledger**: The ledger records the state and ownership of an asset. It consists of two components:
  - The world state describes the state of the ledger at a given point in time. It is the database of the ledger.
  - The blockchain is a transaction log history that records all transactions.
- **Smart Contract**: Hyperledger Fabric smart contracts are called chaincode. Chaincode is a software that defines assets and related transactions; in other words, it contains the business logic of the system. Chaincode is invoked when an application needs to interact with the ledger. It can be written in Golang or Node.js.
- **Peer Nodes**: Peers are a fundamental element of the network because they host ledgers and smart contracts. A peer executes chaincode, accesses ledger data, endorses transactions, and interfaces with applications. Some peers can be endorsing peers, or endorsers. Every chaincode may specify an endorsement policy, which defines the necessary and sufficient conditions for a valid transaction endorsement.

- **Channel**: Channels are a logical structure formed by a collection of peers. This capability allows a group of peers to create a separate ledger of transactions.
- **Organizations**: The Hyperledger Fabric network is built from the peers owned and contributed by the different organizations that are members of the network. The network exists because organizations contribute their individual resources to the collective network. Peers have an identity (digital certificate) assigned by a Membership Service Provider from its owning organization. Peers of different organizations can be on the same channel.
- **Membership Services Provider (MSP)**: The MSP is implemented as a Certificate Authority to manage certificates used to authenticate member identity and roles. No unknown identities can transact in the Hyperledger Fabric network. It manages user IDs and authenticates all participants on the network which enables Hyperledger Fabric as a Private and Permissioned network.
- **Ordering Service**: Ordering service is an open-source collaborative effort created to advance cross-industry blockchain technologies for business use. This global collaboration is hosted by The Linux Foundation.

The ordering service packages transactions into blocks to be delivered to peers on a channel. It guarantees the transaction delivery in the network. It communicates with peers and endorsing peers. The supported configuration mechanisms for the ordering service are **Solo** and **Kafka**.

- **Software Development Kit (SDK)**: SDK is a set of tools provided by the manufacturer of (usually) a hardware platform, operating system (OS), or programming language. The Hyperledger Fabric SDK allows applications to interact with a Fabric blockchain network. It provides a simple API to submit transactions to a ledger or query the contents of a ledger with minimal code.

A software development kit (SDK) is a set of tools that provides a developer with the ability to build a custom app which can be added on, or connected to, another program. SDKs allow programmers to develop apps for a specific platform.

The SDK provides a layer of abstraction on top of the wire-level protobuf-based communication protocol used by client applications to interact with a Hyperledger Fabric blockchain network. It allows Java applications to manage the lifecycle of Hyperledger channels and user chaincode. Ideally, an SDK should include libraries, tools, relevant documentation, samples of code and implementations, process explanations and examples, guides for developer usage, limitation definitions, and any other additional offerings that would facilitate building functions that leverage the API.

An API is a set of libraries that make up the core language that you can work with out of the box, whereas an SDK is a development kit that facilitates usages of an API. Conceptually, both are a way for your program to interface with and control the resources provided by another piece of software.

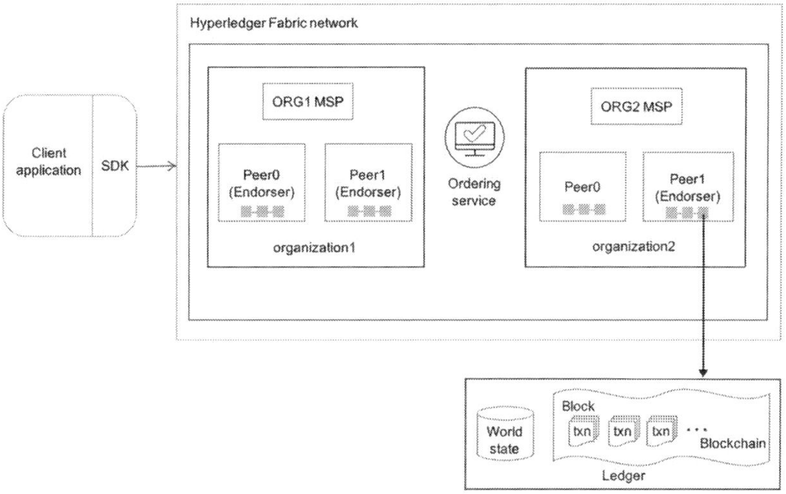

***Figure 8.1**: Components of a Hyperledger Fabric network (for simplicity, channels are not shown)*

Writing a Blockchain Application

In a blockchain solution, the Hyperledger Fabric network serves as a back-end with an application front-end to communicate with the network[2]. SDKs help you set up the communication between front and back end, such as the Node.js SDK and Java SDK. The SDK provides a way to execute user chaincode, perform transactions in the network, monitor events, and more.

To write a blockchain application, you need to:

- Write a chaincode in a supported programming language like Go.
- Deploy a chaincode on Hyperledger Fabric network.
- Develop a client application using an SDK.
- Know how to execute a blockchain transaction.

The high-level request flow of a transaction in a Hyperledger Fabric network flows in the following manner:

1. The client connects to a Hyperledger Fabric network using the Node.js or Java SDK. Using the SDK API, the client creates a transaction and sends it to the endorsing peer.
2. The endorsing peer verifies the client's signature, simulates a transaction, and sends an endorsement signature.

3. If the transaction is endorsed, the client submits the transaction to the ordering service. Otherwise, the transaction is cancelled.
4. The ordering service delivers a transaction to the peers. All peers commit and apply the same sequence of transactions and update their state.

Identity

Identity is an important feature of permissioned blockchain platform. In Hyperledger Fabric, each component needs to be identified before accessing the fabric network. The identity is represented by an X.509 digital certificate. Certificates are managed by way of Certification Authorities (or CA). Fabric CA is the Hyperledger's implementation of the Certification Authority.

For an identity to be verifiable, it must come from a trusted authority.

When interacting with a fabric network, the actor specifies and presents the digital certificate, and the fabric network accepts or denies, based on the policy.

The different actors in a blockchain network include peers, orderers, client applications, administrators and more[3]. Each of these actors – active elements inside or outside a network are able to consume services – has a digital identity encapsulated in an X.509 digital certificate. These identities really matter because they determine the exact permissions over resources and access to information that actors have in a blockchain network.

A digital identity, furthermore, has some additional attributes that Fabric uses to determine permissions. It gives the union of an identity and the associated attributes a special name known as **principal.** Principals are just like **`userIDs`** or **`groupIDs`**, but a little more flexible because they can include a wide range of properties of an actor's identity, such as the actor's organization, organizational unit, role, or even the actor's specific identity. When we talk about principals, they are the properties which determine their permissions.

For an identity to be verifiable, it must come from a trusted authority. A membership service provider (MSP) is how this is achieved in Fabric. More specifically, an MSP is a component that defines the rules that govern the valid identities for this organization. The default MSP implementation in Fabric uses X.509 certificates as identities, adopting a traditional Public Key Infrastructure (PKI) hierarchical model (more on PKI is discussed later).

A Simple Scenario to Explain the Use of an Identity

Imagine that you visit a supermarket to buy some groceries. At the checkout, you see a sign that says only Visa, Mastercard and AMEX cards are accepted. If you try to pay with a different card – let us call it an "ImagineCard" – it does not matter whether the card is authentic and you have sufficient funds in your account. It will be not be accepted.

Figure 8.2: *Use of identity*

Having a valid credit card is not enough – it must also be accepted by the store. PKIs and MSPs work together in the same way – a PKI provides a list of identities, and an MSP says which of these are members of a given organization that participates in the network.

PKI certificate authorities and MSPs provide a similar combination of functionalities. A PKI is like a card provider – it dispenses many different types of verifiable identities. An MSP, on the other hand, is like the list of card providers accepted by the store, determining which identities are the trusted members (actors) of the store payment network. MSPs turn verifiable identities into the members of a blockchain network.

A Public Key Infrastructure (PKI)

PKI is a collection of internet technologies that provides secure communications in a network. It is a PKI that places the S in HTTPS – and if you are reading this documentation on a web browser, you are probably using a PKI to make sure it comes from a verified source.

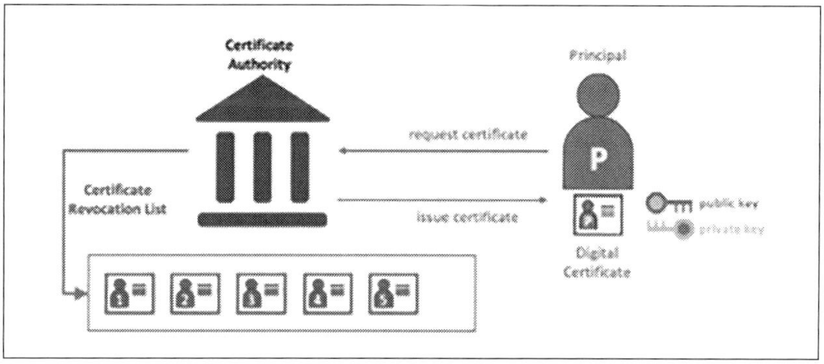

Figure 8.3: *Use of PKI Certification Process: The elements of PKI*

A PKI is comprised of Certificate Authorities who issue digital certificates to parties (example, users of a service, service provider), who then use them to authenticate themselves in the messages they exchange with their environment. A CA's Certificate Revocation List (CRL) constitutes a reference for the certificates that are no longer valid. Revocation of a certificate can happen for a number of reasons. For example, a certificate may be revoked because the cryptographic private material associated to the certificate has exposed.

Although a blockchain network is more than a communications network, it relies on the PKI standard to ensure secure communication between various network participants. It also ensures that messages posted on the blockchain are properly authenticated. It is therefore important to understand the basics of PKI and why MSPs are so important.

There are four key elements to PKI:

- Digital Certificates
- Public and Private Keys
- Certificate Authorities
- Certificate Revocation Lists

Digital Certificates

A digital certificate is a document which holds a set of attributes relating to the holder of the certificate. The most common type of certificate is the one compliant with the X.509 standard, which allows the encoding of a party's identifying details in its structure. Digital Signature Certificates (DSC) are the digital equivalent (that is electronic format) of physical or paper certificates. Few Examples of physical certificates are drivers' licenses, passports, or membership cards. Certificates serve as proof of identity of an individual for a certain purpose. For example, a driver's license identifies someone who can legally drive in a particular country. Likewise, a digital certificate can be presented electronically to prove one's identity, to access information or services on the Internet or to sign certain documents digitally.

The process of obtaining DSC from Certifying Authority includes the following:

- Digital Signature Certificate (DSC) applicants can directly approach Certifying Authorities (CAs) with original supporting documents. Self-attested copies are sufficient in this case.
- DSCs can also be obtained, wherever offered by CA, using Aadhar eKYC-based authentication. Supporting documents are not required in this case.

Certification Agencies:

Certification Agencies are appointed by the office of the Controller of Certification Agencies (CCA) under the provisions of IT Act, 2000. There are a total of eight

Certification Agencies authorized by the CCA to issue Digital Signature Certificates (DSCs).

Certifying Authorities:

Certifying Authorities (CA) has been granted a license to issue a digital signature certificate under Section 24 of the Indian IT-Act 2000. One can procure Class 2 or 3 certificates from any of the certifying authorities. Some of them are :

- National Informatics Center (NIC)
- IDRBT Certifying Authority

Policies in Hyperledger Fabric

The Configuration for a Hyperledger Fabric blockchain network is managed by policies. These policies generally reside in the channel configuration. The primary purpose of this document is to explain how policies are defined in and interact with the channel configuration. However, policies may also be specified in some other places, such as chaincodes. So, this information may be of interest outside the scope of channel configuration.

Understanding Policy

A policy, at its most basic level, is a set of rules that define the structure for how decisions are made and specific outcomes are reached. To that end, policies typically describe a who and a what, such as the access or rights that an individual has over an asset. We can see that policies are used throughout our daily lives to protect assets of value, from car rentals, health, our homes, and many more.

For example, an insurance policy defines the conditions, terms, limits, and expiration under which an insurance payout will be made. The policy is agreed to by the policy holder and the insurance company, and defines the rights and responsibilities of each party.

In Hyperledger Fabric, policies are the mechanism for infrastructure management as compared to an insurance policy that is put in place for risk management. In Fabric, policies represent how members come to an agreement on accepting or rejecting changes to the network, a channel, or a smart contract. Policies are agreed to by the consortium members when a network is originally configured, but they can also be modified as the network evolves. For example, they describe the criteria for adding or removing members from a channel, change how blocks are formed, or specify the number of organizations required to endorse a smart contract. These actions are described by a policy which defines who can perform the action. To sum up, everything you want to do on a Fabric network is controlled by a policy.

At its most basic level, a policy is a function which accepts an input as a set of signed data and evaluates successfully, or returns an error because some aspect of the signed data did not satisfy the policy.

More precisely, policies test whether the signer or signers of some data meet some condition required for those signatures to be considered 'valid'. This is useful for determining that the correct parties have agreed to a transaction, or change.

For example, in Hyperledger Fabric, a policy may define any of the following:

- Administrators from 2 out of 5 possible different organizations must sign.
- Any member from any organization must sign.
- Two specific certificates must be signed by both.

These policy rules are only examples, and other more powerful rules can be constructed.

Need of Policies in Hyperledger Fabric

It is the policies that makes Hyperledger Fabric different from other blockchains such as Ethereum or Bitcoin. In those systems, transactions can be generated and validated by any node in the network. The policies that govern the network are fixed at any point in time and can only be changed using the same process that governs the code. Because Fabric is a permissioned blockchain whose users are recognized by the underlying infrastructure, those users have the ability to decide on the governance of the network before it is launched, and can change the governance of a running network.

The contents of policies allow members to decide which organizations can access or update a Fabric network, and provide the mechanism to enforce those decisions. Policies contain the lists of organizations that have access to a given resource, such as a user or system chaincode. They also specify how many organizations need to agree on a proposal to update a resource, such as a channel or smart contracts. Once they are written, policies evaluate the collection of signatures attached to transactions and proposals, and validate if the signatures fulfill the governance agreed to by the network.

Implementation of Policies Throughout Fabric

In Fabric, policies are implemented at different levels in a network. Each policy domain governs different aspects of how a network operates.

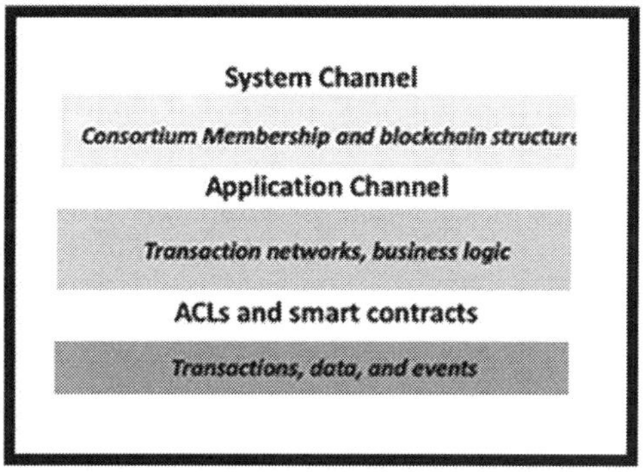

Figure 8.4: *Visual representation of Fabric policy hierarchy*

Every fabric network begins with an ordering system channel. There must be exactly one ordering system channel for an ordering service, and it is the first channel to be created. The system channel also contains the organizations who are the members of the ordering service (ordering organizations) and those that are on the networks to transact (consortium organizations).

The policies existing in the ordering system channel configuration blocks govern the consensus used by the ordering service and define how new blocks are created. The system channel also governs which members of the consortium are allowed to create new channels.

Application Channel Configuration

It is the application channels that are used to provide a private communication mechanism between organizations in the consortium.

The ability to add or remove members from the channel is governed by the policies in an application channel. Application channels also govern which organizations are required to approve a chaincode before the chaincode is defined and committed to a channel using the Fabric chaincode lifecycle. When an application channel is initially created, it inherits all the ordering service parameters from the orderer system channel by default. However, those parameters (and the policies governing them) can be customized in each channel.

Access Control Lists (ACLs)

An access control list (ACL) is a list of rules that specifies which users or systems are granted or denied access to a particular object or system resource. Network administrators will be especially interested in the Fabric use of ACLs, which provide the ability to configure access to resources by associating those resources with existing policies. These "resources" could be functions on system chaincode (example, `"GetBlockByNumber"` on the `"qscc"` system chaincode) or other resources (example, who can receive Block events). ACLs refer to policies defined in an application channel configuration and extends them to control additional resources.

Policy Types

There are presently three different types of policies implemented:

- **Signature Policy**: It is the most powerful and specifies the policy as a combination of evaluation rules for MSP principals. It supports arbitrary combinations of *AND*, *OR*, and *NOutOf*, allowing the construction of extremely powerful rules such as, "An admin of org A and 2 other admins, or 11 of 20 org admins."
- **Implicit Meta Policy**: Less flexible type than Signature Policy, and is only valid in the context of configuration. It aggregates the result of evaluating policies deeper in the configuration hierarchy, which are ultimately defined by Signature Policies. It supports good default rules such as, "A majority of the organization admin policies."
- **Endorsement Policy**: Hyperledger Fabric works as an instruction for endorsing peers to validate whether a transaction is properly endorsed or not. In Hyperledger Fabric, there is a Valid System Chaincode (VSCC) invoked with every chaincode's transaction on each peer after it receives a transaction proposal. Its purpose is to compare the endorsement signatures with which transaction is signed off, as a transaction contains one or more endorsements from many endorsing peers.

Valid System Chaincode (VSCC)

A Validation system chaincode evaluates endorsements in the transaction against the endorsement policy specified for the chaincode. VSCC had been incorporated to determine:

- All transactions endorsements are valid (that is, they contain valid signatures for valid certificates from authorized source).
- The number of transaction endorsements matches the requirement of endorsements declared in the endorsement policy.
- Endorsement is from an authorized expected source.

Roles allowed in the endorsement policy to be checked by VSCC:

- Peer
- Client
- Member
- Admin

NOTE: *These roles must only be defined as strings at the setEnrollment* API *after the registration of the user on the blockchain through the* CA *following any* SDK *implementation.*

VSCC checks the role of the signing identity against the endorsement policy defined. This role must be one of the aforementioned roles for succeeding the approval of endorsement policies, otherwise the "ENDORSEMENT_POLICY_FAILURE" error will be thrown at the endorsing peer where the signature set does not satisfy the endorsement policy or the number of signatures required by the policy cannot be collected.

Let us understand the format of the endorsement policy to be defined for the Node SDK-based client for communicating with the Blockchain.

Access Control

Access Control is a device to limit the access others have to your code. Same package can access each other's variables and methods, except for private members. Outside package can access public classes. Next, can access members that are public.

It is obvious that Fabric uses access control lists (ACLs) to manage access to resources by associating a policy with a resource. Fabric contains a number of default ACLs.

Attribute-Based Access Control (ABAC) in Hyperledger Fabric

ABAC is used for restricting access to the specific user having the necessary attributes in their certificate. First, let us talk about certification creation with attributes.

Generally, the process of creating a certificate are:

1. Enrollment
2. Register

The Enrollment is the process by which a user requests and obtains a digital certificate from a given CA. Registration is usually done by a Registrar, telling a CA to issue the digital certificate. An *admin* (registrar) is enrolled in the CA. Then, the admin receives the signing key and certificate for this admin.

First, the admin registers *user1* into the CA with proper information. The CA returns with a secret. This secret is then used to enroll *user1* to the CA. The result is the signing key and certificate for *user1*.

All the platforms such as Hyperledger Fabric blockchain and IoT devices demonstrate the access control and establish the root of trust for IoT devices. As such, The

Hyperledger Fabric is designed to be secure against unwanted access and use through encryption protocols, access restrictions, and cryptography algorithms.

Access control systems exist to protect resources from unauthorized access[4]. The Auditability feature plays an important role and has its importance increased when it comes to public and private administration, and can be leveraged within a blockchain-based access control system. Hyperledger Fabric will leverage a solution that aims to discourage unauthorized accesses to confidential information while decentralizing trust when it comes to access control. This work action will not only be focused on the implementation of such Proof-of-Concept but also leverages effective techniques to its provisioning and deployment.

It is quiet challenging to build such a system based on the blockchain technology as such distributed ledger technologies are indeed a complex distributed system. Concerning blockchain access control, there are two main challenges:

- Provisioning of features for creating scenarios with requirements for permissions, data privacy, and security.
- The lack of standardized processes for development and operations, that is, continuous integration, continuous deployment, and continuous improvement.

The internship aims to:

- Contribute to the open-source community, by advancing the state-of-the-art on the access control using the blockchain.
- Create a blockchain-based access control system using Hyperledger Fabric.
- Development of an efficient, practical DevOps framework to provision and deploy the created system.
- Propose alterations to Fabric in order to facilitate the creation of such system (that is, creating a tutorial or scripts).
- If time suffices, develop a small web application to help visualize the solution.

Membership Service Provider (MSP)

Membership Service Provider (MSP) is a Hyperledger Fabric component that offers an abstraction of membership operations. In particular, an MSP abstracts away all cryptographic mechanisms and protocols behind, issuing certificates, validating certificates, and user authentication.

Needless to say, a membership service provider (MSP) is a trusted authority in Fabric.

An MSP may define its own notion of identity and rules by which those identities are governed (identity validation) and authenticated (signature generation and verification).

One or more MSPs may govern a Hyperledger Fabric blockchain network. This provides modularity of membership operations and interoperability across different membership standards and architectures.

Channels in Hyperledger System

A channel is a private communication pathway between two or more members of a Hyperledger Fabric network on Amazon Managed Blockchain, in which each transaction on a Hyperledger Fabric network occurs on a channel. All channels in Hyperledger Fabric are the subnet of the main blockchain. Also, a network must contain at least one channel and a network on Managed Blockchain can have up to eight channels.

Peers subscribe to the ordering service of a channel and then receive the channel related blocks from it as they are created. In this procedure:

- Channeling means like splitting the Blockchain (partitioning) and therefore you should imagine that each channel is like an independent chain of blocks with its own incrementing integer sequence number (**seqno**).
- Each transaction broadcast must be done within the scope of a specific Channel (with, a default public Channel).
- Channel is used to create sub network (Private). This network has a number of peers (member). The purpose of this channel is to prepare private network and perform confidential transactions.
- Each transaction of the network is executed on the Channel.
- Each channel has their separate ledger which are stored in each peer on the Channel.
- Channels are seen as independent chains that add privacy and a transaction is done on a specific channel.

Multiple Channels

It is a built-in feature of fabric that is capable of more than just having multiple channels on one peer. Within a chaincode, users are able to call other chaincodes. If the peer is a part of the channel and the chaincode is installed on the peer, it is possible to call chaincodes from others. But on the other channel, no transaction is added to the ledger, so you are only able to make queries (reads) in the other chaincode.

We have learnt just now that Channels are like partitions. User can create a channel and invite peers to join the channel. As such, users are defining which members can have access to the channel. Channels adds in privacy as clients connecting to one channel are unaware of the existence of other channels.

In regards of privacy, we can establish a separate channel per confidential domain where only permitted peers may subscribe to. Transactions sent to a channel will be ordered respective to each other within the channel. So, a batch only contains transactions from the channel and not from any other channels.

Batch means a block. So yes, each Channel is an independent chain of transaction block containing only transaction for this particular Channel. So, with Fabric, you can run multiple Blockchains within the same infrastructure (Ordering service, Membership service, and so on).

Transaction Validation

During the simulation of a transaction by an endorser, a read-write set is prepared for the transaction[5]. The read set contains a list of unique keys and their committed versions that the transaction reads during simulation. The write set contains a list of unique keys and their new values that the transaction writes, though there can be an overlap with the keys present in the read set. A delete marker is set in the place of a new value for the key if the update performed by the transaction is to delete the key. If the transaction writes a value multiple times for a key, only the last written value is retained. Also, if a transaction reads a value for a key, the value in the committed state is returned even if the transaction has updated the value for the key before issuing the read. In other words, read-your-writes semantics are not supported. The versions of the keys are recorded only in the read set; the write set just contains the list of unique keys and their latest values set by the transaction.

There could be various schemes for implementing versions. The minimal requirement for a versioning scheme is to produce non-repeating identifiers for a given key. For instance, using increasing monotonically the numbers for versions can be one such scheme. In the current implementation, we use a blockchain height-based versioning scheme in which the height of the committing transaction is used as the latest version for all the keys modified by the transaction. In this scheme, the height of a transaction is represented by a tuple, **txNumber**, which is the height of the transaction within the block.

The following is an illustration of a sample read-write set prepared by simulating a hypothetical transaction. In the following example, the use of incremental numbers represents the versions.

```
<TxReadWriteSet>
<NsReadWriteSet name="chaincode1">
<read-set>
<read key="K1", version="1">
<read key="K2", version="1">
</read-set>
<write-set>
```

```
<write key="K1", value="V1"
<write key="K3", value="V2"
 <write key="K4", isDelete="true"
 </write-set>
 </NsReadWriteSet>
<TxReadWriteSet>
```

Furthermore, in the event that the transaction executes a range query while in simulation, both the range query and its outcomes will be appended to the read-write set as query data.

Read-Write Set Transaction Validation

In reality, every committer utilizes the write set and read set, of the read-write set, to change the versions and values of the impacted keys, and to verify the legitimacy of a transaction, respectively. Assuming that all previous valid transactions, including those in the same block, are committed, a transaction is deemed valid during the validation phase if the version of each key contained in the transaction's read set matches the version for the same key in the world state. If one or more query pieces are included in the read-write set, then an extra validation is carried out.

Making sure that no key has been added, removed, or altered in the super range—that is, the union of the ranges of results recorded in the query information—should be the goal of the additional validation step. Stated differently, rerunning any of the range queries that the transaction executed during the simulation to confirm the committed state ought to produce the same outcomes that the transaction saw at the time of simulation. This check makes sure that a transaction should be flagged as invalid if it detects phantom objects during commit. An individual object that can exist anywhere is called a phantom and commit denotes the purposeful execution of any action. The **`GetStateByRange`** function in the chaincode, which is not yet implemented for other queries, is the only query type for which this phantom protection is applicable. Other queries should only be used in read-only transactions that are not ordered since they run the danger of phantoms, unless the application can ensure that the result set remains stable between simulation and validation/commit time.

When a transaction passes the validity check, the committer updates the world state using the write set. During the update phase, the value for each key in the write set is updated to the value for the corresponding key in the world state. In addition, the most recent version of the key is reflected in the world state by changing its version.

Flow of Transactions

The transactional processes involved in a typical asset exchange are described in the Transaction Flow paper[6]. Two clients, A and B, who are purchasing and selling radishes, are involved in the situation. They communicate with the ledger and send transactions to each other's peers on the network.

Presumptions:

A channel that is established and operational is assumed by the transaction flow. After registering and enrolling with the organization's Certificate Authority (CA), the application user receives the required cryptographic material in return, which is utilized for network authentication. Thus, the chaincode is published to the channel and placed on the peers. It contains a series of key value pairs that reflect the starting state of the radish market. The logic that defines a set of transaction instructions and the agreed-upon price for a radish is contained in the chaincode. For this chaincode, an endorsement policy has also been established, which stipulates that peerA and peerB must approve of every transaction.

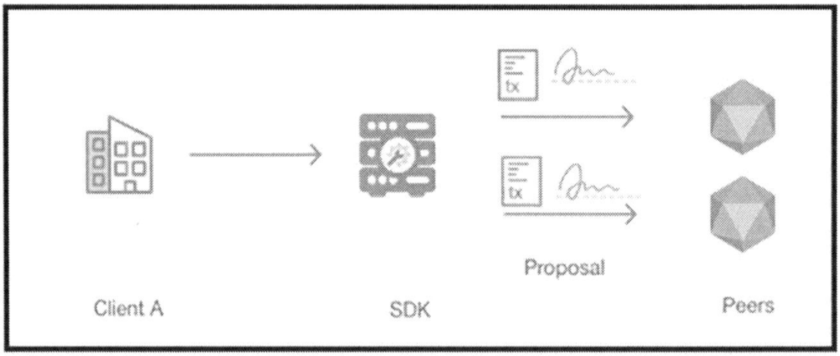

Figure 8.5: *Client A initiates a transaction*

Client A is sending a request to purchase radishes. This request targets peerA and peerB, who are respectively representative of Client A and Client B. The endorsement policy states that both peers must endorse any transaction, therefore the request goes to peerA and peerB.

Next, the transaction proposal is constructed. An application leveraging a supported SDK (*Node, Java, Python*) utilizes one of the available APIs to generate a transaction proposal. The proposal is a request to invoke a chaincode function with certain input parameters, with the intent of reading and/or updating the ledger.

The Software Development Kit (SDK) serves as a shim to package the transaction proposal into the properly architected format (protocol buffer over gRPC) and takes the user's cryptographic credentials to produce a unique signature for this transaction proposal. In the context of Hyperledger Fabric, Shim provides APIs for the chaincode to access its state variables, transaction context, and call other chaincodes. Shim contains the generic means for chaincode and validating peers to communicate with each other.

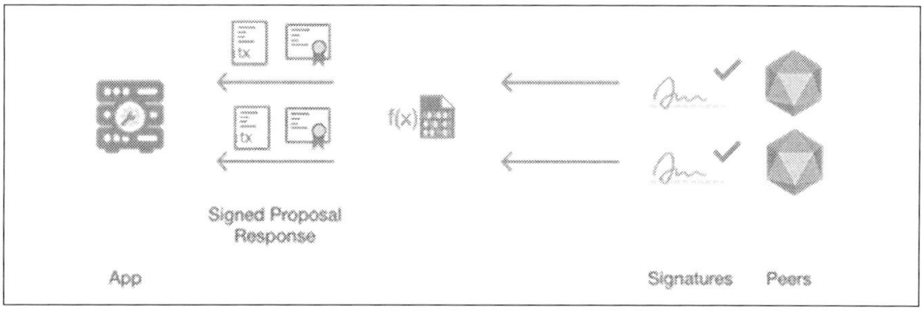

Figure 8.6: *Endorsing peers, verify signature, and executing the transaction*

The endorsing peers verify:

- that the transaction proposal is well formed.
- whether it has not been submitted already in the past (replay-attack protection).
- the signature is valid (using the MSP).
- that the submitter (Client A, in the example) is properly authorized to perform the proposed operation on that channel (namely, each endorsing peer ensures that the submitter satisfies the channel's Writers policy).

The endorsing peers take the transaction proposal inputs as arguments to the invoked chaincode's function. The chaincode is then executed against the current state database to produce transaction results including a response value, read set, and write set (that is, key/value pairs representing an asset to create or update). At this point, no updates are made to the ledger. The set of these values, along with the endorsing peer's signature is passed back as a "proposal response" to the SDK which parses the payload for the application to consume.

Executing Contracts in Blockchain

Computer scientist *Nick Szabo* developed the concept of smart contracts in 1994, where he discussed the method of how contracts could be embedded into computer codes[7]. The emergence of blockchain technology, and especially the launch of Ethereum, has made this an even more vulnerable possibility. This method ensures security and transparency of all records posted on network.

All stakeholders admired the efficiency of sharing and accessing smart contracts. In fact, smart contracts can *automate*, *calculate* and *arrange payments*, and then automatically carry out their terms and conditions. When obligations are met, the contract can be executed instantly, *with benefit of time saving, removing intermediaries, and allowing for multi-party consensus-based validation.*

It is well known that the first well known application of blockchain technology was Bitcoin, *a peer-to-peer* system custom-designed to make value transfer function without relying on a central party. It worked really well and is still working efficiently today, arguably becoming the most robust deployment of blockchain applications. But, one of the innovative blockchain technology smart contracts further elaborated the crypto revolution. There are many business advantages if you choose using smart contracts, including *trust, transparency, security, autonomy, and accuracy.*

The take-away concept as such is that the term **smart contract** refers to a piece of computer program that gets executed by a quorum of blockchain nodes independently in order to record the latest program state.

Basic Definition of Smart Contracts

A smart contract is defined as an agreement between two people in the form of a computer code. They run on the blockchain (apart from several other formats), so they are stored on a public database and cannot be changed. The transactions that happen in a smart contract are processed by the blockchain, which means they can be sent automatically without intervention from a third party (such as central or federal governments, reserve bank, and so on).

Remarkably, smart contracts are carried out by blockchain nodes as a consequence of handling user-submitted transactions. A blockchain transaction consists of the following:

- A target smart contract function that is specified.
- A payload that comprises function call input values.
- Always bears the submitter's signature. Any node in the blockchain network can receive a transaction, which is then broadcasted to all the other nodes in the network for visibility. Every node uses the executable program in the target smart contract at some point to complete the transaction. The blockchain's internal state will be updated if the transaction is successfully executed. In the event that a smart contract determines that the input is invalid and rejects the transaction as unsuccessful, the state remains unaltered.

A majority of blockchain nodes must independently carry out smart contracts. Blockchains have no authority and are decentralized, in contrast to traditional databases. Every node in the network believes that other nodes could be evil, and it never trusts the states that other nodes are maintaining. Rather, by carrying out the transactions using the smart contract code, each node keeps up its own state database.

How is the consistency of state across all nodes ensured by this autonomous execution method in each node? Every node needs to have the same initial state, identical input values, identical execution logic, and both. Applications for smart contracts include lending, borrowing, trading, and investing in the financial sector. They can be applied to real estate, gaming, and healthcare. They can even be utilized to set up whole company hierarchies.

Smart contracts are executable programs[6]. To represent arbitrary business logic or preset conditions to initiate value transfer, they are typically written in high-level computer programming languages. For a smart contracts engine to be effective in supporting a broad range of use cases, the language must be Turing complete, a fancy word in computer science that means the language can be written to handle any computation issue. This is the reason why Bitcoin is not regarded as having smart contracts, even though it is feasible to program in the Bitcoin scripting language due to its extremely limited functionality. When Ethereum first made smart contract support available, it ushered in a period of quick inventions to address some of the most difficult issues facing both society and technology.

According to IBM, smart contracts are essentially blockchain-based algorithms that execute when specific criteria are satisfied. Generally, they are employed to automate the implementation of an agreement so that there is no need for an intermediary and no delay for any parties involved in knowing the outcome right away.

The final state will always be the same if all three components are the same. One of the most important factors in generating consensus among the blockchain nodes is the chain of blocks with the linked hashes reflecting each full list of transactions (input values) and current states (starting state). Lastly, distinct blockchain protocols use various methods to ensure that the transaction is processed using the same smart contract code. When it comes to the cryptocurrency Ethereum, the smart contract code is kept directly as state on the chain. Contract code is kept off-chain in Hyperledger Fabric and Corda, the other two popular commercial blockchain systems; the intended version of the smart contract is represented by an on-chain hash.

Maintaining program states is smart contracts' primary purpose. State is an arbitrary data point that is updated by transaction execution. A blockchain can be thought of as a database in this sense, despite the fact that its architecture places a strong emphasis on data consistency and immutability at the expense of query support and performance. Nearly every blockchain protocol is created with a state transfer conceptual model in mind.

Each smart contract therefore keeps its own set of states. Except for pure value transfers that do not require smart contracts, the majority of transactions submitted to a blockchain are intended to trigger a smart contract. The destination smart contract modifies its state following the execution of a transaction. Additionally, a smart contract has the ability to call another smart contract to update or query the state of the downstream contract.

EOSIO Blockchain

The EOSIO blockchain is designed to emulate the performance of a real computer, and the software itself uses some familiar computing concepts in its operations. There are three types of resources that power the EOSIO blockchain. EOSIO acronym for

Electro-Optical System Input Output, is a smart contract platform that eliminates transaction fees and also executes millions of transactions per second.

An agreement that is modeled, signed, and completed electronically—typically via the internet—is referred to as an online contract or an electronic contract.

An online contract is written in the same way as a typical paper-based contract, using very comparable concepts. In the event of an online contract, the vendor who wants to sell their goods must show the potential customers their goods, prices, and terms of purchase. The purchasers who are interested in purchasing the goods can then choose to sign electronically, or think about using the "I Agree" or "Click to Agree" option to indicate their acceptance of the terms as stated by the vendor.

In reality, there are several methods for executing electronic signatures, such as entering the signer's name in the designated signature field, copying and pasting the scanned copy of the signature, or selecting the appropriate choice. The transaction can be finished once the terms are agreed upon and the money is received. Essentially, servers provide communication between two computers.

In an e-contract, the offer, invitation to offer, counter offer or acceptance, and so on are all by electronic means. This form of electronic communication leads to an agreement contract being drafted.

A **bilateral contract** is a binding agreement between two parties where both exchange promises to perform and fulfill one side of a bargain.

Note: *Anyone can write a smart contract and deploy it to the network. You just need to learn how to code it in a smart contract language, and have enough ETH (Ethereum) to deploy your contract.*

In a nutshell, the smart contracts are *digital agreements* that automatically execute transactions between parties, increasing speed, accuracy, and integrity in payment and performance. It is noteworthy that Smart contracts are legally enforceable if they comply with contract law.

A smart contract may also contain as many clauses as necessary to reassure the parties involved that the work will be finished to their satisfaction. Participants must agree on the "if/when...then..." rules that govern those transactions, investigate any potential exceptions, design a framework for resolving disputes, and decide how transactions and their data are represented on the blockchain in order to construct the terms.

In these situations, a developer can create the smart contract. However, an increasing number of businesses using blockchain technology offer templates, web interfaces, and other online tools to make the process of creating smart contracts easier.

Advantages of Intelligent Contracts

The advantages of smart contracts are as follows:

- **Accuracy, speed, and efficiency**: The contract is carried out right away if a condition is satisfied. Because smart contracts are digital and automated, there is no paperwork to handle in this case, and there is also no time wasted on reconciling errors that can arise from manually filling out documentation.
- **Trust and transparency**: There is no need to wonder if information has been changed for personal gain because there is no involvement from a third party and participants exchange encrypted records of transactions.
- **Security**: It is impossible to hack because blockchain transaction records are encrypted. Furthermore, in order for a hacker to modify a single record on a distributed ledger, they would need to modify the entire chain as every record is linked to the records that come before and after it.
- **Savings**: Because smart contracts handle transactions without the need for middlemen, the corresponding costs and delays, savings are achievable.

Smart Contract Anatomy

Consider smart contracts as program functions, with inputs, outputs, and logic to process the inputs. This will help you grasp how smart contracts work. Smart contract execution frequently produces updated states. The validity of a transaction is verified by the logic embedded in smart contracts. Not operating at the correct level of the initial state, such as trying to spend tokens without having enough balance, is one example of an invalid transaction. Updated states are only the product of valid transactions. Depending on the specific blockchain design, invalid transactions are either rejected by the network and not added to the blockchain or added but recorded as unsuccessful.

Smart contracts may potentially disseminate occurrences as a means of informing the public. When the transaction-containing block is committed to the node's blockchain, event listeners are alerted.

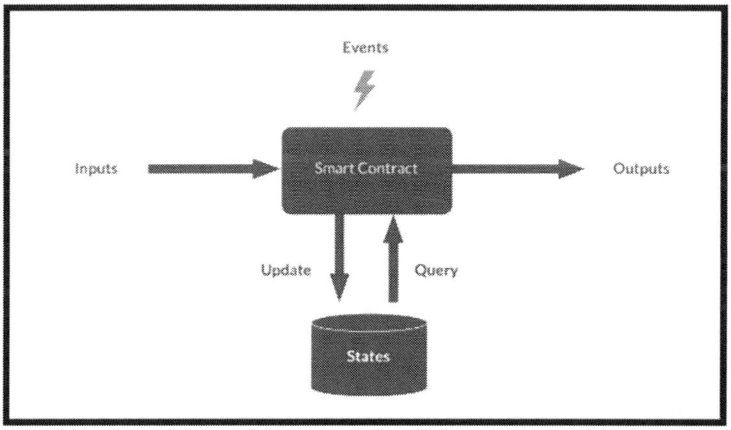

Figure 8.7: *Anatomy of Smart Contract in Blockchain Technology*

A transaction has the ability to call several public functions. Every function has the option to return the most recent state or to update the state itself. For instance, the following features are usually present in a conventional fungible token smart contract and are helpful in situations like commodity trade and payments.

States-updating functions (that call for transactions):

- transfer (amount, to)
- Give approval (assign, sum)
- conveyanceFrom (to, amount, from)
- mint (quantity, to)
- burn (amount, from)

Functions that check the most recent states (that do not need transactions to use):

- accountOf's balance

If the state needs to be changed at any point, a transaction must be created and the entire transaction cycle must be followed. Because blockchain design is decentralized, transactions need to be handled by a consensus mechanism in order to guarantee that all copies kept by the nodes that participate in the blockchain network have the same records.

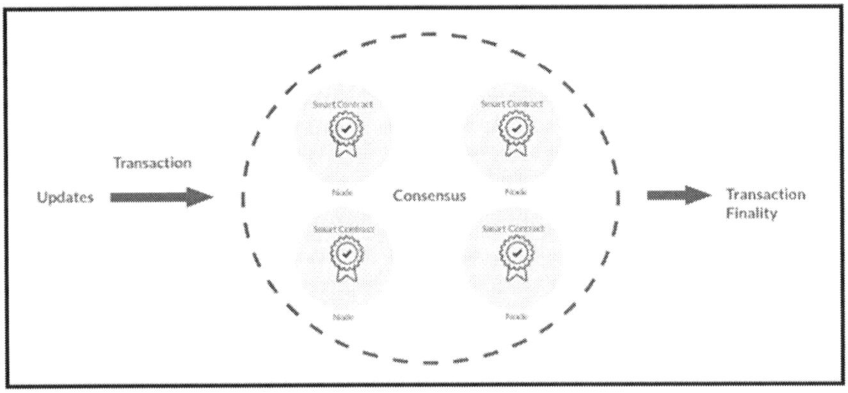

Figure 8.8: *Updating state required transaction processing with consensus from the whole network*

On the other hand, querying for the latest state without updating it can be accomplished much faster and involves only a single node in the network. Any node that has the smart contract installed locally can execute the query request and return the result by reading from the locally maintained state database.

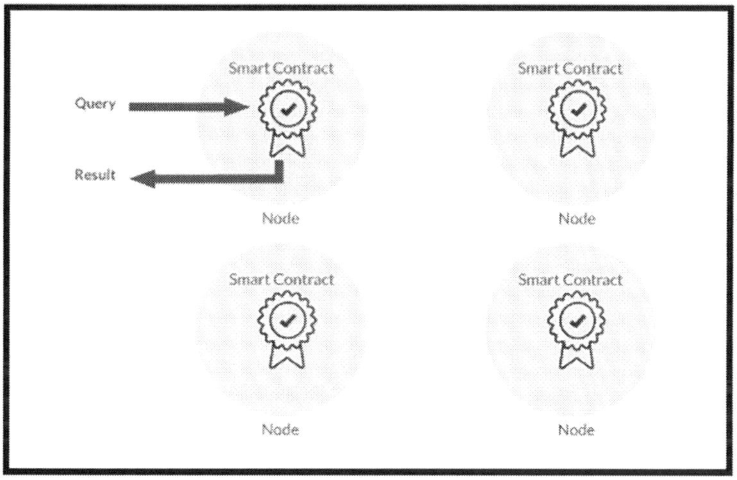

***Figure 8.9**: Querying smart contracts for latest state can be accomplished with a single node*

Smart Contract's Life Cycle

It is necessary to deploy the smart contract on the blockchain before it can handle transactions. Ensuring that every blockchain node has the exact same code is a requirement of the deploy procedure. This requirement is handled differently by different blockchain designs. But, there are generally two ways to handle it: either store the contract code itself in the blockchain, which ensures global consensus (on-chain); or let each node owner determine whether the node should have the code installed locally and use an off-chain reference for code integrity validation (a hash-based commitment in the blockchain).

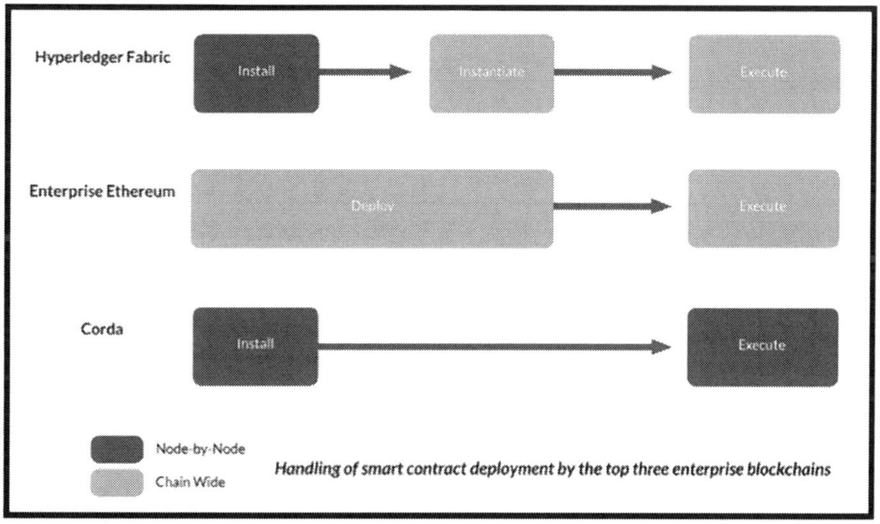

Figure 8.10: *Life cycle of smart contract*

Use Cases of Smart Contracts

Numerous industries, including finance, real estate, healthcare, insurance, and even elections, are already undergoing a transition brought about by smart contracts. Here are a few instances of smart contracts[8]:

A wide range of sectors can employ smart contracts to carry out tasks[9]. Regulatory compliance, enforceability of contracts, international financial transactions, ownership of real estate, purchasing a home, supply management, material provenance, document management, and numerous other uses. Smart contracts are important in a number of domains, including the legal transfer of ownership in the sale of digital financial assets, banking and credit services, logistics, tracing the origin and route of commodities, decentralized storage, and the usage of renewable energy.

- **Supply Chain Management**: This is a field that could benefit from the application of smart contracts. The use of smart contracts to increase supply chain transparency is facilitating the flow of commodities and reestablishing trade confidence. As products pass through the supply chain, smart contracts may track ownership rights and verify who is in charge of the goods at any given moment. Up until it is delivered to the customer, the completed product can be checked at every stage of the procedure.
- **Insurance**: The insurance industry, which now lacks automated administration, could potentially benefit from the usage of smart contracts. The processing and payment of an insurance claim can take several months. When specific circumstances take place, smart contracts can automatically trigger a claim, which helps simplify and streamline the process. Thus, precise information might be documented on the blockchain to ascertain the precise amount of remuneration.
- **Mortgage loans**: The mortgage application process might be made simpler by smart contracts. Here, the conditions of a mortgage contract are determined by evaluating the income, expenses, credit score, and other factors of the mortgagee. For both the lender and the mortgagee, the requirement to conduct these checks—often through third parties—can make the procedure drawn out and challenging. Eliminating intermediaries allowed parties to transact with one another directly.
- **Financial industry**: As money and related documentation move toward electronic forms, this sector continues to employ smart contracts extensively. The financial services industry presents various potential for the use of smart contracts, such as efficient "know your customer" certification, trade finance, payment processing, and financial instrument clearing and settlement.
- **Cutting down on expensive mistakes in trade finance**: Because smart contracts can streamline processes and improve computations, they can also cut down on labor hours. Smart contracts will enable significant adjustments

to the financial service sector's infrastructure and procedures. Distributed ledgers, in their opinion, will emerge as the go-to option for handling large numbers of transactions. By 2022, these savings totaled between $15 and $20 billion annually.

- **Tracking property data in real estate**: By eliminating the need for attorneys or brokers, smart contracts in this sector are utilized to record property ownership of any structure and maximize transaction speed and efficiency. Sellers have the option to direct the procedure. Rob Massey, a prominent figure in the blockchain space, claims that smart contracts make property title management more affordable and transparent. Legal fees may arise from transfers that are impeded by title flaws. Smart contracts, on the other hand, maintain track of a property's history, location, and all other crucial information required for title evaluation. Through safe, tamper-proof encrypted codes, they aid in preventing fraud.
- **Safeguarding private health information**: Blockchain is being used by more healthcare organizations to offer dependable automation and modern security features. Because they have so much sensitive data, hospitals are the main targets of cybercriminals. About 4.5 million patient records have been stolen in data breaches that have affected even well-known companies in the field, such as UCLA Health. Ensuring the safe exchange of patient data among healthcare providers is imperative in this context to uphold care standards. By using smart contracts, patient data can be safely kept on a blockchain, accessible only with the patient's private key. Patients can guarantee that their information is protected and that their medical professionals always have access to the information they require in this way.
- **Increasing election convenience and integrity**: Blockchain voting technologies may be the way of future elections. Blockchain voting systems have the potential to increase accessibility, boost voter turnout, and expedite the tabulation and reporting of votes by enabling secure and simple voting over digital channels. Election hackers frequently want to prevent multiple ballot casting, and smart contracts would be able to verify voters' identities in order to prevent this from happening.
- **Reducing insurance industry claims fraud**: In the insurance business, claims processing costs millions of dollars annually. The bogus claims cause even more money to be lost. Smart contracts assist in managing insurance from individuals or companies by strengthening claim processing through periodic mistake checks. Additionally, customers pay less overall, even for premium rates, as a result of the quicker processing times.
- **One more adaptable example**: Other applications of smart contracts include peer-to-peer transactions, supply chain management, product creation, and stocktaking, among others. Although there is still much space for innovation

and development, the increasing use of smart contracts emphasizes their intended benefits of efficiency, accountability, and transparency.

Smart contracts are key to many use cases and provides us with an opportunity to make transactions and processes more streamlined and automated. Smart contracts are here to stay; the steady increase of deployments year over year only emphasizes their significance within the blockchain ecosystem. The open-source community has fully embraced the concept and have developed many high-quality libraries in various smart contract languages. OpenZeppelin, for example, is widely utilized in the Solidity developer's community for Ethereum-based blockchains.

The currency known as Enterprise Ethereum, with the public Ethereum inheritance, offers a simple one-step process to deploy smart contracts. The deployment is done via a transaction, making it a chain-wide operation by nature. Code for the smart contract is saved on-chain as state. As a result, all nodes are guaranteed to have access to the code and they all have the same version.

Yet another cryptocurrency, Corda adopts a peer-to-peer transaction coordination architecture, without utilizing a globally maintain common ledger of transactions. Because of this, smart contract deployment is done on a per-node basis that is based on the need to perform bi-lateral or multi-lateral transactions. Similar to Fabric, the administrator of the Corda node is responsible for ensuring that the smart contract required to process a transaction has been installed on the node.

Smart Contract Usage Patterns

"Smart" is typically associated with artificial intelligence that is built on massive amounts of data and employs computation intensive algorithms. Despite the name, smart contracts are neither smart nor legally binding. Smart contracts exist to build trust with decentralization, in which multiple parties execute the same code and maintain the same state, independently. In such applications efficiency is sacrificed for security through duplication. This means smart contracts is not a great place to build intelligence through machine learning, or carry out any amount of deep analytics.

Note: Besides duplicating computation, smart contracts also result in state data being stored in every node. When considering what kind of data should be maintained by smart contracts, the best practice is to only use it to keep track of information that either represents commitment of data stored somewhere else, so that they cannot be changed after the fact, or information that need to be updated. Legal documents typically are overly verbose and have a lot of boilerplate content. Saving the whole legal document inside smart contracts would be a very inefficient way to utilize blockchain.

Smart Contract Platforms

These days, there are numerous platforms for smart contracts. Technology, end-user (banking, government, supply chain, real estate, insurance, and more), and regional

(Europe, North America, Asia, or rest of the world orientated) divides could be used to separate them.

Their distinctions are found in:

- Languages used for programming.
- Blockchain consensus.
- The price of upkeep for smart contracts inside an application.
- Variations in blockchain security.
- Confidence in the primary network nodes.
- Transaction confirmation speed, and numerous other factors.

1. **Ethereum**: Ethereum pioneered the introduction of smart contracts to a broader cryptocurrency ecosystem and is the most sophisticated platform for writing and executing them. Because this open-source platform has one of the biggest developer networks out there, it can adapt to the constantly shifting landscape of the blockchain sector.

   However, the first blockchain platform to create codes specifically for dApp creation was Ethereum. Numerous platforms have emerged as a result of their emergence, including Aeternity, Cardano, Qtum, Stellar, and Waves.

2. **Aeternity**: Aeternity provides a way to power so-called Turing-complete smart contracts, which may be executed off-chain. This is done by combining a Proof-of-Work and Proof-of-Stake architecture that provides protection and privacy.

3. **Cardano**: Cardano is a cryptocurrency and decentralized blockchain initiative. Cardano is open source, just like other cryptocurrency initiatives. With Goguen release, the Cardano platform is aiming to integrate smart contract capability. Their smarter contracts should become even more advanced as a result.

4. **Qtum**: Two of the most important features of this open-source blockchain application platform are security and adaptability.

   The Qtum team has put in a lot of effort to ensure that smart contracts can be carried out securely, which makes the platform ideal for companies and their enterprise clientele. Proof-of-Stake and a decentralized governance protocol are used by Qtum.

5. **Stellar**: Unlike many other cryptocurrencies, Stellar was developed by developers for developers, which enables it to manage incredibly intricate smart contracts. Stellar is a clear, user-friendly substitute for basic smart contracts for developers looking to create more efficient smart contracts.

6. **Waves**: Waves is an open-source blockchain project that makes extensive use of Web 3.0 technology and dApps. For developers who may choose to work with Waves, the company provides various online courses to help keep their smart contract project easy in addition to other forms of support. Similar to several smart contract initiatives, Waves uses Proof-of-Stake.

Benefits of Smart Contracts

The smart contracts system provides many benefits over traditional contracts for a wide range of industries. In theory, they are more efficient and trustworthy than traditional contract law, and are also thought to offer better security as all actions are recorded and verified. As a result, they may reduce unnecessary costs and time expenditure while enhancing transparency.

- **Greater efficiency and speed**: Smart contracts are automated so there is no need to spend a lot of time on the paperwork and also correcting the errors that are manually written in the documents. They can be executed in minutes, for a fraction of the cost, from wherever the involved parties are, and without the need for lawyers. Smart contracts are able to improve the efficiency and speed with which commercial arrangements are carried out.
- **Accuracy and transparency**: The fact that the codified terms are fully visible and accessible to all relevant parties, there is no way to dispute them once the smart contract is established. These facilities complete transactional transparency and may remove the likelihood of manipulation, bias, or error. This however, in turn leads to decreased monitoring costs and risks of opportunistic behavior.
- **Trust**: Smart contracts may provide parties with a degree of trust as:
    - They automatically perform transactions following predetermined laws.
    - The encrypted documents of these transactions are distributed over participants.
    - The information on the contract and the terms of the contract are straight.
    - They have specific validation by everyone.
    - The immutability of the work guarantees that the smart contract can never be broken.
- **Security**: Smart contracts are also thought to offer better security as all actions are recorded and verified. This is because blockchain transaction documents are encrypted which makes it extremely difficult to hack. Security features can also be integrated into a smart contract to automatically generate backups and duplicates in the event of damages, data losses to the original ones, or hacks.

Challenges to Smart Contracts Technology

Smart contracts consists of a number of challenges that may prevent more massive adoption:

- **Human Errors**: Similar to paper contracts, smart contracts can still experience fraud, due to human errors. As smart contracts are codes, and these codes are written by people (coders), there is a (high) chance of it consisting bugs. They can be delayed, intercepted, and corrupted. Some mistakes have proven to be very costly.
- **Confidentiality, Security, and Privacy:** Unlike traditional contracts, all transactions executed via a smart contract, are propagated across all of the nodes in the network.
- **Privacy Issues**: Privacy issues may be created, particularly when the accounts of the parties are associated with known entities. Even when the parties rely on pseudonymous accounts, certain identification techniques can be used to discern the identities of parties who transact with a particular smart contract.
- **Lack of Engineering Experience:** As smart contracts begin to proliferate, there will be a need for new types of cryptography experts, and forensic experts, to verify software code and to translate the code into human-readable form. A huge amount of engineering expertise is required to make perfectly operational smart contracts. However, experienced coders are hard to find, and costly.
- **Legal and Regulatory Challenges:** There are also a number of legal and regulatory challenges, which are preventing the widespread utilization of smart contracts. Smart contracts lack a clear legal status and is no official government regulation that applies to them.
- **Interpretation and Enforceability**: If there is a dispute about whether a smart contract accurately memorialized the parties' intentions or whether one party has breached the contract, the parties may still bring legal proceedings or engage in alternative dispute resolution processes. The enforceability of smart contracts is subject to jurisdictional variations in contract law.
- **Jurisdictional Issues**: Smart contracts also raise jurisdictional issues. But as the blockchain operates as a decentralized ledger, smart contracts can be formed and accessed anywhere across the globe. They do not reside in any one location, but exist across multiple locations at one time. Yet, existing laws are jurisdiction-based. The differences in laws across jurisdictions can be highly problematic, and may result in incongruent rights and responsibilities, and confusion regarding the consequences if there is a contract violation.

Conclusion

We have learned that the Fabric is a modular and expandable open-source architecture for implementing and running permissioned blockchains. This was later expanded upon as Hyperledger.

The blockchain stores state and ledger data, performs transactions, and runs programs known as chaincode. We have learnt that various components of the Hyperledger Fabric Network are Assets, Shared Ledger, Smart Contract, and Peer nodes. We also learnt to write a blockchain application and elements of PKI. Furthermore, we have discussed about Hyperledger Fabric policies and its types. Additionally, we learnt about digital certificates and the process of obtaining DSC from Certifying Authority.

In the next chapter, we are going to learn about Blockchain Interoperability, its need, and use cases.

References

[1] Docs » Architecture Reference » Architecture Origins, https://hyperledger-fabric.readthedocs.io/en/release-1.4/arch-deep-dive.html

[2] Blockchain basics: Hyperledger Fabric, Shikha Maheshwari, https://developer.ibm.com/articles/blockchain-basics-hyperledger-fabric/How a blockchain solution works

[3] Identity, https://hyperledger-fabric.readthedocs.io/en/release-1.4/identity/identity.html

[4] Hyperledger Fabric Based Access Control›Introduction›Name: Sara Rouhani, https://wiki.hyperledger.org/display/INTERN/Hyperledger+Fabric+Based+Access+Control?

[5] Hyperledger Fabric: An Overview of its Transaction Validation Feature, https://www.opensourceforu.com/2019/04/hyperledger-fabric-an-overview-of-its-transaction-validation-feature/

[6] Transaction Flow, https://hyperledger-fabric.readthedocs.io/en/release-2.2/txflow.html

[7] What are Smart Contracts and How Do They Work? https://www.kaleido.io/blockchain-blog/what-are-smart-contracts-and-how-do-they-work

[8] Examples of Blockchain Smart Contracts, https://www.kaleido.io/blockchain-blog/5-examples-of-blockchain-smart-contracts

[9] Smart working with blockchain-based smart contracts,30 September 2020,Carlo R.W. De Meijer Owner and Economist MIFSA, https://www.finextra.com/blogposting/19383/smart-working-with-blockchain-based-smart-contracts

CHAPTER 9

Blockchain Interoperability

Introduction

The users of Blockchain utilize this technology through several media, devices, operating systems, and different types of software and programming languages. Interoperability allows for the seamless transfer of data and assets between different blockchain networks, reducing the need for manual processes and intermediaries. But without interoperability, it is almost impossible to adopt blockchain technology, because each individual project would be too isolated. Interoperability solutions allow blockchain to read and write data to other blockchains.

Structure

In this chapter, we will cover the following topics:

- Need for Blockchain Interoperability
- Cross-Chain Technology
- Blockchain Interoperability Projects
- Blockchain Interoperability Architecture
- Blockchain Interoperability Technologies

Need for Blockchain Interoperability

Blockchain technology's development happened very fast and is now being classified into four stages:

- Blockchain 1.0 was devoted to cryptocurrency applications. The common use case was the electronic payment system or cryptocurrency.
- Blockchain 2.0 provides smart contracts, smart property, and more. Ethereum Smart contracts, Hyperledger Fabric, and R3's Corda are examples of Blockchain 2.0.

- Blockchain 3.0 developed decentralized Applications (dApps) that cater to several fields beyond financial applications or asset transfers. Common use cases of Blockchain 3.0 include dApps for sectors such as governance, IoT, healthcare, supply chain, smart city, and many other non-financial applications.

  In a decentralized system, control is distributed amongst the components of the system, while in a distributed system, the components are physically separated and they communicate over a network. Both types of systems can be used to enable the sharing of resources and workloads.

- Blockchain 4.0 has applications for industry 4.0. The key themes of Blockchain 4.0 includes distributed ledger technology and useful blockchain applications for industry 4.0.

To meet their needs, many user groups have created their own versions of blockchain systems. The broad range of uses for distributed ledger systems were made feasible.

Additionally, this led to the internal development of various blockchain projects with various protocols and architectures evolving. These projects make use of various technologies and consensus mechanisms, tailored to particular applications or use cases. Because there are so many initiatives, the development process is extremely fragmented, with little to no compatibility between many.

Wegner stated, "interoperability is the ability of two or more software components to cooperate despite differences in language, interface, and execution platform. As such the objective of blockchain interoperability is to support such cooperation among blockchain systems, despite those kinds of differences."

There are already several blockchain interoperability solutions available[1].

The multinational giant IBM is the largest company in the world embracing blockchain, leading the way for companies to integrate Hyperledger and the IBM cloud into their systems.

The National Institute of Standards and Technology (NIST) defines interoperability in the blockchain architecture as:

"An interoperable blockchain architecture is a composition of distinguishable blockchain systems, each representing a unique distributed data ledger, where transaction execution may span multiple blockchain systems, and where data recorded in one blockchain is reachable, verifiable, and referenceable by another possibly foreign transaction in a semantically compatible manner."

Interoperability technology enables seamless and secure execution of smart contracts among different public permissionless, private, or consortium permissioned blockchains. It is commonly examined from three broad levels, including:

- Foundational
- Structural
- Semantic

Foundationally, data can be transferred smoothly among different systems. But structurally, the aforementioned exchange takes place only if there is a well-defined data format. The data contained by transaction across systems is interpretable by end-users at the semantic level.

Blockchain-Based Initiatives

These blockchain-based apps were compelled to interact with other blockchain apps running on other blockchain networks. This led to the development of a new communication mechanism between several segregated blockchain networks, establishing the groundwork for the idea of blockchain network interoperability.

Blockchain interoperable protocols can be categorized into :

- Cross-Chain Protocols
- Cross Blockchain Protocols

While cross-blockchain interoperability protocols help with communication between heterogeneous blockchains, cross-chain protocols are designed to provide communication between homogeneous blockchains.

The exchange of information between Polygon and Avalanche is an illustration of a cross-chain protocol. One instance of a cross-blockchain protocol is the exchange of data across cryptocurrencies such as Ethereum and Bitcoin. Since the hashing strategy, consensus algorithm, block size, execution environment, and network architecture of the source and target blockchain systems may differ, designing a cross-blockchain protocol is considered challenging.

Avalanche

One well-known Decentralized Finance (DeFi) blockchain is Avalanche. Trader Joe, Wonderland, BenQi, Curve, AAVE, and Wonderland are the main DeFi protocols that leverage Avalanche.

With a transactional throughput of 4,500 transaction per second (TPS), the leading DeFi protocol Avalanche outperforms Bitcoin (7 TPS), Ethereum (14 TPS), and Polkadot (1,500 TPS) astronomically. The native token of Avalanche, known as AVAX, is used for staking, fee payments, and serving as a unit of account across the various subnetworks that have been built atop Avalanche.

Polygon (MATIC)

To address this issue, Polygon offers numerous goods and services.

Note: The blockchain for Ethereum is expensive and slow. Therefore, Polygon's SDK improves upon this by allowing the creation of Ethereum sidechains, which are blockchains connected to Ethereum through a two-way peg. These sidechains come in a variety of forms, including:

- The ability to group transactions into batches and submit them to the Ethereum blockchain as a single batch (Plasma Chains).
- The ability to combine several transfers into a single transaction is known as ZK-Rollups.
- Possessing Ethereum smart contract-scaling Plasma Chains (Optimistic Rollups).

MATIC is Polygon's native token consisting the following uses:

- Pay for transaction fees in the network.
- Incorporate the feature of the unit of payment and settlement in the Polygon ecosystem.
- Power the Polygon proof-of-stake sidechain.

It is not impossible, but rather difficult to identify and verify data recorded in one chain from another chain just by examining the information exchanged between them.

Cross Blockchain token transfer involves several challenges such as:

- Evolving a method of issuing tokens on the blockchains, to disable tokens when they are leaving the blockchain. Tokens are rebalanced throughout the blockchain to preserve liquidity.
- To determine which properties of the blockchain are necessary for cross-chain transfer.
- To choose which blockchain is appropriate for cross-blockchain transfer.

Crypto Tokens

With the increasing number of blockchain systems appearing, even those that support cryptocurrencies, the subject of Blockchain interoperability is becoming a topic of major importance. The objective is to support transferring assets from one blockchain system to another blockchain system.

In technical terms, "token" is simply another synonym for "crypto-asset" or "cryptocurrency." But based on context, it has gradually come to mean a few more distinct things. Firstly, all cryptocurrencies other than Bitcoin and Ethereum (which are also tokens in theory) will be described. The second is to explain specific digital assets, such several decentralized finance (DeFi) tokens, that operate on top of the blockchain of another cryptocurrency. A vast array of potential uses for tokens exist, ranging from the sale of rare items in video games to facilitating the operation of decentralized exchanges. But just like any other cryptocurrency, they may all be owned or exchanged.

THORChain, built on the Cosmos blockchain, is a decentralized liquidity protocol that specializes in cross-chain connectivity, allowing traders to swap tokens between different networks. It uses a decentralized liquidity protocol that allows users to swap assets in a permissionless setting. It enables the exchange of native layer-1 assets such as BTC by acting as a vault manager. THORChain uses Tendermint and Cosmos-SDK to secure its network.

Cross-Chain Technology

The new cross-chain protocol makes it easier for various blockchain networks to communicate with one another and permits data sharing between many networks. Users can communicate with each other directly through cross-chain protocol. As such, blockchains with comparable networks can exchange value and information[2].

Effectively, a cross-chain design promotes interoperability by letting many blockchains trade off features, security, decentralization, and efficiency. This can decrease fragmentation, increase chain efficiency, and facilitate more seamless user and feature flow between different blockchains.

Cross-blockchain interoperability is a characteristic that facilitates communication across several blockchains without the need for middlemen. This basically means that value can be transferred between blockchains that share similar networks.

Main Characteristic Features of Cross-Chain Technology

Following are the main features of the cross-chain technology:

- This technology works on the principle of atomicity.
- It enables proper consistency between several interconnected blockchains.
- It enables the distribution of networks across various platforms.

Cross-chain technology is significant because it allows users to exchange tokens and transfer data without the need for a middleman. This infrastructure makes it easier for two or more blockchains to work together, improve efficiency, balance decentralization and security, and more. It is also crucial since it decreases segmentation, increases chain efficiency, and permits more open communication between users on different blockchains. Thus, cross-chain technology has enormous potential to enable blockchain interoperability, which can resolve multiple problems and eliminate a number of limitations on blockchain and other networks.

Working Approaches of Cross-Chain Technology

Blockchain interoperability is used by each network in a distinct way to facilitate transactions without requiring third-party interfaces. The following are some of the most popular and well-known methods for isolating transactions across different chains:

- **Atomic Swaps:** Exchange brokers known as "atomic swaps" allow two parties to exchange tokens across several blockchains. There is no need for a centralized third party to facilitate the trades with this kind of method. Rather, it facilitates peer-to-peer direct token trading for the user. This mechanism either finalizes the entire processor or does not initiate it in the first place. For instance, two parties can decide to keep a one hour restriction for the atomic swap. In this case, the original owners will receive their deposited tokens once the duration of one hour is over, even though not all the conditions are met. Although it may not be easy for a new user, a professional blockchain developer would find it easy.
- **Relays:** Blockchain networks can monitor events and transactions occurring on other chains because of the Relays feature. They function from chain to chain, allowing a single contract to serve as the core client of other nodes across several chains, all without the need for dispersed nodes. Thus, it may independently validate the complete transaction history and individual central headers. However, the relay approach requires a lot of expenditure to operate and take care of the security of operation. Apart from these two methods, there are various other approaches that cross-chain technology follows to function. Merged consensus is one of the approaches that enables two-way blockchain interoperability between several networks. On the other hand, a specific group of verified parties also comes together to check the events of the chains.

Benefits of Cross-Chain Technology

Although cross-chain mechanisms play a major role in facilitating blockchain interoperability, they also have a number of other advantages. Among the many important advantages that cross-chain technology provides are:

- The ability to establish a solid connection and to facilitate efficient communication across two distinct blockchain networks is one of cross-chain technology's greatest features. It is typically used to start token swaps and asset transfers, therefore blockchain incompatibility is not an issue. Furthermore, it facilitates the transmission of data, including assets, transaction receipts, and virtual contracts, by the user.

- Because current blockchain mechanisms have limited interoperability, cross-chain technology enables better scalability. It is now possible to take advantage of the speed when it comes to many blockchains because this technology facilitates user interaction with various blockchain networks. It is now possible to leverage the speed concerning multiple blockchains that ultimately enhances scalability.
- Improving the data flow and token transfer: Under the existing setup, a user must transmit commands from the source chain. The relayers transfer these instructions to the destination chain after the validator gets them. Cross-chain technology, on the other hand, verifies the transaction immediately upon completion and delays its arrival at the destination change until the verification is finished. It does this by streamlining the entire procedure and facilitating the seamless interchange and transmission of data. You can enroll in any online blockchain course to study the fundamentals if you also want to trade cryptocurrencies on the blockchain.
- The potential of cross-chain technology to deter monopolization by big entities: By deterring monopolization by major firms, cross-chain technology also contributes to market stability. For example, with over 70% of the market share, Bitcoin and Ethereum are the most well-known names in the cryptocurrency sector. Because of this domination, there is no room for new competitors to enter the market, test out their methods, and emerge from the pack. In these kinds of situations, cross-chain technology can be useful because it creates an environment in which transaction processes focus equally on all networks.

Not just a few significant blockchain networks but also additional networks will be the focus. Therefore, by enabling a balanced way to state how cryptocurrency participants participate in the marketplace, cross-chain technology can establish a fair environment.

Blockchain Interoperability Projects

In recent years, a number of projects that addressed public blockchain interoperability have arisen[3]. However, enterprise-level interoperability solutions are very new, and the required standardization work is still in its early stages. While there are other classifications, we may generally divide interoperability solutions into two groups based on distinct methodologies and ideologies. In the first, a permanent infrastructure known as a "settlement" chain (or hub) is established to which other chains (called "sidechains") can connect. The common chain functions as an intermediary for interoperability, providing the sidechains with decentralized trust. This guarantees for the settlement of cross-chain transactions.

This method works especially well with distributed ledgers and public blockchains, as demonstrated by Cosmos and Polkadot.

The modules and features that enable direct network interoperability without reliance on external infrastructure are added to the second category of interoperability solutions. Hyperledger Cactus and the Hyperledger Lab Weaver belong to this second category, which is helpful in business settings where performance and privacy are of important considerations. Each of these strategies have advantages and disadvantages that vary depending on the situation.

Hyperledger Cactus

A new pluggable enterprise-grade architecture called Hyperledger Cactus allows transactions on several distributed ledgers without adding yet another rival blockchain[4]. A SDK of SDKs provides a decentralized, flexible, and secure integration with and between blockchain networks. Furthermore, through an extensible plugin design that allows new protocols or functionality to be added by creating new plugins, it seeks to cover as many protocols as possible.

Key Characteristics of Hyperledger Cactus

- The Open Digital Asset Protocol (ODAP) is supported.
- More examples and better documentation (similar to fabric-samples).
- A greater quantity of maintainers.
- Enabling public testing of a Cactus network.
- Anyone with access to a cloud provider account or a K8s cluster can replicate the Cactus benchmarks in the same manner that they do the functional test cases.

Hyperledger FireFly

An additional Hyperledger called FireFly facilitates interoperability at the application tier by offering an API orchestration layer across several blockchain ledgers. This enables the implementation of common blockchain programming elements across various blockchains in pluggable microservice code modules, such as identity verification, off-chain/on-chain data orchestration, and tokens. One such pattern that has actually been put into practice spans several chains in a single corporate transaction. It involves coordinating tokenized value transfer on an Ethereum blockchain.

Salient Features of Hyperledger FireFly

- Multi-ledger support
- Pluggable DID provider support
- Pluggable API Security (for example, OAuth 2.0)
- Active-active clustering
- NoSQL database support

Weaver

The Hyperledger Lab's Weaver framework and family of protocols allow autonomous networks constructed on heterogeneous DLTs to cooperate for asset transfers and data exchange while maintaining the fundamental security and decentralization principles of blockchain technology.

Weaver-based cooperation eliminates the need for dependable middlemen. The internal governance processes of the networks are used to formulate rules and regulations. Its interoperability is mainly dependent on shared infrastructure, which might offer identification services but is not involved in the fundamental protocols that facilitate the sharing of assets and data. Protocols that rely on the innate consensus mechanisms of counterparty networks to maintain trust enable interoperability.

The protocols for data transfer between ledgers with provenance and authenticity verification are supported by Fabric and Corda.

Salient Features of Weaver

- Implementation of cross-network decentralization.
- The relay module makes ODAP compliant by offering increased resilience (fault tolerance) and message queueing capabilities for distribution and load balancing.
- Invoking cross-network transactions and publishing/subscribing events.
- Complete confidentiality assistance for sharing of states and assets.
- Contains an enhanced data/state sharing mechanism that makes use of verifiable external observation features to confirm the state's freshness.
- Better testing features, tutorials, and documentation.
- Increased capacity for performance evaluation.
- Interoperability with Hyperledger Cactus via combined and combined features.

YUI

Originating from a Japanese term meaning knot, join, and connect, comes the word "YUI." A new initiative from Hyperledger Labs called YUI aims to establish interoperability across several heterogeneous ledgers.

With the help of our Hyperledger Lab, several heterogeneous ledgers can communicate with one another. The lab offers tools and modules for developing cross-chain applications as well as middleware and modules for cross-chain communication.

With enhancements to suit other Hyperledger projects, YUI is built on the Inter Blockchain Communication (IBC) protocol developed by the Cosmos project for cross-chain communication. IBC offers the foundation for arbitrary data transfer and computation between ledgers without relying on a reliable third party.

YUI supports cross-authentication between enterprise ledgers (Fabric, Besu, and Corda). Each actor of ledgers has to interact with only a respective ledger of its interest to complete a cross-chain operation such as an atomic swap of tokens.

Salient Features of YUI

- Supports other ledger (possibly other Hyperledger projects).
- Enhanced support for Solidity and Ethereum-based ledgers.
- Has Enhanced support for connecting the Cosmos ecosystem (such as Tendermint light client for Solidity).
- Improved documentation and release samples.

Interoperability operations can be classified in three categories:

- Cryptocurrency interoperability approaches.
- Blockchain engines.
- Blockchain connectors.

Blockchain Interoperability Architecture

The draft of a blockchain interoperability architecture was produced by several individual IETF participants. The Internet Engineering Task Force (IETF) is the body that defines standard operating internet protocols such as TCP/IP. The IETF is an open standards organization supervised by the Internet Society's Internet Architecture Board (IAB).

The Internet Engineering Task Force (IETF) is an open, global community of network designers, operators, vendors, and academics that are interested in the development of Internet architecture and its seamless functioning. To coordinates the management, development, and operation of the Internet. The IETF was founded in 1986.

The capacity of various blockchain networks to transfer certain kinds of digital assets between the networks' individual blockchains as well as to exchange and utilize data between them is referred to as "blockchain interoperability."

Interoperability is harmed directly by these disparate data standards. Blockchain, which uses APIs to access data, provides a solution to this problem. By doing this, data formats are standardized to allow for smooth data transfer regardless of how well EHRs can interact with various HL7 versions.

A cross-chain is the capacity of two relatively independent blockchains to communicate with one another. In other words, it enables blockchains to communicate with one another due to their uniform construction. Cross-chains overcome the constraints of a single chain.

Currently, there are at least 1,000 blockchains with at least four types of blockchain networks. While the idea of blockchain is a singular data transfer type, there are multiple platforms provided in this industry.

The definition "interoperable blockchain architecture" is incorporated in the NIST definition of "blockchain" (p.50 of [5]):

Interoperable blockchain architecture is a composition of distinguishable blockchain systems, each representing a unique distributed data ledger, where the atomic transaction execution may span multiple heterogeneous blockchain systems, and where data recorded in one blockchain is reachable, verifiable, and referenceable by another possibly foreign transactions in a semantically compatible manner.

In this context it is useful to revisit some key architectural designs of the Trusted Platform Module (TPM) from the late 1990s which provided a basic understanding on trustworthiness[6]. Reusing some of the concepts in trusted computing, a node can be considered to exhibit technical trust if it:

- Operates unhindered and shielded from external influences or interference
- Operates for a well-defined task
- Has the ability to report results of its computations and its internal status truthfully

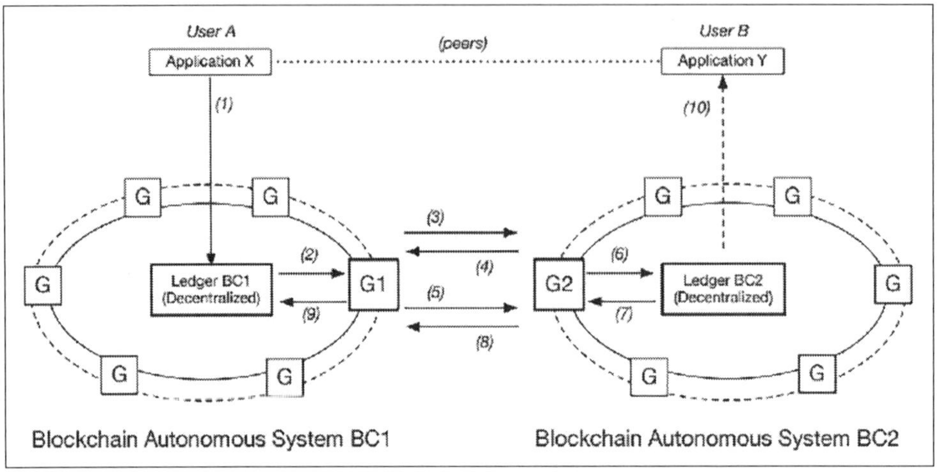

Figure 9.1: *Example of Inter-Domain Transaction across Two Blockchain Systems*

To illustrate **Inter-Domain Transaction**, a simple example is shown in *Figure* 9.1 in which an asset recorded in blockchain system BC1 is to be transferred to blockchain system BC2.

Both blockchain BC1 and BC2 are permissioned/private blockchain systems.

In *Figure* 9.1, a User A with Application X has his or her asset ownership (example, land title deed) recorded on the ledger inside blockchain BC1. The local transaction-identifier for this ledger entry is T x1privateID. The User A wishes to transfer legal ownership of the asset (example, sell) to a different User B running Application Y. However, the User B requires that the asset be "moved" to the blockchain BC2 and be authoritatively recorded on the ledger of BC2.

This would allow User B to later sell the asset locally in blockchain BC2 to other users in BC2. Note that being private blockchain systems, none of the gateways or nodes in BC1 can directly read/write to BC2, and vice versa.

The following is a high-level summary of the transaction flows between BC1 and Bc2 :

In step 1, the User A initiates the transfer to User B by submitting a (candidate) transaction to BC1 with the recipient address being the public-key of User B in BC2 (example, pubkeyB/BC2).

Because the destination blockchain BC2 is a foreign system, only the gateway nodes in BC1 are permitted or have the capability to process this transaction.

In step 2, the gateway G1 selects the candidate (unprocessed) transaction of User A in BC1 and proceeds to process the transaction. Seeing that the pending transaction is destined for pubkeyB/BC2, gateway G1 locates one or more gateways G2 in BC2 and proceeds to perform trust negotiations with G2.

In step 3, identifier value T x1privateID with a new public value T x1publicID. G1 has to persistently maintain this table of mappings (T x1privateID, T x1publicID). In the future, Gateway G1 must provide a means to resolve the public value T x1publicID back to the internal private value T x1privateID, should that be required.

In step 4 and step 5, (multiround) gateways G1 and G2 must establish trust by executing a key establishment protocol that includes the exchange of keying parameters, hardware root of trust certificates (example, AIK certificates in TPM), hardware status reports such as Quote protocol reports, and other relevant trust establishment parameters.

In step 6, after pairwise technical-trust has been established between gateways G1 and G2, the gateway G2 proceeds to submit a new local transaction with identifier T x2privateID into the ledger of BC2 addressed pubkeyB. This local transaction references the asset (in BC1) identified by the public value T x1publicID. In effect, gateway G2 is "registering" this asset T x2privateID as belonging to User B with public key pubkeyB.

In step 7, confirmation has been achieved in the ledger of BC2. Gateway G2 needs to indirectly report this confirmed status of T x2privateID to gateway G1. As such G2 has to mask local transaction-identifier T x2privateID with a new public identifier T x2publicID. Gateway G2 must henceforth maintain a persistent mapping between T x2publicID and T x2privateID.

In step 8, Gateway G2 issues a signed assertion to G1 stating that the asset with transaction identifier T x2publicID has been confirmed on ledger BC2, and includes a hash of the private identifier T x2privateID in the assertion.

In step 9, upon seeing the signed assertion from G2, gateway G1 proceeds to submit a new "invalidation" transaction in BC1, essentially marking that the asset previously known as T x1privateID has been moved to BC2. The invalidation-transaction also includes a reference to the new home of the asset, namely T x2publicID/BC2. It should also include a hash of the signed assertion from G2. Finally, in step 10 the User B is able to see the confirmed transaction T x2privateID/BC2, while User A sees that T x1privateID/BC1 as also being confirmed.

Note: *The above use-case is an abstract example only. Many variations are possible for these flows, including the incorporation of commitment protocols (example, 2-phase commit) in Steps 2 to 9.*

Conclusion

In this chapter, we have learned that these blockchain-based apps were compelled to interact with other blockchain apps running on different blockchain networks. This led to the development of a new communication mechanism between several segregated blockchain networks, establishing the groundwork for the idea of blockchain network interoperability.

For revision, we learned that Blockchain technology development happened very fast and is now being classified into four stages:

- Blockchain 1.0 was devoted to cryptocurrency applications.
- Blockchain 2.0 provides smart contracts and property.
- Blockchain 3.0 developed distributed applications such as governance, IoT, healthcare, supply chain, smart city, and many other non-financial applications.
- Blockchain 4.0 distributed ledger technology.

We have seen that Blockchain interoperable protocols can be categorized into: cross-chain (homogenous) and cross blockchain protocols (heterogeneous).

As a form of money that symbolizes a digital asset kept in a blockchain, crypto tokens are the widely used application of blockchain technology. The new cross-chain protocol makes it easier for various blockchain networks to communicate with one another and permits data sharing between many networks.

In the next chapter, titled *Legal and Environmental Aspects*, we will study implications of using cryptocurrencies and about Non-Fungible Tokens and the Indian rules on cryptocurrency.

References

[1] Belchior, Rafael; Vasconcelos, André; Guerreiro, Sérgio; Correia, Miguel (May 2020). "A Survey on Blockchain Interoperability: Past, Present, and Future Trends"

[2] Blockchain Interoperability – Understanding Cross-Chain Technology, blog by Ayushi Abrol, https://www.blockchain-council.org/blockchain/blockchain-interoperability/

[3] Why is Interoperability Needed?, htRafael Belchior (Hyperledger Cactus), Nicko Guyer (Hyperledger FireFly), Jun Kimura (YUI), Hart Montgomery (Hyperledger Cactus), Venkatraman Ramakrishna (Weaver), Peter Somogyvari (Hyperledger Cactus), Susumu Toriumi (YUI), Dhinakaran Vinayagamurthy (Weaver), and Jim Zhang (Hyperledger FireFly) https://www.hyperledger.org/blog/2022/02/02/why-is-interoperability-needed

[4] D. Yaga, P. Mell, N. Roby, and K. Scarfone, "Blockchain Technology Overview," NIST Draft NISTIR 8202, January 2018, available on https://csrc.nist.gov.

[5] Trusted Computing Group, "TPM Main – Part 1 Design Principles – Specification Version 1.2," Trusted Computing Group, TCG Published Specification, October 2003, available at http://www.trustedcomputinggroup.org/ resources/ tpm main specification.

[6] Belchi D. Yaga, P. Mell, N. Roby, and K. Scarfone, "Blockchain Technology Overview," NIST Draft NISTIR 8202, January 2018, available on https://csrc.nist.gov.

Chapter 10
Legal and Environmental Aspects

Introduction

Cryptocurrency is a new way of payment that has emerged in recent times, as an advancement in Virtual Currency. The use and functioning of Cryptocurrency are fairly different than traditional mode of payment and is not regulated by any government or financial institution.

There are no rules and regulations or any guidelines laid down for regulating and settling disputes while dealing with cryptocurrency. India recently decided to tax digital assets such as cryptocurrencies and non-fungible tokens (NFT), with a 30-percent tax on transfer of such assets as well as a 1-percent tax deduction at source (TDS) on every transaction. We shall read about NFT in this chapter.

Structure

In this chapter, we will cover the following topics:

- Legal Aspects of Cryptocurrencies
- The Transfer of Property
- Digital Ownership and Non-Fungible Tokens (NFT)
- Difference Between NFT and Cryptocurrency
- Working and Use Cases for NFTs
- Use Cases for NFTs
- Electricity Consumption and Environmental Footprints in Usage in Blockchain Operations

- Illicit Contents Scammers
- Transfer of Funds
- Preventing Money Laundering by Blockchain Technology
- Exchange of Blockchain
- Metaverse

Legal Aspects of Cryptocurrencies

All **Fiat** (the conventional) currencies in the world derive their authority as medium of transaction from the government or monetary authorities. For example, each Rupee (paper currency of India) is guaranteed to be returned by Reserve bank of India, the same way as, dollar bill by the Federal Reserve of USA. The currency we use is Fiat currency (money), a government-issued currency, is not backed by a commodity such as gold in all countries. Because central banks can regulate the amount of money generated, fiat money provides them more control over the economy and, consequently leads to inflation.

Legal Status of Cryptocurrencies in Major Countries of the World

Cryptocurrencies such as Bitcoin and Ethereum are not backed or financially supported by any public or private entities. Throughout the world, it is almost difficult to make a case for their legal status in different financial jurisdictions. It is a universal fact that cryptocurrencies are largely functioning outside existing financial infrastructures. The legal status of cryptocurrencies is controversial for their use in daily transactions and trading.

All users as well as financial and banking organizations have come to the conclusion that cryptocurrencies cannot be classified as money, assets, or commodities since they lack intrinsic value and underlying cash flows. They are also similar to Ponzi schemes, if not worse.

In this aspect, the regulators fear the misuse of cryptocurrency as it may erode their attempts to combat money laundering by taking advantage of its anonymity. India, being a part of the Financial Action Task Force (FATF), has to abide by its standards that seek global cooperation between sovereign member nations.

As we know, cryptocurrencies are decentralized systems where transactions are authenticated by participants through consensus. They are cleverly designed to bypass the financial system and all its controls and cannot be traced, confiscated, or frozen by governments. However, in the budget of India (2022), it was made clear that the RBI would launch India's Digital Rupee in FY 2023.

In June 2019, the Financial Action Task Force (FATF) of USA recommended that the wire transfers of cryptocurrencies should be subject to the requirements of its Travel Rule, which requires AML compliance. A **wire transfer** is an electronic way to transfer money and is also known as bank transfer. This mode of transfer is fast and secure and happens from one bank to another.

In the USA, the Bank Secrecy Act, among other things, requires financial institutions, including broker-dealers, to develop and implement anti-money laundering (AML) compliance programs.

El Salvador was the only country in the world to allow Bitcoin as a legal tender for monetary transactions. Japan's Payment Services Act defines Bitcoin as legal property.

However as of April 2022, Cryptocurrency exchanges operating in the country are subject to collect information about the customer and details relating to the wire transfer. **China** has banned cryptocurrency exchanges and mining within its borders.

Notably, cryptocurrencies are legal in the European Union. Derivatives and other products that use cryptocurrencies will need to be certified as "financial instruments." In June 2021, the European Commission released the Markets in Crypto-Assets (MiCA) regulation that lays out guidelines and regulatory safeguards for companies or vendors providing financial services using cryptocurrencies.

The United States of America is known as the biggest and most sophisticated financial market in the world. Crypto derivatives such as Bitcoin futures are available on the Chicago Mercantile Exchange. But the Securities and Exchange Commission (SEC) has iterated that Bitcoin and Ethereum are not securities.

Although cryptocurrencies are considered a form of money, the **Internal Revenue Service** (IRS) treats them as a financial *asset or property*. Additionally, just as with most investments, the government wants a cut of your profits if you sell or trade cryptocurrencies and make capital gains. On May 20, 2021, the U.S. Department of the Treasury announced a proposal that would require taxpayers to report any cryptocurrency transaction of and above $10,000 to the IRS. How the IRS would treat the tax proceeds–as capital gains or ordinary income–depends on how long the taxpayer held the cryptocurrency.

The Transfer of Property

Property is defined by any item that a person or a business has legal title over. Example of Property include tangible items, such as houses, cars, or appliances, or it can also refer to intangible items that carry the promise of future worth, such as stock and bond certificates. Property is mainly divided into two parts, namely movable and immovable. Any offence which is committed in regard to any property whether it is movable or immovable is punishable under the provisions of the law of Crimes or the Indian Penal Code [IPC].

The term transfer of property includes transfer through sale, mortgage, lease, actionable claim, gift, or exchange. The Act does not cover transfers by the operation of law, in the form of inheritance, forfeiture, insolvency, or sale through the execution of a decree.

The Transfer of Property Act 1882 is an Indian legislation which regulates the transfer of property in India. It contains specific provisions regarding what constitutes a transfer and the conditions attached to it. It came into force on 1 July 1882.

According to this Act, 'transfer of property' means an action by which a person conveys the property to one or more persons, or herself/himself. The act of transfer may be done in the present or for the future. The term person may include an individual, company or association, body of individuals, and any kind of property may be transferred, including the transfer of immovable property.

Property is broadly classified into the following categories:

- Immovable Property (excluding standing timber, growing crops, and grass)
- Movable Property (such as watch, timber)

If we interpret the Act, it means "immovable property does not include standing timber, growing crops or grass". Section 3(26), The General Clauses Act, 1897, defines, " immovable property" shall include land, benefits to arise out of the land, and things attached to the earth, or permanently fastened to anything attached to the earth. Also, The Registration Act, 1908, 2(6) states that "immovable property" includes land, buildings, hereditary allowances, rights to ways, lights, ferries, fisheries or any other benefit to arise out of the land, and things attached to the earth or permanently fastened to anything which is attached to the earth, but not standing timber, growing crops nor grass.

Note that a transfer of property passes forthwith to the transferee all the interest which the transferor is then capable of passing in the property unless a different intention is expressed or implied.

As per Section 43 of the Transfer of Property Act 1882:

- In case a person either fraudulently or erroneously represents that she/he is authorized to transfer certain immovable property and does some acts to transfer such property for consideration, then such a transfer will continue to operate in future. It will operate on any interest which the transferor may acquire in such property.
- This will be at the option of the transferee and can be done during the time in which the contract of transfer exists. As per this rule, the rights of the bona fide transferee, who has no notice of the earlier transfer or of the option, are protected. This rule embodies a rule of estoppel that means a person who makes a representation cannot later on go against it.

- Every person who is competent to contract, is competent to transfer property, which can be transferred in whole or in part. He should be entitled to the transferable property, or authorized to dispose of transferable property which is not his own. The right may be either absolute or conditional, and the property may be movable or immovable, present or future. Such a transfer can be made orally unless a transfer in writing is specifically required under any law.
- Even when a person is mentally competent, but physically unable to sign any contract, the property lawyer hired by him, can do that with the help of a power of attorney.

According to Section 6 of the Transfer of Property Act, property of any kind may be transferred. However, the person insisting non-transferability, must prove the existence of some law or custom which restricts the right of transfer. Unless there is some legal restriction preventing the transfer, the owner of the property can transfer it. However, in some cases, there may be a transfer of property by an unauthorized person who subsequently acquires an interest in such property.

In case the property transferred is subject to the condition which absolutely restrains the transferee from parting with or disposing of his interest in the property, the condition is void. The only exception is in the case of a lease where the condition is for the benefit of the lessor or those claiming under him. Generally, only the person having interest in the property is authorized to transfer and can pass on the proper title to any other person.

The rights of the transferees will not be adversely affected, provided: they acted in good faith; the property was acquired for a consideration, and the transferees had acted without notice of the defect in the title of the transferor.

These conditions must be satisfied:

- It is compulsory that there must be a representation by the transferor that he has authority to transfer the immovable property.
- The representation should be either fraudulent or erroneous.
- The transferee must act on the representation in good faith.
- The transfer should be done for a consideration.
- The transferor should subsequently acquire some interest in the property he had agreed to transfer. The transferee may have the option to acquire the interest which the transferor subsequently acquires.

Digital Ownership and Non-Fungible Tokens (NFT)

The digital ownership gives authority to have permission to access and/or use data, information and knowledge about ourselves or about the objects someone own. Alternatively, it also grants or revokes rights on these data. The digital ownership is also a component layer of Internet of Things (IoT) that enables gathering of gigabytes of data on a single thing.

A Non-Fungible Tokens (NFT) is defined as a type of digital asset that represents real-world objects such as art, music, in-game items and videos. They are represented, bought and sold online, frequently with cryptocurrency, and they are generally encoded with the same underlying software as many cryptos have used. Needless to say, that NFTs are unique cryptographic tokens that exist on a blockchain and cannot be replicated.

Despite their existence since 2014, NFTs are currently gaining notoriety due to the fact that, despite their growing popularity, the majority of the capital invested in them comes from unapproved sources.

According to Forbes Advisor India (8.4.2022), a staggering $174 million has been spent on NFTs since November 2017.

Perhaps the most well-known NFT of 2021, "EVERYDAYS: The First 5000 Days," was created by well-known digital artist Mike Winklemann, best known by his stage name "Beeple," using a composite of 5,000 daily drawings. It sold at Christie's for an astounding $610.3 million.

Anyone can view the individual images–or even the entire collage of images online for free. So why are people willing to spend millions on something they could easily screenshot or download?

The reason is that NFT allows the buyer to own the original item that contains built-in authentication, which serves as proof of ownership.

Difference Between NFT and Cryptocurrency

Physical currency (money) and cryptocurrencies are "fungible," meaning they can be traded or exchanged for one another. Another word for fungible are exchangeable, substitutable, Inter-changeable or convertible. Crypto's fungibility makes it a trusted means of conducting transactions on the blockchain.

NFT is built using the same kind of programming as cryptocurrency, such as Bitcoin or Ethereum, but that is where the similarity ends.

Each transaction of NFTs is different as they have a digital signature that makes it impossible for NFTs to be exchanged for or equal to one another (hence, non-fungible).

Working Method of NFT

NFTs exist on a blockchain, which is a distributed public ledger that records transactions. You are probably familiar with blockchain as the underlying process that makes cryptocurrencies possible[1]. NFTs are typically held on the Ethereum blockchain, although other blockchains support them as well.

Typically, an NFT is created, or "minted", from digital objects that represent both tangible and intangible items, including:

- A unique digital artwork or Graphic art
- Videos and sports highlights
- Collectibles related with VIPS, Neta, Abhineta
- Virtual avatars and video game skins
- Designer sneakers
- Music
- A unique sneaker in a limited-run fashion line
- An in-game item
- An essay
- A digital collectible
- A domain name
- A ticket that gives you access to an event or a coupon
- Furniture
- Memes
- Big Sports Moments
- Virtual Fashion
- Real-world assets

Tweets count can also be included. Twitter co-founder Jack Dorsey sold his first ever tweet as an NFT for more than $2.9 million.

Use Cases for NFTs

The following factors are required to be kept in mind while thinking of owning NFTs:

- NFTs are like physical collector's items, only digital. So instead of getting an actual oil painting to hang on the wall, the buyer gets a digital file instead.
- They also get exclusive ownership rights. NFTs can have only one owner at a time, and their use of blockchain technology makes it easier to verify ownership and transfer tokens between owners.
- The creator can also store specific information in an NFT's metadata. For instance, artists can sign their artwork by including their signature in the file.

- Blockchain technology and NFTs provide artists and content creators a unique opportunity to monetize their wares. For example, artists no longer have to rely on galleries or auction houses to sell their art. Instead, the artist can sell it directly to the consumer as an NFT, which also lets them keep more of the profits. In addition, artists can program in royalties so they will receive a percentage of sales whenever their art is sold to a new owner. This is an attractive feature as artists generally do not receive future proceeds after their art is first sold.
- Even celebrities such as Snoop Dogg and Lindsay Lohan are jumping on the NFT bandwagon, releasing unique memories, artwork, and moments as securitized NFTs.

Nyan Cat, a 2011-era GIF of a cat with a pop-tart body, was sold for approximately $600,000 in February. And NBA Top Shot generated more than $500 million in sales as of late March. A single LeBron James highlight NFT fetched more than $200,000.

Users are now able to redeem the virtual currency through third-party vendors, peer-to-peer transfers, and full cash redemptions as the issuer's virtual currency or token becomes more popular. Many exchanges offer fiat-to-cryptocurrency exchanges, trading, and investment services. This has changed digital currencies from being a means of prepaying for goods or services, that can be redeemed with a single company, to being a widely accepted proxy for real currency and a means of transmitting legal tender between multiple parties.

Issuers were required to follow state and federal money transmitter, and money service business laws in what are considered landmark cases for the SEC. Many cryptocurrency startups responded by simply shifting their operations to tax havens and off-shore zones, bypassing numerous financial services laws in the US, Canada, Europe, and Australia.

Digital Ownership with Blockchain

Cryptocurrency and tokens do not have any legal tender status in any jurisdiction. The Internal Revenue Service (IRS) of United States describes tokens and cryptocurrencies as digital representations of value that serve as means of exchange, accounts units, and stores of value.

Assets remain very simple and antiquated, based on current legal concepts about goods, value, and exchange. Thus, depending on the jurisdiction, cryptocurrency may or may not be considered money. The hybrid nature of digital ownership of virtual tokens and property makes this inconsistency even worse. Various countries' laws depend on whether they consider cryptocurrency or token a commodity or a currency.

Cryptocurrencies and virtual goods defy categorization from a legal perspective because their legal status is open to many interpretations. This will likely continue to happen until the industry grows and lawmakers and other authorities are better equipped to predict and understand its details and consequences.

Indeed, the absence of regulations has not stopped anybody, including investors, from taking cryptocurrency in return for digital tokens, virtual products, or in-game items. Game producers are incorporating exclusive digital products into their game's arena to entice users and establish closed economies.To purchase so-called digital assets, such as collectible (non-fungible) tokens like virtual cats, players fork over millions of dollars in real estate.

The blockchain game "CryptoKitties" was created by Dapper Labs, a Canadian firm, using Ethereum. Players could generate, purchase, and sell non-fungible tokens in the game. These NFTs stand for digital felines. The Digital Felines is a marketing agency based in Thessaloniki, Greece, with the sole purpose of creating, managing, and expanding your business's image.

Soon after CryptoKitties, other blockchain and game developers began to offer eager fans spells, weapons, textures, skins, property, islands, and other digital assets.

Despite the lack of governance, investors and the general public continue to accept cryptocurrencies for the exchange and purchase of virtual products, in-game items, and digital tokens. A growing number of developers are adding exclusive digital goods to their games in an effort to pique players' interest and establish "closed economies." Millions are spent by players on so-called "digital assets," including virtual kittens and other collectible, non-fungible tokens.

NFT proponents assert that the technique is groundbreaking in two respects. First of all, it assists artists, particularly up-and-coming ones, in escaping the grasp of intermediaries such as record labels and art galleries, who have traditionally kept the majority of the earnings for themselves. Direct interaction and mutually beneficial agreements might be made between the artists and the audience. A wide range of celebrities, including Ellen DeGeneres, Eminem, and Salman Khan, have joined the NFT marketplace.

CryptoKitties is among the initial endeavors to utilize blockchain technology for leisure and entertainment purposes. The Ethereum network experienced congestion in December 2017 due to the game's popularity, which resulted in an all-time high in transactions and markedly slowed down the network[2]. Virtual cats with unique visual characteristics and differing degrees of rarity can be bought, bred, and traded by players. To play the game, players must buy the cryptocurrency Ether, which they must use to complete all trading and breeding tasks.

The underlying blockchain network of Ethereum powers CryptoKitties' operations. Every CryptoKitty token is non-fungible (NFT).Everyone is distinct, belongs to the user, is verified by the blockchain, and is subject to market fluctuations in value. Even the game developers are unable to copy or redistribute CryptoKitties without the user's consent.

Is Ownership of Digital Items Real or Fake?

The practice of using real money to buy virtual products, in-game items, tokens, and digital currencies is becoming more and more common, despite the lack of regulations.

Whether it is $11,000 for an Eve Online Revenant Titan, $170,000 for a virtual cat on CryptoKitties, or $38,000 for a Dota 2 courier, people are spending a lot of money on digital goods, with the intention of reselling them.

In theory, each of these objects is valuable–at least to the individuals who paid for them. However, governments are still at odds over whether to classify that value as a commodity or as money. This distinction is crucial because, if they were seen as currency, they would be governed by a central bank, but if they were regarded as commodities, they would be subject to regulation by the appropriate commodity authority and would have tax ramifications.

Apps, media, in-game goods, and cryptocurrency libraries are being gathered by users, who may then give, share, and sell these collections to other users. However, the terms and conditions that users accept when they register for a game or service almost always specify that the digital goods, they purchase are non-transferable. The question here is whether the real accounts are transferable or not. Other kinds of accounts have highly defined but intangible values, such digital exchange profiles that hold a certain quantity of cryptocurrencies.

The European Court's 2012 Oracle v. UsedSoft decision made it lawful to sell used software, including digital and physical games, as long as the seller removed it from their computer. Rentals of used software were nonetheless prohibited.

However, downloaded digital content was not covered by a June 2014 verdict from the regional court in Hamm, Germany. Furthermore, the law can be confusing when it comes to digital goods and in-game purchases, even though it is generally straightforward about music, movies, and books.

The increasing popularity and global pervasiveness of virtual assets will inevitably lead to a heightened awareness of digital ownership concerns. Governments will eventually need to have a crucial conversation about what they should and should not be able to control, as well as the best ways to go about it.

A boutique law company in San Francisco, The Gamma Law represents a restricted group of clients in innovative industries. They push the boundaries of innovation, give their clients the support they need to flourish in complicated and dynamic business situations, and help them accomplish their goals both domestically and globally.

Electricity Consumption and Environmental Footprints in Usage in Blockchain Operations

It is undeniable that Bitcoin has gone mainstream, within the past one decade, but perhaps not in quite the way Nakamoto imagined. According to Nakamoto's founding white paper, the Bitcoin was to enable instantaneous, borderless transactions without the high fees or foreign exchange barriers that exist today.

When the enigmatic, possibly nonexistent Satoshi Nakamoto minted the world's first cryptocurrency in 2009, the plan was to create a decentralized payments platform that would revolutionize the way we buy and sell everything[3].

Conceptually, it does not seem like Bitcoin should require enormous amounts of electricity. To purchase and sell bitcoin on your smartphone, all you have to do is point and click or tap. And for decades, we have had electronic networks that perform essentially the same functions for different kinds of digital transactions.

This method did not require nation-state levels of electricity in the early days of Bitcoin. However, the arithmetic puzzles in the cryptocurrency are designed to get much, much tougher as more people fight to solve them. This dynamic will only get stronger as more people try to invest in Bitcoin.

Bitcoin demands computers to do ever-more difficult mathematical operations. Verifying transactions on centralized networks requires a far lower energy consumption than this proof of work consensus method.

New sets of transactions (blocks) are added to Bitcoin's blockchain roughly after every 10 minutes by so-called miners. While working on the blockchain, these miners are not required to trust each other. The only thing miners have to trust is the code that runs Bitcoin. The code includes several rules to validate new transactions. For example, a transaction can only be valid if the sender actually owns the sent amount. Every miner individually confirms whether transactions adhere to these rules, eliminating the need to trust other miners.

Ever since its inception, Bitcoin's trust-minimizing consensus has been enabled by its proof-of-work algorithm (vide *Chapter 4, Distributed Consensus in Open Environments*). The machines performing this work are consuming huge amounts of energy while doing so. Moreover, the energy used is primarily sourced from fossil fuels. The Bitcoin Energy Consumption Index was created to provide insight into these amounts, and raise awareness on the unsustainability of the proof-of-work algorithm.

An increasing number of rigs, or dedicated computers, are joining the battle to combat this, putting enormous amounts of electrical and processing energy into the ecosystem in an attempt to be the first to solve Bitcoin math puzzles and get the associated prize. Although there may be hundreds of thousands of computers racing to solve the same problem, only one can ultimately receive the Bitcoin honorarium.

It also takes a very long time to complete this process: A Bitcoin transaction can take up to ten minutes. Other digital transactions, like those powered by Visa, take less than a second and use roughly 1/500,000 the energy because they rely on a centralized authority to verify transactions.

Instead of enabling regular transactions, cryptocurrencies, like Bitcoin, have mostly evolved into speculative assets (a kind of digital gold), drawing investors who think they may sell their holdings for significant gains in the future. However, because the Bitcoin gold rush involves tremendous electricity usage, it has had a severe ecological impact on humanity.

The Fortune magazine states that each Bitcoin transaction consumes 1,173 kilowatt hours of electricity. That is the volume of energy that could "power the typical American home for six weeks," the authors add. The Bitcoin mining that enables a purchase, sale or transfer, it posits, uses a punch of electricity that costs $176.

Based on the data from the Bitcoin Energy Consumption Index from Digiconomist, an online tool created by data scientist Alex de Vries, the carbon footprint of Bitcoin, the world's largest cryptocurrency, is equivalent to that of New Zealand, with both emitting nearly 37 megatons of carbon dioxide into the atmosphere every year.

The Bitcoin Energy Consumption Index provides the latest estimate of the total energy consumption of the Bitcoin network.

The CBECI is an ongoing project created and maintained by the Digital Assets Programme (DAP) Team at the Cambridge Centre for Alternative Finance, an independent research institute based at The University of Cambridge, Judge Business School.

The Cambridge Bitcoin Electricity Consumption Index provides a real-time estimate of the total annual electricity consumption of the bitcoin network. The underlying model updates the network power estimate every thirty seconds based on live price and hash rate data.

Since 2020, Cambridge provides detailed insights into the localization of Bitcoin miners over time.

From Cambridge calculations, it is estimated that at an average efficiency of 48.7 it takes around 142,498 kWh to produce one bitcoin. This is equivalent to 142 MWh or 0.142 GWh. To get the daily amount of energy the network uses, we take the kWh to mine one bitcoin times the daily production rate of 900 coins.

It is essential to distinguish between electricity consumption and environmental footprint. The former concerns the total amount of electricity used by the Bitcoin mining process whereas, the latter is concerned with the environmental implications of Bitcoin mining. An environmental footprint takes into account the entirety of supply and demand of goods and services that is counted as energy used by any user or group of users. In doing so, it is assumed that the entire population follows a certain lifestyle characterized by a known person or a group of people. What ultimately matters for the environment is not the level of electricity consumption per se, but the carbon intensity of the energy sources used to generate that electricity.

Just to have an idea of this concept, let us use the annualized power consumption estimate from CBECI as of July 13th, 2021, which corresponds to roughly 70 TWh. Let us also assume that all this energy comes exclusively from coal (the most-polluting fossil fuel) and is generated in one of the world's least efficient coal-fired power plants (the now-decommissioned Hazelwood Power Station in Victoria, Australia). In this worst-case scenario, the Bitcoin network would be responsible for about 111 million metric tons (Mt) of carbon dioxide emissions, accounting for roughly 0.35% of the world's total yearly emissions.

Although Bitcoin is not unique among cryptocurrencies in terms of its environmental burden, but its high profile and uniquely inefficient transaction approval system makes it an easily condemnable scapegoat.

Combating Bitcoin's Energy Problem

The energy consumption issue with Bitcoin, which is almost the size of a continent, may be resolved without forcing humanity to go back to centralized systems, as demonstrated by Visa's network. As was the central promise of Bitcoin, the elimination of intermediaries like the card networks and their concentrated power over finance is needed. But if that is not possible then Bitcoin's advocates have more than a few options:

- Switching to Renewable Energy
- Transiting to Proof-of-Stake Systems
- Force Embracing Pre-Mining
- Introduction Carbon Credits or Fees
- Switch to Renewable Energy

In the year 2022, an estimated 39-percent of proof-of-work mining was performed using renewable energy. So, perhaps the most obvious and suggestable course of action was to enforce the user companies to adopt green means at the time of giving electric service connections to them by governments.

Countless startups have emerged to address this gap, each targeting new ways to bring more environmental friendly energy to Bitcoin. Hong Kong-based LiquidStack, aims to lower the temperature of mining rigs more efficiently, or Genesis Mining in Iceland, which exclusively uses renewable energy sources.

- **Transition to Proof-of-Stake Systems**

According to Simon Peters, an eToro cryptocurrency market analyst, cryptocurrencies may transition from proof-of-work to proof-of-stake (see Review section 4.5 of this book), which does not necessitate the same frenzy of problem-solving.

The basic notion behind this is that in order to be eligible to validate transactions through proof-of-stake, network users must front a modest sum of cryptocurrency and enter a lottery.

The thought is that if you are putting up some amount of value as collateral, you are less likely to approve fraudulent transactions that would devalue the currency and cost you your stake.

In contrast to proof-of-work (PoW) systems, where a number of machines race to answer the same problem (spending energy), proof-of-stake systems eliminate the competitive computational element while saving energy and enabling each machine to work on one problem at a time. Whereas Proof of Work (POW) uses a competitive validation process to confirm transactions and add new blocks to the blockchain, Proof of Stake (POS) uses randomly chosen miners to validate transactions.

Ethereum, the blockchain system powering Ether and most NFTs, is in the process of converting to proof of stake from proof of work. This will dramatically reduce the energy consumption of Ethereum-based cryptos and blockchains by an estimated 910.5%.

- **Embrace Pre-Mining**

To avoid the rush in wasteful computing involved in solving math problems quickly to earn digital coins, some cryptos have introduced pre-mining that is a system which functionally works similar to fiat currency or stocks. A central authority, such as the U.S. government (in the case of dollars) or a company (in the case of stocks), creates a set amount of an item and then carefully releases it into the economy depending on what is going on in the world or their business.

Several other crypto assets such as XRP (also popularly referred to as **Ripple**) were not mined at all but were instead produced algorithmically. This idea eliminates the need for dedicated high-speed mining equipment.

In these systems, transactions are still verified by a decentralized network of validators before they are added to the currency's blockchain record. But those involved in the transaction may have to pay a small transaction fee to compensate the validators for their effort since the currency system itself does not always reward them. In the case of XRP, currently this fee is a fraction of a cent.

It is said that transitioning Bitcoin to a proof-of-stake or pre-mined system would not be easy. For making any fundamental change in Bitcoin protocol someone would have to convince the majority of miners to agree to the new system. This is rather a tough task when billions are at stake in the existing system that works slowly and electrically inefficiently. The last time a change of this magnitude happened, it was not accepted universally by miners, resulting in a so-called "hard fork" that created a separate cryptocurrency called Bitcoin Cash, which itself later hard forked into Bitcoin SV, among others.

- **Introduce Carbon Credits or Fees**

The government-sanctioned ability of a company to emit a certain amount of carbon emission into the environment is called the Carbon credits. They remain often securitized, as such they can be traded (sold) to by companies that can afford to produce a lessor amount of emissions to other companies. Thus, this provides an incentive to a company to produce less than its allotment—as well as penalizes those that go over. In the case of a crypto mining company, this might mean it purchases carbon credits from another company to help offset the amount of emissions it creates or switches to greener energy so it can earn a profit from selling its credits.

The Environmental Future of the Blockchain

According to Digiconomis's estimate, in year 2022, electricity costs consume up to an estimated 28-percent of Bitcoin mining's profitability each year.

The smart contracts similar to those enabled by Ethereum will allow companies to automate much of their complex payment and business process systems by automatically checking to make sure that a purchase order, for example, complies with the terms and conditions of a contract. This might allow a company to reduce the number of employees who need to commute into an office to process orders, resulting in fewer transportation-related carbon emissions.

Though we may not know the full potential of green applications of blockchain technology for years to come, there are talks of using it to combat big issues, such as helping companies to better log carbon emissions or even, in a truly meta move, using blockchain-powered carbon credits to move to a carbon-neutral future.

Blockchain is a powerful tool that can significantly improve the transparency, accountability, and traceability of greenhouse gas emissions. It helps companies provide more accurate, reliable, standardized, and readily available data on carbon emissions. Blockchain has the potential to ease the process of finding and buying real estate through tokenization, using digital real estate tokens to represent physical assets. This would aid in easing transfers between the buyer and seller by cutting out the need for a middleman.

Illicit Contents

Illicit contents usually refer to something that is not morally proper or acceptable, and is considered improper or socially forbidden. Illicit activities such as smuggling or counterfeiting does happen but they are under the radar of the law. They may or may not be illegal but they go against social norms and values.

In *Chapter 1, Overview of Blockchain Technology*, we learned that every Bitcoin transaction is stored in the distributed database known as the Bitcoin blockchain. However, people have found ways to hack the Bitcoin protocol to store more than just transactions.

Few years back, people started noticing all sorts of things embedded in the Bitcoin blockchain such as the Bitcoin logo, advertisements, and several prayers. There was even illegal pornography and leaked classified documents. All of these were put in by anonymous Bitcoin users. But none of this, so far, appears to seriously threaten those in power in governments and corporations. Once someone adds something to the Bitcoin ledger, it becomes sanctified that is sacrosanct.

Meanwhile, a 2014 tech blog (presented at the SXSW festival in the US) reveals the extraordinary range of material that the writer of the blog had already found stored in the Bitcoin blockchain[4].

This included photographs, illegal primes, an image of Nelson Mandela, Python software, leaked firmware keys, Valentine's Day messages, Wikileaks data, an email, unknown encrypted content, and a Hex-encoded image of Ben Bernanke, then chairman of the Federal Reserve, and the original paper describing Bitcoin by its alleged founder, the pseudonymous Satoshi Nakamoto.

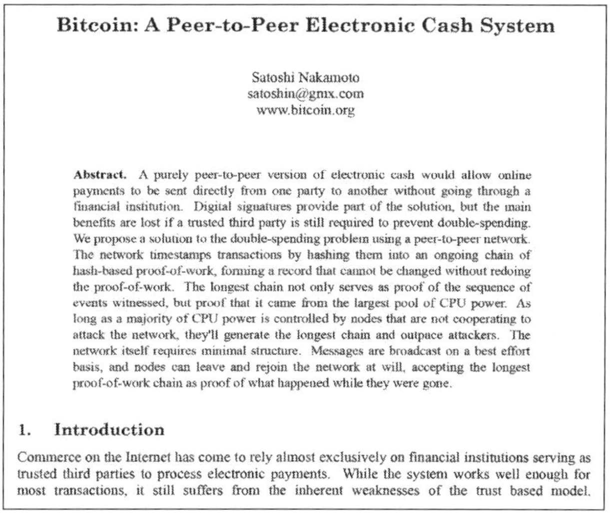

Bitcoin: A Peer-to-Peer Electronic Cash System

Satoshi Nakamoto
satoshin@gmx.com
www.bitcoin.org

Abstract. A purely peer-to-peer version of electronic cash would allow online payments to be sent directly from one party to another without going through a financial institution. Digital signatures provide part of the solution, but the main benefits are lost if a trusted third party is still required to prevent double-spending. We propose a solution to the double-spending problem using a peer-to-peer network. The network timestamps transactions by hashing them into an ongoing chain of hash-based proof-of-work, forming a record that cannot be changed without redoing the proof-of-work. The longest chain not only serves as proof of the sequence of events witnessed, but proof that it came from the largest pool of CPU power. As long as a majority of CPU power is controlled by nodes that are not cooperating to attack the network, they'll generate the longest chain and outpace attackers. The network itself requires minimal structure. Messages are broadcast on a best effort basis, and nodes can leave and rejoin the network at will, accepting the longest proof-of-work chain as proof of what happened while they were gone.

1. Introduction

Commerce on the Internet has come to rely almost exclusively on financial institutions serving as trusted third parties to process electronic payments. While the system works well enough for most transactions, it still suffers from the inherent weaknesses of the trust based model.

Figure 10.1: *Hacked copy of original paper describing Bitcoin by its alleged founder, the pseudonymous Satoshi Nakamoto*

The initial cryptocurrency Bitcoin has raised financial concerns for governments worldwide. Despite its use for buying goods and services, there are still no uniform international laws that regulate Bitcoin or other cryptocurrencies. Many developed countries allow Bitcoin to be used, such as the U.S., Canada, and the U.K.

A fork in the blockchain is necessary to remove anything, causing Bitcoin to split into several rival cryptocurrencies (and related blockchains). Although they do occasionally occur, fork transactions are not currently the result of legal coercion.

Repeated forking involves the possibility of destroying Bitcoin's standing as a stable(ish) currency.

It is well known that in Bitcoin and most other public blockchains there are no central, trusted authorities. Anyone in the world can perform transactions or become a miner.

For cryptographic computations to be performed, hardware and electricity must be available to all.

This openness is also a vulnerability, that opens the door to asymmetric threats and small-time malicious actors. Anyone can put information in the Bitcoin blockchain.

While nasty people will always exploit technology to do evil things, the blockchain fraternity should not succumb to a moral panic and fall in the trap of blaming the entire type of technology for that evil. This technique of including arbitrary data in the Bitcoin blockchain, that is irregularly being used perversely and unreasonably, is the same technique that is being used systematically every day to do socially beneficial record endorsing (notarizing), like tracking land title on the blockchain. The related elements of humanity should be careful not to criticize and disparage technology because of fear, uncertainty, and doubt.

Blockchains are a permanent record of any kind of data, from images to brief messages. Users should be aware that there is some danger involved because each participant must locally duplicate the entire blockchain, including any potentially hazardous material. Expert investigation finds that over 1600 files on the blockchain, more than 99-percent of which are texts or images, can make the mere ownership of a blockchain illegal due to certain content, such as illicit pornography. These files contain content that is clearly offensive and sly, including links to child pornography that is shared with all Bitcoin users.

Scammers

In general, **spam** is unsolicited email, instant messages, or social media messages. These messages are fairly easy to spot and can be damaging if you open or respond. **Scammers** use email or text messages to trick you into giving them your personal information. They may try to steal your passwords, account numbers, or Social

Security numbers. If they get that information, they could gain access to your email, bank, or other accounts.

Scammers launch thousands of phishing attacks like these every day and often successful. **Phishing** is an email sent from an Internet criminal disguised as an email from a legitimate, trustworthy source. Phishing is a type of online scam that targets consumers by sending them an email that appears to be from a well-known source such as an internet service provider, a bank, or a mortgage company. It asks the consumer to provide personal identifying information.

Scams and phishing attacks come in many forms in the crypto world. Here is a list of some of the most common scams you should watch out for[5]:

- **Impersonation**: One might receive correspondence from someone posing as a Blockchain.com employee by phone, social media, or email. Workers never call or get in touch with on social media. All emails will originate from an official Blockchain.com email account that ends in blockchain.com or blockchain.info. Login credentials are not asked under any circumstances. Open a Support Center Ticket to verify the legitimacy of a request if you are unsure.
- **Phishing Emails or Websites**: Always be wary when receiving an email that was not prompted by you. If an email asks you to go to a website and reset your password, do not do it unless you have specifically requested this. These types of scams often result in a malicious third party recording your login details and stealing your funds. Blockchain.com employees will never ask you for your Secret Private Key or Recovery Phrase. In case anyone asks you to provide this information, you can report it in their Support Center.
- **Fake Investment Proposals**: This type of scam may ask you to "pay a fee" or "pay a tax" in order to release a bigger amount of funds to you. The scammers usually refer to official authorities such as the SEC or other institutions. Fraudsters can go as far as to forge official-looking documents or fake ID cards.
- **Fake Refunds**: Blockchain.com does not provide refund services of lost funds from third-party platforms. If someone asks for payment in order to recover/ refund lost or previously scammed funds from third-party platforms or old forgotten wallets, then this request is definitely a fraud. Payments are never asked for such services.
- **Romance Scam**: This is a deceptive practice involving impersonation of an eventual partner or a promise of a fake relationship that can be used as a persuasion technique to manipulate victims in order to extract funds or sensitive data, such as login credentials, recovery phrases, and so on. Be very cautious when you come across a new person on social media.
- **Money Transfers/Deposits/Withdrawals**: Never perform money transfers on behalf of another individual, either for them or by giving them your login details. Not only is this a potential violation of Money Laundering and Terrorist

Financing regulations, but you are also putting your own funds at risk if you give someone access to your account.

- **Platform Clones**: Be cautious of modified URLs such as b1ockchain.com, bl0ckchain.com, blockchain.io, and so on. Make sure you are using our official website with the correct URL to access your account. The login page of the Wallet platform is https://login.blockchain.com/#/login and their Exchange platform is https://exchange.blockchain.com/trade/login.

Other types of scams and phishing attacks could include blackmail, fake exchanges, fake airdrops, malware such as one that can affect Clipboard, an XLM transaction with malicious link as MEMO, Sim Swap, and "pump and dump" schemes, among others.

Please take care of the following as well:

- Any email that ends in a domain other than blockchain.com or blockchain.info but appears to be from original is probably malicious.
- It is probably a scam if you get a call from someone posing as an employee of Blockchain as they never make a call.
- If an email ended up in your spam or junk mail folder, please check the email's headers to be sure the sender is who they say they are.
- Avoid clicking on links or downloading files from unsolicited emails or sources in general.

Transfer of Funds

The illicit practice of obtaining substantial sums of money through criminal conduct, such as sponsoring terrorism, honey trapping, or drug trafficking, is known as money laundering. Money laundering can be done in many different ways[6]. If the quantity is within a realistic range of expectations, the easiest way to register these illicit gains is as sales by a genuine business. Some techniques for money laundering include:

- Bulk cash smuggling
- Black salaries
- Gambling on cricket or any other game
- Trade-based laundering
- Round tripping

Preventing Money Laundering by Blockchain Technology

Blockchain technology possesses inherent characteristics that can potentially prevent money laundering. Every transaction done over blockchain leaves behind a permanent trail of records which is impossible to be altered. Thus, it makes easier for authorities to track the original source of the money[7].

In *Chapter 1, Overview of Blockchain Technology*, we learned that a public blockchain ledger can supervise, validate, and record each transaction's complete history. The in-built security of Blockchain system is such that the public ledger's readers, members, and crypto miners get immediate notification of transactions as they occur. If all the transaction phases, including destination wallet, departure wallet, currency type, and amount, are anyhow left unverified, the transaction gets immediately blocked.

Blockchain can potentially be used to facilitate risk analysis and reporting for money laundering. Rather than only keeping an eye on entry and exit points, it enables comprehensive system analysis.

Immutable Ledger for Regulatory Oversight

The network is extremely secure since Blockchain is a decentralized system where every user or node must validate changes. Every node has access to the complete ledger record and is able to compare and identify any unlawful changes. Blockchain gives data integrity and immutability by removing unwanted modifications.

Because the ledger is verifiable and unchangeable, user trust is naturally incorporated. Blockchain easily and safely creates trust for any transaction facilitating the international transfer of funds or other sensitive data.

Transactions Monitoring in Smart Contracts

The integration facility of Smart Contracts in a Blockchain-based AML platform automates the process of fraud detection in the system. In-built algorithms keep a continuous check on every transaction, automatically generate an alert for a suspicious transaction, and immediately block the transaction. Thus, implementing blockchain in AML enables in gaining oversight over all the transactions.

Exchange of Blockchain

The company's exchange is focused on mainstream adoption and ease of use.

Here, the bitcoin aspirant can view the markets, check the status of previously placed orders, can make deposits, withdraw funds, and trade crypto-assets. In some locations, you can also buy crypto using fiat. The Blockchain Exchange was built aiming towards the trader that is looking for a fast, intuitive, and simple trading experience.

A cryptocurrency exchange refers to a website or service where people may purchase, sell, or exchange fiat money for digital currency. This is in contrast to a cryptocurrency wallet, which is a program that allows an investor to keep all of their cryptocurrency.

Coinbase Global, Inc., selling the branded **Coinbase**, is an American company that operates a cryptocurrency exchange platform. Coinbase is a distributed company; despite not having a physical headquarters, every employee works remotely. By trading volume, it is the biggest cryptocurrency exchange in the US, handling over 30 different cryptocurrencies.

Coinbase Pro, the robust exchange powering Coinbase, is one of the largest and safest platforms out there.

According to the Bloomberg Billionaire Index, Changpeng Zhao–founder of cryptocurrency exchange Binance–is estimated to be worth $96 billion, making him the richest person in cryptocurrencies.

FTX is a fast-growing cryptocurrency exchange that offers advanced trading options such as margin and futures trading. While residents of the United States cannot use it due to strict regulations, a separate exchange–FTX.US–is available, but with fewer crypto offerings. FTX offers a wide array of services in addition to spot trading. It supports Bitcoin and Ethereum derivatives trading, as well as NFT trading. U.S. residents cannot trade on FTX's global platform: due to strict regulations for the crypto space in the United States, residents of the U.S. have limited access to FTX. The exchange has a U.S. partner, FTX.US, but its offerings are more limited than the global platform.

Both FTX.US and Coinbase prioritize security and have excellent track records as of April 2022. Of these two, Coinbase has been around much longer without any data breaches or hacks. But each of these crypto exchanges does well from a security perspective. Two-factor authentication (2FA) is available on FTX.US and Coinbase.

MetaMask Exchange for Ethereum

The Metamask application includes an integrated service for exchanging **Ethereum** tokens by aggregating several decentralized exchanges (DEXs) to find the best exchange rate. This feature, branded as MetaMask Swaps, charges a service fee of 0.875% of the transaction amount.

MetaMask provides an essential utility for blockchain newcomers, token traders, crypto gamers, and developers. MetaMask provides the simplest yet most secure way to connect to blockchain-based applications. You are always in control when interacting on the new decentralized web-2. MetaMask generates passwords and keys on your device, so only you have access to your accounts and data. You always choose what to share and what to keep private. The attractiveness of Web 3.0 is that it is decentralized, meaning that rather than consumers accessing the internet through services mediated by companies such as Google, Apple or Facebook, individuals, themselves, own and govern sections of the internet. Web 3.0 ensures that its users always have control over their online data by utilizing decentralized networks. The next version of the internet is also expected to be more reliable due to its decentralized nature, which eliminates the possibility of a single point of failure. But it is very much different than VPN.

Web 2.0 (also known as participative or participatory web or social web) refers to websites that emphasize user-generated content, ease of use, participatory culture, and interoperability (that is, compatibility with other products, systems, and devices) for end users.

Web 3.0, also known as the next evolution of the World Wide Web. Some literature calls it as 4th gen Web. It provides a data-driven Semantic Web employing a machine-based understanding of data with the objective of developing a more intelligent and connected web experience for users. The three crucial foundations of Web 3.0 are Artificial intelligence (AI), Internet of things (IoT), and blockchain technology. Blockchain will help in achieving decentralized data storage and foster faith in the virtual world. Web3 is the name some technologists have given to the idea of a new kind of internet service that is built using decentralized blockchains – the shared ledger systems used by cryptocurrencies such as Bitcoin and Ethereum. The term has been around for years, but it has come into Vogue in 2021 or so.

Frailty

Frailty is often defined as an aging-related syndrome of physiological decline, characterized by marked vulnerability to adverse health outcomes. Some bitcoin watchers, such as Swanson, also worry about the risk of one of the big exchanges being suddenly shut by authorities.

In July, U.S. authorities shut down the website of the BTC-e exchange, saying it had facilitated transactions involving ransomware, computer hacking, identity theft, tax refund fraud schemes, public corruption, and drug trafficking.

BTC-e, which is no longer operating, could not be reached for comment. The top three exchanges out of more than 100 - Bitfinex, GDAX, and bitFlyer - are home to more than 60 percent of all trading, according to data provider Bitcoinity.

The bitcoin blockchain will stop synchronizing in the event of an internet shutdown. The ledgers will immediately stop recording bitcoin transactions, leading to a temporary break in transaction processing. The network will resume if the transactions are consistent. A blockchain-based alternative can address this problem by replacing Internet giants with a decentralized, peer-to-peer network of providers. In such an alternative, members of the community would own and operate the infrastructure used for storage and computing.

What would happen if there was an internet shutdown? For the everyday person, some cell phone services and text messaging would be unavailable, all mobile apps and social networking sites would be down, cloud storage would be inaccessible, any pending electronic payments would fail, and more.

No person, company, organization or government runs the Internet. It is a globally distributed network comprising many voluntarily interconnected autonomous networks. It operates without a central governing body with each constituent network setting and enforcing its own policies. The cryptocurrency Bitcoin has raised financial concerns for governments worldwide. Despite its use for buying goods and services, there are still no uniform international laws that regulates Bitcoin.

Nowadays, virtual ledgers used by banks and other financial institutions hold 93% of the world's money. There is no denying that we are moving towards a cashless future given the growing digitalization of financial services; the only question is, what that future will entail?

What is the lifespan of cryptocurrency?

Furthermore, blockchain projects only average a lifespan of roughly 1.22 years.

However, there is good news with the sharp rise in bitcoin use in 2021: illegal activity is at an all-time low. According to Chainalysis, the percentage of cryptocurrency transactions involving illegitimate addresses dropped to 0.15% in 2021 from 0.62% in 2020.

Metaverse

A metaverse is a network of 3D virtual worlds focused on social connection. In futurism and science fiction, it is often described as a hypothetical iteration of the Internet as a single, universal virtual world that is facilitated by the use of virtual and augmented reality headsets.

The term "metaverse" refers to a hybrid technology environment where users "live" in a virtual reality, augmented reality, and video. The metaverse's proponents see their users engaging in anything from virtual international travel to concerts and conferences as well as working, playing, and maintaining social connections with friends.

The metaverse can be defined as a simulated digital environment that uses augmented reality (AR), virtual reality (VR), and blockchain, along with concepts from social media, to create spaces for rich user interaction mimicking the real world.

The metaverse has also been described as a place where users can connect, interact, and transfer themselves and their belongings across multiple digital locations. With the metaverse, customers will be able to take a 3D virtual hotel tour and research the location of the hotel where they are considering staying using VR platforms and hardware. Before booking a hotel room, travelers can put on their 3D digital avatars and take a virtual tour of the facility.

There is a debate about what the metaverse, the next-generation virtual reality-powered version of the Web, might look like. Yet despite the uncertainty of this hybrid physical/virtual landscape, the metaverse is inevitably going to be a fully functioning marketplace – among other things – where users can dart around from one place to another as digital replicas of themselves, purchasing products in virtual stores.

Although not owned by any one company – Google, Microsoft, and Samsung are also participating with Facebook with their involvement in the XR Association – Facebook has placed the biggest stake in this virtual land with an elaborate marketing campaign, which included renaming itself, Meta.

Think Ready Player One, but more accessible and pragmatic. Think of social media as it exists today, but more integrated and immersive. The notion of the metaverse – recently propelled into the mainstream by Facebook's rebranding as Meta – will transform how we inhabit the world around us.

This has several implications:

- In addition to two-dimensional digital spaces, users will now have an immersive reality that they can occasionally inhabit.
- Content creators and designers (especially 3D modelling and VR world-building experts) can expect new opportunities on the road ahead.
- The metaverse opens up a new economy where wealth can be created, traded, and enhanced using a currency distinct from but related to the real world.
- The metaverse necessitates the evolution of new technologies for its execution. For example, you need a "Digital me" or the digital twin of a person to simulate real-world presence.
- There are concerns around data privacy, security, diversity, and ethical behavior – problems of the real world that may take on a new dimension in a virtual one.

The Origins of the Metaverse

While the term metaverse may be new to some, it has been around as a concept for nearly three decades. American science fiction author Neal Stephenson introduced the metaverse in his 1992 novel, Snow Crash. In the novel (like others in its genre), users use metaverse as an escape from a futuristic, largely dystopian world.

Over the last 30 years, the industry has laid the foundations for a non-fictional metaverse, brick by brick. Virtual reality headsets have become more ergonomic and affordable. Global internet penetration has steadily risen. The popularity of online gaming, often reaching tournament levels, has made it possible to envision and execute sophisticated digital avatars, tradable digital assets, and even digital real estate.

Decentraland is a 3D virtual world browser-based platform. Users may buy virtual plots of land in the platform as NFTs via the MANA cryptocurrency, which uses the Ethereum blockchain. It was opened to the public in February 2020, and is overseen by the nonprofit Decentraland Foundation. The platform's MANA coin is the cryptocurrency that is used to buy virtual goods and services, while LAND is an NFT token that defines ownership of land parcels that represent digital real estate. Decentraland is backed by $25.5 million in funding and provides users with a VR environment builder, customizable avatars, a crypto-enabled marketplace, digital wallets, and a governance system. Facebook is looking to build a similar experience, but one that intersects with pre-existing, non-AR/VR social media. It announced its pivot into AR/VR in September 2021, along with launching its own take on the metaverse.

Conclusion

All Fiat (the conventional) currencies, worldwide, derive their authority as being the media of transaction from the government or monetary authorities.

We have learnt about Legal status of cryptocurrencies in major countries of the world including India, USA, and China. El Salvador, EU, and Japan were the only countries in the world to allow Bitcoin as legal tender for monetary transactions. Japan's Payment Services Act defines Bitcoin as legal property.

We have learnt about Transfer of Property and its related Acts, Non-Fungible Tokens (NFT) and its role in cryptocurrency.

In the next chapter, we will go through some practical questions related to blockchain network.

References

[1] What Is An NFT? Non-Fungible Tokens Explained, https://www.forbes.com/advisor/investing/cryptocurrency/nft-non-fungible-token/

[2] Risks, Issues, and Concerns Related to Digital Ownership, https://gammalaw.com/risks-issues-and-concerns-related-to-digital-ownership/

[3] Why Does Bitcoin Use So Much Energy? by John Schmidt, https://www.forbes.com/advisor/investing/cryptocurrency/bitcoins-energy-usage-explained/

[4] Ken Shirriff's blog, http://www.righto.com/2014/02/ascii-bernanke-wikileaks-photographs.html

[5] What are the most common scams?, https://support.blockchain.com/hc/en-us/articles/4413805384852-What-are-the-most-common-scams

[6] How Can Blockchain Simplify KYC and AML Processes? https://www.leewayhertz.com/blockchain-in-aml/

[7] "CryptoKitties craze slows down transactions on Ethereum". 5 December 2017. Retrieved 7 October 2018

CHAPTER 11

Exercises for Practical

Introduction

For reading purpose, the practical is divided into three different sections each containing an exercise. The base material had been derived from the archived series of IBM.

Structure

In this chapter, we will discuss the following topics:

- Practical 1: How to Get Started with Docker
  - Container
  - Docker Container
- Practical 2: Create and Deploy a Blockchain Network
  - Code Pattern
  - Networks of Blockchains
  - Blockchain Network Types
  - Packaging the Smart Contract
  - Creating IBM Cloud Services
- Practical 3: Interact with a Blockchain Network
  - Developer Pattern
  - Elements of a Blockchain
  - Developing Services for IBM Cloud
  - Building a Network

Practical 1: How to Get Started with Docker Container

Install and understand Docker container, Node.js, Java and Hyperledger Fabric, and

Ethereum. Perform necessary software installation on local machine/create instance on Cloud to run. Refer to the following links:

https://github.com/hyperledger/

https://docs.docker.com/get-started/

https://console.ng.bluemix.net/docs/services/block chain/index.htm

Containers

Programmable application environments that are totally separated are known as containers. In other words, they share the same operating system kernel but can each have its own networking interface, mounts, processes, and services, just like virtual machines.

At the heart of an operating system on a computer is a computer program called the kernel, which has total authority over all system functions. It is the area of the operating system code that is permanently stored in memory and allows the software and hardware to communicate with one another.

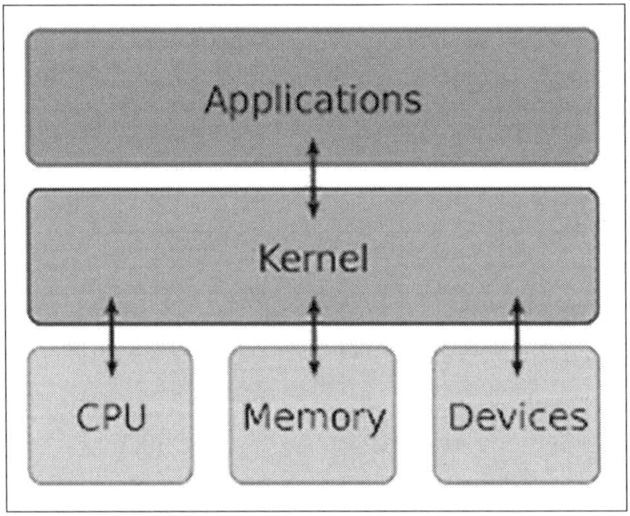

Figure 11.1: *Kernel of operating System*

It is important to note that containers are not new with Docker.

Containers have been in existence for the past ten years. Among the various containers are LXC, LXD, LXCFS, and so forth. LXC containers are utilized by Docker. Because these container environments use very low-level code applications, the setup process is very complicated. On the other hand, Docker provides end users like us with a very easy-to-use collection of high-level tools that have multiple strong features.

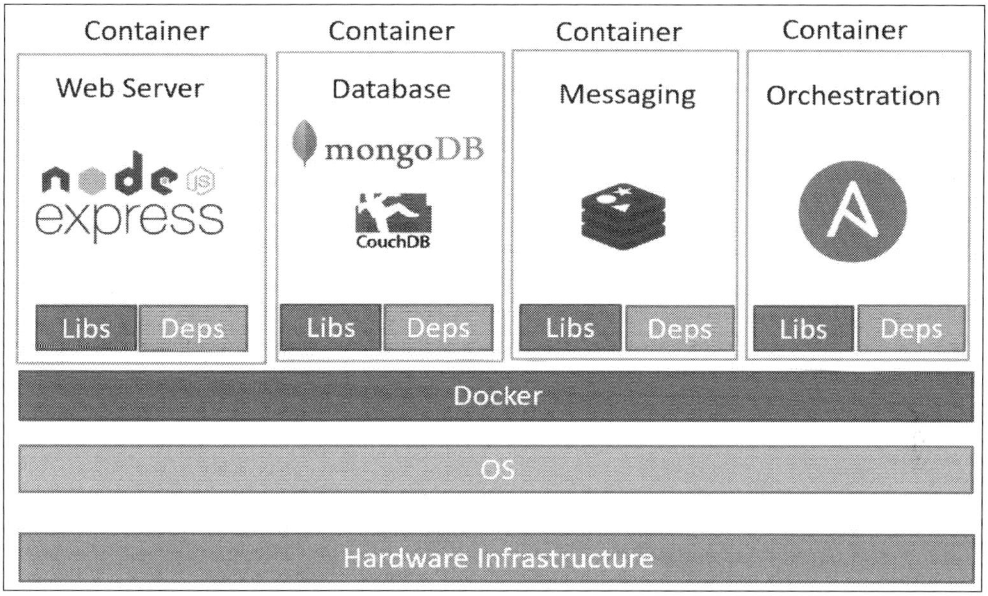

Figure 11.2: *Containers and Docker Management*

The docker technology utilizes several container technologies as shown in *Figure 11.2*.

Linux Containers (LXC)

Linux Containers (LXC) is designed to be an operating-system-level **virtualization** method for running multiple isolated Linux systems (containers) on a control host using a single Linux kernel. LXC is a well-known Linux container runtime that consists of tools, templates, and library and language bindings.

Linux containers are designed for running applications, whereas Virtual Machines are designed for running Operating Systems. Docker is developed in the Go language and utilizes LXC, cgroups, and the Linux kernel itself. Since it is based on LXC, a Docker container does not include a separate operating system; instead, it relies on the operating system's own functionality as provided by the underlying infrastructure. Go was originally built for programs related to networking and infrastructure. It was intended to replace popular high-performance server-side languages such as Java and C++. Today, Go is used for a variety of applications such as cloud and server-side applications, DevOps, command line tools, and much more.

Control Groups (cgroups) is a Linux kernel feature that limits, accounts for, and isolates the resource usage (CPU, memory, disk I/O, network, and so on) of a collection of processes or process containers. One of the design goals of cgroups is to provide a unified interface to many different use cases, from controlling single processes (by using nice, for example) to full operating system-level virtualization.

The Docker Dashboard

The Docker Dashboard gives the user a quick view of the containers running on their machine. The Docker Dashboard is available for Mac and Windows. The user can simply manage the container lifecycle (stop, delete, and more), can easily access container logs, and get a shell inside the container.

The Docker Dashboard provides a simple interface that enables you to manage your containers, applications, and images directly from your machine without having to use the **Command Line Interface** (CLI) to perform core actions.

Remember that CLI, is a non-graphical, text-based interface to the computer system, where the user types in a command and the computer then successfully executes it. The **Terminal** is the platform or the IDE that provides the command line interface (CLI) environment to the user.

Docker Container

Docker is a set of platform as a service (PaaS) products that use OS-level virtualization to deliver software in packages called containers. The service has both free and premium tiers. The software that hosts the containers is called Docker Engine. It was first released in 2013 and is developed by Docker, Inc.

The following are the characteristic feature of the Docker Container:

- An executable bundle of programs and their dependencies is called a Docker container.
- All the instructions needed to run the solution are included in this package for the programmer.
- The integrated structural redundancy makes it incredibly light.
- The container is naturally transportable as well.
- Its total isolation during operation is an additional advantage. Unlike with a virtual machine or non-containerized environment, it is guaranteed not to be affected by any host OS security measures or special configurations even if you are running a container.
- The memory for a Docker environment can be shared across multiple containers, which is really useful, especially when you have a virtual machine that has a defined amount of memory for each environment.

The container is built using Docker images, and the command to run those images is Run.

Let us go through the basic steps of running a Docker image in this section for Practical 1 on Docker.

Docker's Working Method

First, let us review some fundamental operating system ideas[1]. Examine operating systems such as Windows, Fedora, Ubuntu, and CentOS, among others. They are all made up of an operating system kernel and a collection of programs. The software that runs on top of the operating system kernel (in this case, Linux) is what distinguishes different operating systems from one another. The operating system kernel is in charge of communicating with the underlying hardware.

Different user interface drivers, compilers, file managers, developer tools, and so on, may be included in the software. Thus, all operating systems use a similar Linux kernel, and some specialized software sets each operating system apart from the others.

Any OS version can be run on top of Docker, provided that each one is built upon the same kernel–in this case, Linux/Windows.

However, Docker is far more capable than this. Docker has the following features available:

- Docker is an OS virtualized software platform that makes it easy for IT organizations to build, distribute, and run applications in containers that contain all of the dependencies. The container is actually a very compact package that includes all of the instructions and dependencies, such as libraries, bins, and frameworks.
- It is relatively easy to shift the container itself from one environment to another.
- When deploying a solution, you want to be able to ensure that the tested code will function as intended in the production environment. This is where Docker really shines in a DevOps life cycle. Furthermore, it is advantageous to have a container running the solution while you are developing and testing the code since it allows you to verify your work in the same environment that is used for production.

A server and a client are the two main components of the Docker engine, which is used to operate Docker. REST API is used for communication between the two components. The **`instructComponents`** of Docker are communicated by the server.

Docker can build images automatically by reading the instructions from a Dockerfile. A Dockerfile is a text document that contains all the commands a user could call on the command line to assemble an image. It executes any command on top of the current image and creates a new layer giving the result.

`RUN <command>` (the command is run in a shell)

`CMD`:- The **`CMD`** command defines a default command to run when your container starts.

Important instructions used in Dockerfile:

- **`RUN`**: A RUN instruction is used to run specified commands.

  `ENTRYPOINT`: The difference between **`ENTRYPOINT`** and **`CMD`** is that, if you try to specify default arguments in the docker run command, it will not ignore the **`ENTRYPOINT`** arguments. For example, **`WORKDIR /usr/src/app`**.

- **`EXPOSE`**:

  There are four components of Docker:

  - Docker client
  - Docker server
  - Docker image
  - Docker registry Docker Image

Docker Client and Server

This is a solution that requires you to utilize the terminal on your Mac or Linux computer to send commands to the Docker daemon from the Docker client. A REST API is used to facilitate communication between the Docker host and client. Similar instructions can be given, like the Docker Pull command, which instructs the daemon to carry out the task via interacting with other components (image, container, registry). In actuality, the Docker daemon functions as a server that communicates with the operating system and provides services. As one might expect, the Docker daemon continuously scans the REST API for requests to see if it needs to execute any particular ones. If you want to start the process from scratch, you can use the Docker command inside your Docker daemon to start all of your performances. The Docker daemon and registry ions to the client can then be executed on a Docker host.

Image Docker

A template with instructions for the Docker container is called a Docker image. Yet Another Markup Language (YAML), is the language used to write the template.

The YAML file contains the Docker image, which is then hosted as a file on the Docker registry. Docker-**`compose.yml`** is only utilized during the setup of local projects. There are multiple important layers in the image, and each layer is dependent on the layers below it. Each command in the Dockerfile is executed to produce an image layer, which is in read-only format. There is a layer of dependencies above your base layer, which is normally where your base image and base operating system are located. These then make up the read-only file that would eventually form your Dockerfile, including the instructions.

The instructions are delivered in four layers: **`From`**, **`Pull`**, **`Run`**, and **`CMD`**. Following is an explanation of their goal:

- **`From`**: After a layer based on Ubuntu is created using the From command, files from the Docker repository are added to the base command of that base layer.
- **`Pull`** : Adding files from your Docker repository is done using Pull.
- **`Run`**: Constructs the container.
- **`CMD`**: Indicates the command to execute inside the container. In this case, to run Python is the command. One of the things that will happen when we add more containers is that each new container will introduce a fresh layer of images to the Docker environment.

Since every container in the Docker environment is independent of every other container, you can write unique read-write instructions for every layer. It is interesting to note that removing a layer will also remove the layer above it.

The Docker Registry

The Docker registry is the location from which you would distribute and host different image formats. The repository is nothing more than an assembly of Docker images, which are created using YAML instructions and are incredibly simple to share and save. The Docker images can be named and tagged to make it simple for users to locate and distribute them inside the Docker registry. Using the publicly accessible Docker hub registry, which is open to everyone, is one method to begin administering a registry. For internal usage only, you can also establish your own register.

You can build both public and private photos for the registry that you internally establish. **`Push`** and **`Pull`** are the commands you would use to link the registry.

- To push a newly generated container environment from your local management node to the Docker registry, use the push command.
- To receive newly produced clients (Docker images) from the Docker registry, use the pull command.

Once more, a **`Pull`** command pulls and retrieves a Docker image from the Docker registry, while a **`Push`** command enables you to push a newly produced command to the registry—whether it be your own private registry or Docker hub.

Containerized Docker

Take a look at this simple Docker run command example, which launches a single redis container:

```
$ Docker run redis
```

It will be taken from the registry if the Redis image is not installed locally. Following this, you will be able to use the newly created Docker container Redis in your environment.

Let us now examine why containers are so thin. The reason for this is that they lack some of the extra layers that virtual machines have. The hypervisor is the most significant layer that Docker lacks, and it is not dependent on a host operating system.

The following is a list of prerequisites for creating and using Docker containers:

- **Docker Engine**: This software builds and operates containers on the host computer.
- **Docker Daemon**: This program controls Docker containers.
- **Docker Client:** It executes instructions. The Docker Daemon receives the translated command over a REST API.
- **Docker Compose**: This allows you to run two containers within one service.

Step-by-Step Docker Installation on Windows

Here are the step-by-step instructions for Docker installations on Windows:

1. Go to the website https://docs.docker.com/docker-for-windows/install/ and download the Docker file.

   Note: A 64-bit *processor and* 4GB *system* RAM *are the hardware prerequisites required to successfully run Docker on Windows 10.*

2. Then, double-click on the **`Docker Desktop Installer.exe`** to run the installer.

   Note: *Suppose the installer (**`Docker Desktop Installer.exe`**) is not downloaded; you can get it from Docker Hub and run it whenever required.*

3. Once you start the installation process, always enable the Hyper-V Windows feature on the Configuration page. Docker installation on Windows Docker is an OS-level virtualization software platform that helps users build and manage applications in the Docker environment.
4. Then, follow the installation process to allow the installer and wait until the process is done.
5. After completion of the installation process, click Close and restart all its library dependencies.

Starting the Docker Desktop Tool

After the installation process is complete, the tool does not start automatically. To start the Docker tool, search for the tool, and select Docker Desktop in your desktop search results.

Before starting the application, Docker offers an onboarding tutorial. The tutorial explains how to build a Docker image and run a container. You are now successfully running Docker Desktop on Windows.

Next, follow the instruction below to install the Docker engine on your system. Go to Docker CLI and run the Docker version to verify the version of Docker installation on the system. You have already installed Docker Installation on Windows and now, you are ready to build and run Docker images and containers on the Docker ecosystem.

Getting Started with Docker Container

This section give a step-by-step instructions on how to get started with Docker.

In this exercise for Practical 1, user intend to learn how to:

- Build and run an image as a container
- Share images using Docker Hub
- Deploy Docker applications using multiple containers with a database

Running Applications Using Docker Compose

In addition, you will also learn about the best practices for building images, including instructions on how to scan your images for security vulnerabilities.

If you are looking for information on how to containerize an application using your favorite language, see guides on Language-specific getting started.

Downloading and Installing Docker

This tutorial assumes you have a current version of Docker installed on your machine. If you do not have Docker installed, choose your preferred operating system below to download Docker:

- Mac with Intel chip
- Mac with Apple chip
- Windows
- Linux

If you have already run the command to get started with the tutorial, congratulations! If not, open a command prompt or bash window, and run the command:

```
$ docker run -d -p 80:80 docker/getting-started
```

You will notice a few flags being used. Here is an explanation of the aforementioned command:

- **-d:** It runs the container in detached mode (in the background).

- **`-p 80:80`**: It maps port 80 of the host to port 80 in the container.

  docker/getting-started: The name of the Docker image from which the container will be created.

Tip: *You can combine single character flags to shorten the full command. As an example, the command above could be written as:*

```
$ docker run -dp 80:80 docker/getting-started
```

The Docker Dashboard

Before going too far, we will highlight the Docker Dashboard, which gives you a quick view of the containers running on your machine. The Docker Dashboard is available for Mac and Windows

To access the dashboard, follow the instructions in the Docker Desktop manual.

Advantages of Working with Docker on Windows

Some of the top benefits of working with Docker on Windows are as below:

- Enables integrated user interface to view and monitor Docker containers
- Quickly starts Docker within ten seconds
- Easy to use Linux Workspaces
- Allots required resource and memory space
- Consists of CA synchronization
- Supports HTTP proxy settings

Container Revisited

Now that you have run a container, what is a container?

In short, a container is a process that is isolated from all other processes on the host machine and runs inside of a sandbox on your computer. This separation makes use of kernel namespaces and cgroups, two long-standing Linux features. Docker has made an effort to simplify and make these features accessible. In conclusion, a container:

- Is an executable version of an image. The DockerAPI or CLI can be used to create, stop, relocate, or destroy containers.
- May be installed in the cloud, run locally, or run in virtual machines.
- Is OS-neutral (meaning it runs on any PC).

Run independently of one another, each container has its own software, binaries, and configurations.

Container image: It makes use of an isolated filesystem when operating a container. A container image provides this custom filesystem. All dependencies, configuration, scripts, binaries, and other components required to run an application must be included in the image since it houses the container's filesystem. Additional container options, including environment variables, a default command to run, and other metadata, are also contained in the image.

Practical Exercise 2: Create and Deploy a Blockchain Network

Create and deploy a blockchain network using the Hyperledger Fabric SDK for Java. Set up and initialize the channel, install and instantiate chaincode, and perform invoke and query on your blockchain network.

Code Pattern

Blockchain is a secure, distributed, and open technology that is lowering costs, speeding up processes, and building a new level of trust in transactional applications. This developer code pattern gets you started with blockchain by showing you how to build a blockchain network using IBM Blockchain Platform Extension for VS Code and the IBM Blockchain Platform on IBM Cloud[2].

When something as big as a blockchain emerges, developers who understand and can implement the technology are in the driver's seat. But first you have to learn it. In this developer pattern, the first in a series of "hello world" blockchain patterns, you will learn how to build a blockchain network using Hyperledger Fabric. You will create a smart contract that defines the participants, tradeable assets, and allowable transactions. You will then deploy the packaged contract onto a configured Hyperledger Network on the IBM Hyperledger Platform on IBM Cloud.

When you have finished this code pattern, you will understand how to:

- Package up your blockchain smart contracts using the IBM Blockchain Platform Extension for VS Code.
- Set up a Hyperledger Fabric network on IBM Blockchain Platform.
- Install and instantiate a smart contract package through IBM Blockchain Platform.
- Test out your blockchain network by executing a Node.js application with the Hyperledger Fabric SDK to interact with the deployed network by issuing transactions.
- Discover how easy it is to set up and configure a basic network that includes a peer, orderer, channel, and certificate authority. Refer to the Getting Started

with IBM Blockchain Platform in IBM Cloud Docs to learn more about these significant components of a blockchain. Business networks also include the participants who interact with them, each of which can be associated with a unique identity, across multiple business networks. This is your chance to climb on the blockchain train and build the skills every business will need. Complete this developer pattern, watch for future blockchain patterns, and make yourself indispensable.

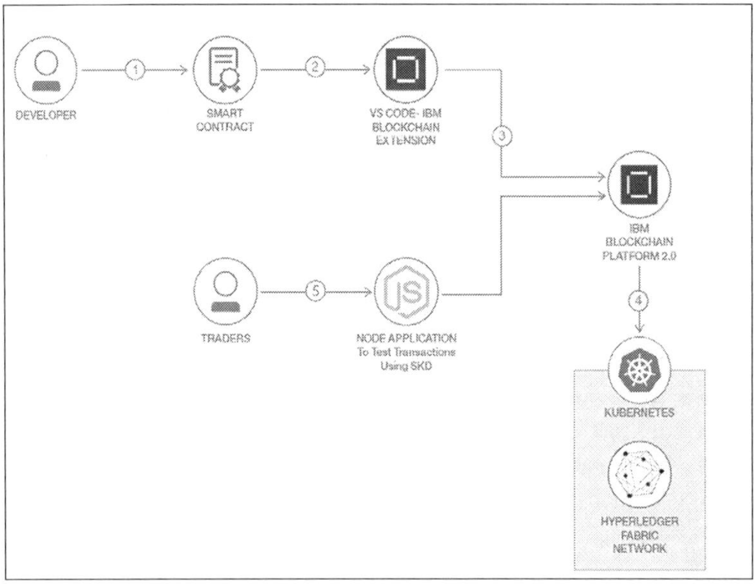

Figure 11.3: *Architectural flow depiction of creating a node in Hyperledger Fabric Network*

1. The developer uses Node.js to create a smart contract.
2. Use the IBM Blockchain Platform Extension for VS Code to package the smart contract.
3. Configure and start the IBM Blockchain Platform application.
4. The installation and instantiation of the smart contract on the network is made possible by the IBM Blockchain Platform, which facilitates the construction of a network onto an IBM Kubernetes service.
5. The Node.js program communicates with the IBM Blockchain Platform's deployed network and performs transactions via the Fabric Software Development Kit (SDK).

Networks of Blockchains

Applications can access ledger and smart contract services over a blockchain network, which is a type of technological infrastructure[3]. The main function of smart contracts is to start transactions. These are then sent to all peer nodes in the network and permanently recorded on each one's copy of the ledger. App users include end users who use client applications and blockchain network administrators.

A blockchain can track orders, accounts, payments, production, and a lot more.

Since all members have access to the same version of the truth, you can see every detail of a transaction from beginning to end, giving you more confidence as well as more opportunities and efficiency.

Blockchain Network Types

There are numerous approaches to building a blockchain network. They can be built by a consortium of persons or they can be private, public, authorized, or both.

Creating Blockchain Network-IBPV20 Using the IBM Blockchain Platform

A blockchain platform allows users and developers to create novel uses for an existing blockchain infrastructure. One example is Ethereum, which has a native cryptocurrency known as ether (ETH). But the Ethereum blockchain also allows the creation of smart contracts, programmable tokens used in initial coin offerings (ICOs), and non-fungible tokens (NFTs). These are all built up around the Ethereum infrastructure and secured by nodes on the Ethereum network.

Building a Blockchain Application Using the IBM Blockchain Platform

You will learn how to configure your Blockchain network on the IBM Cloud in Part 1. For novice developers, these will be the standard "Hello World" style Hyperledger samples utilizing the IBM Blockchain Platform. In this practical, the Hyperledger Fabric V1.4 network is utilized.

The pattern of using the IBM Blockchain Platform extension for VS Code to package your smart contract and then publishing it into the network, demonstrates how to test your network.

One of the Hyperledger initiatives run by The Linux Foundation is the blockchain framework implementation known as Hyperledger Fabric. The Hyperledger Fabric is meant to serve as a basis for creating solutions or applications with a modular design that enables plug-and-play elements such as membership services and consensus. After completing this code pattern, you will know how to:

- Use the IBM Blockchain Platform Extension for VS Code to package the smart contract.

- Create a network using Hyperledger Fabric on the IBM Blockchain Platform.
- Set up the IBM Blockchain Platform to host the smart contract bundle.
- Use the SDK to interact with the contract and carry out transactions.

IBM Blockchain Platform Components:

- With an intuitive user interface that can expedite and streamline the process of deploying and managing blockchain components on the IBM Cloud Kubernetes Service, the IBM Blockchain Platform grants you complete command over your blockchain network.
- Highly available containers are deployed and a cluster of compute hosts is created by IBM Cloud Kubernetes Service. You can swiftly build, scale, and update apps by managing the resources you require with a Kubernetes cluster in a secure manner.
- The IBM Blockchain Platform Extension for VS Code helps users create, test, and implement smart contracts, as well as establish connections with Hyperledger Fabric settings.

Highlighted Functionalities:

- The distributed ledger platform of Hyperledger Fabric v1.4 is built on a modular design that offers excellent levels of secrecy, resilience, flexibility, and scalability.
- The cross-platform, open-source Node.js JavaScript runtime environment runs JavaScript scripts on the server.

Needs:

- A Cloud account with IBM.
- Npm v6.0 or above with Node v8.x or v10.x.
- Using VSCode version 1.38.0 or above.
- VSCode API for the IBM Blockchain Platform Extension.

Launching the Software:

To configure and execute this code pattern, consider the following actions:

1. Make a copy of the repository.
2. Put the smart contract in the package.
3. Establish IBM Cloud offerings.
4. Establish a network.
5. Install smart contracts with a blockchain on the network.

6. Attach the program to the network.
7. Launch the software.

Clone the repo:

Clone this repository in a folder of your choice:

git clone https://github.com/IBM/Create-BlockchainNetwork-IBPV20

Packaging the Smart Contract

We will use the IBM Blockchain Platform extension on VS Code to package the smart contract.

In order to install the IBM Blockchain Platform VS Code extension, you must first install the most recent version of VS Code if you have not previously. Go to **`Help -> Check`** for updates to find out if you are running the most recent version. If you do not have the recent version, use the previously provided link to update your VS Code, and then click on **`extensions`** on the left-hand sidebar of your screen. Look for IBM Blockchain Platform in the marketplace extensions at the top, then select **`Install`**. Following **`"Installing"`** and **`"Installed",`** you ought to be able to select **`"Reload".`**

Launch Visual Studio Code and navigate to the contract folder located in the previously cloned **`Create-Blockchain Network`** repository. You will encounter an error stating that it does not understand the programming language you are using if you open the contract folder instead of the complete **`Create-Blockchain Network`** directory.

F1 can be used to view the various VS Code choices.

1. Select the **`Package Open Project`** option for the IBM Blockchain Platform.

Figure 11.4: *IBM Blockchain Platform: Package Open Project*

2. Press the left-hand **`IBM Blockchain Platform`** extension button. This will display the blockchain links at the bottom and the bundled contracts at the top.

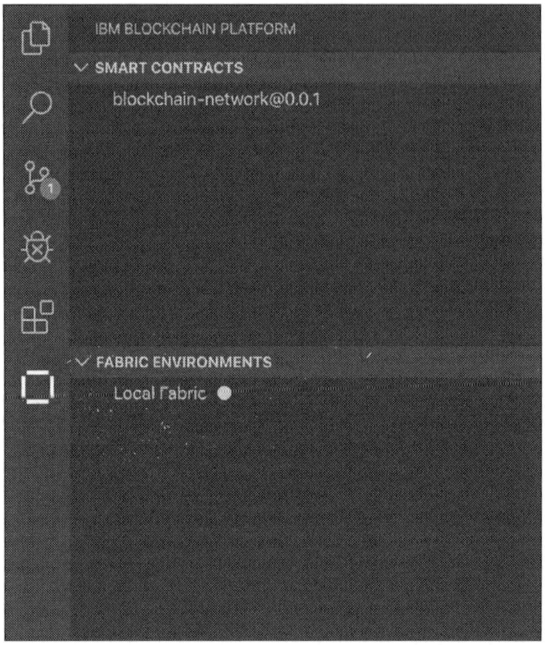

Figure 11.5: *Displaying of bundled contracts and blockchain links*

3. After that, when you right-click on the packed contract, pick Export Package from the context menu (in this example, blockchain-network@0.0.1).

4. Select a location on your computer where the **.cds** file should be saved. This packed smart contract will be used when we eventually publish it on the IBM Blockchain Platform service.

We will now begin configuring the various services needed to build up our Hyperledger Fabric network on the IBM Cloud and to operate our application on this network.

Creating IBM Cloud Services

Blockchain services refer to third-party cloud-based infrastructure and management for companies building and operating blockchain apps. BaaS functions like a sort of web host, running the back-end operation for a blockchain-based app or platform.

Blockchain-as-a-service (BaaS) is a cloud-managed platform that allows people and organizations to more easily and quickly build, host, and manage blockchain applications.

1. Create the IBM Cloud Kubernetes Service. You can find the service in the Catalog. For this code pattern, we can use the Free cluster, and give it a name.

   Note: *The IBM Cloud allows one instance of a free cluster which expires after 30 days.*

- It could take 20 minutes for the IBM Cloud Kubernetes Service setup to complete.

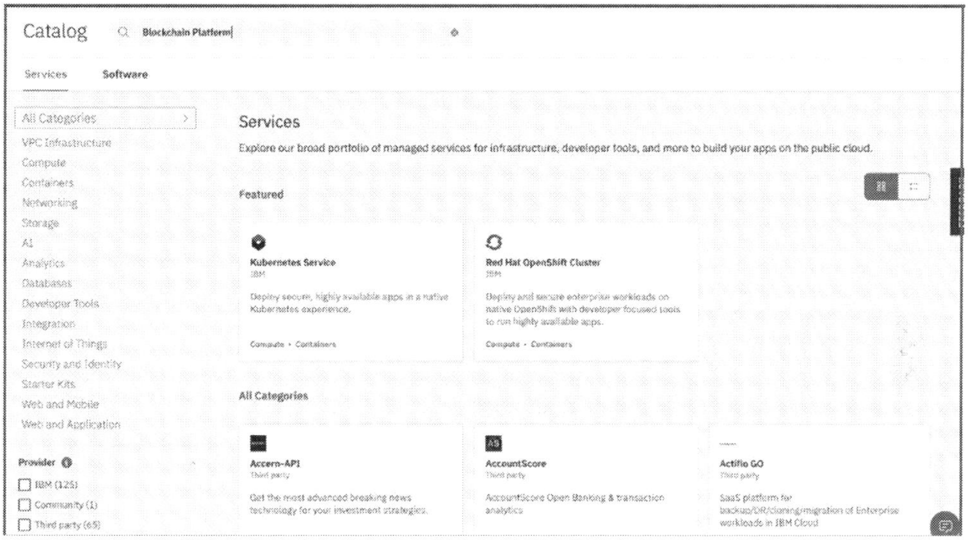

***Figure 11.6**: Catalog for selecting services*

2. Go to **`Create a new cluster`** Window. From here, first you have to select a plan from the given two options:

- **`Free`**
- **`Standard`**

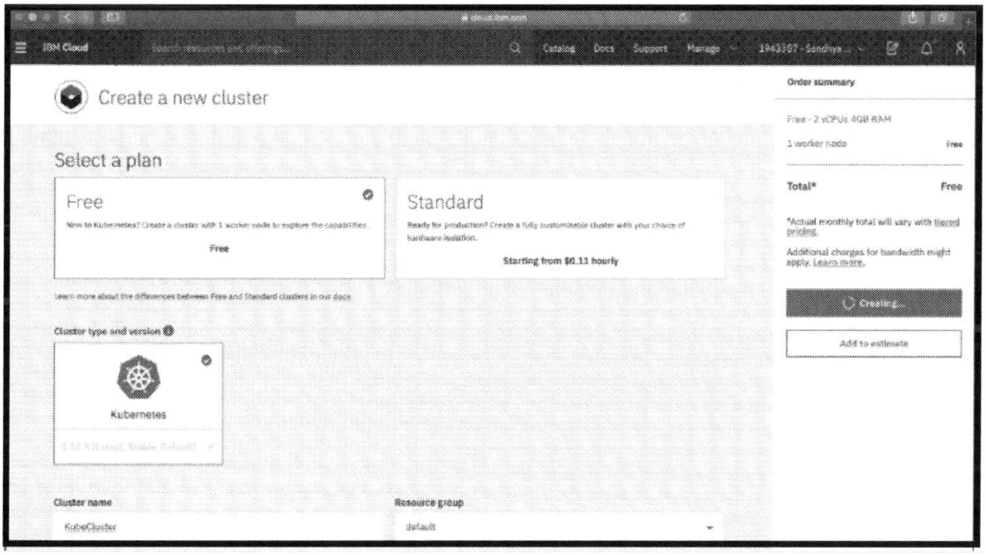

***Figure 11.7**: Selecting a plan*

3. If you choose KuberCluster, the following shall be displayed:

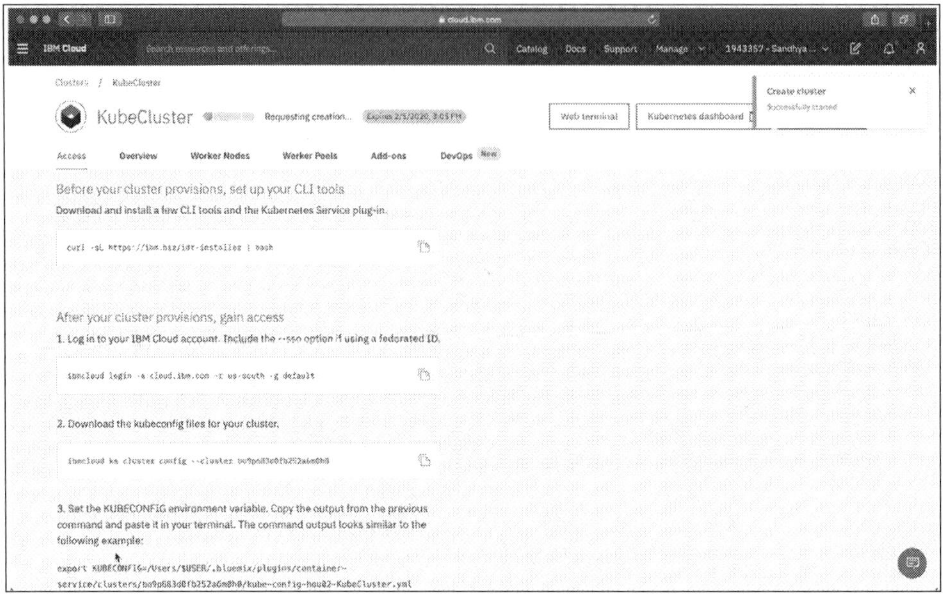

Figure 11.8: *CLI Tools Kuber Cluster*

4. After your Kubernetes cluster is up and running, you can deploy your IBM Blockchain Platform on the cluster. Again, wait for the IBM Cloud Kubernetes service to indicate it was deployed. The IBM Blockchain Platform service walks through a few steps and finds your cluster on the IBM Cloud to deploy the service on.

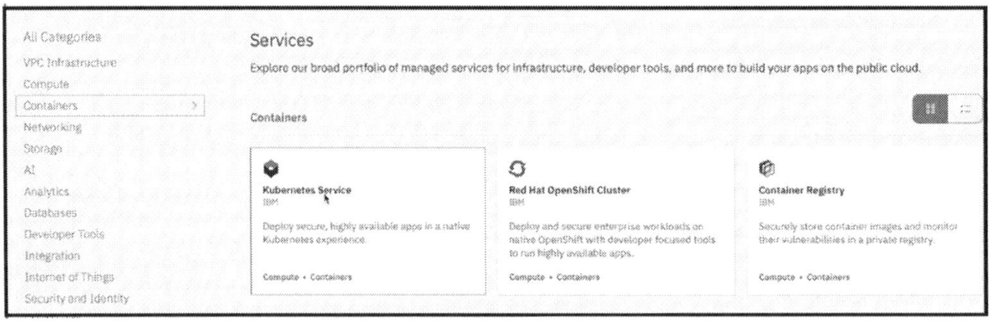

Figure 11.9: *Creating the IBM Blockchain Platform service on the IBM Cloud*

5. You can find the service in the Catalog, and give it a name.

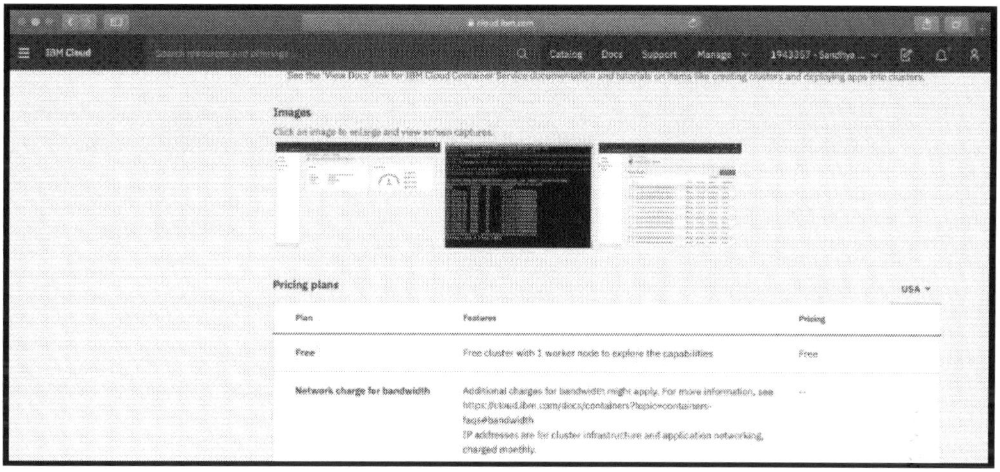

Figure 11.10: *Selecting cloud services*

6. Create the IBM Blockchain Platform service on the IBM Cloud.

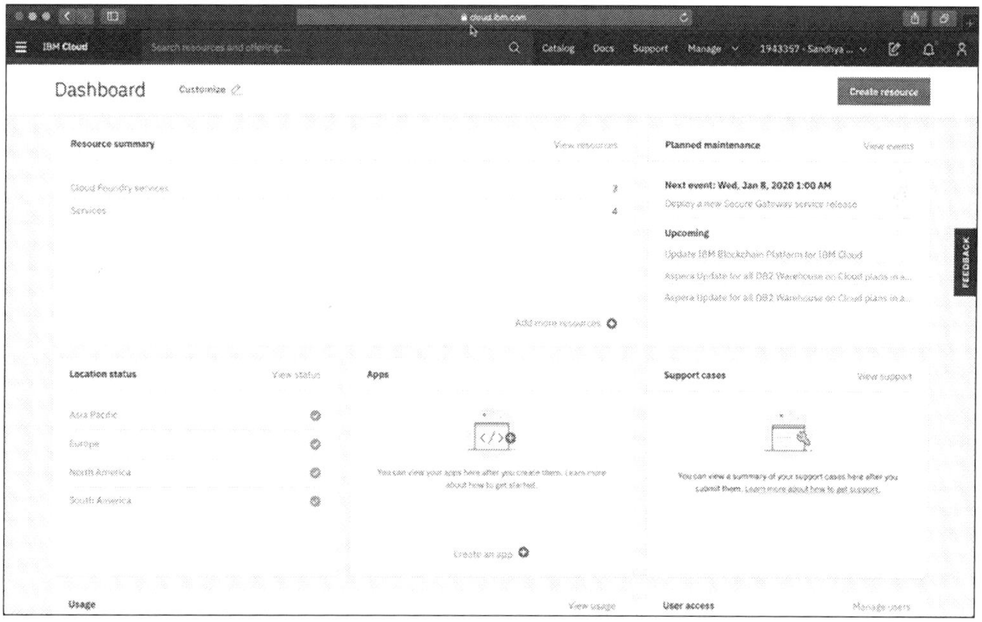

Figure 11.11: *Dashboard*

A cloud is a cyberspace where users can access information online. In turn, blockchain implies an encrypted system that utilizes various styles of encryption and hash to keep data in secured databases.

With IBM Cloud® Kubernetes Service, you can manage your containers by using Kubernetes clusters. You can manage a cloud infrastructure where you can use

Kubernetes as an orchestration tool to load-balance, scale, and monitor your containers.

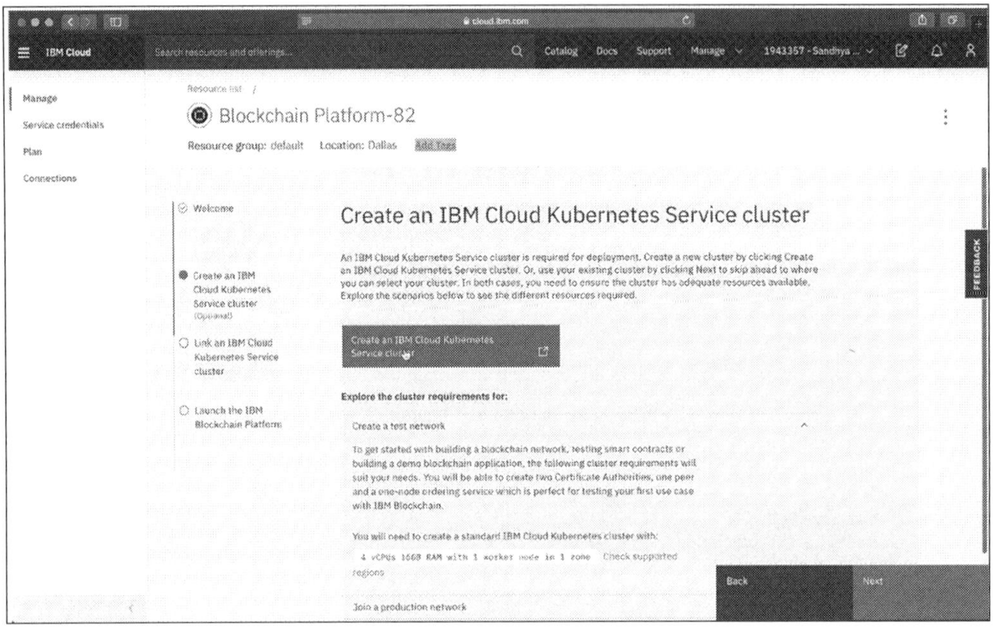

***Figure 11.12**: IBM Cloud® Kubernetes Service*

Practical Exercise 3: Interact with a Blockchain Network

Execute transactions and requests against a blockchain network by creating an app to test the network and its rules (https://developer.ibm.com/patterns/interacting-with-a-block chain-network/).

Developer Pattern

Blockchain is a secure, distributed, and open technology that is lowering costs, speeding up processes, and building a new level of trust in transactional applications. This developer code pattern gets you started with blockchain by showing you how to build a blockchain network using IBM Blockchain Platform Extension for VS Code and the IBM Blockchain Platform on IBM Cloud.

Any software design pattern is a general, reusable solution to a commonly occurring problem within a given context in software design. It is not a finished design that can be transformed directly into source or machine code.

A pattern (or design pattern) is a written document that describes a general solution to a design problem that recurs repeatedly in many projects. Software designers adapt the pattern solution to their specific project.

Note: *This developer pattern is the first in a series of patterns designed to get you started with blockchain.*

Design patterns can speed up the development process by providing tested, proven development paradigms.

Every blockchain consists of a cluster of nodes functioning on a peer-to-peer (P2P) network system. Every node in a network has a copy of the shared ledger which gets updated timely. Each node can verify transactions, initiate or receive transactions, and create blocks.

Once you have your network, with participants and transactions defined, the next step is to create an application that tests that the network is set up correctly and operates as expected. One might call this a unit test, which repeatedly exercises the functionality of code. You should always build test cases to verify the logic of your code. In this case, you want to ensure that each participant can only execute transactions defined for that participant. Additionally, you want to validate that all the transactions are working as expected. This effort is fundamental to the development lifecycle process.

This developer code pattern helps you take what you built in the first step of this composite pattern, testing out the transactions. If you have not deployed the network in step 1, check out Explore Hyperledger Fabric through a complete set of APIs and set it up now. Then you are ready for this pattern, where you will build the application, deploy it, and step through issuing transactions.

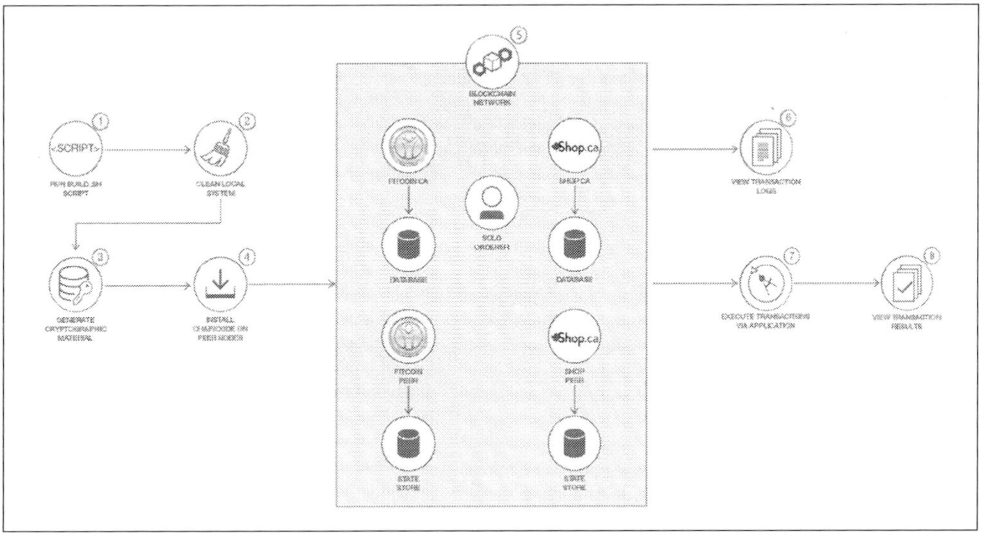

Figure 11.13: *Flow Diagram for the Developer Code Pattern*

Deploy Blockchain Network Smart Contract on the Network

1. Install a smart contract.
2. Navigate to the **`Smart Contracts`** tab in the left navigation and click **`Install Smart Contract.`**
3. Browse to the location of the Blockchain Network smart contract package file (it is probably named blockchain-network@0.0.1.cds), which we packaged earlier using the IBM Blockchain Platform extension for Visual Studio code.
4. Click on **`Add file`** and find your packaged smart contract.
5. Once the contract is uploaded, click **`Install Smart Contract`**.

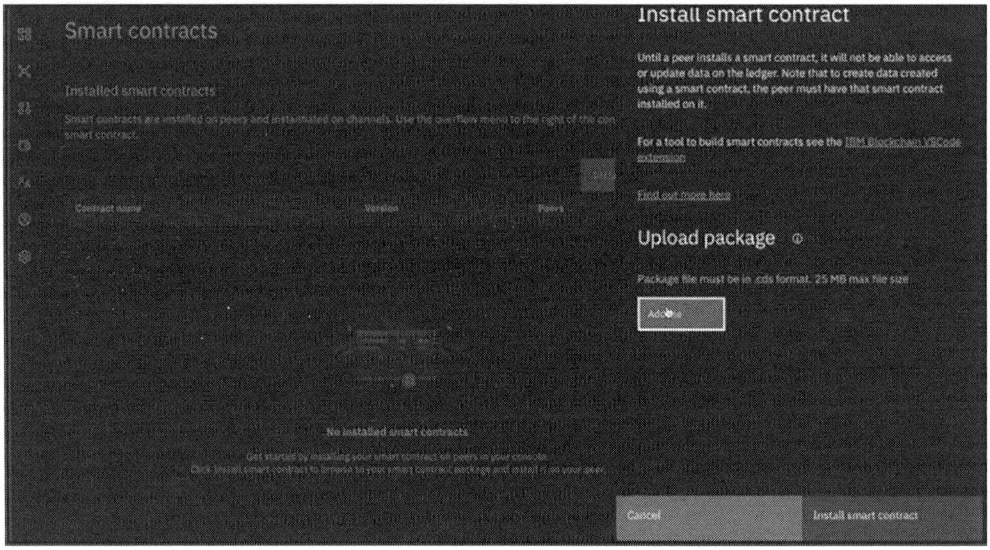

Figure 11.14: *Smart Contract Installation window*

Instantiate Smart Contract

1. Under **`Installed Smart Contracts`**, find the **`Smart Contract`** from the list (here, our is called blockchain-network) installed on our peer and click Instantiate from the overflow menu on the right side of the row.
2. On the side panel that opens, select the channel, **`mychannel,`** on which to instantiate the smart contract. Click **`Next`**.
3. Select the organization members to be included in the endorsement policy. In our case, we need to select **`Org1MSP`**. Click **`Next`**.

4. We can skip the **`Setup Private Data Collection`** step and simply click **`Next`**.
5. Give the **`Function`** name of instantiate and leave **`Arguments`** blank.

   Note: *Instantiate is the method in the* ***`my-contract.js`*** *contract file that initiates the smart contracts on the peer. Some may name this* ***`initLedger`****.*

6. Click **`Instantiate`**.

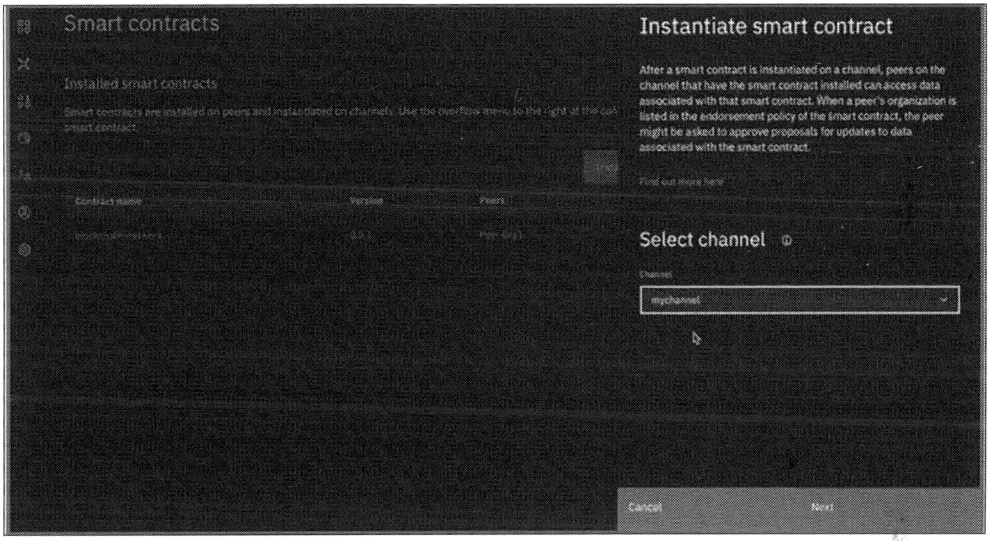

Figure 11.15: *Selecting a channel using Instantiate Contract window*

Connect Application to the Network

1. Connect with SDK through connection profile.
2. Scroll down to the **`Instantiated Smart Contracts`** section and find the **`"blockchain-network"`** contract in the list. Click on **`Connect with SDK`** from the overflow menu on the right side of the row.
3. From the dropdown for **`MSP`** for connection, choose **`Org1MSP`**.
4. From the dropdown for **`Certificate Authority`**, choose **`Org1 CA`**.
5. Download the connection profile by scrolling down and clicking **`Download Connection Profile`**. This will download the connection JSON which we will use to establish a connection between the Node.js web application and the Blockchain Network.
6. You can click **`Close`** once the download completes.

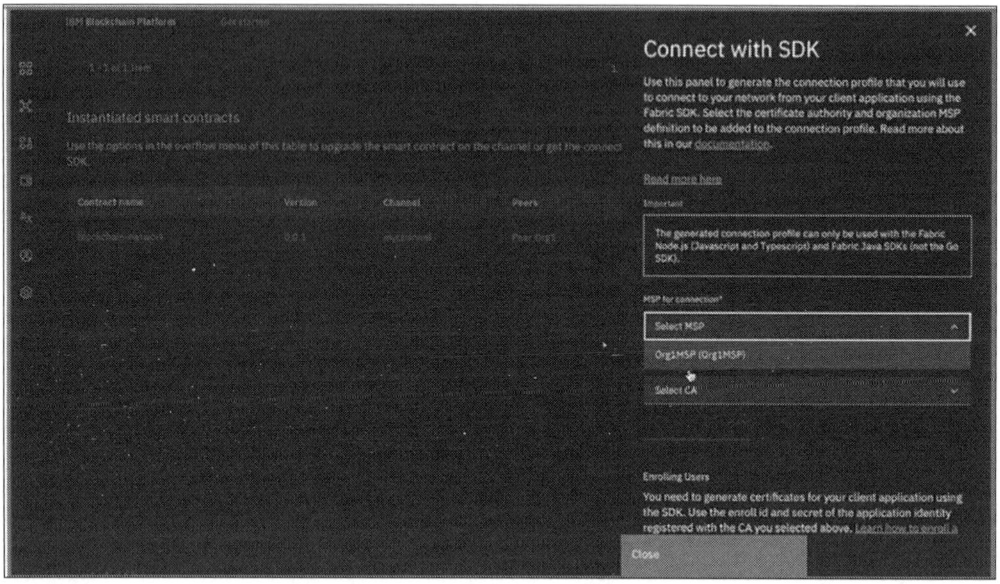

***Figure 11.16**: Connecting with SDK window*

Create an Application Admin

1. Navigate to the **Nodes** tab in the left navigation, and under **Certificate Authorities**, choose your organization **CA**, **Org1 CA**.
2. Click on **Register user**.
3. Give an **Enroll ID** of app-admin and **Enroll Secret** of **app-adminpw**. Set the **Type** for this identity as client. We can specify to use root affiliation or uncheck this field and select from any of the affiliated organizations from the drop-down list. We will leave the **Maximum Enrollments** field blank. Click **Next**.
4. Under **Attributes**, click on **Add attribute**. Give attribute as **hf.Registrar.Roles**. This will allow this identity to act as a registrar and issue identities for our app. Click **Add attribute**.
5. Click **Register user**.

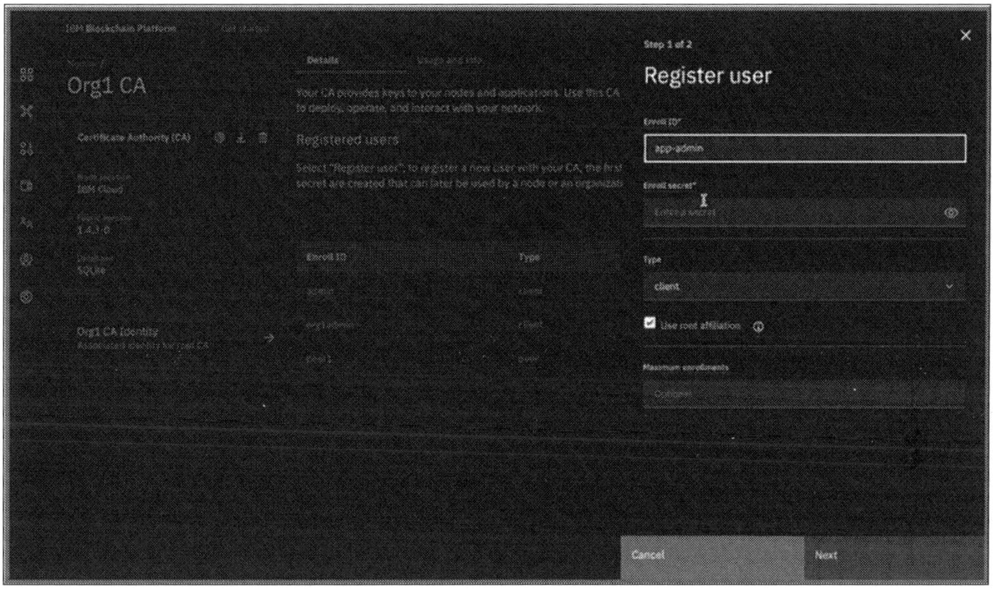

Figure 11.17: *Register user window*

Update Application Connection

1. Copy the connection profile you downloaded into the application folder.
2. Update the **`config.json`** file with:
   - The name of the downloaded connection JSON file.
   - Your app admin's enroll id and enroll secret, which we previously supplied as **`app-admin`** and **`app-adminpw`**.
   - The **`orgMSP`** ID, **`Org1MSP`**, which we supplied.
   - The **`caName`**, which is located under **`"organization"`** -> **`"Org1MSP"`** -> **`certificateAuthorities`**" in your connection's JSON file. This would resemble a port and an IP address.
   - The username you wish to set up.
3. To connect to the IBM Blockchain Platform, update the gateway discovery to { `enabled: true, asLocalhost: false }`.

```
{
    "connection_file": "mychannel_blockchain-network_profile.json",
    "channel_name": "mychannel",
    "smart_contract_name": "blockchain-network",
    "appAdmin": "app-admin",
    "appAdminSecret": "app-adminpw",
```

```
    "orgMSPID": "org1msp",
    "caName": "169.46.208.151:30404",
    "userName": "user1",
    "gatewayDiscovery": { "enabled": true, "asLocalhost": false }
}
```

Run the Application

Enroll admin.

First, navigate to the application directory, and install the node dependencies.

```
cd application
npm install
```

Run the **enrollAdmin.js** script

```
node enrollAdmin.js
```

You should see the following in the terminal:

```
msg: Successfully enrolled admin user app-admin and imported it into the wallet.
```

Run the invoke-transactions.js script to execute the transactions on the smart contract.

```
node invoke-transactions.js
```

You should see the following in the terminal:

```
Wallet path: /Users/snyk/CognitiveApps/code-patterns/Create-Blockchain-Network-IBPV20/Create-BlockchainNetwork-IBPV20/application/wallet

Submit AddTrader transaction.
addTraderAResponse:
{"traderId":"traderA","firstName":"Carlos","lastName":"Roca"}
addTraderAResponse_JSON.parse:
{ traderId: 'traderA', firstName: 'Carlos', lastName: 'Roca' }

Submit AddTrader transaction.
addTraderBResponse:
{"traderId":"traderB","firstName":"Lisa","lastName":"Smith"}
addTraderBResponse_JSON.parse:
{ traderId: 'traderB', firstName: 'Lisa', lastName: 'Smith' }
```

```
Submit AddCommodity transaction.
addCommodityResponse:
{"tradingSymbol":"commodityA","description":"farm-commodity","trade-
rId":"traderA"}
addCommodityResponse_JSON.parse:
{ tradingSymbol: 'commodityA',
  description: 'farm-commodity',
  traderId: 'traderA' }

Submit Commodity trade transaction.
commodityTradeResponse:
{"description":"farm-commodity","traderId":"traderB","tradingSymbol-
":"commodityA"}
commodityTradeResponse_JSON.parse:
{ description: 'farm-commodity',
  traderId: 'traderB',
  tradingSymbol: 'commodityA' }
```

Troubleshooting

If you receive the following error on submitting transaction:

```
error: [Client.js]: Channel not found for name mychannel
```

It is safe to ignore this error because the IBM Blockchain Platform service has service discovery enabled by default. (In order to use service discovery to find other peers, please define anchor peers for your channel in the UI). If you really want the message to go away, you can add the channels section to the connection profile, but it is a warning rather than a true error telling the user the channel is found but not in the connection profile.

As an example, you can manually add the following JSON and update the IP address and ports manually:

```
"channels": {
        "mychannel": {
            "orderers": [
                "169.46.208.151:32078"
            ],
            "peers": {
                "169.46.208.151:31017": {}
            }
        }
    },
```

Extending the Code Pattern

This application can be expanded in a couple of ways:

Create a wallet for every member and use the member's wallet to interact with the application.

Add a UI application in place of the invoke.js node application to execute the transactions.

Conclusion

In this chapter, we have completed three exercises to test our efficacy in learning Blockchain. We have first understood what is the need of Docker container and then installed it. The software that hosts the containers is called Docker Engine. We have understood in detail all the four components of Docker.

We have learnt the process of installing Docker on Windows.

In the second exercise, we learnt to create and deploy a Blockchain Network and the types of Blockchain Networks. For packaging the Smart Contract, we used the IBM Blockchain Platform extension on VS Code to package the smart contract.

We have understood how to interact with a Blockchain Network in the third exercise.

References

[1] What is Docker: Advantages and Components, https://www.simplilearn.com/tutorials/docker-tutorial/what-is-docker

[2] Create a basic blockchain network using the IBM Blockchain Platform, https://developer.ibm.com/patterns/build-a-blockchain-network/By Ishan Gulhane, Laura Bennett

[3] A beginner's guide to the different types of blockchain networks, https://cointelegraph.com/blockchain-for-beginners/a-beginners-guide-to-the-different-types-of-blockchain-networks

Index

A

B

L

M

N

O

P

R

Made in United States
Orlando, FL
04 November 2026

90201558R00197